T0181549

Lecture Notes of the Institute for Computer Sciences, Social Informatics and Telecommunications Engineering 514

The LNICST series publishes ICST's conferences, symposia and workshops.
LNICST reports state-of-the-art results in areas related to the scope of the Institute.
The type of material published includes

- Proceedings (published in time for the respective event)
- Other edited monographs (such as project reports or invited volumes)

LNICST topics span the following areas:

- General Computer Science
- E-Economy
- E-Medicine
- Knowledge Management
- Multimedia
- Operations, Management and Policy
- Social Informatics
- Systems

Tanya Zlateva · Georgi Tuparov
Editors

Computer Science and Education in Computer Science

19th EAI International Conference, CSECS 2023
Boston, MA, USA, June 28–29, 2023
Proceedings

 Springer

Editors
Tanya Zlateva
Boston University
Boston, MA, USA

Georgi Tuparov 🆔
New Bulgarian University
Sofia, Bulgaria

ISSN 1867-8211 ISSN 1867-822X (electronic)
Lecture Notes of the Institute for Computer Sciences, Social Informatics
and Telecommunications Engineering
ISBN 978-3-031-44667-2 ISBN 978-3-031-44668-9 (eBook)
https://doi.org/10.1007/978-3-031-44668-9

This Springer imprint is published by the registered company Springer Nature Switzerland AG
The registered company address is: Gewerbestrasse 11, 6330 Cham, Switzerland

Paper in this product is recyclable.

Preface

We are delighted to introduce the proceedings of the nineteenth edition of the Computer Science and Education in Computer Science International Conference (EAI CSECS 2023). The event is endorsed by the European Alliance for Innovation, an international professional community-based organization devoted to the advancement of innovation in the field of Information and Communication Technologies. The conference took place in Boston, USA between 28 and 29 June 2023 and was also transmitted online for remote participants from Bulgaria, Germany, India, Pakistan, Senegal, Portugal, China, and North Macedonia.

EAI CSECS 2023 was dedicated to a wide range of Computer Science research areas starting from software engineering and information systems design and ending with cryptography, the theoretical foundations of algorithms, and implementation of machine learning and big data technologies. Another important topic of the conference was education in computer science, which includes the introduction and evaluation of computing programs, curricula, and online courses, to syllabus, laboratories, teaching, and pedagogy aspects. The fields of teaching and education have evolved multiple existing and emerging technologies, solutions, and services for design and training providing a heterogeneous approach towards the delivery of Software 5.0 and Education 5.0 to a broad range of citizens and societies. CSECS 2023 brought together technology experts, researchers, and industry representatives contributing to the design, development, and deployment of modern solutions based on recent technologies, standards, and procedures.

The technical program of EAI CSECS 2023 consisted of 22 full and 9 short papers in oral presentation sessions on-site or online in the main conference tracks. All papers have been selected from more than 100 submissions. Every paper has been reviewed double-blind by at least 3 reviewers. The papers cover many systems technologies, applications, and services as well as solutions. Multiple topics have been addressed including the theory of computation, models of computation, computational complexity and cryptography, logic, design and analysis of algorithms, network architectures, performance evaluation, network services, software engineering, software creation and management, applied computing, machine learning, and education.

Coordination with the steering chair, Imrich Chlamtac, as well as the valuable support of Ivan Landjev, Tanya Zlateva, Vladimir Zlatev, Lou Chitkushev, Dimitar Atanasov, Constandinos Mavromoustakis, Eugene Pinsky, Petya Asenova, Rossitza Goleva, Metodi Traikov, Irena Vodenska, and Vijay Kanabar were essential for the success of the conference. We sincerely appreciate their continuous work and support. We are also grateful to the Conference Manager, Kristina Havlickova from EAI, for her support and to all the authors who submitted their papers to the EAI CSECS 2023 conference.

We strongly believe that CSECS 2023 provides a good forum for all researchers, developers, and practitioners to discuss all science and technology aspects that are relevant to computer science and education in the field. We also expect that the future

EAI CSECS 2024 conference will be as successful and stimulating, as indicated by the contributions presented in this volume.

July 2023   Tanya Zlateva
                                                                                                    Georgi Tuparov

Organization

Steering Committee

Imrich Chlamtac   University of Trento, Italy

Organizing Committee

General Chair

Ivan Landjev   New Bulgarian University, Bulgaria

General Co-chair

Tanya Zlateva   Boston University, USA

TPC Chairs and Co-chairs

Tanya Zlateva (Chair)	Boston University, USA
Rossitza Goleva (Chair)	New Bulgarian University, Bulgaria
Lou Chitkushev (Co-chair)	Boston University, USA
Constandinos X. Mavromoustakis (Co-chair)	University of Nikosia, Cyprus
Ciprian Dobre (Co-chair)	University Polytehnica of Bucharest, Romania

Sponsorship and Exhibit Chair

Vijay Kanabar   Boston University, USA

Local Chairs

Tanya Zlateva (Chair)	Boston University, USA
Reza Rawassizadeh	Boston University, USA

Workshops Chair

Eugene Pinsky   Boston University, USA

Publicity and Social Media Chair

Rossitza Goleva   New Bulgarian University, Bulgaria

Publications Chair

Rossitza Goleva   New Bulgarian University, Bulgaria

Web Chair

Metodi Traikov   New Bulgarian University, Bulgaria

Posters and PhD Track Chair

Irena Vodenska   Boston University, USA

Panels Chair

Dimitar Atanasov   New Bulgarian University, Bulgaria

Demos Chair

Gregory Page   Boston University, USA

Tutorials Chair

Vladimir Zlatev   Boston University, USA

Community and Industry Outreach Chair

Vijay Kanabar   Boston University, USA

Technical Program Committee

Ruksana Khan   Boston University, USA
Kathleen Park   Boston University, USA

Farshid Alizadeh-Shabdiz	Boston University, USA
Hanbo Yu	Boston University, USA
Jack Polnar	Boston University, USA
Linpeiyu Ji	Boston University, USA
Zhaoyu Li	Johns Hopkins University, USA
Mary Lucas	Drexel University, USA
Guanglan Zhang	Boston University, USA
Huey Fern Tay	Boston University, USA
Victor Obionwu	Institut für Technische und Betriebliche, Germany
David Broneske	German Centre for Higher Education Research and Science Studies, Germany
Gunter Saake	Otto von Guericke University, Magdeburg, Germany
Elissaveta Gourova	Sofia University St. Kliment Ohridski, Bulgaria
Boris Evstatiev	University of Ruse, Bulgaria

Contents

Health Informatics

Computer Architecture and Networks

Business Informatics

Education in Computer Science

Computational Math

α-Based Similarity Metric in Computational Advertizing: A New Approach to Audience Extension

Sarthak Pattnaik and Eugene Pinsky[✉]

Department of Computer Science, Met College, Boston University, Boston, MA, USA
{spattna1,epinsky}@bu.edu

Abstract. Over the past few decades, advertising has undergone significant evolution, with online advertising now the most widely used form to reach potential audiences globally. Advertisers face the challenge of targeting the right audience through media channels while working within limited budgets. However, campaigns often attract small audiences, which has led to extensive research into inducing preferable attributes from campaign data to reach a wider range of customers. Audience expansion techniques offer a promising solution to identifying potential audiences with similar characteristics to the seed users, who are likely to achieve the business goal of a targeted campaign. Typically, the ultimate goal is to achieve the maximum impressions possible at a certain cost per thousand impressions. In this paper, we propose a distance-based approach that uses a hyperparameter to compute the weighted average to find the nearest neighbors of a target campaign from the historical dataset (seed audience). This approach will be used to determine the total impressions and cost per thousand impressions. To extend our potential audience, we will use heuristic measures to find the best set of features to render the maximum impressions at a reasonable cost per thousand impressions [1].

Keywords: computational advertising · audience extension · similarity metrics · nearest neighbors

1 Introduction

Online advertisers rely on audience segments to group users based on various characteristics such as demographics, location, behavior, and intent. These segments are created using first-party data collected by advertisers or third-party data provided by external sources [2]. However, sometimes these segments do not produce the expected number of impressions at the desired cost per thousand impressions. To address this issue, advertisers can use audience extension, which uses feature selection techniques to identify the set of features that will provide the advertiser with the highest possible audience [3]. In other words, audience

T. Zlateva and G. Tuparov (Eds.): CSECS 2023, LNICST 514, pp. 3–29, 2023.
https://doi.org/10.1007/978-3-031-44668-9_1

extension enables advertisers to expand their target audience beyond the existing segments. This can help advertisers find more potential customers to meet their targets [4]. Audience extension requires calculating nearest neighbors for an advertising campaign, which involves using various distance and similarity measures as metrics to identify nearest neighbors [5].

2   Computational Advertising

Advertising plays a critical role in modern business, allowing companies to effectively reach their target audiences and promote their products and services. The use of machine learning techniques in computational advertising has become increasingly popular, enabling advertisers to develop more sophisticated and data-driven campaigns. One of the key challenges in computational advertising is achieving optimal results while minimizing the cost of the campaign. To address this challenge, Dave and Varma [1] provide a comprehensive guide to computational advertising techniques, covering topics such as ad targeting, ad ranking, and ad delivery. The authors describe the key algorithms and metrics used in these processes and the various ethical considerations and challenges involved in advertising. In recent years, machine learning optimization has emerged as a powerful approach to improving the effectiveness and efficiency of advertising campaigns. Truong and Hoang [6] conducted a systematic literature review to provide an overview of the current state of machine learning optimization in computational advertising. The authors emphasize the importance of data preprocessing, feature engineering, and model selection in achieving optimal results.

3   Similarity Metrics for Advertisement Campaigns

Similarity measures and distance measures are statistical measures of how two advertisement campaigns are related to each other. In our analysis, we propose a combination of Hamming distance and Jaccard distance to calculate the distance between two user advertisement campaigns. This would allow us to consider scenarios where we emphasize commonality and priority for our targets.

3.1   Hamming Distance

Hamming distance is a distance measure used to compare two strings of equal length. It counts the number of positions at which the corresponding symbols are different between the two numeric strings, A and B. In other words, it measures the minimum number of substitutions required to change one string into the other [7,8]. Below are two strings of length 6 each (see Fig. 1):

$$A : 123456 \qquad B : 165438$$

Hamming distance is used to measure the difference between two strings of equal length. It represents the number of positions at which the symbols differ, making it a critical distance measure for comparing data in various fields, including error-correcting codes, data compression, and DNA analysis. Strings A and B differ at exactly 4 positions. Therefore, the hamming distance between A and B is 4 [9].

Normalized Hamming Distance: The normalized hamming distance is a measure of dissimilarity between two strings that takes into account the length of the strings. It is obtained by dividing the hamming distance by the length of the strings, which gives a value between 0 and 1. A value of 0 means that the two strings are identical, while a value of 1 means that the two strings are completely different. In strings, A and B, the normalized hamming distance are $4/6 = 0.67$, which means that the two strings are 67% dissimilar. Equation (1) represents the normalized hamming distance between two strings A and B.

$$d_H(A, B) = \frac{1}{n} \sum_{i=1}^{n} [A_i \neq B_i] \tag{1}$$

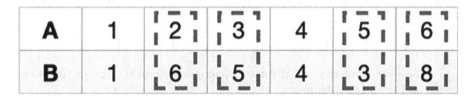

Fig. 1. Illustration of the Hamming Distance

3.2 Jaccard Similarity

The Jaccard coefficient is a similarity metric commonly used to measure the similarity between finite sample sets. It is defined as the ratio of the size of the intersection of the sets to the size of their union. In other words, the Jaccard coefficient measures the proportion of common elements in the two sets. The Jaccard coefficient has been widely used in various fields, such as data mining, information retrieval, and social network analysis. In information retrieval, it has been used to measure the similarity between documents based on the presence or absence of certain terms [10]. In social network analysis, it has been used to measure the similarity between users based on their shared interests or activities [11]. The union and intersection of two sets A and B has been illustrated in the Venn diagram below (See Fig. 2) [12].

Equations (2) show how to calculate Jaccard similarity and Jaccard distance, respectively. The Jaccard similarity $S_J(A, B)$ and the Jacard distance $D_J(A, B)$ between two sets of items A and B can be defined as:

$$S_J(A, B) = \frac{|A \cap B|}{|A \cup B|} \quad \text{and} \quad D_J(A, B) = 1 - S_J(A, B) \tag{2}$$

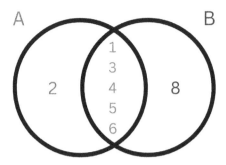

Fig. 2. Illustration of Jaccard Similarity

Similar to the case of hamming distance, let us consider the two sets below:

$$A = \{1, 2, 3, 4, 5, 6\}, \qquad B = \{1, 6, 5, 4, 3, 8\}$$

To calculate the Jaccard similarity between these sets, we first need to find their intersection and union:

Intersection: $A \cap B = \{1, 3, 4, 5, 6\}$,   Union: $A \cup B = \{1, 2, 3, 4, 5, 6, 8\}$

The Jaccard similarity and distance is computed from the size of the intersection and the size of the union:

$$S_J(A, B) = |A \cap B|/|A \cup B| = 5/7 = 0.71, \qquad D_J(A, B) = 1 - S_J(A, B) = 0.29$$

3.3 α-Based Weighted Average

The α-based weighted average is a method of calculating the distance between two values. It is a linear interpolation between two values, and the weight given to each value is controlled by the parameter α, which ranges from 0 to 1 [13]. We are interested in calculating the distance between two campaigns, A and B, in our dataset. To do this, we calculate a weighted average of the Jaccard score and hamming distance score [14].

The distance metric between campaigns A and B can be expressed as follows:

$$d_\alpha(A, B) = \alpha \cdot D_H(A, B) + (1 - \alpha) \cdot D_J(A, B) \tag{3}$$

Here, α represents the weight assigned to the Hamming distance score, and $(1 - \alpha)$ represents the weight assigned to the Jaccard score. The values of α used in the calculation of the distance between campaigns can have a significant impact on the results [15]. We plan to study the effect of varying α values on the nearest neighbors and the value of total impressions and cost per thousand impressions. The α values we will be using are as follows:

- $\alpha = 1$ (Priority Only)
- $\alpha = 0.75$ (Mostly Priority)
- $\alpha = 0.50$ (Priority and Commonality Equally)
- $\alpha = 0.25$ (Mostly Commonality)
- $\alpha = 0$ (Commonality Only)

By exploring the effects of these α values on the distance metric between campaigns, we can better understand the impact of prioritizing either the Jaccard score or the hamming distance score and determine which approach is most effective for our specific use case. In the above examples, we have calculated the hamming distance and Jaccard distance for set A and set B. Substituting the value into Eq. (1) we get:

$$\text{For } \alpha = 0.00, \quad d_\alpha(A, B) = 0 \times 0.67 + (1 - 0) \times 0.29 = 0.29$$
$$\text{For } \alpha = 0.25, \quad d_\alpha(A, B) = 0.25 \times 0.67 + (1 - 0.25) \times 0.29 = 0.385$$
$$\text{For } \alpha = 0.50, \quad d_\alpha(A, B) = 0.50 \times 0.67 + (1 - 0.50) \times 0.29 = 0.48$$
$$\text{For } \alpha = 0.75, \quad d_\alpha(A, B) = 0.75 \times 0.67 + (1 - 0.75) \times 0.29 = 0.575$$
$$\text{For } \alpha = 1.00, \quad d_\alpha(A, B) = 1 \times 0.67 + (1 - 1) \times 0.29 = 0.67$$

3.4 Significance of Hyperparameter α

let us recall our previous example. We have two strings (campaigns) A and B: $A =$ "1 2 3 4 5 6" and $B =$ "1 6 5 4 3 8". The Hamming and jacard distances between these two campaigns are: $D_H(A, B) = 0.67$ and $D_J(A, B) = 0.29$. Let us add one more string $C =$ "6 5 4 3 2 1". This gives us $D_H(A, C) = 1$ and $D_J(A, C) = 0$. We can now compute the α-weighted distance $d_\alpha(A, C)$ between A and C.

$$\text{For } \alpha = 0.00, \ d_\alpha(A, C) = 0 \times 1 + (1 - 0) \times 0 = 0$$
$$\text{For } \alpha = 0.25, \ d_\alpha(A, C) = 0.25 \times 1 + (1 - 0.25) \times 0 = 0.25$$
$$\text{For } \alpha = 0.50, \ d_\alpha(A, C) = 0.50 \times 1 + (1 - 0.50) \times 0 = 0.50$$
$$\text{For } \alpha = 0.75, \ d_\alpha(A, C) = 0.75 \times 1 + (1 - 0.75) \times 0 = 0.75$$
$$\text{For } \alpha = 1.00, \ d_\alpha(A, C) = 1 \times 1 + (1 - 1) \times 0 = 1$$

The graph below shows how the α based weighted average distance changes for a pair of different advertisement campaigns with different values of α (See Fig. 3). We can observe that at a certain value of α, A is closer to B than it is closer to C. There is a point beyond which the distance metric between a pair of advertisement campaigns changes.

3.5 Calculating Nearest Neighbours

The radius-based method is a type of clustering algorithm that groups data points together based on their distance from a central point (or centroid). In

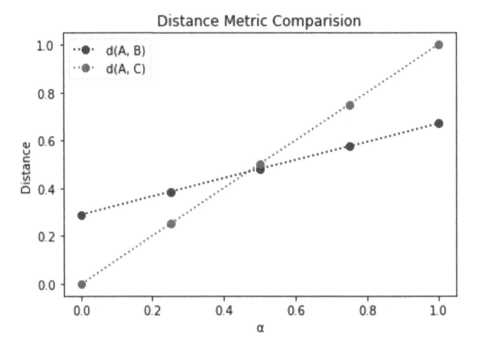

Fig. 3. Comparing distances $d(A, B)$ and $d(A, C)$ (intersection around $\alpha = 0.5$)

this method, a fixed radius is chosen, and all data points within that radius are grouped together into a cluster. The radius-based method is often used in geospatial analysis and location-based services, where the goal is to identify clusters of points that are close to each other in physical space. It is also used in outlier detection and data cleaning applications, where the goal is to identify and remove data points that are far from any cluster. This is the technique which we will be using to calculate the nearest neighbours of a target campaign based on their distance from the campaigns which are part of the dataset [16,17].

3.6 Commonality vs Priority: α as Hyperparameter

Facebook user interests are topics, activities, and hobbies that users are interested in and have indicated on their Facebook profiles. Facebook can use these interests to show relevant content, ads, and suggestions to users based on their preferences. Facebook users can add interests to their profiles by selecting from a list of predefined categories or by entering custom interests. We will be calculating Hamming and Jaccard's distance from the interests of multiple users. Using these metrics, we calculate the α based weighted average. This metric indicates how similar the two users are. These conclusions can be used in many applications like social media clustering to group similar users. We will be illustrating two examples to show how the metric of similarity changes with the value of α:

Example 1:

- Campaign U_1: Book, Movies, Travel
- Campaign U_2: Book, Travel, Swimming

For this example, we have $d_H(U_1, U_2) = 1/3$, $S_J(U_1, U_2) = 0.5$, $D_J(U_1, U_2) = 1 - 0.5 = 0.5$ Substituting these values in Eq. (2) we get:

$$\text{For } \alpha = 0.00, \ d_\alpha(U1, U2) = 0 \times 0.33 + (1 - 0) \times 0.50 = 0.50$$
$$\text{For } \alpha = 0.25, \ d_\alpha(U_1, U_2) = 0.25 \times 0.33 + (1 - 0.25) \times 0.50 = 0.4575$$
$$\text{For } \alpha = 0.50, \ d_\alpha(U_1, U_2) = 0.50 \times 0.33 + (1 - 0.50) \times 0.50 = 0.415$$
$$\text{For } \alpha = 0.75, \ d_\alpha(U_1, U_2) = 0.75 \times 0.33 + (1 - 0.75) \times 0.50 = 0.3725$$
$$\text{For } \alpha = 1.00, \ d_\alpha(U_1, U_2) = 1 \times 0.33 + (1 - 1) \times 0.50 = 0.33$$

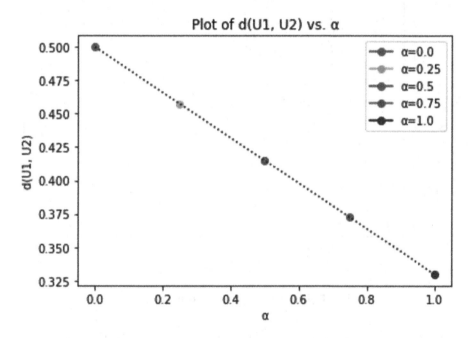

Fig. 4. Distance increases as α increases.

Example 2:

- Campaign U_1: Book, Travel, Movies
- Campaign U_2:: Book, Travel, Swimming

For this example, we have $D_H(U_1, U_2) = 2/3 = 0.67$, $S_J(U_1, U_2) = 0.5$ and Jaccard distance $D_J(U_1, U_2) = 1 - 0.5 = 0.5$ Substituting these values in Eq. (2) we get:

For $\alpha = 0.00$, $d_\alpha(U_1, U_2) = 0 \times 0.67 + (1 - 0) \times 0.50 = 0.50$

For $\alpha = 0.25$, $d_\alpha(U_1, U_2) = 0.25 \times 0.67 + (1 - 0.25) \times 0.50 = 0.5425$

For $\alpha = 0.50$, $d_\alpha(U_1, U_2) = 0.50 \times 0.67 + (1 - 0.50) \times 0.50 = 0.585$

For $\alpha = 0.75$, $d_\alpha(U_1, U_2) = 0.75 \times 0.67 + (1 - 0.75) \times 0.50 = 0.6275$

For $\alpha = 1.00$, $d_\alpha(U_1, U_2) = 1 \times 0.67 + (1 - 1) \times 0.50 = 0.67$

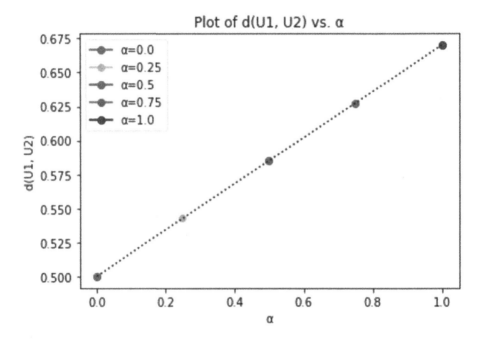

Fig. 5. Distance decreases as α increases.

In the first case, the value of the Hamming distance is less than the Jaccard distance. We observe that as we increase the weight associated with the Hamming distance, the value of the distance metric reduces, and the users become more similar (See Fig. 4).

In the second case, the value of the Hamming distance is more than the Jaccard distance. We observe that with an increase in weight, the value of the distance metric increases, and the users become more dissimilar (See Fig. 5).

Therefore, we can conclude that when the commonality metric is higher than the priority metric, the users become more similar as we increase the value of α, and vice versa.

4 Use Case Description

Our dataset consists of advertisement campaigns from Facebook with five target features. The details of those features are mentioned below:

- **Age**: This is the age range of the audience you want to target with your ads. You can choose to target a specific age range, such as 18–24, or a broader range, such as 18–34.
- **Gender**: This refers to the gender of the audience you want to target with your ads. You can choose to target men, women, or all genders.
- **Interest_1**: This is one of the interests or behaviors that the user has specified in his or her Facebook profile.
- **Interest_2**: This is another interest or behavior that the user has specified in his or her Facebook profile.
- **Interest_3**: This is a third interest or behavior that the user has specified in his or her Facebook profile.

The targeted advertisement campaign curated by advertisers has specific values for each of its features. The advertiser's objective is to maximize impressions for the advertisement campaign at a specific cost per thousand impressions. Therefore, to estimate the cumulative impressions for the target campaign, we calculate the distance of the target campaign from all the campaigns present in our dataset using α based weighted average of the Jaccard distance and Hamming distance. Once we have calculated this metric, we select the nearest neighbors by applying the Radius-Based Method with a specific threshold. To calculate the total impressions obtained for the target campaign, we sum up the impressions of all the nearest neighbors of our target campaign. To calculate the cost, we take the weighted average of the impressions and the cost of each campaign. This method ensures that we can accurately estimate the total impressions and cost for the target campaign. Let us illustrate the above steps using a detailed example where we will be taking a target campaign and a sample historical dataset with a couple of records [18, 19].

4.1 An Illustrative Example

A targeted campaign is a marketing initiative aimed at a specific group of consumers with the goal of driving specific actions, such as product purchases or website visits [20]. A targeted campaign can be informed by audience segmentation, where audiences are divided into groups based on demographics, interests, or behaviors [21]. An example of a sample target campaign for our case study is given below (See Table 1).

Table 1. Sample target Campaign

Age	Sex	Interest_1	Interest_2	Interest_3
30–34	M	1	2	3

A historical dataset refers to a collection of data points about the behavior and characteristics of previous audiences that engaged with similar campaigns or products. This data can include information about demographics, browsing behavior, interests, and purchase history [22]. Historical data can be used to create a profile of the target audience and inform the targeting and messaging of the current campaign [23]. For our example, we will be considering a dataset with 3 records (See Table 2). Let us calculate the distance metric between the target campaign and each of the campaigns that are part of the historical dataset. We will be using α based weighted average distance metric to calculate the same, and then based on our threshold, we will be selecting the campaigns which are the nearest neighbors to our target campaign.

Table 2. A Sample historical dataset

Age	Sex	Interest_1	Interest_2	Interest_3	Imps	Cost
30–34	M	2	3	6	2000	30
35–39	F	1	2	5	1500	25
40–44	F	3	4	5	2500	50

- **Target T: 30–34, M, 1, 2, 3**
- **Campaign C_1: 30–34, M, 2, 3, 6**

Normalized Hamming Distance $= d_H(T, C_1) = \frac{3}{5} = 0.60$
Jaccard Similarity $= J(T, C_1) = \frac{|30-34, M, 2, 3|}{|30-34, M, 1, 2, 3, 6|} = \frac{4}{6} = 0.67$
Jaccard distance $= d_J(T, C_1) = 1 - 0.67 = 0.33$

Substituting these values in Eq. (2) we get:

For $\alpha = 0.00$, $d_\alpha(T, C_1) = 0 \times 0.60 + (1 - 0) \times 0.33 = 0.33$
For $\alpha = 0.25$, $d_\alpha(T, C_1) = 0.25 \times 0.60 + (1 - 0.25) \times 0.33 = 0.40$
For $\alpha = 0.50$, $d_\alpha(T, C_1) = 0.50 \times 0.60 + (1 - 0.50) \times 0.33 = 0.45$
For $\alpha = 0.75$, $d_\alpha(T, C_1) = 0.75 \times 0.60 + (1 - 0.75) \times 0.33 = 0.53$
For $\alpha = 1.00$, $d_\alpha(T, C_1) = 1 \times 0.60 + (1 - 1) \times 0.33 = 0.60$

- **Target T: 30–34, M, 1, 2, 3**
- **Campaign C_2: 35–39, F, 1, 2, 5**

Normalized Hamming Distance $= d_H(T, C_2) = \frac{3}{5} = 0.60$
Jaccard Similarity $= J(T, C_2) = \frac{|1, 2|}{|30-34, 35-39, M, F, 1, 2, 3, 5|} = \frac{2}{8} = 0.25$
Jaccard distance $= d_J(T, C_2) = 1 - 0.25 = 0.75$

Substituting these values in Eq. (1) we get:

For $\alpha = 0.00$, $d_\alpha(T, C_2) = 0 \times 0.60 + (1 - 0) \times 0.75 = 0.75$

For $\alpha = 0.25$, $d_\alpha(T, C_2) = 0.25 \times 0.60 + (1 - 0.25) \times 0.75 = 0.71$

For $\alpha = 0.50$, $d_\alpha(T, C_2) = 0.50 \times 0.60 + (1 - 0.50) \times 0.75 = 0.68$

For $\alpha = 0.75$, $d_\alpha(T, C_2) = 0.75 \times 0.60 + (1 - 0.75) \times 0.75 = 0.64$

For $\alpha = 1.00$, $d_\alpha(T, C_2) = 1 \times 0.60 + (1 - 1) \times 0.75 = 0.60$

- **Target T: 30–34, M, 1, 2, 3**
- **Campaign C_3: 40–44, F, 3, 4, 5**

Normalized Hamming Distance $= d_H(T, C_3) = \frac{5}{5} = 1.00$

Jaccard Similarity $= J(T, C_3) = \frac{|3|}{|30-34,40-44,M,F,1,2,3,4,5|} = \frac{1}{9} = 0.11$

Jaccard distance $= d_J(T, C_3) = 1 - 0.11 = 0.89$

Substituting these values in Eq. (1) we get:

For $\alpha = 0.00$, $d_\alpha(T, C_3) = 0 \times 1.00 + (1 - 0) \times 0.89 = 0.89$

For $\alpha = 0.25$, $d_\alpha(T, C_3) = 0.25 \times 1.00 + (1 - 0.25) \times 0.89 = 0.92$

For $\alpha = 0.50$, $d_\alpha(T, C_3) = 0.50 \times 1.00 + (1 - 0.50) \times 0.89 = 0.94$

For $\alpha = 0.75$, $d_\alpha(T, C_3) = 0.75 \times 1.00 + (1 - 0.75) \times 0.89 = 0.97$

For $\alpha = 1.00$, $d_\alpha(T, C_3) = 1 \times 1.00 + (1 - 1) \times 0.89 = 1.00$

The distance between the target campaign and the records which are part of the historical dataset for all 5 values of α are summarized in the table given below (see Table 3).

Table 3. α based weighted average of target campaign from historical dataset.

α	Campaign1	Campaign2	Campaign3
0	0.33	0.75	0.89
0.25	0.40	0.71	0.92
0.50	0.45	0.68	0.94
0.75	0.53	0.64	0.97
1	0.6	0.6	1.0

Once we have calculated the distance metric using weighted average for each of the 5 values of α, we find out the nearest neighbours of the target campaign. This is done by taking a subset of those campaigns whose distance metric is less than a specific radial distance. For this example let us consider radial distance to be **0.7**. Suppose for a campaign x, we have obtained two nearest neighbors, y and

z. To calculate the total impressions, cost, and cost per thousand impressions for y, we use the below equations:

$$I(x) = I(y) + I(z)$$
$$P(x) = (I(y) \times P(y) + I(z) \times P(z))/(I(y) + I(z))$$
$$P^*(x) = \frac{P(x)}{I(x)} \times 1000$$

Using these equations, we will perform the calculations for our target campaign. Let us look at the values of these parameters for different values of α. We observe that for $\alpha = 0$ and $\alpha = 0.25$ only campaign1 can be considered a nearest neighbor since its distance from the target campaign is less than the threshold. The calculations for cumulative impressions, cost and cost per thousand impressions is given below:

$$I = 2000 \quad P = 30 \quad P^* = \frac{30}{2000} \times 1000 = 15$$

For $\alpha = 0.50$ and $\alpha = 0.75$ and $\alpha = 1.00$ campaign1 and campaign2 can be considered nearest neighbors since their distance from the target campaign is less than the threshold. The calculations for cumulative impressions, cost, and cost per thousand impressions are given below (See Table 4).

$$I = 2000 + 1500 = 3500$$
$$P = (2000 * 30 + 1500 * 25)/3500 = 27.85$$
$$P^* = \frac{27.85}{3500} \times 1000 = 7.95$$

Table 4. Total impressions and cost for the Target Campaign.

α	Total Imps (I)	Total Cost (P)	CPTI (P^*)
0	2000	30.00	15.00
0.25	2000	30.00	15.00
0.50	3500	27.85	7.95
0.75	3500	27.85	7.95
1	3500	27.85	7.95

We can observe that we have obtained maximum impressions of 3500 with 7.95$ per 1000 impressions at α values 0.5, 0.75, and 1.

Suppose the advertiser is not satisfied with the reach of the advertisement campaign and expects the campaign to reach a wider audience. In such a case, we will use Sequential Backward Selection (SBS) Algorithm in order to select the best set of features that will return the maximum possible impressions at a reasonable cost. In the SBS algorithm, we remove features one by one in a round-robin manner and calculate our result metrics. From the above calculations, we can generalize the process of calculating the hamming and Jaccard distance for a set of campaigns.

Relax Interest_1

We start with relaxing Interest1 (See Table 5). Below are a few examples of campaigns that are part of our dataset (Table 6).

Table 5. Sample target Campaign with relaxation in Interest1

Age	Sex	Interest_1	Interest_2	Interest_3
30–34	M	*	2	3

Table 6. A Sample historical dataset with relaxation in Interest1

Age	Sex	Interest_1	Interest_2	Interest_3	Imps	Cost
30–34	M	*	3	6	2000	30
35–39	F	*	2	5	1500	25
40–44	F	*	4	5	2500	50

- **Target T: 30–34, M, *, 2, 3**
- **Campaign C_1: 30–34, M, *, 3, 6**

Normalized Hamming Distance $= D_H(T, C_1) = \frac{2}{5} = 0.40$

Jaccard Similarity $= J(T, C_1) = \frac{|30-34,M,3|}{|30-34,M,2,3,6|} = \frac{3}{5} = 0.60$

Jaccard distance $= d_J(T, C_1) = 1 - 0.60 = 0.40$

Substituting these values in Eq. (1) we get:

For $\alpha = 0.00$, $d_\alpha(T, C_1) = 0 \times 0.40 + (1 - 0) \times 0.40 = 0.40$

For $\alpha = 0.25$, $d_\alpha(T, C_1) = 0.25 \times 0.40 + (1 - 0.25) \times 0.40 = 0.40$

For $\alpha = 0.50$, $d_\alpha(T, C_1) = 0.50 \times 0.40 + (1 - 0.50) \times 0.40 = 0.40$

For $\alpha = 0.75$, $d_\alpha(T, C_1) = 0.75 \times 0.40 + (1 - 0.75) \times 0.40 = 0.40$

For $\alpha = 1.00$, $d_\alpha(T, C_1) = 1 \times 0.40 + (1 - 1) \times 0.40 = 0.40$

- **Target T: 30–34, M, *, 2, 3**
- **Campaign C_2: 35-39, F, *, 2, 5**

If the value of the interest in the position that we have relaxed is the same as the value in the target campaign, we do not consider those campaigns as the nearest neighbor in order to avoid double counting. Normalized Hamming Distance $= d_H(T, C_2) = 1.00$

Jaccard distance $= d\_J(T, C2) = 1.00$ Substituting these values in Eq. (1) we get:

$$\text{For } \alpha = 0.00, \ d_\alpha(T, C_2) = 0 \times 1.00 + (1 - 0) \times 1.00 = 1.00$$
$$\text{For } \alpha = 0.25, \ d_\alpha(T, C_2) = 0.25 \times 1.00 + (1 - 0.25) \times 1.00 = 1.00$$
$$\text{For } \alpha = 0.50, \ d_\alpha(T, C_2) = 0.50 \times 1.00 + (1 - 0.50) \times 1.00 = 1.00$$
$$\text{For } \alpha = 0.75, \ d_\alpha(T, C_2) = 0.75 \times 1.00 + (1 - 0.75) \times 1.00 = 1.00$$
$$\text{For } \alpha = 1.00, \ d_\alpha(T, C_2) = 1 \times 1.00 + (1 - 1) \times 1.00 = 1.00$$

- **Target T: 30–34, M, *, 2, 3**
- **Campaign C_3: F, *, 4, 5**

Normalized Hamming Distance $= d_H(T, C_3) = \frac{4}{5} = 0.80$
Jaccard Similarity $= J(T, C_3) = \frac{||}{|30-34,40-44,M,F,2,3,4,5|} = \frac{0}{8} = 0$
Jaccard distance $= d_J(T, C_3) = 1 - 0 = 1$

Substituting these values in Eq. (1) we get:

$$\text{For } \alpha = 0.00, \ d_\alpha(T, C_3) = 0 \times 0.80 + (1 - 0) \times 1.00 = 1.00$$
$$\text{For } \alpha = 0.25, \ d_\alpha(T, C_3) = 0.25 \times 0.80 + (1 - 0.25) \times 1.00 = 0.95$$
$$\text{For } \alpha = 0.50, \ d_\alpha(T, C_3) = 0.50 \times 0.80 + (1 - 0.50) \times 1.00 = 0.90$$
$$\text{For } \alpha = 0.75, \ d_\alpha(T, C_3) = 0.75 \times 0.80 + (1 - 0.75) \times 1.00 = 0.85$$
$$\text{For } \alpha = 1.00, \ d_\alpha(T, C_3) = 1 \times 0.80 + (1 - 1) \times 1.00 = 0.80$$

Based on the distances we can say that for each of the five values of α we can observe that only campaign1 is the nearest neighbour (See Table 15). The

Table 7. Calculation of α based weighted average from Target with Interest_1 Relaxed

α	Campaign1	Campaign2	Campaign3
0	0.40	1.00	1.00
0.25	0.40	1.00	0.95
0.50	0.40	1.00	0.90
0.75	0.40	1.00	0.85
1	0.40	1.00	0.80

cumulative values of impressions and costs are calculated using Eqs. (2), (3), and (4) (See Table 8).

$$I = 2,000, \qquad P = 30, \qquad P^* = \frac{30}{2000} \times 1000 = 15$$

Table 8. Total impressions and cost from nearest neighbours relaxing Interest_1

α	Total Imps (I)	Total Cost (P)	CPTI (P^*)
0	2000	30.00	15.00
0.25	2000	30.00	15.00
0.50	2000	30.00	15.00
0.75	2000	30.00	15.00
1	2000	30.00	15.00

The calculations illustrating the results of cumulative costs and impressions by relaxing Interest_2 and Interest_3 is given in the appendix section. The metrics that we have got from all possible scenarios is provided in Table 9. To maximize the success of an advertising campaign, it's crucial to evaluate the impact of different features on the campaign's reach. In particular, advertisers need to determine whether dropping certain features will help them achieve their desired reach at a lower cost. In our example, we set out to achieve a maximum of 3500 impressions at a cost of $7.95 per thousand impressions. After the first iteration, we observed that we had already achieved the best result possible without relaxing any features. This suggests that our campaign is highly effective, and we can expect to achieve our desired reach without any additional adjustments. However, it's important to note that if the advertiser is not satisfied with the reach of the campaign, further processing may be necessary. For example, we might explore different targeting options or adjust the ad copy to increase its appeal to the target audience. By continuing to evaluate and refine the campaign, we can ensure that we achieve our goals and maximize our return on investment. Overall, our analysis demonstrates the importance of carefully evaluating the impact of different features on an advertising campaign's reach and cost. By making data-driven decisions and continuously refining our approach, we can achieve optimal results and drive the success of our advertising efforts.

Table 9. Summary table for results of all scenarios

α	No Relax			Relax Interest_3			Relax Interest_2			Relax Interest_1		
	I	P	P^*	I	P	P^*	I	P	P^*	I	P	P^*
0	2000	30.00	15.00	3500	27.85	7.95	2000	30.00	15.00	2000	30.00	15.00
0.25	2000	30.00	15.00	3500	27.85	7.95	2000	30.00	15.00	2000	30.00	15.00
0.5	3500	27.85	7.95	3500	27.85	7.95	2000	30.00	15.00	2000	30.00	15.00
0.75	3500	27.85	7.95	3500	27.85	7.95	2000	30.00	15.00	2000	30.00	15.00
1	3500	27.85	7.95	3500	27.85	7.95	2000	30.00	15.00	2000	30.00	15.00

4.2   Algorithm Summary

The Algorithm below summarizes the approach followed to calculate the total impressions and cost of the target campaign by calculating the α based weighted average from all the campaigns present in our historical dataset and finding out the nearest neighbours using radial distance approach (See Algorithm 1).

5   Case Study: Kaggle Facebook Ad Campaign Dataset

The simple example above provides an explanation of the mathematical calculations involved in determining the nearest neighbors of a target campaign from a historical dataset using distance metrics and radial distance methods. We will now proceed to apply this technique to our advertisement campaign that is at our disposal. We have selected several target campaigns and attempted to analyze how the value of impressions and costs change with the value of α, as well as how these values change when we apply Sequential Backward Selection (SBS) to these campaigns. The following observations are provided below:

5.1   Case Study 1

The comprehensive details of our first target campaign, carefully selected for analysis (See Table 10) We have determined the distance of this campaign from all other campaigns that are part of our Facebook advertisement campaign historical dataset. Figure 6 illustrates the relationship between cumulative impressions and cost with the tuning parameter α. This example reveals that when none of the features are relaxed, the cost and the values of α are directly proportional. However, post $\alpha = 0.5$, the impressions have steadily reduced. This implies that the nearest neighbors of our target campaign have a higher cost associated with them for higher values of α. Thus, we must employ the Selective Backward Selection algorithm to observe how this trend changes. Upon removing each feature iteratively, we noticed that both the cost and total impressions vary linearly with the value of α. Consequently, a spike in the number of impressions and cost was observed. However, this offset was balanced by the cost per thousand impressions (See Tables 11).

Algorithm 1. Calculate impressions and cost

Require: α: hyperparameter controlling the commonality vs priority index *data*: Consists of the value of features of the target campaign and seed user dataset with impressions and cost.

Ensure: *Imps(I)*: array of impressions for α *Cost(P)*: array of cost for each α

1: Calculate the d_h and d_J for each row in *data*
2: Initialize I and P to empty arrays
3: **for** each weight i in α **do**
4:     Calculate the d_α for each row in *data*
5:     Select the nearest neighbors with an average distance of 0.5 or less
6:     Calculate the impressions from the nearest neighbors
7:     **if** $I > 0$ **then**
8:         Calculate the P from the nearest neighbors
9:     **else**
10:         Set the P to 0
11:     **end if**
12:     Append the impression and cost to the result array
13: **end for**
14: **return** I and P

Table 10. Target Campaign for Case Study 1

Age	Sex	Interest_1	Interest_2	Interest_3
30–34	F	17	16	19

5.2   Case Study 2

Table 12 presents the comprehensive details of our second target campaign, carefully selected for analysis. We have determined the distance of this campaign from all other campaigns that are part of our Facebook advertisement campaign historical dataset. Figure 7 illustrates the relationship between cumulative impressions and cost with the tuning parameter α. This example reveals that when none of the features are relaxed, the value of cumulative impressions and cost change after $\alpha = 0.5$. Here also we observe that a higher value of α attracts campaigns with high cost associated with it. Thus, we must employ the Selective Backward Selection algorithm to observe how this trend changes. Upon removing each feature iteratively, we noticed that there is an inverse relationship between impressions and costs. This is a consequence of having a lot of nearest neighbours which have no cost associated with them (See Table 13).

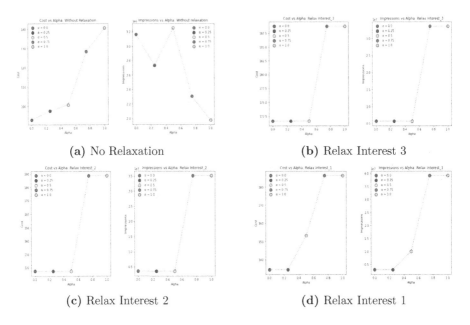

(a) No Relaxation   **(b)** Relax Interest 3

(c) Relax Interest 2   **(d)** Relax Interest 1

Fig. 6. impressions and costs vs. α for target campaign 1.

Table 11. Summary Table for Case Study 1

α	No Relax			Relax Interest_3		
	Imps (I)	Cost (P)	CPTI (P^*)	Imps (I)	Cost (P)	CPTI (P^*)
0	3,165,899	92.73	2.90	5,703,896	171.60	3.0
0.25	2,732,929	97.61	3.60	5,703,896	171.60	3.0
0.5	3,252,310	100.68	3.10	5,703,896	171.60	3.0
0.75	2,309,434	128.36	5.60	33,571,260	188.72	0.6
1	1,977,152	140.64	7.10	33,571,260	188.72	0.6
α	Relax Interest_2			Relax Interest_1		
	Imps (I)	Cost (P)	CPTI (P^*)	Imps (I)	Cost (P)	CPTI (P^*)
0	3,614,343	117.323	3.20	2,944,133	134.438	4.6
0.25	3,614,343	117.323	3.20	2,944,133	134.438	4.6
0.5	3,614,343	117.323	3.20	10,033,388	153.255	1.5
0.75	35,132,532	188.568	0.50	39,118,142	186.298	0.5
1	35,132,532	188.568	0.50	39,118,142	186.298	0.5

Table 12. Target Campaign for Case Study 2

Age	Sex	Interest_1	Interest_2	Interest_3
35-39	M	29	31	33

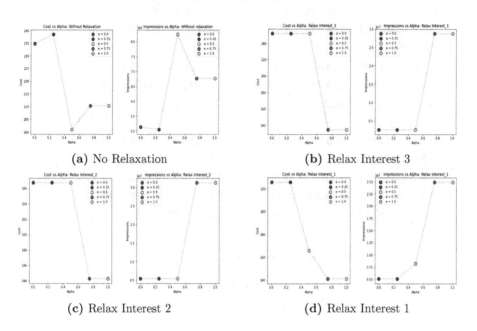

(a) No Relaxation   (b) Relax Interest 3

(c) Relax Interest 2   (d) Relax Interest 1

Fig. 7. Impressions and costs vs. α for target campaign 2.

5.3 Case Study 3

Table 14 presents the comprehensive details of our second target campaign, carefully selected for analysis. We have determined the distance of this campaign from all other campaigns that are part of our Facebook advertisement campaign historical dataset. Figure 8 illustrates the relationship between cumulative impressions and cost with the tuning parameter α. This example reveals that when none of the features are relaxed, the value of cumulative impressions is highest at a different alpha value than the highest cost (See Table 15).

Table 13. Summary table for Case Study 2

α	No Relax			Relax Interest_3		
	Imps (I)	Cost (P)	CPTI (P^*)	Imps (I)	Cost (P)	CPTI (P^*)
0	5,132,042	234.842	4.60	2,581,594	251.742	9.8
0.25	5,047,848	238.433	4.70	2,581,594	251.742	9.8
0.5	8,241,967	201.066	2.40	2,581,594	251.742	9.8
0.75	6,765,186	210.34	3.10	28,710,998	134.534	0.5
1	6,765,186	210.34	3.10	28,710,998	134.534	0.5
α	Relax Interest_2			Relax Interest_1		
	Imps (I)	Cost (P)	CPTI (P^*)	Imps (I)	Cost (P)	CPTI (P^*)
0	5,382,884	156.732	2.90	5,072,066	225.661	4.4
0.25	5,382,884	156.732	2.90	2,944,133	134.438	4.6
0.5	5,382,884	156.732	2.90	8,206,737	165.99	2.0
0.75	31,255,377	144.266	0.50	24,883,863	141.082	0.6
1	31,255,377	144.266	0.50	24,883,863	141.082	0.6

Table 14. Target Campaign for Case Study 3

Age	Sex	Interest_1	Interest_2	Interest_3
45-49	F	24	27	30

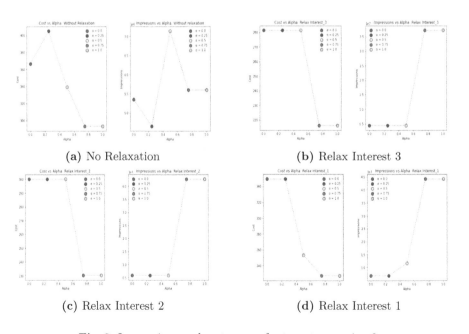

(a) No Relaxation

(b) Relax Interest 3

(c) Relax Interest 2

(d) Relax Interest 1

Fig. 8. Impressions and costs vs. α for target campaign 3.

Table 15. Summary table for Case Study 3

α	No Relax			Relax Interest_3		
	Imps (I)	Cost (P)	CPTI (P^*)	Imps (I)	Cost (P)	CPTI (P^*)
0	5,351,420	366.807	6.90	4,406,144	281.342	6.4
0.25	4,654,708	405.017	8.70	4,406,144	281.342	6.4
0.5	7,138,515	339.087	4.80	4,406,144	281.342	6.4
0.75	5,599,004	293.093	5.20	37,100,269	216.254	0.6
1	5,599,004	293.093	5.20	37,100,269	216.254	0.6
α	Relax Interest_2			Relax Interest_1		
	Imps (I)	Cost (P)	CPTI (P^*)	Imps (I)	Cost (P)	CPTI (P^*)
0	5,914,824	299.974	5.1	6,898,159	349.214	5.1
0.25	5,914,824	299.974	5.1	6,898,159	349.214	5.1
0.5	5,914,824	299.974	5.1	11,680,241	253.523	2.2
0.75	42,676,162	230.354	0.50	44,142,592	227.478	0.5
1	42,676,162	230.354	0.50	44,142,592	227.478	0.5

6   Conclusion

In this study, our objective was to measure the reach of an advertisement campaign by computing its distance from all campaigns in our dataset using a weighted average of hamming and jaccards distance. By employing the radial distance metric, we determined the nearest neighbors of the target campaign at a specific distance. We then estimated the cumulative impressions of the target campaign by adding the impressions of its nearest neighbors and the total cost of our target campaign by calculating the weighted average of impressions and cost of its nearest neighbors. Our analysis revealed the variation of total impressions and total cost with respect to α and the impact of Sequential Backward Selection (SBS) on the increase in the reach of the advertisement campaign. Our future work includes comparing the effectiveness of the SBS method for feature selection with other heuristic methods such as SFS and collaborative filtering techniques. Our methodology has broad applications, but it is particularly relevant in recommendation systems. In social media and OTT networks, user segments can be created by analyzing the similarity in the content that specific users view. Sequential Backward Selection can be applied to recommend specific content to a wider group of users for greater viewership. Overall, our study presents a robust methodology for measuring the reach of advertisement campaigns and highlights the potential applications of our approach in recommendation systems.

A   Appendix

Relax Interest_3
We will begin applying Sequential Backward Selection from Interest3. We will be calculating all our metrics by using 4 out of the 5 constraints that we have (see Table 5, 6, 16 and 17).

Table 16. Sample target Campaign with relaxation in Interest3

Age	Sex	Interest_1	Interest_2	Interest_3
30–34	M	1	2	*

Table 17. A Sample historical dataset with relaxation in Interest3

Age	Sex	Interest_1	Interest_2	Interest_3	Imps	Cost
30–34	M	2	3	*	2000	30
35–39	F	1	2	*	1500	25
40–44	F	3	4	*	2500	50

Below are a few examples of campaigns that are part of our dataset.

- **Target T: 30–34, M, 1, 2, ***
- **Campaign C_1: 30–34, M, 2, 3, ***

Normalized Hamming Distance $= d_H(T, C_1) = \frac{2}{5} = 0.40$

Jaccard Similarity $= J(T, C_1) = \frac{|30-34,M,2|}{|30-34,M,1,2,3|} = \frac{3}{5} = 0.60$

Jaccard distance $= d_J(T, C_1) = 1 - 0.60 = 0.40$

Substituting these values in Eq. (1), we get:

For $\alpha = 0.00$, $d_\alpha(T, C_1) = 0 \times 0.40 + (1 - 0) \times 0.40 = 0.40$

For $\alpha = 0.25$, $d_\alpha(T, C_1) = 0.25 \times 0.40 + (1 - 0.25) \times 0.40 = 0.40$

For $\alpha = 0.50$, $d_\alpha(T, C_1) = 0.50 \times 0.40 + (1 - 0.50) \times 0.40 = 0.40$

For $\alpha = 0.75$, $d_\alpha(T, C_1) = 0.75 \times 0.40 + (1 - 0.75) \times 0.40 = 0.40$

For $\alpha = 1.00$, $d_\alpha(T, C_1) = 1 \times 0.40 + (1 - 1) \times 0.40 = 0.40$

- **Target: 30–34, M, 1, 2, ***
- **Campaign C_2: 35-39, F, 1, 2, ***

Normalized Hamming Distance $= d_H(T, C_2) = \frac{2}{5} = 0.40$

Jaccard Similarity $= J(T, C_2) = \frac{|1,2|}{|30-34,35-39,M,F,1,2|} = \frac{2}{6} = 0.33$

Jaccard distance $= d_J(T, C2) = 1 - 0.33 = 0.67$

Substituting these values in Eq. (1) we get:

For $\alpha = 0.00$, $d_\alpha(T, C_2) = 0 \times 0.40 + (1 - 0) \times 0.67 = 0.67$

For $\alpha = 0.25$, $d_\alpha(T, C_2) = 0.25 \times 0.40 + (1 - 0.25) \times 0.67 = 0.60$

For $\alpha = 0.50$, $d_\alpha(T, C_2) = 0.50 \times 0.40 + (1 - 0.50) \times 0.67 = 0.53$

For $\alpha = 0.75$, $d_\alpha(T, C_2) = 0.75 \times 0.40 + (1 - 0.75) \times 0.67 = 0.46$

For $\alpha = 1.00$, $d_\alpha(T, C_2) = 1 \times 0.40 + (1 - 1) \times 0.67 = 0.40$

- **Target T: 30–34, M, 1, 2, ***
- **Campaign C_3: 40–44, F, 3, 4, ***

Normalized Hamming Distance $= d_H(T, C_3) = \frac{4}{5} = 0.80$

Jaccard Similarity $= J(T, C_3) = \frac{||}{|30-34,40-44,M,F,1,2,3,4|} = \frac{0}{8} = 0$

Jaccard distance $= d_H(T, C_3) = 1 - 0 = 1.00$

Substituting these values in Eq. (1) we get:

For $\alpha = 0.00$, $d_\alpha(T, C_3) = 0 \times 0.80 + (1 - 0) \times 1.00 = 1.00$

For $\alpha = 0.25$, $d_\alpha(T, C_3) = 0.25 \times 0.80 + (1 - 0.25) \times 1.00 = 0.95$

For $\alpha = 0.50$, $d_\alpha(T, C_3) = 0.50 \times 0.80 + (1 - 0.50) \times 1.00 = 0.90$

For $\alpha = 0.75$, $d_\alpha(T, C_3) = 0.75 \times 0.80 + (1 - 0.75) \times 1.00 = 0.85$

For $\alpha = 1.00$, $d_\alpha(T, C_3) = 1 \times 0.80 + (1 - 1) \times 1.00 = 0.80$

The α-based weighted average is calculated based on the hamming and Jaccard distance (See Table 7). Based on the distances we can say that for each of the five values of α, we can observe that campaign1 and campaign2 are the nearest neighbors. The cumulative values of impressions and costs are calculated using equations (2), (3), and (4) (See Table 8, 18 and 19).

$$I = 2000 + 1500 = 3500$$
$$P = (2000 * 30 + 1500 * 25)/3500 = 27.85$$
$$P^* = \frac{27.85}{3500} \times 1000 = 7.95$$

Table 18. Calculation of α based weighted average with Interest_3 Relaxed

α	Campaign1	Campaign2	Campaign3
0	0.40	0.67	1.00
0.25	0.40	0.60	0.95
0.50	0.40	0.53	0.90
0.75	0.40	0.46	0.85
1	0.40	0.40	0.80

Table 19. Results calculated on nearest neighbors using Radial Distance relaxing Interest_3

α	Total Imps (I)	Total Cost (P)	CPTI (P^*)
0	3500	27.85	7.95
0.25	3500	27.85	7.95
0.50	3500	27.85	7.95
0.75	3500	27.85	7.95
1	3500	27.85	7.95

Relax Interest_2

Now we relax Interest2 in our target campaign (See Table 9, 20 and 21).

Accordingly, we will also relax Interest 2 in our historical dataset (See Table 10).

Table 20. Sample target Campaign with relaxation in Interest2

Age	Sex	Interest_1	Interest_2	Interest_3
30–34	M	1	*	3

- **Target: 30–34, M, 1, *, 3**
- **Campaign1: 30–34, M, 2, *, 6**

Normalized Hamming Distance $= d_H(T, C_1) = \frac{2}{5} = 0.40$
Jaccard Similarity $= J(T, C_1) = \frac{|30-34,M|}{|30-34,M,1,2,3,6|} = \frac{2}{6} = 0.33$

Table 21. A Sample historical dataset with relaxation in Interest2

Age	Sex	Interest_1	Interest_2	Interest_3	Imps	Cost
30–34	M	2	*	6	2000	30
35–39	F	1	*	5	1500	25
40–44	F	3	*	5	2500	50

Jaccard distance $= d_J(T, C_1) = 1 - 0.33 = 0.67$

Substituting these values in Eq. (1) we get:

For $\alpha = 0.00$, $d_\alpha(T, C_1) = 0 \times 0.40 + (1 - 0) \times 0.67 = 0.67$
For $\alpha = 0.25$, $d_\alpha(T, C_1) = 0.25 \times 0.40 + (1 - 0.25) \times 0.67 = 0.60$
For $\alpha = 0.50$, $d_\alpha(T, C_1) = 0.50 \times 0.40 + (1 - 0.50) \times 0.67 = 0.53$
For $\alpha = 0.75$, $d_\alpha(T, C_1) = 0.75 \times 0.40 + (1 - 0.75) \times 0.67 = 0.46$
For $\alpha = 1.00$, $d_\alpha(T, C_1) = 1 \times 0.40 + (1 - 1) \times 0.67 = 0.40$

- **Target T: 30–34, M, 1, *, 3**
- **Campaign C_2: 35-39, F, 1, *, 5**

If the value of the interest in the position that we have relaxed is the same as the value in the target campaign, we do not consider those campaigns as the nearest neighbor in order to avoid double counting.

Normalized Hamming Distance $= d_H(T, C_2) = 1.00$
Jaccard distance $= d_J(T, C_2) = 1.00$

Substituting these values in Eq. (1) we get:

For $\alpha = 0.00$, $d_\alpha(T, C_2) = 0 \times 1.00 + (1 - 0) \times 1.00 = 1.00$
For $\alpha = 0.25$, $d_\alpha(T, C_2) = 0.25 \times 1.00 + (1 - 0.25) \times 1.00 = 1.00$
For $\alpha = 0.50$, $d_\alpha(T, C_2) = 0.50 \times 1.00 + (1 - 0.50) \times 1.00 = 1.00$
For $\alpha = 0.75$, $d_\alpha(T, C_2) = 0.75 \times 1.00 + (1 - 0.75) \times 1.00 = 1.00$
For $\alpha = 1.00$, $d_\alpha(T, C_2) = 1 \times 1.00 + (1 - 1) \times 1.00 = 1.00$

- **Target T: 30–34, M, 1, *, 3**
- **Campaign C_3: 40-44, F, 3, *, 5**

Normalized Hamming Distance $= d_H(T, C_3) = \frac{4}{5} = 0.80$
Jaccard Similarity $= J(T, C_3) = \frac{|3|}{|30-34,40-44,M,F,1,3,5|} = \frac{1}{7} = 0.14$
Jaccard distance $= d_J(T, C_3) = 1 - 0.14 = 0.86$

Substituting these values in Eq. (1) we get:

For $\alpha = 0.00$, $d_\alpha(T, C_3) = 0 \times 0.80 + (1 - 0) \times 0.86 = 0.86$
For $\alpha = 0.25$, $d_\alpha(T, C_3) = 0.25 \times 0.80 + (1 - 0.25) \times 0.86 = 0.84$
For $\alpha = 0.50$, $d_\alpha(T, C_3) = 0.50 \times 0.80 + (1 - 0.50) \times 0.86 = 0.83$
For $\alpha = 0.75$, $d_\alpha(T, C_3) = 0.75 \times 0.80 + (1 - 0.75) \times 0.86 = 0.81$
For $\alpha = 1.00$, $d_\alpha(T, C_3) = 1 \times 0.80 + (1 - 1) \times 0.86 = 0.80$

Table 22. Calculation of α based weighted average with Interest_2 Relaxed

α	Campaign1	Campaign2	Campaign3
0	0.67	1.00	0.86
0.25	0.60	1.00	0.84
0.50	0.53	1.00	0.83
0.75	0.46	1.00	0.81
1	0.40	1.00	0.80

For all the values of α we can observe that only Campaign1 is the nearest neighbour (See Table 11). Therefore, calculating the cumulative impressions and cost using Eqs. (2), (3), and (4) (See Table 12, 22 and 23).

$$I = 2000 \qquad C = 30 \qquad P^* = \frac{30}{2000} \times 1000 = 15$$

Table 23. Total impressions and cost calculated on nearest neighbors

α	Total Imps (I)	Total Cost (P)	CPTI (P^*)
0	2000	30	15
0.25	2000	30	15
0.50	2000	30	15
0.75	2000	30	15
1	2000	30	15

References

1. Vasudeva Dave, Kushal Varma (2014)
2. Lotame. Audience extension: a strategic guide for advertisers (2019)
3. Liu, H., Yu, L.: Feature selection for high-dimensional data: a fast correlation-based filter solution. In: Proceedings of the Twentieth International Conference on Machine Learning (ICML-03), pp. 856–863. ACM (2005)
4. AdRoll. Audience extension: tips for finding more of your best customers, n.d.
5. Andoni, A., Indyk, P.: Nearest neighbors in high-dimensional spaces. In: Proceedings of the Annual Symposium on Foundations of Computer Science, pp. 459–468. IEEE (2006)
6. Truong, V., Hoang, V.: Machine learning optimization in computational advertising-a systematic literature review. In: Abdul Karim, S.A. (ed.) Intelligent Systems Modeling and Simulation II, pp. 97–111. Springer, Cham (2022). https://doi.org/10.1007/978-3-031-04028-3_8
7. MacKay, D.J.C.: Information Theory, Inference, and Learning Algorithms. Cambridge University Press, Cambridge (2003)

8. Hamming, R.W.: Error detecting and error correcting codes. Bell Syst. Tech. J. **29**, 147–160 (1950)
9. Wang, S., Zhao, Z., Hong, X.: The research on collaborative filtering recommendation algorithm based on improved clustering processing. In: 2015 IEEE International Conference on Computer and Information Technology; Ubiquitous Computing and Communications; Dependable, Autonomic and Secure Computing; Pervasive Intelligence and Computing, pp. 1012–1015. IEEE (2015)
10. Manning, C.D., Raghavan, P., Schütze, H.: Introduction to Information Retrieval. Cambridge University Press, Cambridge (2008)
11. Liben-Nowell, D., Kleinberg, J.: The link-prediction problem for social networks. J. Am. Soc. Inform. Sci. Technol. **58**(7), 1019–1031 (2007)
12. Ali, N., Neagu, D., Trundle, P.: Evaluation of k-nearest neighbour classifier performance for heterogeneous data sets. SN Appl. Sci. **1**, 1–15 (2019)
13. Lombardi, G., Testa, C., Pellegrino, R.: Fuzzy decision making in multi-criteria decision analysis: a review. Int. J. Approx. Reason. **93**, 708–728 (2018)
14. Pavlov, D., Kostic, B., Pekar, V.: Similarity measures for categorical data: a comparative study. IEEE Access **8**, 45784–45805 (2020)
15. Fakhouri, M., Hilson, G., Mina, J.: An overview of similarity measures for clustering and classification of complex data. J. Big Data **7**(1), 1–24 (2020)
16. Wang, T., Ren, C., Luo, Y., Tian, J.: NS-DBSCAN: a density-based clustering algorithm in network space. ISPRS Int. J. Geo-Inf. **8**(5), 218 (2019)
17. Jain, R.: A hybrid clustering algorithm for data mining. Comput. Sci. Inf. Technol. **2**, 05 (2012)
18. Hancock, J.: Jaccard Distance (Jaccard Index, Jaccard Similarity Coefficient) (2004)
19. Weller-Fahy, D., Borghetti, B., Sodemann, A.: A survey of distance and similarity measures used within network intrusion anomaly detection. IEEE Commun. Surv. Tutor. **17**, 70–91 (2015)
20. Dholakia, U.M., Bagozzi, R.P., Pearo, L.K.: A social influence model of consumer participation in network-and small-group-based virtual communities. Int. J. Res. Mark. **33**(3), 603–624 (2016)
21. Kumar, V., Reinartz, W.: Customer Relationship Management: Concept, Strategy, and Tools. Springer, Heidelberg (2016). https://doi.org/10.1007/978-3-642-20110-3
22. Cohen, J., Venkatesan, R., Kumar, V.: Developing optimal customer segmentation using RFM analysis. J. Interact. Mark. **27**(2), 63–73 (2013)
23. Lee, K.H., Yoo, B., Lee, J.: Improving digital marketing performance using a sentiment analysis and target identification approach. J. Bus. Res. **80**, 82–94 (2017)

On the p-Rank of the Incidence Matrix of a Projective Hjelmslev Plane

Maryam Bajalan[1], Ivan Landjev[1,2(✉)], and Assia Rousseva[3]

[1] Institute of Mathematics and Informatics, Bulgarian Academy of Sciences, 8 Acad. G. Bonchev str., 1113 Sofia, Bulgaria
ivan@math.bas.bg
[2] New Bulgarian University, 21 Montevideo str., 1618 Sofia, Bulgaria
i.landjev@nbu.bg
[3] Faculty of Mathematics and Informatics, Sofia University, 5 J. Bourchier blvd., 1164 Sofia, Bulgaria
assia@fmi.uni-sofia.bg

Abstract. In this paper we estimate the p-rank of the points-by-lines incidence matrix of a projective Hjelmslev plane over a chain ring with 4 or 9 elements. The proof uses a characterization of all divisible arcs in the corresponding projective planes. Furthermore, we prove lower and upper bounds on the p-rank of the incidence matrix of the projective Hjelmslev plane over an arbitrary finite chain ring of nilpotency index 2.

Keywords: projective Hjelmslev plane · finite chain ring · incidence matrix · p-rank

1 Preliminaries

In this paper we shall use the basic definitions and notations from [1,2,4,5].

A set of points X in $\mathrm{PG}(2,q)$ or $\mathrm{PHG}(2,R)$, $R/\mathrm{Rad}\,R \cong \mathbb{F}_q$, is said to be linearly independent if there exists an arc $\mathcal{K}$ with support $\mathrm{Supp}\,\mathcal{K} \subseteq X$ such that every line has multiplicity $0 \mod p$, i.e. for every line L it holds $\mathcal{K}(L) \equiv 0$ (mod p). If X is a linearly independent set of points in a finite plane $(\mathrm{PG}(2,q)$ or $\mathrm{PHG}(2,R))$, and A is the incidence matrix of that plane then we have the following inequality

$$\mathrm{rk}\,A \geq |X|. \tag{1}$$

It is known that the rank of the points-by-lines incidence matrix of $\mathrm{PG}(2,q)$, $q = p^h$, is

$$\left(\frac{p(p+1)}{2} \right)^h + 1.$$

The research of the second and the third author was supported was supported by the Science Research Fund of Sofia University under Contract 80-10-72/25.04.2023.

T. Zlateva and G. Tuparov (Eds.): CSECS 2023, LNICST 514, pp. 30–39, 2023.
https://doi.org/10.1007/978-3-031-44668-9_2

The incidence matrix of $\mathrm{AG}(2,q)$ has rank

$$\left(\frac{p(p+1)}{2}\right)^h.$$

In the case $q = p$, the rank of $\mathrm{PG}(2,p)$ (resp. $\mathrm{AG}(2,p)$) is $\binom{p+1}{2}+1$, resp. $\binom{p+1}{2}$. It is known that the neighbor classes of points in $\mathrm{PHG}(2,R)$, are affine planes of order q [2]. This implies the following lemma.

Lemma 1. *Let R be a finite chain ring with, $|R| = q^2$ and $R/\mathrm{Rad}\,R \cong \mathbb{F}_q$. If X is a linearly independent set of points in $\mathrm{PHG}(2,R)$ then for every neighbor class of points $[P]$, it holds*

$$|X \cap [P]| \le \left(\frac{p(p+1)}{2}\right)^h.$$

Corollary 2. *(i) If $|R| = 4$ then $|X \cap [P]| \le 3$.*
(ii) If $|R| = 9$ then $|X \cap [P]| \le 6$.

Theorem 3. *Let A be the incidence matrix points-by-lines of the projective plane $\mathrm{PHG}(2,R)$, where $R/\mathrm{Rad}\,R \cong \mathbb{F}_q$. Then*

$$\mathrm{rk}\,(A) \le \left(\frac{p(p+1)}{2}\right)^h (q^2 + q + 1).$$

Proof. The theorem follows immediately by Lemma 1.

An arc in which every line has multiplicity $c \mod p$ is called a $(c \mod p)$-arc.

Lemma 4. *Let Y be linearly independent set of points in $\mathrm{PHG}(2,R)$, and let $\mathcal{K}$ be a $(0 \mod p)$-arc with $\mathrm{Supp}\,\mathcal{K} \subseteq Y$. Then there exist a constant c such that for every neighbor class of points $[P]$, it holds*

$$\mathcal{K}[P] \equiv c \pmod{p}.$$

Proof. Let $[L]$ be a neighbor class of points, and let $[P_i]$, $i = 0, \ldots, q$, be the neighbor classes of points incident with this class of lines. Let $L_1 \in [L]$ and denote by $L_1, \ldots, L_q$ all lines that contain the line segment $L_1 \cap P_0$.
    Set
$$x_{ij} = \mathcal{K}([P_i] \cap L_j), i = 0, \ldots, q, i = 1, \ldots, q.$$
Counting the multilicities of the points through the segment $[P_0] \cap L_1$, one gets

$$x_{01} + x_{11} + x_{21} + \cdots + x_{q1} \equiv 0 \pmod{p}$$
$$x_{01} + x_{12} + x_{22} + \cdots + x_{q2} \equiv 0 \pmod{p}$$
$$\vdots$$
$$x_{01} + x_{1q} + x_{2q} + \cdots + x_{qq} \equiv 0 \pmod{p}$$

This implies

$$\mathcal{K}[P_1] + \mathcal{K}[P_2] + \cdots + \mathcal{K}[P_q] \equiv 0 \pmod{p}.$$

Thus we have that

$$\mathcal{K}[L] - \mathcal{K}[P_j] \equiv 0 \pmod{p}, \tag{2}$$

for every $j = 0, 1, \ldots, q$. This in turn implies

$$\mathcal{K}[P_0] \equiv \mathcal{K}[P_1] \equiv \cdots \equiv \mathcal{K}[P_q] \pmod{p}.$$

Theorem 5. *Let R be a finite chain ring with $|R| = q^2$, $R/\mathrm{Rad}\,R \cong \mathbb{F}_q$, $q = p^h$, where $p \geq 3$. Denote by A the points-by-lines incidence matrix of $\mathrm{PHG}(2, R)$. Then*

$$\mathrm{rk}_p\, A \geq \binom{p+1}{2}^h (q+1) + 2q^2 - 1.$$

Proof. Define the pointset X as follows: select a line class $[L]$, i.e. a line in the factor geometry, and sets of $\binom{p+1}{2}^h$ points in each point class on $[L]$. These points in each of the classes on $[L]$ should form an independent set (i.e. an independent set in $\mathrm{AG}(2, q)$). Further select a point in the point class $[P_0] \notin [L]$ and two points in each of the remaining point classes not on $[L]$ or different from $[P_0]$. There are no restrictions on the point in $[P_0]$ and the remaining $2(q^2 - 1)$ points are selected in the following way.

Let $[L']$ be any line class through $[P_0]$. Denote by $[P_i]$, $i = 0, \ldots, q-1$, the point classes on $[L']$. Consider a line segment in $[L] \cap [L']$ that has the direction of L' and denote by L'_i, $i = 1, \ldots, q$, the lines through this segment. Now the two points of X in each of the point classes $[P_i]$, $i = 1, \ldots, q-1$, are selected so that $[P_i]$ contains points incident with L'_i and L'_{i+1}. These two points from $X \cap [[P_i]$ are denoted by P'_i and P''_i. The same selection is made for the points in all line classes through $[P_0]$ (see Fig. 1).

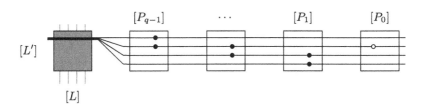

Fig. 1. A neighborclass of lines in $\mathrm{PG}(2, 2)$

Hence by construction we have that

$$|X| = \binom{p+1}{2}^h (q+1) + 2q^2 - 1.$$

We are going to prove that X is an independent set. It is enough to demonstrate that every $(0 \mod p)$-arc with support contained on X is the trivial zero-arc.

Let $\mathcal{K}$ be a $(0 \mod p)$-arc in $\mathrm{PHG}(2, R)$ with $\mathrm{Supp}\,\mathcal{K} \subseteq X$. By Lemma 4 every point class has the same multiplicity modulo p. Since $p + 12 \equiv 0 \pmod{p}$ we get that every point class has multiplicity $0 \pmod{p}$. This implies in particular that $\mathcal{K}([P_0]) = 0$.

Furthermore, since $\mathcal{K}(L'_i) \equiv 0$, $i = 1, \ldots, q$, we get that

$$\mathcal{K}(P'_i) \equiv a \pmod{p}, \mathcal{K}(P''_i) \equiv b \pmod{p},$$

for some constants $a, b \in \{0, \ldots, p-1\}$. Moreover we have

$$a \equiv a + b \equiv b \pmod{p}.$$

This implies that $a \equiv b \equiv 0 \pmod{p}$, i.e. $a = b = 0$. We have obtained so far that for all points P in $X \setminus [L]$ we have $\mathcal{K}(P) = 0$.

Let $[L]$ contain the points $[Q_0], [Q_1], \ldots, [Q_q]$. Consider one of them, $[Q_0]$ say. Clearly $\mathcal{K}([Q_0]) \equiv 0 \pmod{p}$. All line segments in $[Q_0]$, except for those contained in one parallel class (the one with the direction of L), have multiplicity $0 \pmod{P}$. Now an easy counting gives that also the segment in this parallel class have multiplicity $0 \pmod{P}$. Hence $\mathcal{K}|_{[Q_0]}$ is a $(0 \mod p)$-arc. By the fact that $X \cap [Q_0]$ is an independent set, $\mathcal{K}(P) = 0$ for all points $P \in [Q_0]$. Similarly, $\mathcal{K}(P) = 0$ for all points $P \in [Q_i]$ for all $i = 1, \ldots, q$. Thus $\mathcal{K}$ is the trivial zero arc on X. This implies that X is an independent set and

$$\mathrm{rk}_p A \geq |X| = \left(\frac{p+1}{2}\right)^h (q+1) + 2q^2 - 1.$$

This theorem can be improved slightly by taking suitably a line class with a maximal number of independent points, a line in the affine part containing one point in each neighbour class, and sets of three points (suitably chosen) in each of the remaining point classes.

Theorem 6. *Let R be a finite chain ring with $|R| = q^2$, $R/\mathrm{Rad}\,R \cong \mathbb{F}_q$, $q = p^h$, where $p \geq 3$. Denote by A the points-by-lines incidence matrix of $\mathrm{PHG}(2, R)$. Then*

$$\mathrm{rk}_p A \geq \left(\frac{p+1}{2}\right)^h (q+1) + 3q^2 - 2q.$$

2   The Case $|R| = 4$

In this case the point multiplicities are contained in $\{0, 1, \ldots, p-1\} = \{0, 1\}$. If X is a set that supports a $(0 \mod p)$-arc by Lemma 4, all point classes contain even or odd number of points. Therefore we have for all points P either $|X \cap [P]| \in \{0, 2, 4\}$, or else $|X \cap [P]| \in \{1, 3\}$.

We can also make the following observation. If X is a $(0 \mod 2)$-arc and if we replace the intersection of this arc with some point class by its complement in the point class, the result is again a $(0 \mod 2)$-arc. In other words, if X is a $(0 \mod 2)$-arc then

$$(X \setminus (X \cap [P])) \cup ([P] \setminus (X \cap [P]))$$

is again a $(0 \mod 2)$-arc.

Let A_R, where $R = \mathbb{Z}_4$ or $\mathbb{F}_2[u]/(u^2)$, be the rank of the points-by-lines incidence matrix of the plane $\mathrm{PHG}(2, R)$. In both cases, we have (by Theorem 5)

$$\mathrm{rk}\, A_r \geq 12.$$

Denote by V the vector space of all $(0 \mod 2)$-arcs in $\mathrm{PHG}(2, R)$, $|R| = 4$. This vector space can be viewed as a subspace of $\mathbb{F}_2^{28}$. More generally, the vector space of all $(0 \mod p)$-arcs in $\mathrm{PHG}(2, R)$, $|R| = q^2, q = p^h$, can be viewed as a subspace of $\mathbb{F}_p^{q^2(q^2+q+1)}$ by identifying each arc with its characteristic vector $\boldsymbol{x}$.

If $\boldsymbol{x}$ is the characteristic vector of a $(0 \mod 2)$-arc then $\boldsymbol{x}A_R = \boldsymbol{0}$ and $\boldsymbol{x}$ is a solution to a homogeneous system of linear equations with a coefficient matrix A_R. Hence

$$\mathrm{rk}_p A_R + \dim V = 28.$$

In the general case, we have

$$\mathrm{rk}_p A_R + \dim V = q^2(q^2 + q + 1).$$

Note that all $(0 \mod 2)$-arcs that have an even number of points in each point class form a subspace V_0 of V. Now we are going to construct all $(0 \mod 2)$ arcs from V_0.

(1) Every neighbor class contains 0 or 4 points. The number of such arcs is 2^7.
(2) Every neighbor class with 2 points, where the two points in every class determine all possible directions (i.e. they determine a all lines in the factor geometry $\mathrm{PG}(2, q)$). Two points P, Q are said to determine the line class $[L]$ if $\langle P, Q \rangle \in [L]$. If B is the incidence matrix of $\mathrm{PG}(2, 2)$ then the number of such arcs is $\mathrm{per}(B) \cdot 2^7$, i.e. this number is $24 \cdot 2^7$. Here $\mathrm{per}(B)$ is the permanent of the of B.
(3) Four classes have 0 or four points and three classes with two points. The classes with two point should form a triangle. The two points in each of these classes should determine directions that point at the nucleus. Since the number of triangles is $\dfrac{7 \cdot 6 \cdot 4}{3!} = 28$, the total number of such arcs is $28 \cdot 2^7$ (see Fig. 2).
(4) Three classes have 0 or four points and the remaining four classes have two points. The classes with 2-points form a hyperoval and the 0/4-classes are collinear. The pairs of points in each of the 2-point classes determine a line which points at the same point class on the line of 0/4-points (see Fig. 3). Altogether we have 7 choices for the 0/4 line and 3 possibilities for the point on it. So, altogether we have $21 \cdot 2^7$ such arcs.

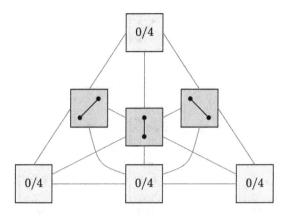

Fig. 2. An arc of type (3) in $PG(2,2)$

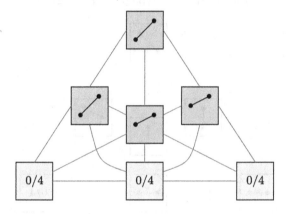

Fig. 3. An arc of type (4) in $PG(2,2)$

(5) Two classes have 0 or 4 points, and the remaining five classes have 2 points. The two points in the class which is the third point on the line $[L]$ defined by the 0/4-point classes define a line in the class $[L]$. In the remaining four 2-point classes the directions are as introduced on Fig. 4. The point classes $[Q_1]$ and $[Q_2]$ can be selected in $\binom{7}{2} = 21$ ways. Furthermore, the two point classes with two points that define a line pointing at $[Q_i]$, $i = 1, 2$, can be selected in four ways. Hence the number of such arcs is equal to $84 \cdot 2^7$.

(6) One class with 0/4 points (see Fig. 5).
Total number of arcs: $98 \cdot 2^7$

Summing up, the total number of (0 mod 2) arcs with an even number of points in each point class is:

$$2^7 + 24 \cdot 2^7 + 28 \cdot 2^7 + 21 \cdot 2^7 + 84 \cdot 2^7 + 98 \cdot 2^7 = 256 \cdot 2^7 = 2^{15}.$$

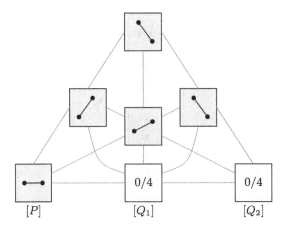

Fig. 4. An arc of type (5) in PG(2, 2)

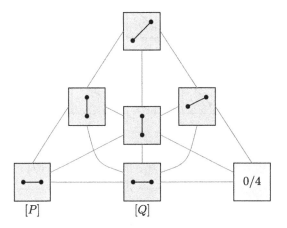

Fig. 5. An arc of type (6) in PG(2, 2)

Hence dim $V_0 = 15$.

Now it remains to count the number of all (0 mod 2)-arcs with an odd number of points in each neighbor class of points.

In the case when $R = \mathbb{F}_2[u]/(u^2)$ there exist no hyperovals and hence no (0 mod 2)-arcs with an odd number of points in each class. Hence dim $V = 15$.

In the case $R = \mathbb{Z}_4$ there exist (0 mod 2)-arcs that have an odd number of points in each point class [3]. If we select arbitrarily four points in general position in the point classes $[U]$, $[U_0]$, $[U_1]$, $[U_2]$, where

$$U = (1,1,1), U_0 = (1,0,0), U_1 = (0,1,0), U_2 = (0,0,1),$$

then they can be extended uniquely to a hyperoval. Therefore the number of the (0 mod 2)-arcs with an odd number of points in each neighbor class is $4^4 \cdot 2^7 = 2^{15}$. Thus in the case $R = \mathbb{Z}_4$, we get that dim $V = 16$.

Thus we have proved the following theorem.

Theorem 7.
$$\mathrm{rk}_2\,(A_R) = \begin{cases} 12 & \text{if } R = \mathbb{Z}_4, \\ 13 & \text{if } R = \mathbb{F}_2[u]/(u^2). \end{cases}$$

3   The Case $|R| = 9$

Since $\mathrm{rk}_3\,A_{\mathrm{AG}(2,3)} = 6$, we have the upper bound

$$\mathrm{rk}_3\,A_{\mathrm{PHG}(2,R)} \leq 6 \cdot 13 = 78.$$

On the other hand, by Theorem 6 we get also a lower bound, which gives altogether

$$45 \leq \mathrm{rk}_3\,A_{\mathrm{PHG}(2,R)} \leq 76.$$

Lemma 8. *Let R be a chain ring with $|R| = 9$. Consider two lines $[L_1]$ and $[L_2]$ in the factor geometry of $\mathrm{PHG}(2, R)$. Let X be an arbitrary point set containing six points in each of the point classes in $[L_1]$ and $[L_2]$ but not in the point class $[L_1] \cap [L_2]$. Then X is a linearly dependent set.*

Proof. Denote the nonempty point classes on $[L_1]$ by $[P_1]$, $[P_2]$, and $[P_3]$, and the nonempty point classes on $[L_2]$ by $[Q_1]$, $[Q_2]$, and $[Q_3]$. Without loss of generality $[P_i] \cap X$ and $[Q_j] \cap X$ are independent sets and hence a triangle. Otherwise there is nothing to prove.

Consider any of these six point classes. We can prescribe multiplicities to the points in these sets in such way that all lines in the same direction have the same multiplicity, and the multiplicities in the four directions are either $(1, 1, 1, 0)$, or $(2, 2, 2, 0)$. This can be done in two ways. The two possibilities are presented on Fig. 6.

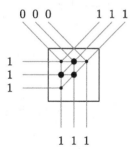 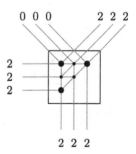

Fig. 6. A neighbor class of points in PG$(2, 3)$

The same multiplicities are obtained from two line segments with points of multiplicity 1 or 2 (see Fig. 7).

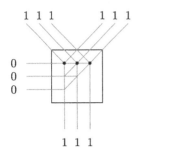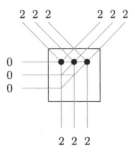

Fig. 7. A neighbor class of points in PG(2, 3) with six non-zero points

Each of the classes $[P_i]$, $[Q_j]$ contains a triangle whose sides (the line segments with three points) determine three directions. We are going to prove that no matter how the directions of the sides of the triangle are selected we can prescribe multiplicities to the points from X in such way that the obtained arc is a (0 mod 3)-arc.

Assume that some class $[P_i]$ (or, $[Q_i]$) has a triple of collinear points that determine the line $\langle [P_i], [R] \rangle$ (or $\langle [Q_j], [R] \rangle$). Then we prescribe to these three points multiplicity 1 if they are in some $[P_i]$, and multiplicity 2 if they are in some $[Q_j]$.

If in some $[P_i]$ (resp., $[Q_j]$) the sides of the triangle determine all directions different from $\langle [P_i], [R] \rangle$ (resp., $\langle [Q_j], [R] \rangle$) then we select the multiplicities in such way that the lines in the direction of the point $[R]$ have multiplicities 0 mod 3 and in all other directions multiplicity 1 mod 3 (resp., 2 mod 3). Now it is easily checked that all lines have multiplicity 0 mod 3 (Fig. 8).

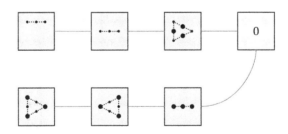

Fig. 8. Two neighbor classes of lines in PG(2, 3) with three non-zero points

Corollary 9. *Let X be a linearly independent set of points. Then at most seven of the point classes can have six points. Consequently for every independent set X, it holds $|X| \leq 72$.*

Proof. If there are eight neighbor classes with six points, we necessarily have two line classes satisfying the conditions of Lemma 8 and hence the set X is dependent. Therefore the number of neighbor classes with 6 points is at most seven and hence

$$|X| \leq 7 \cdot 6 + 6 \cdot 5 = 72.$$

Now by Theorem 6 and Corollary 9

$$45 \leq \mathrm{rk}_3 \, A_{\mathrm{PHG}(2,R)} \leq 72.$$

References

1. Hirschfeld, J.W.P.: Projective Geometries over Finite Fields, 2nd edn. Oxford University Press, Oxford (1998)
2. Honold, T., Landjev, I.: Linear codes over finite chain rings. Electronic J. Combin. **7**, R11 (2000)
3. Honold, T., Landjev, I.: On maximal arcs in projective Hjelmslev planes of even characteristic. Finite Fields and Their Appl. **11**, 292–304 (2005)
4. Landjev, I., Rousseva, A.: Divisible arcs, divisible codes, and the extension problem for arcs and codes. Probl. Inform. Transm. **55**(3), 30–45 (2019)
5. Ward, H.N.: Divisibility of codes meeting the Griesmer bound. J. Combin. Theory Ser. A **83**, 79–93 (1998)

On Some Alternative Probability Density Metrics for Analyzing Empirical Datasets

Sidney Klawansky[1], Brielle Balswick[2], Meaad Alsayel[2], Iryna Charvachidze[2], Anuka Manghwani[1,2], Pearl Almeida[2], Dharmit Dalvi[2], Janvi Vora[2], and Eugene Pinsky[2(✉)]

[1] Department of Health Policy and Management, Harvard Chan School of Public Health 2, 677 Huntington Ave, Boston, MA 02115, USA
sidney.klawansky@alum.mit.edu
[2] Department of Computer Science, Metropolitan College, Boston University, 1010 Commonwealth Avenue, Boston, MA 02215, USA
{brielleb,sayelmm,irynach,palmeida,dharmit,epinsky}@bu.edu

Abstract. We propose a simple set of probability density shape metrics with intuitive interpretability and complement the Classical statistical metrics of Variance, Skewness, and Kurtosis. These Classical metrics involve squaring of deviations and computation of third and fourth moments. Therefore, they may be overly sensitive to outliers. Therefore, we take The Mean Deviation around the mean, rather than the standard deviation, as the primary measure of data dispersion. This work presents some of our initial results using Mean Deviation and the new metrics of Tailness (an analog of Kurtosis) and Asymmetry (an analog of Skewness). These new metrics use only first and second moments. They have simple interpretations and directly allow us to compare datasets with different measurement units. As such, they give us additional tools for data analysis. We illustrate the proposed metrics for several public datasets.

Keywords: mean absolute deviation · skewness · asymmetry · kurtosis · tailness

1 Introduction

Standard deviation, skewness, and kurtosis are widely used measures in statistical analysis. In computing σ, we use the squares of the distances from the mean μ. For skewness and kurtosis, we use higher-order moments. As noted by Pham in [1], using the L_2 norm is convenient in differentiation, estimation, and optimization. The additive property of variance σ^2 for independent variables is also cited as one of the prime reasons for using the L_2 norm.

In recent years, there has been an increased interest in using the L_1 metrics in data analysis (e.g. [2–6]). Using the L_1 norm is not new. The L_1 norm was considered independently by both Boscovitch and Laplace as early as the 18th

T. Zlateva and G. Tuparov (Eds.): CSECS 2023, LNICST 514, pp. 40–47, 2023.
https://doi.org/10.1007/978-3-031-44668-9_3

century. A historical survey using the L_1 norm is presented in [7,8] and a survey of more recent results is given in [1].

Our starting point is the mean absolute deviation defined as follows: Consider a real-valued random variable X on a sample space $\Omega \subseteq R$ with density $f(x)$, finite mean μ, and cumulative distribution function $F(x)$. If X is a discrete random variable, then Ω is some countable sample space, and $f(x)$ is the probability mass function (or discrete density function).

For any a, we define the mean absolute deviation of X from a as

$$d(X, a) = \mathrm{E}(|X - a|) = \int_{\Omega} |x - a| f(x)\, dx \tag{1}$$

If $a = \mu$, then $d(X, \mu)$ is the mean absolute deviation from the mean μ. If we take $a = M$, then $d(X, M)$ is the mean absolute deviation from the median. Both of these are denoted as MAD (mean absolute deviation) in the statistical literature, leading to some confusion [1]. In this paper, we use MAD to denote **mean absolute deviation** from the mean and denote it by d. A detailed discussion of mean absolute deviation from the median is presented in [9].

The measure d can be interpreted as the average distance of values of X to the mean μ. It is well-known that $d \leq \sigma$ for any distribution. Therefore, one can expect metrics based on d to be less sensitive to outliers and therefore more robust.

Note that we can remove the absolute magnitude sign in (1) and derive d by computing contributions from points less than or equal to μ and points greater than μ:

$$d = d_- + d_+, \qquad d_- = \int_{x \leq \mu} (\mu - x) f(x)\, dx, \qquad d_+ = \int_{x > \mu} (x - \mu) f(x)\, dx \tag{2}$$

By separately computing the integrals over the left and right sub-spaces, we have eliminated the absolute sign. Similarly, although σ^2 is usually thought of as a single number, for the proposed metrics we explicitly compute contributions to variance from the left ($X \leq \mu$) and right ($X > \mu$) sub-spaces.

$$\sigma^2 = \sigma_-^2 + \sigma_+^2, \qquad \sigma_-^2 = \int_{x \leq \mu} (\mu - x)^2 f(x)\, dx, \qquad \sigma_+^2 = \int_{x > \mu} (x - \mu)^2 f(x)\, dx \tag{3}$$

These contributions from the left and right subspaces in (2) and (3) must be computed separately. As a result, they form the building blocks of the more transparent asymmetry and tailness metrics proposed below. In this paper, we define the following Alternative Metrics:

1. Mean deviation d - instead of standard deviation σ
2. Tailness $T = 2\sigma^2/d^2$ - instead of kurtosis $K = \mathrm{E}((X - \mu)/\sigma)^4$
3. Asymmetry $A = (\sigma_+^2 - \sigma_-^2)/\sigma^2$ - instead of skewness $S = \mathrm{E}(((X - \mu)/\sigma)^3)$

Let us make a few quick observations. The mean absolute deviation d always satisfies $d \leq \sigma$. For example, in Gaussian distributions $d = \sigma\sqrt{2/\pi}$ or about

20% lower than σ. For tailness T, we normalize the variance σ^2 by $d^2/2$ to bring the value $T = \pi$ for the Gaussian distribution close to the kurtosis value $K = 3$. Finally, for asymmetry A, we can show that, unlike Skewness that can be unbounded, Asymmetry is always in the range $-1 \leq A \leq 1$. For this reason, the proposed measure of Asymmetry allows us to compare datasets across different measurement units.

The above definitions for Mean Deviation d, Asymmetry, A, and Tailness, T, allow the computation of these measures without calculating 3rd or 4th moments. Many fields including medicine, epidemiology, psychology, economics, finance, and biology are heavy users of statistical tools. We are optimistic that the proposed metrics can provide a self-consistent system of measurement that will make more results in these fields easier to interpret.

2   Examples: Gaussian, Laplace and Exponential

In this section, we present these Alternative Metrics the for some well known distributions. We start with the normal distribution. The standard representation of the Normal or Gaussian distribution is given in Eq. (4)

$$f(x, \mu, \sigma) = \frac{1}{\sigma\sqrt{2\pi}} \exp\left(-\frac{(x-\mu)^2}{2\sigma^2}\right) \tag{4}$$

For this distribution, the relationship of d to standard deviation σ, is given by [10]

$$d = \sqrt{\frac{2}{\pi}}\sigma \qquad \text{or} \qquad \sigma = \sqrt{\frac{\pi}{2}}d \tag{5}$$

For the Normal Distribution, $d \approx 0.798\sigma$. Using (5), we re-express the Normal Distribution as a function of d rather than σ.

$$f(x, \mu, d) = \frac{1}{\pi d} \exp\left(-\frac{(x-\mu)^2}{\pi d^2}\right) \tag{6}$$

The representation of the Gaussian distribution using the d in (6) is simpler than the representation using the σ in (4) in that there is no square root in the factor multiplying the exponential. We also note that in Equation (5) for the Gaussian, when we square both sides, we obtain $\sigma^2/d^2 = \pi/2$. This relationship led to the definition of Tailness as discussed previously.

Similarly, for Laplace and exponential distribution, we have

1. Laplace: mean deviation $d = b$ [11]

$$\text{Classical:} \qquad f(x, \mu, b) = \frac{1}{2b} \exp\left(-\frac{|x-\mu|}{b}\right)$$

$$\text{Alternative:} \qquad f(x, \mu, d) = \frac{1}{2d} \exp\left(-\frac{|x-\mu|}{d}\right)$$

This distribution is symmetric and therefore $\sigma_-^2 = \sigma_+^2$. The asymmetry is therefore $A = 0$ and its tailness $T = 4$. The classical kurtosis for this distribution is $K = 6$.

2. Exponential: density is $f(x) = \lambda e^{-\lambda x}$ with $x > 0$. The standard deviation is $\sigma = 1/\lambda$ and the mean deviation $d = 2/(e\lambda)$ [11]

$$\text{Classical:} \quad f(x,\sigma) = \frac{1}{\sigma} \exp\left(-\frac{x}{\sigma}\right)$$

$$\text{Alternative:} \quad f(x,d) = \frac{2}{ed} \exp\left(-\frac{2x}{ed}\right)$$

This distribution is not symmetric and, therefore, $\sigma_-^2 \neq \sigma_+^2$. We compute σ_-^2 and σ_+^2 as follows. For this distribution, $\mu = 1/\lambda$ and integrating by parts we obtain,

$$\sigma_-^2 = \int_0^{1/\lambda} \left(\frac{1}{\lambda} - x\right)^2 \lambda e^{-\lambda x}\, dx = (1-2/e)\sigma^2, \qquad \sigma_+^2 = \int_{1/\lambda}^{\infty} \left(x - \frac{1}{\lambda}\right)^2 \lambda e^{-\lambda x}\, dx = (2/e)\sigma^2$$

For this distribution, the Asymmetry $A = (\sigma_+^2 - \sigma_-^2)/\sigma^2 = 4/e - 1 \approx 0.47$ and Tailness $T = e^2/2 \approx 3.69$. By contrast, the classical Skewness and Kurtosis for exponential distribution are $S = 2$ and $K = 9$ respectively. These values are noticeably larger than the corresponding A and T metrics.

A summary comparison of these distributions is given in Table 1.

Table 1. Comparison of Alternative Distribution Metrics with Classical Distribution Metrics for Several Common Distributions

Distribution	Gaussian	Exponential	Laplace
Mean (μ)	μ	$1/\lambda$	μ
Median (M)	$M = \mu$	$(\log 2)/\lambda$	μ
Standard Deviation	σ	$1/\lambda$	$b\sqrt{2}$
Mean Deviation d	$\sigma\sqrt{2/\pi} \approx 0.80\,\sigma$	$(2/e)\sigma \approx 0.74\,\sigma$	b
σ_-^2	$0.5\sigma^2$	$(1 - 2/e)\sigma^2 \approx 0.26\,\sigma^2$	b^2
σ_+^2	$0.5\sigma^2$	$(2/e)\sigma^2 \approx 0.74\,\sigma^2$	b^2
Tailness T	$\pi \approx 3.14$	$e^2/2 \approx 3.69$	4
Kurtosis K	3	9	6
Asymmetry A	0	$4/e - 1 \approx 0.47$	0
Skewness S	0	2	0

The Alternative Metrics reintroduce the natural constants. In Table 1, the Tailness for the Normal Distribution is π, while the Tailness of the Exponential Distribution is $e^2/2$. Correspondingly, the Asymmetry of the Exponential Distribution is $4/e - 1$.

As expected, the numerical values of $T = 3.69$ for the Exponential and $T = 4$ for Laplace Distributions are noticeably muted compared to the corresponding values of K for these distributions, 9.0 and 6.0, respectively. Note that for the

Exponential distribution Kurtosis $K = 9$ is greater than for the Laplace distribution where $K = 6$. However, for the exponential, Tailness $T = 3.69$ is less than for the Laplace distribution where Tailness $T = 4.0$. The latter inequality as compared to the former Classical inequality might be partially explained because the Laplace distribution has two fat tails while the Exponential Distribution has only one fat tail.

We have made the point that the Variance, σ^2, while treated in Classical Statistics as a single number, is the sum of two numbers, $\sigma^2 = \sigma_-^2 + \sigma_+^2$. This composition of σ^2 is well illustrated in Table 1 for the Case of the asymmetric Exponential Distribution: $\sigma_-^2 = (1 - 2/e)\sigma^2$ and $\sigma_+^2 = (2/e)\sigma^2$. Clearly, the sum of σ_-^2 and $(\sigma)_+^2$ is σ^2. The Asymmetry is then $A = (s_+^2 - s_-^2)/s^2 = 4/e - 1 \approx 0.47$.

3   A Case Study with Empirical Datasets

To illustrate the utility of the Alternative metrics, we consider the following empirical datasets: the NHANES Height, Cholesterol, and Creatinine data and the 2018 Boston Marathon finishing times data [12–14]. These are presented in Table 2.

Table 2. Comparison of Alternative and Classical metrics for Empirical Datasets

Dataset	Cholesterol		Height		Creatinine		Marathon	
metrics	Female	Male	Female	Male	Female	Male	Female	Male
pop. size	3,461	3,277	2,814	2,630	7,120	6,711	11,982	14,675
Min−Max	79–446	76–431	138–189	148–198	0.3–10.7	0.4–13.9	144–446	128–464
Mean μ	182.94	176.68	159.76	173.53	0.98	1.21	245.32	223.02
Median M	179	172	160	173	0.9	1.2	236	212
d	31.57	31.9	5.59	6.14	0.14	0.17	32.4	36.55
St. dev σ	40.58	40.37	7.02	7.67	0.28	0.38	40.95	45.77
σ/d	1.29	1.27	1.26	1.25	2.00	2.24	1.26	1.25
T	3.31	3.20	3.15	3.12	8.26	9.99	3.19	3.14
K	4.68	4.18	3.07	2.95	445.98	390.55	3.40	3.45
A	0.19	0.19	0.04	0.01	0.71	0.76	0.26	0.28
S	0.82	0.75	0.15	0.01	15.82	15.52	0.85	0.91

Table 2 presents results comparing Classical and Alternative distribution shape metrics for the four datasets in a side-by-side fashion to facilitate comparison. The first two datasets are taken from the 2018 National Health and Nutritional Examination Survey [13]. They are the female and male values of Height and Serum Cholesterol. The Serum Creatinine data are from the 1994 NHANES [14]. Creatinine, part of the routine laboratory chemistry profile, is a metabolite of creatine, a muscle component excreted in the urine. Because males typically have more muscle mass than females, they have higher mean values. The fourth dataset comprises the female and male finishing times of the 2018 Boston Marathon [12].

The following are some of the observations:

- Ratio of Standard Deviation to Mean Deviation, σ/d: we see in Table 2 that for Cholesterol, Height and Marathon, the Standard Deviation is about 25% greater than the Mean Deviation for both males and females. This ratio of about 1.25 is similar to that of the normal distribution and is due to the weight given to the outliers. The Creatinine dataset for both males and females is notable for the very long tails in the empirical PDFs. In the Creatinine data, the Standard Deviation for males, $\sigma = 0.38$, is more than double the Mean Deviation $d = 0.17$ due to the exaggerated influence of these much longer tails. As a result, for both male and female Creatinine, ratios of σ/d are of the order of 2, noticeably higher than the roughly 1.25 ratio for the other three data sets.

- Tailness T and Classical Kurtosis K for the approximately normal male and female Height have comparable values in the general range of 3.0–4.0 as seen in Table 2. By contrast, a very convincing example of the practical utility of Tailness vs. Kurtosis is demonstrated in the case of creatinine.

  We compare Tailness vs. Kurtosis for Creatinine. In Table 2, Classical Kurtosis for the male Creatinine $K = 390.55$ and for the female $K = 445.98$. These numerical results are a typical case where the 4th Moment blows up. In the case of Creatinine, the greatest contribution to the Variance and Kurtosis arises from the outlier points in the very long tail. These highly elevated patient data points likely reflect patients with renal failure and perhaps even dialysis. Yet, these patients are still an intrinsic component of this population-based sample of individuals. There is no scientific reason to prune these high values.

  By contrast with the very high values for Kurtosis, the Tailness for the male Creatinine $T = 9.99$ and for the female $T = 8.26$ are orders of magnitude lower. Even for a noticeably narrowly peaked and long-tailed distribution like the Creatinine, the numerical values for leptokurtic Tailness are a more reasonable multiple of the Tailness $= \pi \approx 3.1416$ of the Normal Distribution.

- Asymmetry vs. Skewness: Suppose that we wish to compare the Asymmetry A for two datasets across two different measurement systems. If the Asymmetry of dataset 1 is $A_1 = 0.3$ and The Asymmetry of dataset 2 is $A_2 = 0.6$; then we can say that dataset 2 is twice as right asymmetric or right skewed as dataset 1. We cannot make a similar statement for the Skewness S metric. In Table 2, Classical Skewness for the female Creatinine $S = 15.82$. Classical Skewness for female Marathon finishing times is $S = 0.85$. If we tried to compare these two measures of Skewness by taking the ratio, we might be tempted to say that the Creatinine is $15.82/0.85 = 18.61$ times more right-skewed than the Marathon finishing times. Such a direct comparison of these values would not make statistical sense. By contrast, the normalized Asymmetry for the female Creatinine is $A = 0.71$ while the normalized Asymmetry for the Marathon is $A = 0.26$. Then the ratio $0.71/0.26 = 2.73$ allows us to assert that the Creatinine empirical distribution is about 2.73 times more asymmetric or skewed to the right than the Marathon empirical distribution.

The above numerical examples highlight the benefits of using Mean Deviation, Tailness, and Asymmetry to analyze and compare empirical datasets.

4   Summary and Conclusion

We believe the proposed metrics will provide valuable and understandable tools for data analysis. We summarize some of the comparisons between the proposed and classical metrics:

- Simpler to compute and interpret: the Alternative metrics use only 1st and 2nd Moments, whereas classical metrics use higher order moments (for skew and kurtosis). By computing the upside and downside components of variance, we gain additional information to calculate Asymmetry and provide more information about both tails.
- Mean Deviation d is an unbiased measure of data dispersion and does not exaggerate the impact of outliers. By contrast, the Standard Deviation σ is a biased measure of data dispersion that exaggerates the impact of tails and may influence the final result.
- Tailness T that uses the 2nd is more robust to outliers than classical Kurtosis, K that uses the 4th moment. By using Tailness, it may be less necessary to prune outlier points.
- Asymmetry A is always in the range $(-1, 1)$ and therefore allows us to compare datasets across different measurement scales. By contrast, the classical measure of skewness S which is not bounded cannot be used to compare datasets across different measurement scales.

We hope that users will appreciate the additional informational value provided by the new metrics.

References

1. Pham-Gia, T., Hung, T.L.: The mean and median absolute deviations. J. Math. Comput. Modell. **34**, 921–936 (2001)
2. Dodge, Y.: Statistical Data Analysis Based on the L_1 Norm and Related Topics. North-Holland, Amsterdam (1987)
3. Elsayed, K.M.T.: Mean absolute deviation: analysis and applications. Int. J. Bus. Stat. Anal. **2**(2), 63–74 (2015)
4. Gorard, S.: An absolute deviation approach to assessing correlation. Br. J. Educ. Soc. Behav. Sci. **53**(1), 73–81 (2015)
5. Gorard, S.: Introducing the mean deviation "effect" size. Int. J. Res. Method Educ. **38**(2), 105–114 (2015)
6. Rousseeuw, P.J., Croux, C.: Alternatives to the median absolute deviation. J. Am. Stat. Assoc. **88**(424), 1273–1283 (1993)

7. Farebrother, R.W.: The historical development of the l_1 and l_∞ estimation methods. In: Dodge, Y. (ed.) Statistical data Analysis Based on the L_1-Norm and Related Topics, pp. 37–63. North-Holland, Amsterdam (1987)
8. Portnoy, S., Koenker, R.: The gaussian hare and the Laplacian tortoise: computability of square-error versus Abolute-error estimators. Stat. Sci. **2**(88), 279–300 (1997)
9. Pinsky, E., Klawansky, S.: Mad (about median) vs. quantile-based alternatives for classical standard deviation, skewness, and kurtosis. Front. Appl. Math. Stat. **9** (2023). https://doi.org/10.3389/fams.2023.1206537
10. Johnson, N.L., Kotz, S., Balakrishnan, N.: Continuous Univariate Distributions, vol. 1, 2nd edn. Wiley-Interscience, New York (1994)
11. Johnson, N.L., Kotz, S.: Distributions in Statistics. Wiley, New York (1970)
12. Boston marathon archives; Boston athletic association. Boston Athletic Association. http://registration.baa.org
13. NCHS. Nhanes (2017–2018) laboratory data. Centers for Disease Control and Prevention (2018). https://wwwn.cdc.gov/nchs/nhanes
14. NCHS. National center for health statistics; plan and operation of the third national health and nutrition examination survey, 1988–1994, vital health stat, vol. 1, no. 32, pp. 0094–1308. DHHS Publication (1994)

Expository Clustering Visualizations: Keeping it Simple

Greg Page(⊠)

Boston University, Boston, USA
gpage@bu.edu

Abstract. In this paper, the authors present a very basic overview of k-means clustering, before using statistical summaries to demonstrate how such a model separates records in a dataset into distinct groups.

The author then shows how simple visualizations can effectively "tell the story" behind a clustering model, to include the key distinctions that tend to differentiate one group from another.

The author then explores Principal Component (PC) plots, a tool often misused by analysts seeking to convey information about the clusters identified by their models. Such plots are based not on original variables from the data, but upon linear combinations of those variables. While PC plots are colorful and impressive-looking, their meaning often eludes the students who use them in end-of-semester project presentations.

PC plots serve some value as a diagnostic tool for kmeans modelers; however, these plots should not be used in an expository way by someone who wishes to convey the main findings of a clustering model. Instead, boxplots, scatterplots, barplots, and histograms can much more effectively convey the major takeaways for such a model.

Keywords: data mining · k-means clustering · computer science education

1 Introduction

Clustering, a form of unsupervised learning, is commonly taught in data mining and marketing analytics courses. While clustering can be done with many distinct methods, each approach boils down to the same basic principle – placing the observations into distinctive groups, in a way that maximizes within-group similarity as well as between-group difference. [1] In marketing analytics, clustering models identify specific customer personas, which are often characterized by pithy descriptions such as "Single and Carefree" or "Cruising through the Golden Years."

To communicate the results of a clustering model, the modeler may rely on several methods. Among these are: Presenting the groups with descriptive labels, backed by qualitative statements; delivering per-group summary statistics, often starting with the group means for each of the variables used in the model; and using visualizations to offer insights about the model and its clusters.

© ICST Institute for Computer Sciences, Social Informatics and Telecommunications Engineering 2023
Published by Springer Nature Switzerland AG 2023. All Rights Reserved
T. Zlateva and G. Tuparov (Eds.): CSECS 2023, LNICST 514, pp. 48–57, 2023.
https://doi.org/10.1007/978-3-031-44668-9_4

In our experience, students are too quickly drawn to Principal Component (PC)-based plots, which can serve a diagnostic purpose during model-building time, but are simply ineffective for explaining the meaningful differences from cluster to cluster. Students may encounter such plots in course material, or through online searches, and feel that these must somehow be the right way to "show" their clustering model.

In order to explain the key distinctions among clusters, analysts should instead rely on simple visualizations, based on original variables from the dataset.

In this paper, we will first build a clustering model, using the kmeans() function from the R language.

2 Building a k-means Clustering Model in R

The dataset *portland_families.csv* contains simulated info about 15,000 households in the vicinity of Portland, Maine.

After isolating the dataset's numeric variables, we will be build a model using the following variables: total_ppl (total people per household); square_foot (square footage of primary household residence); household_income (estimated household income from previous year); number_pets (estimate of number of household pets); entertainment_spend_est (estimated total household entertainment spending from previous year); travel_spend_est (estimated total household travel spending from previous year); and under_12 (number of household members under the age of 12).

Given the different scales, and the different units of measurement associated with these variables, we will scale the original values into z-scores before building the model with the kmeans() function from R. [2] After some iteration through various possible k-values, we decided to build this model with six clusters.

After building the model, the questions that naturally arise include, "What does this really mean? What can we learn from this model?" As we show immediately below, a segmentation model can be assessed with per-cluster summary stats (Fig. 1).

```
> model$centers
    total_ppl square_foot household_income number_pets entertainment_spend_est travel_spend_est     under_12
1  1.60477638  -0.2408347      0.0007955225   0.04655520              0.06949739       -0.0647511  -0.3433841
2 -0.02651803   0.8298155      0.1096830284  -0.96622633              0.24382259        0.6811863   0.2695893
3 -0.90492036  -0.2672496      0.0913109899  -0.06254586             -0.24377267       -0.1216444  -1.2068592
4  0.05062574  -0.6012920      0.5479376714   0.02546871             -0.70504780       -0.4143889   0.7417900
5 -0.14956028  -0.6940049     -0.8784297372  -0.02902584              0.57304837       -0.8002412   0.2774678
6 -0.10135708   0.8720494      0.0487035289   0.99291182              0.14749940        0.6530828   0.2011637
```

Fig. 1. Per-Cluster Summary Stats, as Centroid Values

This table with per-cluster centroid values helps us to identify distinguishing features from group to group [3].

For instance, the output above shows us that Cluster 1 stands out for having the largest number of people per household. Their homes are slightly smaller than the dataset average, and they have the second-lowest average number of children under 12. Perhaps many of its members are college students, or recent graduates who share apartments with other twentysomethings.

Cluster 5's members have the lowest incomes, yet their entertainment spending ranks the highest among all groups. Meanwhile, they have the smallest residences and the lowest travel spending. Perhaps this cluster includes bored retirees, or maybe just some die-hard entertainment fans. Either way, marketers can use the centroid values shown above to assist with the tailored marketing approaches that they may wish to use for each segment.

The centroid values may not appeal to all audiences, though. Visualizations tend to be more eye-catching and memorable than descriptive summary stats for most audiences and in most contexts – and clustering is no exception.

While visualizations are both effective and appropriate for expressing the key differences among groups in a clustering model, some types are more effective than others. Before demonstrating the superiority of simple visualizations for conveying group differences in clustering models, we will first show an alternative plot type.

3   So What are those Principal Component Plots Showing, Exactly?

To generate PC plots for a k-means clustering model, we will use the fviz-cluster() function from the factoextra package [4].

For a k = 3 solution for the *portland_families* dataset, this function renders the image shown below.

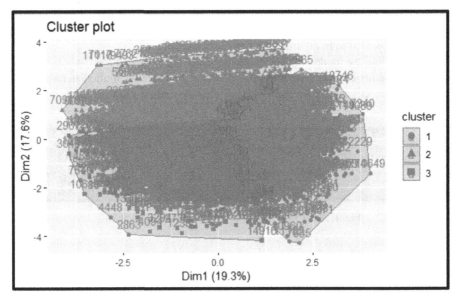

Fig. 2. Principal Component Plot for k = 3 Solution

In the plot shown above, the x-axis is labeled "Dim1" while the y-axis is labeled "Dim2." Dim1 refers to the first PC, which explains 19.3% of the variation among the values in the dataset. "Dim2" refers to the second PC, which captures a further 17.6% of the variation among the input variables.

This can be verified by calling the prcomp() function on the matrix of standardized values that went into this clustering model. The results shown below indicate that seven PCs are needed to capture all of the variation among the variables in this data. Note also that collectively, the first two PCs based on this data explain less than 40% of the total variation (Fig. 3).

```
> summary(pc)
Importance of components:
                          PC1    PC2    PC3    PC4    PC5    PC6     PC7
Standard deviation     1.1627 1.1114 1.0039 0.9994 0.9877 0.8734 0.81729
Proportion of Variance 0.1931 0.1764 0.1440 0.1427 0.1394 0.1090 0.09542
Cumulative Proportion  0.1931 0.3696 0.5135 0.6562 0.7956 0.9046 1.00000
```

Fig. 3. Principal Component Stats for the Portland families dataset

As for the PCs themselves, each one can be viewed as a 7 × 1 array. In the plot shown above, the labeled points correspond to the product of that record's standardized values, multiplied by each of those first two PCs.

We can see the values for each of the seven PCs below (Fig. 4).

```
> pc
Standard deviations (1, .., p=7):
[1] 1.1626579 1.1113566 1.0039463 0.9994144 0.9876935 0.8734305 0.8172860

Rotation (n x k) = (7 x 7):
                             PC1          PC2          PC3          PC4          PC5          PC6          PC7
total_ppl             0.086230040 -0.70097276  0.031685065  0.007936918  0.04868452 -0.70506029 -0.025582015
square_foot           0.686941731  0.08043302 -0.007052183 -0.060218475  0.11881583  0.03697669 -0.708859021
household_income      0.195923697  0.01223611 -0.181059808  0.633001660 -0.72536683 -0.03986776  0.015618877
number_pets           0.009382622 -0.01082705 -0.710073168 -0.609170398 -0.34907700 -0.05115935  0.005498643
entertainment_spend_est 0.119523481 -0.04343833  0.674296162 -0.471601831 -0.54949695  0.04288193  0.054386511
travel_spend_est      0.679139790  0.09624475 -0.044769462 -0.034915535  0.18240662 -0.02789282  0.701592837
under_12              0.081759355 -0.70053611 -0.072664619  0.030061320  0.01678559  0.70334851  0.037414735
```

Fig. 4. The vectors associated with PC1 through PC7

Towards the bottom left corner of the plot, we can see a clearly labeled point for observation 2863. Why does that point land in that particular spot on the graph? It's because observations 2863's standardized values, multiplied by the first two PCs, yield values of −2.43 for PC1 and −3.93 for PC2. Along with many other observations whose standardized values yield negative results when multiplied by PC 1 and PC2, this observation lands in Cluster 3 (Fig. 5).

Such plots can serve a valuable diagnostic purpose for a modeler. The plot shown in Fig. 2 indicates that when this dataset's standardized values are multiplied by the first two principal components, a three-cluster solution very neatly cleaves the observations into distinct groups, with little overlap.

A four-cluster solution, by contrast, does not separate the data in such a way. While the plot below shows a strong separation between clusters 1 and 3, many of the observations in clusters 2 and 4 overlap, in terms of where they fall along the data's first two PCs (Fig. 6).

```
> pc1 <- c(0.086230040, 0.686941731, 0.195923697, 0.009382622, 0.119523481, 0.679139790,0.081759355)
> pc2 <- c(-0.70097276, 0.08043302, 0.01223611, -0.01082705, -0.04343833, 0.09624475, -0.70053611)
> first_two <- data.frame(pc1, pc2)
> new_matty <- as.matrix(first_two)
>
> combo <- port_scaled %*% new_matty
> combo[2863,]
      pc1      pc2
-2.343664 -3.932016
```

Fig. 5. Connecting the Dots between an observation from the the dataset and its position on the PC plot

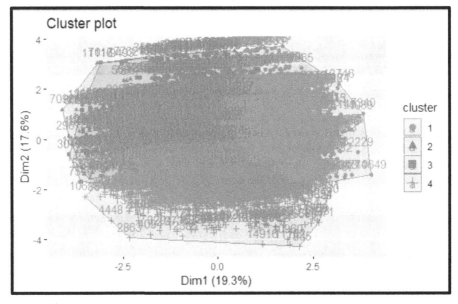

Fig. 6. PC plot for a k = 4 solution

However, some important limitations of such plots should be noted here. First, this plot is limited to just two dimensions, and only shows Principal Components 1 and 2. For some datasets, the first two principal components may account for the overwhelming proportion of overall variance, but here, these two only explain 36.96% of the variance; therefore, PC analysis may not prove to be a particularly valuable aid when it comes to this particular dataset. Second, and perhaps even more important, a purely statistical answer to the "How many clusters?" question may not align with the associated business goals. Clustering is an unsupervised learning task, for which there is no solution. Furthermore, there is no threshold for statistical significance when it comes such models.[5] In fact, a company may choose the number of clusters to use in a segmentation model before any analysis of the data has even begun.[6].

In student-led presentations, such plots are frequently misused. Students often present a graph such as the one in Fig. 2, perhaps because they have been told that such plots are effective for demonstrating clustering results. When asked simple, straightforward questions such as "What does this graph show you about your model?" students tend to stammer and struggle at first, before ultimately responding with something along the lines of "one of the clusters is red, another one of them is green, and yet a third one is blue."

Even the most data-savvy presenter, speaking to a completely data-savvy audience, cannot use such a plot to effectively explain the key distinctions from group to group. At best, a plot such as this could be used to indicate the level of differentiation among clusters for those first two PCs. However, such a plot does not enable the presenter to make statements such as "This cluster stands out for having more people per household, but that other cluster stands out for the way its members spend money on travel." For this reason, alternative visualization methods should be employed instead.

4 Simple Visualizations as a Far More Effective Option

Simple visualizations can convey the essential information about a clustering model.

1. *Such visualizations should depict original variables from the dataset, along with information about the model's cluster assignments.*
2. *Such visualizations do not need to depict all of the model's input variables, or all of the model's clusters.*
3. *Such visualizations can include variables that were not used as inputs in the original model.*

To demonstrate the power of a simple illustrative visualization, we will start with a boxplot, built with R's ggplot package [7].

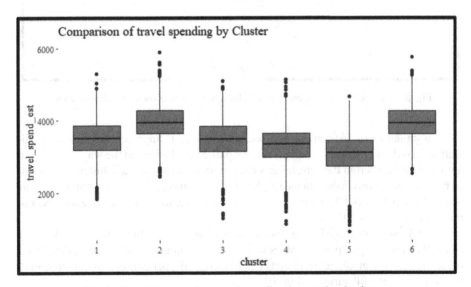

Fig. 7. Boxplot comparing travel spending among the six clusters

The plot shown in Fig. 7 clearly identifies a distinction among clusters – from this plot, we know that Cluster 2 and Cluster 6's households tend to be bigger travel spenders, compared to households in the other clusters. We also know that Cluster 5's households have the lowest average travel spending, and that this cluster contains several outliers with very low travel spending amounts.

Effective cluster model visualizations do not need to depict every single segment. Reviewing subsets of the original data may be helpful for marketers who wish to zero in on particular groups. In the visualization below, we can come away with a clear takeaway regarding Clusters 5 and 6 – for the most part, these groups are well-separated in terms of their members' estimated household incomes, as well as their annual spending on travel (Fig. 8).

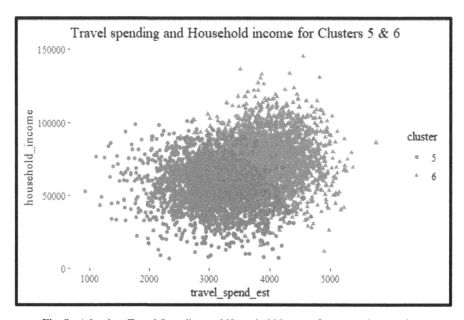

Fig. 8. A Look at Travel Spending and Household Income for a two-cluster subset

In a similar spirit, we could use a "one versus the rest" approach to a cluster visualization, in order to emphasize a point about a particular cluster and the way it stands out among the others. From the per-cluster summary stats, we know that Cluster 6 stands for its high rate of pet ownership. In the graph below, we compare the average number of pets owned by members of Cluster 6, compared with the overall average among members of the other five clusters (Fig. 9).

Even though categorical variables are not used as inputs in the k-means model, they can still be used as grouping variables in statistical summaries and visualizations based on the model. The graph below depicts counts of records, per cluster, along with county information as the fill variable (Fig. 10).

From the plot above, we can know that the clusters generally contain similar numbers of records, with Cluster 1 showing slightly fewer than the others. We can also know something interesting about the way the counties are represented among the six clusters – Sagadahoc, the least-represented county in the dataset, makes up a larger

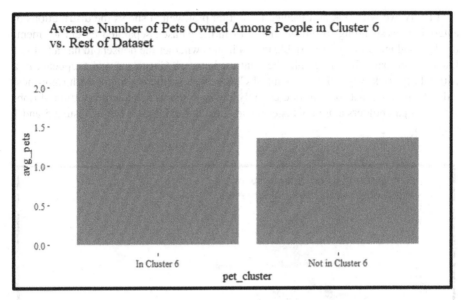

Fig. 9. Comparing Pet Ownership between Cluster 6 and the rest of the data

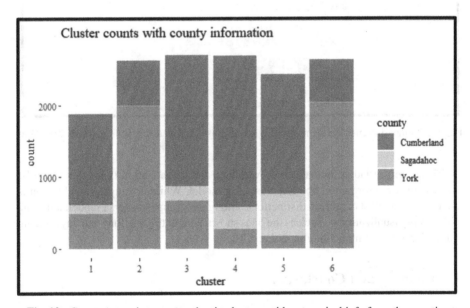

Fig. 10. Count comparison among the six clusters, with categorical info from the counties

proportion of Cluster 5, compared with its proportion of the others. Meanwhile, York County households comprise the overwhelming majority of Clusters 2 and 6, but do not comprise a majority of any of the others.

Finally, we will look at a faceted histogram plot, which shows the distributions of entertainment spending for all observations in the dataset, separated by cluster membership, and including a fill variable that indicates whether the household has a Lobster Land season pass. In this graph, the contrast between Clusters 4 and 5 appears in a particularly stark way – the midpoint of Cluster 5's distribution aligns with right-most tail of Cluster 4's distribution. Interestingly, this also shows a higher proportion of Lobster Land passholders among Cluster 6 and Cluster 2, compared with Clusters 5 and 1 (Fig. 11).

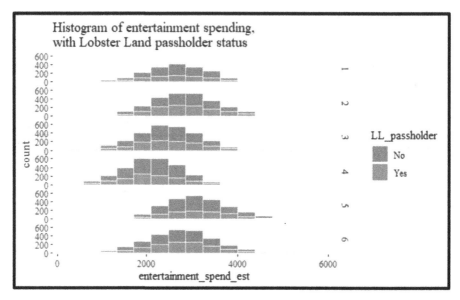

Fig. 11. Comparing entertainment spending across clusters, with an insight into passholder status

There are myriad combinations of variables and visualization types that could be used to convey information about a clustering model. While no single visualization is universally "best" at capturing distinctions among the groups in such a model, a mosaic of different visualizations – such as the ones shown here in this section – can lay a strong foundation for communicating model results.

5   Summary and Conclusion

Clustering is one of the most practically useful skills taught in data mining and marketing analytics courses. It is used every day, by companies large and small, in many different contexts.

Furthermore, data visualization is one of the most fundamental elements of the toolkit of any data analytics professional.

Data visualizations can serve an essential role in the way that a modeler communicates the results of a clustering solution to an audience. However, it is not enough to "just" have data visualizations for expressing model results – it is also vital that these visualizations are built in a sensible way.

Plots based on Principal Components may appeal to students for their sophisticated look – however, such plots offer very little expository value when it comes to explaining clustering models. While these plots can have diagnostic value during the model-building process, they are not an appropriate choice for situations in which an analyst seeks to explain the key distinctions among the segments formed by such a model.

Instead, simple visualizations should be used for this purpose. These visualizations should depict original variables from the dataset. They do not need to include every single cluster, or every single variable – instead, they might just feature a tiny "slice" of the clusters or the variables to make some particular point.

References

1. James, G., Witten, D., Hastie, T., Tibshirani, R.: An Introduction to Statistical Learning, p. 385. Springer, New York (2013). https://doi.org/10.1007/978-1-0716-1418-1
2. R Core Team, R: A language and environment for statistical computing. R Foundation for Statistical Computing, Vienna, Austria (2022). https://www.R-project.org/
3. Ahmed, M., et al.: The k-means algorithm: a comprehensive survey and performance evaluation. Electronics **9**, 1295 (2020)
4. Kassambara, A, Mundt, F.: _factoextra: Extract and Visualize the Results of Multivariate Data Analyses_. R package version 1.0.7 (2020). https://CRAN.R-project.org/package=factoextra
5. Yuan, C., Yang, H.: Research on K-value selection method of K-means clustering algorithm. Multidisc. Sci. J. **2**, 226–235 (2019)
6. Artun, O., Levin, D.: Predictive Marketing: Easy Ways Every Marketer Can Use Customer Analytics and Big Data, p. 94. Wiley, New York (2015). The authors note that "Strategy informs segmentation and not the other way around"
7. Wickham, H.: Ggplot2: Elegant Graphics for Data Analysis. Springer-Verlag, New York (2016). https://doi.org/10.1007/978-0-387-98141-3

Signal Prediction on Catalonia Cell Coverage

Yang Xing, Xinyue Zeng[✉], and Farshid Alizadeh-Shabdiz

Boston University Metropolitan College, Boston, MA 02215, USA
zengxiny@bu.edu

Abstract. The GenCat Mobile Coverage app is designed to collect information on the mobile telephone network coverage in Catalonia. Through an Android app, citizens can contribute to this initiative by recording data. The dataset compiled by the platform offers a comprehensive view of the data collected between 2015 and 2017, encompassing 20 features with 11,744,914 observations. This research aims to predict signal strengths of the mobile network in Catalonia using various factors, including location, network supplier, signal strength and other relevant features.

Keywords: Spark · Classification · Regression · Stacking · Model Evaluation

1 Introduction

The dataset was acquired from Google Cloud Big Query [1], we utilized SQL queries to partition it into three segments on the platform. Subsequently, we combined these segments locally using Python. Following data preprocessing, the number of observations decreased from 11,744,914 to 8,281,531, while the number of features increased from 20 to 36. We employed classification and regression algorithms to predict the target variable "signal" and compared the Root Mean Square Error (RMSE) of each model. Hyperparameter tuning was performed for each algorithm to identify the optimal model. Lastly, we applied stacking techniques with regression models to enhance performance.

2 State of Art

With the rising popularity of Python, numerous free libraries and packages have been developed to facilitate the implementation of distributed computation frameworks for machine learning algorithms [2]. Among the most widely used tools are Spark and Hadoop, both of which offer flexible, fault-tolerant, and scalable environments. Spark utilizes RDD (Resilient Distributed Dataset) as its primary data structure, whereas Hadoop relies on HDFS (Hadoop Distributed File System). Notably, Spark leverages RAM memory to store temporary results, resulting in faster processing times compared to Hadoop in most scenarios. As stated by Samadi [3], Spark outperforms Hadoop in terms of execution time for typical algorithms such as PageRank and Word-count.

T. Zlateva and G. Tuparov (Eds.): CSECS 2023, LNICST 514, pp. 58–72, 2023.
https://doi.org/10.1007/978-3-031-44668-9_5

Regarding Hadoop, Python offers several libraries that supports its functionalities. One such library is Hadoop Streaming, which was utilized by Dede [4] to process the extensive dataset, Cassandra. Additionally, another option available is Mrjob [5], an open-source wrapper designed for Hadoop Streaming.

When it comes to Spark, the primary package supporting it is PySpark. Within PySpark, MLlib serves as Apache Spark's scalable machine learning library [6]. Spark demonstrates exceptional performance in iterative computation, which makes it well-suited for MLlib's fast execution. Moreover, MLlib incorporates high-quality algorithms that leverage iteration, often yielding superior results compared to one-pass approximations commonly used in MapReduce.

Machine learning is a well-established research field within computer science, and it plays a crucial role in the development of classification and predictive analysis systems. MLlib in PySpark supports two main categories of algorithms in supervised learning: classification and regression [7]. For classification, MLlib provides support for logistic regression, decision trees, random forests, gradient-boosted trees, Support Vector Machine (SVM), and Naïve Bayes algorithms. However, the number of algorithms for regression is relatively limited. For instance, SVM is solely implemented for classification purposes.

In terms of ensemble methods, generalized forms like stacking, boosting, and voting algorithms are not supported. However, Kaur [8] implements an ensemble method using a voting algorithm. It is important to note that algorithms are not applicable for regression problems. Therefore, our objective is to construct a pipeline that implements a stacking ensemble method using PySpark's MLlib packages within the Spark environment.

3   Data Preprocessing

3.1   Coding Environment and Package Versions

PySpark was utilized to execute Python code within the Spark framework for our experiment. Throughout the entire study, we employed Python 3.9 and Spark 3.3.

3.2   Dataset Overview

The raw dataset utilized in this study was obtained from Google Big Query Dataset Platform. It consists of a total of 11,744,914 data samples and encompasses 20 features, including 'date', 'hour', 'lat', 'long', 'signal', 'network', 'operator', 'status', 'description', 'net', 'speed', 'satellites', 'precision', 'provider', 'activity', 'downloadSpeed', 'uploadSpeed', 'postal code', 'town name', and 'position geom'. These features can be categorized into three groups: time features ('date' and 'hour') related to the record's timestamp, geographical features ('lat', 'long', 'postal code', 'town name', and 'position geom') dependent on end-users' location, and business features associated with cell phone service providers.

To enhance the clarity and meaningfulness of the dataset, we performed several feature transformations. Firstly, we converted the 'hour' feature from a 12-h to a 24-h format. Additionally, we categorized the operators, listing only the top seven by name, while grouping the remaining operators into a single category called 'others'. This approach was employed to address the presence of numerous small companies in the real market, which would lead to a large sparse one-hot encoded matrix if included individuality. Thus, the 'operator' feature was reclassified into nine distinct groups. Furthermore, we applied other preprocessing methods to the dataset.

3.3   Feature Selection

Examine Irrelevant Features. Five features, namely 'date', 'signal', 'hour', 'activity', and 'speed' were considered.

Seasonal Effect. We extracted month information from both 'date' and 'month' features. Subsequently, we examined the correlation between 'month' and the class feature 'signal'. The results indicated no substantial evidence suggesting a seasonal effect on the signal. As a result, the 'date' feature was deemed irrelevant and excluded from further analysis.

Signal and Hour. We explored the correlation between 'hour' feature and the class feature 'signal' to determine if the signal exhibited variations throughout the day. After conducting the analysis, we concluded that 'hour' feature had no relevance to the signal and thus was eliminated from the feature set.

Speed and Activity. We investigated the relationship between the 'speed' and 'activity' features. The interpretation of the 'speed' feature could either represent the network communication speed or the moving speed of the signal source. To discern its nature, we examined the distribution of speeds across different activity groups. The results revealed a significant difference in the distribution, indicating that the 'speed' feature primarily represents the moving speed of the signal source.

Deleted Features. Six features were removed from the analysis for various reasons. The first feature to be eliminated was 'description' since it held the same meaning as 'status' feature. The second and third features, 'download speed' and 'upload speed', were excluded due to the excessive number of missing values present in both. Additionally, the fourth, fifth, and sixth features, namely 'postal code', 'town name' and 'position_geom', duplicating the information already captured by the 'lat', and 'long' features.

3.4   Preparation and Transformation

To prepare the data for analysis, several preprocessing steps were performed. Firstly, we addressed outliers in the dataset by applying the IQR (Interquartile Range) method to all remaining features, effectively removing any extreme values. Subsequently, for categorical features, we employed the StringIndexer() and OneHotEncoder() functions from the pyspark.ml.feature module, enabling us to convert the categorical variables into numerical representations through one-hot encoding. This process ensured compatibility with the machine learning algorithms employed in the study. Finally, to facilitate fair comparisons and optimize the performance of numerical features, we employed the StandardScaler() function from the pyspark.ml.feature module to standardize the data. This step improved the interpretability and convergence of the models utilized in subsequent analysis.

4   Classification Algorithms

4.1   Approach Overview

In this section, we present an overview of our approach, which involves the utilization of quantile-based grouping for conducting a multidimensional analysis of mobile network coverage data obtained through the GenCat Mobile Coverage app. The class feature, denoted as 'signal', consists of integer values ranging from 0 to 33, making it amenable to classification-based prediction. Our approach involves dividing the class feature into three distinct groups based on quantiles: below Q1, between Q1 and Q3, and above Q3. This grouping enables us to perform classification analysis and facilitates the comparison of results from regression algorithms, thereby allowing us to evaluate different approaches.

To conduct the analysis, we employ two models: Support Vector Machine (SVM) and logistic regression. The data is partitioned into three groups on the quantiles, with the first model classifying data below Q1 and the second model classifying data above Q3. The remaining data falling between Q1 and Q3 are labeled as within the IQR. Labels are assigned to each group based on the quality of network coverage, with a value of 2 denoting poor coverage, 1 representing good coverage, and 0 indicating moderate coverage.

In evaluating the performance of the classification models, it is essential to consider various metrics that provide insight into their effectiveness. One such metric is the confusion matrix, which presents a comprehensive view of the classification results by indicating the number of true positives (TP), true negatives (TN), false positives (FP), and false negatives (FN) for a given set of predictions. TP and TN represent correct predictions, while FP and FN represent incorrect predictions.

Furthermore, to enable a comparative evaluation between classification and regression models, we estimate the numeric value of the predicted class by taking the mean value within each range. This approach provides a more nuanced understanding of network coverage quality across different locations in Catalonia and facilities comparisons with regression analysis by calculating the Root Mean Square Error (RMSE). By combining both classification and regression analyses and assigning labels based on the quality of network coverage, out approach yields valuable insights that can directly inform policy decisions and drive improvements in network infrastructure.

4.2   Support Vector Machine

Algorithm Description. Support Vector Machines (SVM) is a powerful supervised learning algorithm used for both classification and regression tasks. It is particularly effective in scenarios where the data has complex decision boundaries. SVM seeks to find an optimal hyperplane that separates the data points of different classes with the maximum margin.

Implementation. In our implementation, we utilized the Support vector Machine algorithm for classification tasks in PySpark. Specifically, we employ the LinearSVC() function from the pyspark.ml.classificaiton.

Hyperparameters. When applying LinearSVC(), we focused on tuning three key hyperparameters. The first hyperparameter, maxIter, represents the maximum number of iterations performed during the training process. Careful selection this parameter can ensure convergence to an optimal solution.

The second hyperparameter, regParam, plays a crucial role in balancing the tradeoff between bias and variance in the SVM model. It determines the regularization strength, controlling the complexity of the model. By finding the optimal value for regParam, we can strike a balance between underfitting and overfitting.

The third hyperparameter, fitIntercept, is related to the inclusion of an intercept term in the linear equation of the SVM model. This intercept term allows the decision boundary to be shifted vertically, potentially improving the accuracy of the SVM model. When fitIntercept is set to True, an intercept term is incorporated during training process.

4.3 Logistic Regression

Algorithm Description. Logistic Regression is a widely used statistical model for binary classification. It extends the concept of linear regression by applying the logistic function to estimate the probability of the binary response variable. Logistic Regression is known for its simplicity and interpretability, making it a popular choice for various classification tasks.

Implementation. In our implementation, we utilize the PySpark Logistic Regression algorithm for classification problems. We employ the LogisticRegression() function from the pyspark.ml.classification module.

Hyperparameters. LogisticRegression() offers several hyperparameters for customization. One significant hyperparameter is regParam, which controls the strength of L1 or L2 regularization applied to the logistic regression model. By adjusting the regParam value, we can control the extent of regularization applied to the model, which helps prevent overfitting and improves the generalization performance.

The second hyperparameter, elasticNetParam, determines the balance between L1 and L2 regularization in the logistic regression model. When regParam is set to a positive value, the model applies L1 or L2 regularization based on the regularization type specified by the elasticNetParam parameter. A value of 0 for regParam indicates no regularization, resulting in a standard logistic regression model.

5   Regression Algorithms

5.1   Approach Overview

In addition to considering signal with categorical labels and applying classification algorithms, we can also treat signals as numerical features and leverage regression algorithms for analysis. When running regression algorithms, the output of predictions will be in the form of float numbers. To align with the integer labels of 'signal', we will employ the round() function to map the predicted numbers to integers.

Another distinction between classification and regression lies in evaluating the performance of a specific algorithm. For this purpose, we will utilize packages in pyspark.mllib.evaluation and employ the RegressionEvaluator to access performance. Specifically, we will employ the Root Mean Square Error (RMSE) as the evaluation metric. RMSE is a widely used measure for evaluating the quality of predictions, representing the Euclidean distance between predictions and the true measured values.

To compute RMSE, calculate the residual (difference between prediction and truth) for each data point, compute the norm of the residuals, calculate the mean of the residuals, and finally take the square root of this mean. RMSE is commonly employed in supervised learning applications as it requires true measurements at each predicted data point. Equation (1) expresses the computation of RMSE:

$$RMSE = \sqrt{\frac{\sum_{i=1}^{N}||y(i) - \hat{y}||^2}{N}} \tag{1}$$

In our investigation of regression models supported by Spark, we found that it offers a limited number of regression algorithms, including Linear Regression, Random Forest, Gradient Boosted Trees, Survival Regression, Isotonic regression, Factorization machines regression and Decision Trees Regression. Given the nature of our problem, we have opted to utilize linear regression, random forest regression and gradient-boosted tree regression. Since random forest and gradient-boosted tree algorithms are both derived from decision trees, we have chosen not to consider decision tree regression.

We also explored whether Spark supports sklearn (scikits.learn). It appears that in Spark 2.0, there was a package called spark-sklearn, but it has been deprecated subsequently. Currently, the functionality of spark-sklearn has been incorporated into Joblib-spark, which provides an Apache Spark backend for Joblib to distribute tasks on a Spark cluster. However, it does have certain limitations. For instance, it does not generally support running model inference and feature engineering in parallel.

5.2 Linear Regression

Algorithm Description. Linear Regression is a fundamental and widely used regression algorithm that models the relationship between a dependent variable and one or more independent variables. It measures a linear relationship between the input features and the target variable, making it a simple yet effective approach for regression analysis.

In Linear Regression, the algorithm estimates the coefficients of a linear equation that best fits the given data points. It aims to minimize the difference between the predicted values and the actual values by adjusting the coefficients using optimization techniques such as gradient descent.

Implementation. Linear regression is implemented as a supervised algorithm that utilizes the ordinary least squares method to estimate the coefficients of the linear equation. In out implementation, we employ the LinearRegression() function from the PySpark MLlib to perform the training process.

Hyperparameters. In the context of LinearRegression(), our focus was on three key hyperparameters. The first one is maxIter, which specifies the maximum number of iterations. Since linear regression employs Newton's method for gradient descent, it typically converges swiftly. By appropriately setting maxIter, we can optimize computational efficiency by avoiding unnecessary iterations.

The second hyperparameter is regParam, which determines the fraction of a regularization applied to the overall loss function. Generally, increasing regParam imposes a greaeter penalty from regularization. Additionally, in conjunction with regParam, we utilized the elastic net param to regulate the mixture of L1 and L2 penalties.

5.3 Random Forest

Algorithm Description. Random Forest is a popular machine learning algorithm that leverages ensemble learning and decision trees to construct a robust and accurate predictive model. It excels in both classification and regression tasks due to its versatility and effectiveness.

The name "Random Forest" stems from the algorithm's approach of building an ensemble or a "forest" of decision trees. Each tree is trained on a random subset of the training data and features, ensuring diversity, and reducing overfitting [9].

Implementation. Random Forest is implemented as a meta estimator that fits multiple decision trees on different subsets of the dataset and employs averaging to enhance predictive accuracy while mitigating overfitting. In our implementation, we utilize the RandomForestRegressor() function from the pyspark.ml.regression library.

Hyperparameters. Two key parameters are selected for tuning: the number of trees and the depth of trees. It is important to note that increasing either the depth or the number of trees substantially impacts the runtime of the algorithm.

5.4 Gradient Boosted Trees

Algorithm Description. Gradient Boosted Tree is a powerful machine learning algorithm that combines the principles of decision trees and gradient boosting to create a highly accurate predictive model. It builds the model in a stage-wise manner by sequentially adding multiple decision trees. The algorithm works by minimizing a loss function using gradient descent, thereby improving the model's predictive performance iteratively.[10].

Implementation. Gradient boosting regression trees are implemented by utilizing the GBTRegressor() function from the pyspark.ml.regression library. This algorithm builds an ensemble of decision trees, where each tree is trained on a subset of the training data and learns to make predictions based on the residuals from the previous trees.

Hyperparameters. To tune the Gradient Boosted Trees algorithm, we focus on three key hyperparameters: stepSize, maxDepth, and maxIter.

The stepSize parameter controls the learning rate, determining the contribution of each tree to the final prediction. A smaller stepSize value leads to a more cautions learning approach.

The maxDepth parameter determines the maximum depth of each individual decision tree in the ensemble. A deeper tree allows the model to capture more complex patterns but can also increase the risk of overfitting.

Finally, the maxIter parameter specifies the maximum number of iterations or boosting stages for the algorithm.

6 Hyperparameter Tuning

6.1 GridSearch and Parameter Setting

To optimize the performance of our models, we employed the GridSearch method in PySpark for hyperparameter values and identify the optimal configuration for each model. In our implementations, we utilized the ParamGridBuilder() function to set the parameters for each estimator in the pipeline.

6.2 Model Tuning Methods

Pyspark.ml.tuning provides two main functions for model tuning: CrossValidator() and TrainValidationSplit(). These functions assist in selecting the best hyperparameter values by performing systematic evaluations of the models. While CrossValidator generally yields better results, it requires a longer training time, making it more suitable for cases where data size is limited. In our study, however, we are dealing with a large dataset, and training time is a critical consideration. Therefore, we chose to utilize TrainValidationSplit() for the entire hyperparameter tuning process.

6.3 Pipeline Model and Training

To streamline the entire workflow, we constructed a Pipeline model that integrates all the components, including data preprocessing and the models themselves. The Pipeline model allows us to apply a consistent set of transformations to the data and train the models efficiently. We used the fit() function to train the pipeline model on the training data, ensuring that all necessary preprocessing steps and model training were execute in a unified manner.

By employing the GridSearch method, setting appropriate parameters, and utilizing the TrainValidationSplit() function within the Pipeline model, we were able to systematically explore different hyperparameter combinations and select the optimal settings for our models, this approach ensures that our models are fine-tuned and capable of providing accurate predictions on the mobile network coverage data.

6.4 Best Params

(See Tables 1 and 2).

Table 1. Best params for classification.

Support Vector Machine		Logistic Regression	
Model 1	Model 2	Model 1	Model 2
maxIter = 2, regParam = 0.005, fitIntercept = True	maxIter = 10, regParam = 0.01, fitIntercept = True	elasticNetParam = 0.0, regParam = 0.005	elasticNetParam = 0.0, regParam = 0.001

Table 2. Best params for regression.

Linear Regression	Random Forest	Gradient Boosted Tree
maxIter = 100, regParam = 0.02, elasticNetParam = 0.0	numTrees = 22, maxDepth = 15	stepSize = 0.5, maxDepth = 10, maxIter = 20

7   Outputs from the Google Cloud Platform

7.1   Outputs from Classification

Since we are doing multi-class classification, it is important to evaluate the performance of our algorithms using appropriate metrics. In addition, we select logistic regression as a baseline algorithm to compare the performance of the other algorithms (Tables 3 and 4).

Table 3. Confusion matrix from logistic regression.

Actual |Prediction	TP	FP	TN	FN
Label = 0	892704	747579	10116	5917
Label = 1	9208	6777	1267180	373151
Label = 2	33	15	1280965	375303

Table 4. Confusion matrix from SVM.

Actual |Prediction	TP	FP	TN	FN
Label = 0	896267	757201	1601	1688
Label = 1	198	946	1273085	382528
Label = 2	470	1675	1279006	375606

7.2   Outputs from Regression

Linear Regression.   When evaluating the performance of regression algorithms, we rely on RMSE as the key measurement. To assess the performance of different algorithms and parameter combinations, we compute the RMSE for both the training and testing datasets (with a ratio of 0.8:0.2). By comparing these values, we can evaluate how well the algorithms generalize to unseen data and identify potential overfitting or underfitting issues.

Linear regression is chosen as the baseline algorithm for comparison with other approaches, including random forests and gradient-boosted trees. By comparing the performance of these algorithms to the baseline linear regression, we can gain insights into their relative effectiveness and suitability for our regression task.

Through our experiments and analysis using From the Google Cloud Platform (GCP) statistics, we have observed that different parameter combinations have minimal impact on the performance of linear regression. This observation supports the notion that linear regression can serve as a robust and reliable baseline for our regression task (Tables 5).

Table 5.   RMSE from linear regression.

maxIter	regParam	elasticnet	trainRMSE	testRMSE
20	0.1	0	7.02	7.03
20	0.1	0.25	7.02	7.03
20	0.1	0.5	7.02	7.03
20	0.1	0.75	7.03	7.03
20	0.1	1	7.04	7.04
20	0.05	0	7.02	7.03
20	0.05	0.25	7.02	7.03
20	0.05	0.5	7.03	7.03
20	0.05	0.75	7.03	7.03
20	0.05	1	7.03	7.03
20	0.01	0	7.02	7.02
20	0.01	0.25	7.02	7.03
20	0.01	0.5	7.02	7.03
20	0.01	0.75	7.02	7.03
20	0.01	1	7.02	7.03

Random Forest.   When applying the random forest algorithm, we carefully consider two crucial parameters: numTrees and maxDepth. These parameters play a significant role in controlling the performance and behavior of the random forest model.

During our analysis, we examine the effect of varying these parameters on the performances of the random forest algorithm. By observing the RMSE values obtained from the testing set and comparing them with the RMSE values from the training set, we can gain insights into the model's generalization capabilities and potential overfitting tendencies. If there is a significant increase in RMSE on the testing set or a large gap between the training and testing set RMSE, it indicates that the model may be overfitting to the training data.

By carefully analyzing the relationship between these parameters and the performance metrics, we can determine the optimal values for numTrees and maxDepth that strike a balance between capturing complex patterns in the data and avoiding overfitting. This analysis allows us to select the best performing random forest model (Tables 6).

Table 6. RMSE from random forest.

numTrees	maxDepth	RMSE train	RMSE test
21	11	6.73	6.74
21	13	6.65	6.67
21	15	6.54	6.59
22	11	6.73	6.74
22	13	6.65	6.67
22	15	6.54	6.59

Gradient Boosted Trees. When utilizing the gradient boosted trees algorithm, we pay close attention to two critical parameters: stepSize and maxDepth. These parameters play a significant role in controlling the behavior of the gradient boosted trees and addressing the issue of overfitting.

By observing the RMSE values on the test set and comparing them with the RMSE values on the training set, we can conclude that if there is a significant increase in RMSE on the testing set or a substantial gap between the training and testing set RMSE, it indicates that the model may be overfitting to the training data (Tables 7 and 8).

Table 7. RMSE from gradient boosted trees.

stepSize	maxDepth	maxIter	RMSE train	RMSE test
0.5	5	10	6.8	6.8
0.5	5	15	6.78	6.79
0.5	5	20	6.77	6.77
0.5	10	10	6.58	6.62
0.5	10	15	6.53	6.59
0.5	10	20	6.5	6.57
0.5	15	10	6.13	6.67
0.5	15	15	5.96	6.75
0.5	15	20	5.83	6.83

Using the combinations of parameters that yield the best RMSE score on the test set for each algorithm, we compare the performances between the different algorithms. The results as follows:

Table 8. Best RMSE from all models.

Model	RMSE test
SVM	11.78
Logistic Regression	8.63
Linear Regression	7.02
Random Forest	6.59
Gradient Boosted Tree	6.57

8 Stacking Models

8.1 Algorithm

Stacking, also referred to as Stacked Generalization, is an ensemble machine learning technique that leverages a meta-learning algorithm to learn the optimal combination of predictions from multiple base machine learning algorithms. The fundamental advantage of stacking lies in its capability to exploit the strengths of diverse models, leading to predictions that surpass those of individual models in the ensemble.

In our study, we will utilize the three - Linear Regression, Random Forest Regression, and Gradient Boosted Trees Regression - as the base algorithms for stacking. Linear regression will be selected as the ensemble algorithm to fuse the predictions generated by the base models. To facilitate the stacking process, we have implemented two distinct training pipelines, each with its own merits and considerations.

The first training pipeline involves a straightforward split of dataset into training and testing sets. Within this pipeline, both the base algorithms and the ensemble algorithm are trained on the training data. This approach offers the advantage of consolidating all model training procedures into a single pipeline, streamlining the training process. However, it is crucial to note that this method may expose the ensemble algorithm to the risk of severe overfitting, as it heavily relies on the predictions generated by the base models.

The second training option involves a three-part split of the data, consisting of train data, validation data, and test data. The train data is exclusively utilized for training the base models, while the validation data is employed to train the ensemble algorithm using the predictions generated by the base models as input features. Finally, the performance of the stacked model is evaluated using the test data. This approach allows for improved control over overfitting concerns by utilizing the validation data to fine-tune the hyperparameters of the ensemble algorithm.

8.2 Implementation

In our implementation, we employ linear regression, random forest regression, and gradient boosted trees regression as the base models. Each base model is carefully selected based on the best set of parameters determined in the previous sections of our study. The stack algorithm is then utilized to combine the results from each individual model. The detailed process involves training each base algorithm separately and utilizing the predicted values – outputted by the base models – as new features for predicting values based on linear regression.

To facilitate the implementation, we utilize the pipelines functionality from the PySpark library. However, it is important to note that the usage of pipelines introduces certain considerations. Notably, pipelines operate on the same RDD (Resilient Distributed Dataset), resulting in two different methods being implemented based on whether the training set it divided for the base models and the stack model.

In the first method, a single pipeline is established to encompass the entire workflow, including data preprocessing, training of the individual models, prediction of values, transformation of predicted values into new features, and training of stack model. This single pipeline computation takes place sequentially on the training set. The model saved from this pipeline is subsequently applied to the test set to calculate the RMSE. Utilizing a single pipeline enhances computational efficiency by involving only one RDD in the training process. However, it may raise concerns regarding overfitting, as each data sample is utilized twice – once in the base models and once in the stack model.

The second method involves the establishment of two pipelines: one for the base models and another for the stack model. In this approach, the training set is split into two parts. The first part is employed to train the base models, while the second part is used to train the stack model. This two-stage training process begins with training the base models on training set 1, followed by passing all model information to stage 2. In stage 2, the stack model is trained on training set 2 using predicted values generated by the models saved in stage 1. Notably, in this method, each data sample will only be used once. But it will cause longer time to proceed.

8.3 Outputs from Google Cloud Platform

The stack model was executed on the Google Cloud Platform, and the training process took approximately 49 min to complete. The performance of the ensemble model surpassed that of the individual base models, highlighting the efficacy of the stacking approach. We observed a notable discrepancy between the train RMSE and test RMSE suggests the presence of overfitting when utilizing the first option, proving the importance of employing appropriate validation techniques to mitigate overfitting risks.

RMSE for each base model. LR: 7.02, RF: 6.59, GBT: 6.57.
RMSE for single pipeline. Train: 5.59, Test: 6.92.
RMSE for two pipelines. Train: 6.512, Test: 6.517.

9 Conclusion

9.1 Findings on Running GCP

(1) Classification and regression models can be considered when dealing with integer type labels. Both types of models have shown potential effectiveness in handling such labels, and the choice depends on the specific problem and desired outcome.

(2) When tuning hyperparameters, it is advisable to start with smaller values to reduce the overall running time on the GCP. This approach allows for faster experimentation and exploration of different parameter settings.

(3) Splitting the training data appropriately for base models and ensemble models is crucial when creating the stack ensemble model. This separation ensures that the base models capture relevant patterns and provide reliable predictions as inputs to the ensemble model.

9.2 Findings on Signal Coverage Prediction

(1) The dataset is sufficiently large, indicating that removing null values and outliers will not significantly reduce the dataset's size. However, due to the dataset's large volume, careful feature selection is essential. Including irrelevant features can increase computational complexity and potentially lead to decreased model performance.

(2) When dealing with multiple classes in the class feature, grouping them into two or three classes for classification models and assigning the mean value from each group's range may not yield optimal. Instead, directly fitting regression models to the data can potentially provide better predictions.

(3) The obtained RMSE values for both the train and test data are not satisfactory, suggesting the presence of other influential features not included int the dataset. Exploring additional relevant features or collecting more comprehensive data may lead to improved prediction accuracy.

References

1. Dataset: Catalonia cell coverage. https://console.cloud.google.com/marketplace/product/gen cat/cell_coverage?hl=zh-cn&project=firm-retina-379321&pli=1
2. Stančin, I, Jović, A.: An overview and comparison of free Python libraries for data mining and big data analysis. In: 42nd International Convention on Information and Communication Technology, Electronics and Microelectronics (MIPRO), pp. 977–982, Opatija, Croatia (2019). https://doi.org/10.23919/MIPRO.2019.8757088
3. Samadi, Y., Zbakh, M., Tadonki, C.: Performance comparison between Hadoop and Spark frameworks using HiBench benchmarks. Concurrency Comput. Pract. Exp. **30**(12), e4367 (2018)
4. Dede, E., Sendir, B., Kuzlu, P., Weachock, J., Govindaraju, M., Ramakrishnan, L.: Processing Cassandra datasets with hadoop-streaming based approaches. IEEE Trans. Serv. Comput. **9**(1), 46–58 (2016). https://doi.org/10.1109/TSC.2015.2444838
5. Mrjob, version 0.7.4, David, Marin. The Python MapReduce library (2020). https://pypi.org/project/mrjob/
6. Tellez, A., Pumperla, M., Malohlava, M.: Mastering Machine Learning with Spark 2.x (2017)
7. Yadav, R.: Spark Cookbook: over 60 recipes on spark, covering spark core, spark SQL, spark streaming, MLlib, and GraphX libraries (2015)
8. Kaur, G.: A comparison of two hybrid ensemble techniques for network anomaly detection in spark distributed environment. J. Inf. Secur. Appl. **55**, 102601 (2020). https://doi.org/10.1016/j.jisa.2020.102601
9. Ho, T.K.: Random decision forests. In: Proceedings of 3rd International Conference on Document Analysis and Recognition, vol.1, pp. 278–282, Montreal, QC, Canada (1995). https://doi.org/10.1109/ICDAR.1995.598994
10. Duffy, N., Helmbold, D.: Boosting methods for regression. Mach. Learn. **47**, 153–200 (2002). https://doi.org/10.1023/A:1013685603443

Branching Process Simulator in R

A. Tchorbadjieff[1], L. Tomov[2]([⊠]), and P. Mayster[3]

[1] Institute of Mathematics and Informatics, Bulgarian Academy of Sciences, Sofia, Bulgaria
atchorbadjieff@math.bas.bg
[2] Department of Informatics, New Bulgarian University, 1618 Sofia, Bulgaria
lptomov@nbu.bg
[3] Institute of Mathematics and Informatics, Bulgarian Academy of Sciences, Sofia, Bulgaria
penka.mayster@math.bas.bg

Abstract. We developed a set of software functionalities in R for simulation of branching processes. Originally it was designed for simulating the branching mechanism of a cosmic ray atmosphere cascade, beginning with electron-photon cascade. Further this simulator was adapted for applications epidemiology with extended set of probability distributions such as Poisson, Negative Binomial, shifted Geometric and Polya-Aepply used either for modeling the initial conditions for linear birth-death processes or branching process mechanism following predefined probabilistic distribution. The simulator is applied mostly when analytical solutions give convergent infinite series. It uses the capability of R for parallel computation and applies the Object-Oriented Programming paradigm (a secure type encapsulation).

Keywords: Branching processes · R · parallel computing · epidemiology · physics

1 The simulator

1.1 Purpose

The cosmic rays are the biggest natural permanently occurring branching process. Partially, the electron-photon pair production induced cascades naturally imply connection to Yule-Furry process and age-dependent Markov branching processes. This is the reason that it is the first mathematically modelled particle showers during the down of nuclear era [1, 2]. However, the explicit solution of the backward Kolmogorov equation for more complicated and larger multi-type branching processes is extremely difficult, even analytically insolvable. This makes the need of numerical solutions and computer simulation important and indispensable part in research.

As a part of this effort a new simulator[1] is developed as a modeling tool for cosmic ray air shower using branching processes [3]. It works as a generator of multiple independent

---

[1] https://gitlab.com/Tchorbadjieff/covid-19.

© ICST Institute for Computer Sciences, Social Informatics and Telecommunications Engineering 2023
Published by Springer Nature Switzerland AG 2023. All Rights Reserved
T. Zlateva and G. Tuparov (Eds.): CSECS 2023, LNICST 514, pp. 73–86, 2023.
https://doi.org/10.1007/978-3-031-44668-9_6

trials, with their aggregated results serving as a good approximation to the real result. Not surprisingly, soon the tool began to evolve in different directions, not limiting only to cosmic rays. One of the initially developed functionalities is the implementation of linear birth-death process induced from different random initial conditions [4]. Later, the available functionalities have been extending with inclusion the option of different branching mechanism, basically following well-known probabilistic distributions.

The mathematical formalism from the very beginning is based on assumption of existence some probabilities p, $0 < p < 1$, that either photon splits on electron and positron, or a new photon production due to charged particles deacceleration by breaking radiation. The simulator is developed in R and uses Object Oriented Programming paradigm. These processes are naturally simulated better with multiple parallel threads and the simulator is written for this purpose. We run it on the Avitohol supercomputer, belonging to Bulgarian Academy of Sciences (IICT-BAS[2]). Since the start of the COVID-19 pandemic, this simulator has been easily adapted also for modeling the disease spread in conjunction with changepoint analysis [5].

1.2 Structure and Functionality

Structure. The epidemiology version of simulator actually implements linear birth-death process with initial conditions following either Negative Binomial or Poisson distribution. It consists of two files with core functionalities – Cascade.R and Run_Cascade.R and two specialized files for epidemiology – Branching_MP.R and CPoints_Init3.R.

The Cascade.R defines the class, which contains the information about given particle (reinterpreted later as infected person) which has some properties relevant only to the electron-photon cascade and other sub-atomic processes that can be used in different context. The specific properties are *type, energy, angle of scattering*, while *age, time, number and depth* are more general. The angle of scattering and the energy are main properties of any natural particle cascades. However, despite of that in the current version they are not completely implemented yet, they provide preserved definition for further reinterpretation beyond particle physics constraints, to address conditions of infection in epidemiology modeling – like environmental and social factors. The last one, depth, gives the position of the particle on the cascade chain or the depth of the branching tree. We give here the class definition without the constructor and the validity check.

We apply S4 as a formal approach to OOP, which has specialized methods for creating classes, such as setClass() [6]. It provides multiple inheritance which we do not use in our simulator due to the issues with extensibility and maintainability it introduces [7]. S4 defines slots, named components of the object accessed with the subsetting operator @ (at). These are the class members. There is a setMethod() function that defines accessor functions for the members of class and assigns them. This is analogous to the properties in C# classes, a way to get and set the values without separating these two logically independent functionalities. In our code we do not use inheritance, but with the extension of the functionality we may have to – and if we do, S4 supplies us with the necessary functionality. The setClass() method can use the argument "contains" to specify the base

---

[2] https://www.iict.bas.bg/avitohol/.

class. Employing the idea of Alan Kay "Until real software engineering is developed, the next best practice is to develop with a dynamic system that has extreme late binding in all aspects." [8] In R the class definition and the object construction both occur at run time. This makes impossible to create invalid object, by redefining the class after an object has been constructed. Every class definition in R should have a prototype, for default values (analogous to the role of parameter less constructor in C#). Validation can be done with function SetValidity() or as in our case with user supplied function for simple objects. The SetValidity() however, in the general context is more appropriate, because we want to have meaningful and informative error messaging to improve maintainability and prevent dangerous errors [9].

```
ParticleInfo = setClass(
  "ParticleInfo",

  slots = c(
    type= "numeric" , #"gamma"==1, "e-"==2, "e+"==3
    #type = "character", # "gamma", "e-", "e+"
    E = "numeric", # Energy, in MeV
    t = "numeric", # Time
    theta = "numeric", # Total scattering angle
    age = "numeric", # Age
    number="numeric",
    depth="numeric"
  ),
prototype = list(type = 2, E = 1000, t = 0, theta = 0,
age = 0, depth=0),

  # Check for validity after construction
  validity = function(object) {
    return(!((object@type < 1 | object@type > 3) | ob-
ject@E <= 0 | object@t<=0 | (object@theta < -180 | ob-
ject@theta > 180) | object@age < 0 | object@number < 0 |
object@depth < 0))
  }
```

The ParticleInfo class is being used as part of array, in which each element holds the number of particles at a given discrete step of time t. For each given element of the structure, a random number is being generated (for instance with random binomial outcome as it is shown in example) [10].

```
trial=function(i,strct, p)
{
  return (rbinom(1,strct[[i]]@number, p))
}
```

Main Method for Cascade. The branching cascade is calculated iteratively. At each state the survival of the previous step is doubled, the depth of the tree increases with one, and the discrete time step also increases with one. The age of particles here is fixed every time. The current version of the simulator works with the symmetric process with equal lifespans for all particles and the survived particles from previous step are doubled (each particle is replaced by two new particles), so the half of them is "reincarnated"[3], exactly in line with the famous myth of Hydra – "cut one head and two new shall arise). Every particle has a certain probability of dying, so survived particles at a given time step are a subset of the generated particles at the previous subset, combined with the newly generated particles at this step t. This process is inside the for loop in the code, shown below.

The most important part in this process is the definition of probabilities. The software relies on values in the classical probabilistic range between 0 and 1. However, usually these values rely on conversion from other measurement units. In high energy particle physics this measure is cross section. For the case of Covid-19 simulation, the probabilities are obtained from the rate of daily infection changes.

```
spawnYule_basic=function(part.atDepth, depth, p.dead)
{
  photons.which = getIndexByType(part.atDepth,1)
  photons= unlist(sapply(photons.which , FUN=iter,
strct=part.atDepth))
  p=1/(p.dead+1)
  n.dead = unlist(sapply(1:length(photons), FUN=trial,
strct=photons, p=1-p))
  surv=unlist(sapply(1:length(photons), FUN=function(i,
strct){ return (max(0,strct[[i]]@number-n.dead[i]))},
strct=photons))

  for (i in 1:length(photons))
  {
    photons[[i]]@number = 2*surv[i]
    photons[[i]]@depth = photons[[i]]@depth +1
    photons[[i]]@age = 1
    photons[[i]]@t = photons[[i]]@t +1
  }

  ret= c(photons)

  return (ret)
}
```

---

[3] https://www.rand.org/content/dam/rand/pubs/reports/2009/R381.pdf.

Cascade Shower. It is in the same file Cascade.R, with default probability of dying set to ½ and with asymmetric process set to false. Asymmetric processes with different lifespans for particles are to be implemented in the future with asynchronous programming model.

```
shower.Extention = function(part, depth, p.dead=1/2,
isAssym=FALSE)
{
  idx=getIndexByDepth(part, depth)
  pool=part[idx]
  ph.index=getIndexByType(pool,1)

  result=NULL
  if(!is.null(ph.index))
  {
    tmp = spawnYule_basic(pool[ph.index],depth, p.dead )
    if(length(tmp)>0)
      result= tmp
  }

  return (result)
}
```

Running the Cascade

Important properties of any branching process are initial conditions and the phenomenology of the process development. For the formal, the importance of initial conditions for linear birth-death process is considered in [2–4]. Later, this assumption is empirically observed as a pure migration of infected population due to first days of Covid-19 pandemic in [5]. In the current available software implementation as options for initial conditions are considered Poisson, Binomial, Negative Binomial and related Geometric distribution, Polia Aeply distributions and Polia urn generator.

Initially, the process of branching is assumed only as binary outcome – death or multiple births. However, with functionalities extension of the code the realization of trial function is extending by inclusion of another probability branching mechanisms – Negative Binomial and Poisson distributions.

The effectiveness and precision of the results from the simulator depend on the number of computed trajectories. This is a direct result of the stochastic nature of every trajectory due to random trials. This implies the requirement of very high number of repeated computations and their statistical aggregation. These receptions are implemented through multiple independent instances of cascade trajectories. They are executed by function main_iter() that runs the cascade iteratively, calling the *shower.Extention()* from Cascade.R in a **for** loop with extending the depth at each step and with a probability of dying, calculated at every step.

Main_iter() is called in *main()* function iteratively, bringing the complexity to $O(n^2)$. This is the place where trajectory repetitions are executed. To extend computational effectiveness of contemporary computer multi-processing hardware, the independent calculations of different trajectories are implemented on parallel computation with doParallel library in R [11]. In the following code block we show how in R we can combine resources for shared memory between nodes and processes, by loading packages and sources and calling linear_predict() with *lapply()* for linux systems. Separate applications of a function to members of list are prerequisite for parallel processing.

```
no_cores <- detectCores() - 1
cl <- makeCluster(no_cores)
registerDoParallel(cl)
system.time(foreach(i = 1:n_sel, .combine = list, .ex-
port= c('distr.pois','data.by.country'),.pack-
ages=c('readxl', 'xts', 'changepoint', 'MASS', 'grDevic-
es')) %dopar%{
   source("Run_Cascade.R")
   library(kSamples)
   library("dgof")
   set.seed(1)
   output=linearPredict(i, bridge[i])
   lapply(1:length(output), function(j) {is.append=TRUE;
if(j==1){is.ap-
pend=FALSE;};write.table(output[[j]],file=paste("Results/
/predicted_",selection[i],".csv", sep=""), append =
is.append,col.names = !is.append, row.names = FALSE,
sep=",")})})
```

Verification.

The simulator is designated to implement stochastic process, resulting to stochastic outcome. This lack of deterministic results implies the requirement for different software verification process. At first, the outcome is designed to consist of large number repeated runs generated by random generator, creating multiple trajectories, as much as possible. The expected results are obtained from averaging over all generated directories. The variability is also represented by results variation in generated directories.

Having different outcome in every run, the classical debugging procedure becomes non-effective and obsolete. Thus, the process of software verification and debug fixing is designed as a statistical learning process, starting from the comparison between already available analytical results and their computer modelling by software. This process is permanently repeated after every new development. For instance, the influence of initial conditions on linear birth-death process was tested by comparison between analytical results and model outcome in [4]. The same comparison is done for geometric distribution, using the analytical results in [12].

The trial mechanism is verified separately during development by directly analytical computing branching processes. For instance, let us consider the following branching cascade of 3 particles with its generating function:

$$
\begin{aligned}
h1(s_1, s_2, s_3) &= (1 - 2p) + ps_1 + ps_1s_2 \\
h2(s_1, s_2, s_3) &= (1 - 2p) + ps_2 + ps_1s_2 \\
h3(s_1, s_2, s_3) &= (1 - 2p) + ps_2 + 2ps_1s_3
\end{aligned}
\tag{1}
$$

The probability of reproduction is $0 < p < 1/2$, having that the process is without particle deaths when $p = 1/2$. The matrixes of expectations $\mathbf{M}_{ij}$ and characteristic determinant Λ are computed as follows:

$$
\mathbf{M}_{ij} = \begin{bmatrix} p & p & p \\ p & 2p & 0 \\ p & 0 & 2p \end{bmatrix}
\tag{2}
$$

$$
\Lambda = \begin{bmatrix} p - \lambda & p & p \\ p & 2p - \lambda & 0 \\ p & 0 & 2p - \lambda \end{bmatrix}
\tag{3}
$$

As straightforward computations show, the process is critical when $\mathbf{p} = 1/3 < 1/2$. The process is subcritical and supercritical, respectively, when $\mathbf{p}$ is less or above $1/3$. The simulated results are in complete agreement with the predicted results after only 10000 runs (Fig. 1). Note, that critical process acquires quickly stable asymmetry proportion between electrons and positrons.

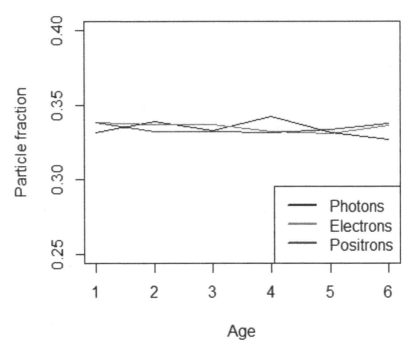

Fig. 1. Software verification with 1000 runs of the electron-photon branching cascade

2 Applications

Application to Covid – When the Covid-19 outburst occurred the need for large number re-computations and predictions of newly infected persons grew. To keep track with it, we automated completely the process[4] by development of the dedicated method linear_predict(). The process, which is fully described in our paper [5], combines linear birth-death process with Poisson and negative Binomial initial conditions with changepoint analysis to detect any regime changes of daily infection rates and to recalculate due probability distributions. This works due to the Markov property of the branching process of linear birth-death. The changepoint operations are implemented in CPoins Init3.R[5], separately from the core functionality in order for it to remain reusable and extendable. It allows continuous adaptive and relatively precise short-term prediction of daily cases for an ongoing pandemic with rapid viral evolution, multiple variants and wide spectrum of measures and adaptive reactions from the public to the pandemic. It can be relatively easily adapted to predict cases by age group, bed occupancy in hospitals, and deaths for the initial waves of pandemics (there is recurrent relation between lethality in a given wave and in previous waves). We show some results of the work of Branching_MP.R on Fig. 2 and Fig. 3

---

[4] https://gitlab.com/Tchorbadjieff/covid-19/-/blob/main/Branching_MP.R.
[5] https://gitlab.com/Tchorbadjieff/covid-19/-/blob/main/CPoints_Init3.R.

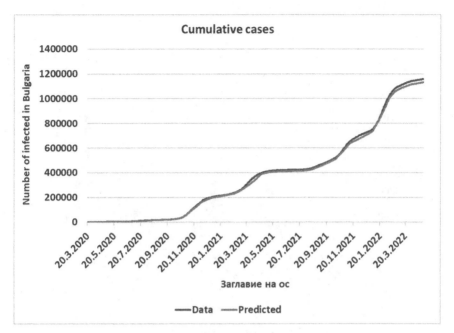

Fig. 2. Predicted cumulative number of infected individuals in Bulgaria for 20.3.2020–30.4.2022

Applications for Branching Inference: An important application of this simulator is for study of industrial scale processes driven by branching mechanism following different distributions and occurring in changing environments when the analytical solutions are not feasible. An example of analytically solvable process is the one driven by geometric branching mechanism [12].

However, the difficulty of solution grows enormously when other distributions are in consideration for branching modelling. For instance, when the branching process consists of multiple number of reactions **r, r > 0** until the experiment stops. In this case, it follows Negative Binomial distribution NB(r,p) with probability of **p**; $0 < p < 1.$. Then, the multiplicity depends on mean (energy) E(N) and Variations (dissipation)D(N):

$$E(N) = \frac{(1-p)r}{p} \tag{4}$$

$$D(N) = \frac{(1-p)r}{p2} \tag{5}$$

Another, possible case is when the branching concerns equally distributed molecules in volume **V** of a continuous region **T**, $V = \int_T d\xi$. The expected mean value of random variable X in this case is [13], see:

$$E(X) = V^{-n} \int_T d\xi_1 \int_T d\xi_2 ... \int_T d\xi_n X(\xi_1, \xi_2, ..., \xi_n)$$

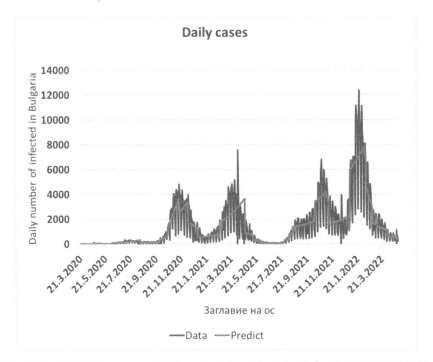

Fig. 3. Predicted daily number of infected individuals in Bulgaria for 20.3.2020–30.4.2022

Then, due to the binomial trial for $T_1 \subset T$ and using probability $p = V_1/V$ and densities $\rho = n/V$ we obtain Poisson distribution (Po(n)):

$$P(R = r) = \frac{e^{-\rho V_1}(\rho V_1)^r}{r!} \tag{7}$$

The variety of possible reasons to use these three distributions, Ge, NB and Po, could be extended to larger class of branching processes. For their probability generating function (p.g.f.) in critical case, $h(s) = p(0) + p(1)s + p(2)s^2 + \ldots$, there is a vertical asymptote for Ge and NB distributions, but not for Poisson (Fig. 4). Moreover, the Po distribution yields the best fit to the tangent $x = y$ in the neighbourhood of $s = 1$ (Fig. 5).

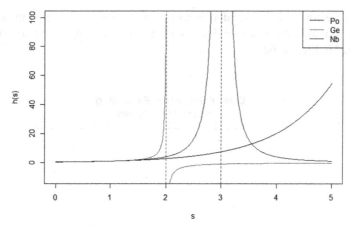

Fig. 4. Probability generating function (p.g.f.) h(s) in critical case for Po, NB and Ge distributions.

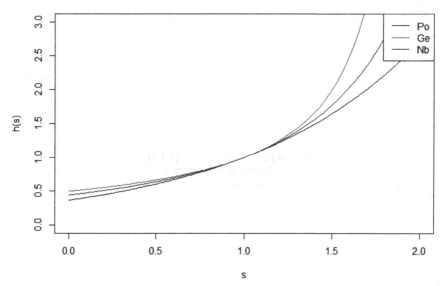

Fig. 5. Probability generating function (p.g.f.) h(s) in the neighbourhood of s = 1 for critical case for Po, NB and Ge distributions.

However, the solutions either for sub-critical of super-critical processes with these three distributions or for any other more complicated distributed processes is not so straight forward. This is not only due to computational complications, but also because the correct identification of exact branching nature of the process, mainly in cases of small data sizes. In this case, the simulator could be used to generate multiple results to test different hypotheses about fit to the real data. The process can be easily implemented by redefining the trial() function[6] with the opted definition and generate enough large

---

[6] https://gitlab.com/Tchorbadjieff/branching-simulator.

number of trajectories. This procedure is also used to calibrate and verify the simulator work to already available results in [12]. Some random trajectories are computed and demonstrated in Fig. 6a–6d.

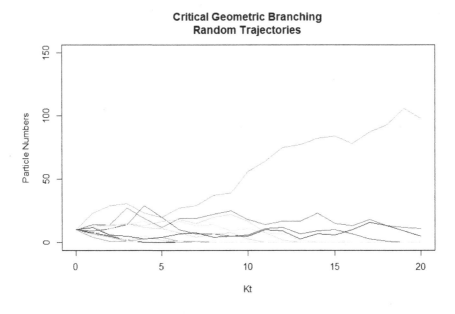

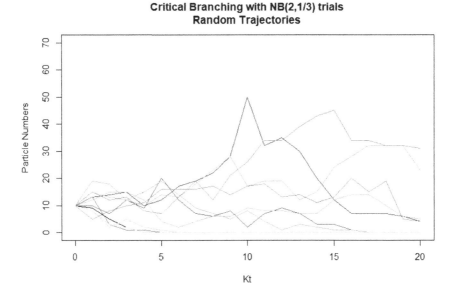

Fig. 6. a. Critical branching process with shifted geometric distribution. **b.** Critical branching process with negative binomial distribution with $r = 2$ and $p = 1/3$. **c.** Critical branching process with negative binomial distribution with $r = 3$ and $p = 1/4$. **d.** Branching process with Poisson distribution.

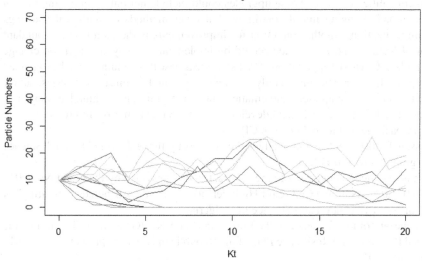

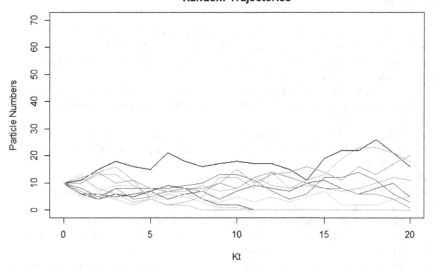

Fig. 6. (*continued*)

3 Conclusions and Future Work

The presented here branching simulator already produced some unexpected practical results – simulated very well development of Covid-19 outbursts, proving that even the most complex ongoing pandemic could be predicted without certain knowledge either of the characteristics of the viral variants, the measures that the governments take or the ability to predict the evolution of variants. The tool is open source and open for functionalities upgrade. These upgrades could include not only particle interaction processes and changing initial conditions, but other methods of statistical learnings and automatization. Another direction for improvements is the inclusion of abundant graphical features. These upgrades could be implemented easily, as inclusion change point tools in Covid-19 application. The list of ideas how this simulator can be extended and improved, may not be limited only to epidemiology and cosmic rays' physics, but for general application in applied mathematical modeling, training machine learning tools or educational purposes. A logical development in the medium-term future is to create a library package and to include it in CRAN.

Assen Tchorbadjieff acknowledges the support by the Bulgarian National Science Fund, grant No KP-06-H22/3.

We acknowledge the access to the e-infrastructure provided by the Grant No. D01–168/28.07.2022 "National Centre for High Performance and Distributed Computing" of the Ministry of Education and Science of Bulgaria.

Latchezar Tomov is grantee of the European Union-NextGenerationEU, through the National Recovery and Resilience Plan of the Republic of Bulgaria, project № BG-RRP-2.004–0008-C01.

References

1. Harris, T.E.: The Theory of Branching Processes. Springer-Verlag, Berlin (1963)
2. Sevastyanov, B.A.: Branching Processes. Nauka, Moscow (1971). (in Russian)
3. Tchorbadjieff, A.: Using branching processes to simulate cosmic rays cascades. Pliska Studia Math. Bulgarica **27**, 103–114 (2017)
4. Tchorbadjieff, A., Mayster, P.: Models induced from critical birth–death process with random initial conditions. J. Appl. Stat. **47**(13–15), 2862–2878 (2020). https://doi.org/10.1080/026 64763.2020.1732309
5. Tchorbadjieff, A., Tomov, L.P., Velev, V., Dezhov, G., Manev, V., Mayster, P.: On regime changes of COVID-19 outbreak. J. Appl. Stat. (2023). https://doi.org/10.1080/02664763. 2023.2177625
6. Wickham, H.: Advanced R. CRC Press (2019)
7. Wang, Y, [王焱林]: Revisiting multiple inheritance for modularity and reuse. (Thesis). University of Hong Kong, Pokfulam, Hong Kong SAR (2019)
8. https://wiki.c2.com/?AlanKaysDefinitionOfObjectOriented. Accessed 10 July 2023
9. Leveson, N.G., Turner, C.S.: An investigation of the Therac-25 accidents. Computer **26**(7), 18–41 (1993). https://doi.org/10.1109/MC.1993.274940
10. Kachitvichyanukul, V., Schmeiser, B.W.: Binomial random variate generation. Commun. ACM. ACM **31**, 216–222 (1988)
11. Microsoft Corporation, Weston, S., doParallel: Foreach Parallel Adaptor for the 'parallel' Package (2019). https://CRAN.R-project.org/package=doParallel
12. Tchorbadjieff, A., Mayster, P.: Geometric branching reproduction Markov processes. Mod. Stochast.: Theory Appl. **7**(4), 357–378 (2020). https://doi.org/10.15559/20-VMSTA163
13. Whittle, P.: Probability. Penguin Books (1976). ISBN: 0140800859, 9780140800852

List of Optimal Solutions of the Minimum Cost for Minimum Time Assignment Problem

Lasko M. Laskov$^{(\boxtimes)}$ ⓘ and Marin L. Marinov ⓘ

Informatics Department, New Bulgarian University, Sofia, Bulgaria
{llaskov,mlmainov}@nbu.bg

Abstract. One of the fundamental problems in the disciplines of combinatorial optimization and operation research is the *assignment problem* (AP). Even though the AP and its variants has been explored extensively in the specialized literature, most of the resources are focused on the calculation of a single optimal solution. In this paper we propose an approach that generates a list of optimal solutions.

We focus on the bi-criteria variant of the AP in which two objectives are minimized: *cost* and *time*. Our approach finds the maximal subset of assignments that are Pareto optimal, and have minimal cost. In particular, the method finds a list of all assignments that are optimal with respect to the cost criterion.

Keywords: Pareto optimal · Assignment problem · Branch and bound

1 Introduction

The *assignment problem* (AP) [5] is a fundamental problem in the fields of combinatorial optimization and operation research [11,22,24]. It has been explored since the middle of the 20th century [9,15,16], and continued to be in the focus of investigations [1,20,27]) with the progress of information technologies and computer science until now-a-days (see for example [4,8,14]). The applications of AP are numerous, and can be found in many scientific disciplines such as economics [10], data science, machine learning and pattern recognition [23], distributed computer systems [25,26], and many others.

In its basic form, the AP can be formulated as the problem of finding an assignment of n *tasks* (jobs, projects, processes) to n other *agents* (workers, companies, processors) that is efficient according to a certain formal criterion. Most commonly the criterion is to minimize the total cost of the proposed plan. In the above informal definition the number of tasks and agents is equal, and in this case the AP called *balanced*. In the case in which the number of tasks and agents differ, the AP is said to be *unbalanced* [5].

© ICST Institute for Computer Sciences, Social Informatics and Telecommunications Engineering 2023
Published by Springer Nature Switzerland AG 2023. All Rights Reserved
T. Zlateva and G. Tuparov (Eds.): CSECS 2023, LNICST 514, pp. 87–101, 2023.
https://doi.org/10.1007/978-3-031-44668-9_7

The naive solution of AP results in a full exhaustion algorithm that leads to unfeasible factorial complexity $O(n!)$, which makes the problem hard to solve even for relatively small values of n. However, different algorithms exist that solve the AP in polynomial time, with the first known such method called *Hungarian algorithm* published in 1956 in the famous work of Kuhn [15], and an year latter extended to its variants in [16]. The computational complexity of the initial version of the Hungarian algorithm was $O(n^4)$ which latter is shown that can be improved to $O(n^3)$ [7,28]. Different versions and improvements of the Hungarian algorithm continue to be a subject of research in more recent works (see for example [8,25]).

A whole section of methods treat AP as a network flow problem [1,7] and adopt the tools of graph theory [2,6] to find an efficient solution. Most of the methods in this category bring the AP to the problem of searching for matchings in bipartite graphs [12,26].

At the same time, a global optimization technique known as *branch & bound* (see [13,17,19]) has been shown to lead to efficient solutions to other combinatorial optimization problems such as the *Travelling Salesman Problem* (TSP) (see [18,21]), and some versions of the *knapsack problem* [8].

Most of the existing methods and algorithms in the literature aim to find an efficient approach to find a single optimal solution of the AP. The main goal of this paper is to present an effective approach for composition of a list of all assignments that have minimal cost and satisfy an additional condition. This approach is presented with a solution of the AP in the case in which two independent optimization criteria are defined: time and cost. The main problem is brought to finding of the maximal subset of Pareto optimal solutions that have minimal cost.

The paper is organized as follows. In Sect. 2 we introduce the main notations and definitions. In Sect. 3 we present the solution of the main problem. In Sect. 4 we solve the problem for description of all solutions of the AP. The solution follows from the presented approach in Sect. 3. Finally, Sect. 5 contains discussion of the presented methods and conclusions.

2   Main Notations and Definitions

In this section we will introduce the basic notations.

With $N(n) = \{1, 2, \ldots, n\}$ we denote the set of the first n natural numbers, for each natural number n. With P^n we denote the permutations of the first n natural numbers. We denote the permutation

$$w = \begin{pmatrix} 1 & 2 & \cdots & n \\ j_1 & j_2 & \cdots & j_n \end{pmatrix} \tag{1}$$

with the shorter $w = (j_1, j_2, \ldots, j_k)$. Also, $w(s) = j_s$, $\forall s \in N(n)$.

Let B is an arbitrary matrix. With $B(i, j)$ we denote the element of B on the ith row and jth column. We denote with

$$[B]_{j_1, j_2, \ldots, j_s}^{i_1, i_2, \ldots, i_k} \tag{2}$$

the sub-matrix that results from B after we delete the rows with indexes $i_1, i_2,$ $\ldots, i_k$, and columns with indexes $j_1, j_2, \ldots, j_s$.

For an arbitrary square *cost matrix* A of order n and an arbitrary permutation $w \in P^n$, we define the *cost function*:

$$F_A(w) = \sum_{i=1}^{n} A(i, w(i)). \tag{3}$$

Similarly, for an arbitrary square *time matrix* T of order n and an arbitrary permutation $w \in P^n$, we define the *time maximization function*:

$$G_T(w) = \max_{i \in N(n)} \{T(i, w(i))\}. \tag{4}$$

The function t assigns to each variation $w = (j_1, j_2, \ldots, j_k)$, $k \in N(n)$ of the first n natural numbers the number

$$t(w) = \max\{T(1, j_1), T(2, j_2), \ldots, T(k, j_k)\}.$$

It is clear that when $k = n$, $t(w) = G_T(w)$.

2.1   Main Problem

Let n independent tasks must be distributed among n agents. The agent i can execute the task j for time t_{ij} that results in costs a_{ij}, $i, j \in N(n)$. The objective is to find the maximal set of plans that are executed for minimal cost, and for shortest possible time.

Let the cost matrix $A(a_{ij})$ and the time matrix $T(t_{ij})$ are predefined square matrices of order n.

We will call each permutation $w \in P^n$ a *plan*.

Definition 1. *We will call an **optimal plan** each plan $\widetilde{w}$, for which the following equalities hold:*

$$F_A(\widetilde{w}) = r_0 \text{ and } G_T(\widetilde{w}) = t_0$$

where:
$r_0 = \min\{F_A(w) : w \in P^n\}$, $t_0 = \min\{G_T(w) : w \in P^n \text{ and } F_A(w) = r_0\}$.

Now let us define the two sets:
$W = \{w \in P^n : F_A(w) = r_0\}$ and $V = \{w \in W : G_T(w) = t_0\}$.

Definition 2. *The plan $\widehat{w}$ is called **Pareto optimal** when there does not exist a plan w, for which one of the following holds:*

- $F_A(w) < F_A(\widehat{w})$ and $G_T(w) \leq G_T(\widehat{w})$, or
- $F_A(w) \leq F_A(\widehat{w})$ and $G_T(w) < G_T(\widehat{w})$.

Remark 1. The set V of all optimal plans is the set of all Pareto optimal solutions that have minimal cost r_0.

Now the main problem that we will call *Minimum Cost for Minimum Time* (MCMT) is defined in the following way.

Problem 1 (MCMT). For arbitrary square matrices A and T of the same order, and an arbitrary chosen natural number n_0, compile a list S_0 of optimal plans with the following properties.

1. If more than $n_0 - 1$ optimal plans exist, then S_0 contains n_0 elements.
2. If the optimal plans are less than n_0, then S_0 contains all the optimal plans.

To solve the MCMT problem, we will use the procedure $\mathcal{H}$ and the function $\mathcal{T}$.

With $\mathcal{H}$ we denote the procedure that for an arbitrary square matrix M of order k calculates the pair $\{r_0, w_0\}$, where $r_0 = \min_{w \in P^k} \{F_M(w)\}$, $w_0 \in P^k$ and $F_M(w_0) = r_0$. In our implementations of $\mathcal{H}$, we use the Hungarian algorithm [7,15,28] to solve the classical AP with computational complexity $O(n^3)$.

With $\mathcal{T}$ we denote the function

$$T(M) = \max\{\max\{M_r\},\ \max\{M_c\}\}, \tag{5}$$

where M_r is the set of row minima of M and M_c is the set of column minima of M.

3   Solution of MCMT Problem

The challenging feature of the MCMT problem is that the optimal plan is determined by two criteria:

– the *cost* criterion, for which the function F_A is minimized;
– the *time* criterion, for which the function G_T is minimized.

Moreover, the function G_T is not a linear function, and for that reason the whole problem is nonlinear.

3.1   General Structure of the Solution

Step 1. Calculate a plan w_0 that is executed with a minimal cost. Define:

– minimal cost $r_0 = F_A(w_0)$;
– the current record $S_0 = \{\}$ and $t_0 = G_T(w_0)$.

Step 2. Define the stack $S = \{X_0\}$, where X_0 is storage of the initial problem.

Step 3. While $S \neq \varnothing$, update t_0 and S_0.

When the loop from *Step 3* completes, S_0 stores the solution of the MCMT problem, and t_0 stores the minimal time.

In *Step 1* of the solution, the procedure $\mathcal{H}$ applied on $Z = A$ calculates the minimal possible cost r_0 and a plan w_0, for which $F_A(w_0) = r_0$. Also, the initial record is defined $t_0 = G_T(w_0)$.

We store the sub-problems that result from the branching process in *Step 3* in a list of the form $\{w, B, Bt, k, dt\}$, where w is a vector; B and Bt are matrices, and k, dt are special numbers.

The *initial problem* is stored with $X_0 = \{w, B, Bt, k, dt\}$ where: $w = (\ ) = \varnothing$; $Bt = T$; $dt = T(Bt)$; $k = n$ and B is a $(n+1) \times n$ matrix with elements

$$B(i, j) = \begin{cases} A(i, j), & \text{if } i \in N(n) \text{ and } j \in N(n) \\ j, & \text{if } i = n + 1 \text{ and } j \in N(n). \end{cases} \quad (6)$$

In *Step 2* the set $S = \{X_0\}$ is defined.

The update of t_0 and S_0 in *Step 3* combines the branching process with the bound by the cost and time criteria.

3.2   Branching Procedure

If $n > 2$, the branch of X_0 replaces X_0 in S with a finite number of sub-problems, resulting from the following inductive procedure.

The **base case** of the induction is composed by the following two stages.

1. For each $j \in \{1, 2, \ldots, n\}$ we define $w_j = (j)$, $B_j = [B]_j^1$, $Bt_j = [Bt]_j^1$ and $dt_j = \max\{Bt(1, j), T(Bt_j)\}$.
2. For each $j \in \{1, 2, \ldots, n\}$:
   - using the procedure $\mathcal{H}$ for $Z = [B_j]^n$ we calculate $\{\tilde{r}, \tilde{w}\}$;
   - if $B(1, j) + \tilde{r} = r_0$, we push the sub-problem $X_{w_j} = \{w_j, B_j, Bt_j, n-1, dt_j\}$ into the stack S.

The first stage of the base case implements branching, while the second stage implements bound by the cost criterion.

Inductive Step. Let $X_{w'} = \{w', B', Bt', k, dt'\}$ is a sub-problem that is a result of the previous branching and $w' = (j_1, j_2, \ldots, j_{n-k})$, where j_s are different $n-k$ natural numbers, for which $j_s \leq n$. If $k > 2$, then the branching procedure replaces $X_{w'}$ in S with the finite number of its sub-problems, that are a result from the following two stages.

1. For each $i \in \{1, 2, \ldots, k\}$ we define $w_i = (j_1, j_2, \ldots, j_{n-k}, B'(k+1, i))$; $B'_i = [B']_i^1$; $Bt'_i = [Bt']_i^1$ and $dt'_i = \max\{t(w_i), T(Bt'_i)\}$.
2. For each $i \in \{1, 2, \ldots, k\}$:
   - using the procedure $\mathcal{H}$ for $Z = [B'_i]^k$ we calculate $\{\tilde{r}, \tilde{w}\}$;
   - if $\sum_{s=1}^{n-k} B(s, j_s) + B(n-k+1, B'(k+1, i)) + \tilde{r} = r_0$, we push the sub-problem $X_{w_i} = \{w_i, B'_i, Bt'_i, k-1, dt'_i\}$ into the stack S.

Again, the first stage of the inductive step implements branching, while the second stage implements bound by the cost criterion.

3.3   Update of t_0 and S_0

The current values of t_0 and S_0 will be updated only after the extraction of a sub-problem $X_{w'} = \{w', B', Bt', 2, dt'\}$ from the stack S. In this case $w' = (j_1, j_2, \ldots, j_{n-2})$ is a variation of the first n natural numbers from $(n-2)$ class, and there exists exactly two permutations

$$w_1 = (j_1, j_2, \ldots, j_{n-2}, x, y) \quad \text{and} \quad w_2 = (j_1, j_2, \ldots, j_{n-2}, y, x)$$

from P^n.

We will suppose that a function edn is defined, such that for an arbitrary variation w' of the first n natural numbers from class $(n-2)$, calculates the pair of permutations $end(w') = \{w_1, w_2\}$.

If $X_{w'} = \{w', B', Bt', 2, dt'\}$ is at the top of the stack S, then we define $\{w_1, w_2\} = end(w')$ and pop $X_{w'}$ out from S.

For each $i \in \{1, 2\}$, if $F_A(w_i) = r_0$ and $G_T(w_i) < t_0$, then we define $t_0 = G_T(w_i)$ and $S_0 = \{w_i\}$. Otherwise, if $F_A(w_i) = r_0$ and $G_T(w_i) = t_0$, then we push w_i into S_0, if $|S_0| < n_0$.

3.4   Bound Procedure

The current record t_0 allows us to implement a bound procedure based on time criterion.

Let for the sub-problem $X_{w'} = \{w', B', Bt', k, dt'\}$ the inequality is fulfilled

$$t_0 < dt' \tag{7}$$

From the definition of dt' it follows that if $w \in P^n$ and $w(i) = w'(i), \forall i \in \{1, \ldots, n-k\}$, then it is fulfilled that

$$G_T(w) \geq dt' > t_0.$$

Therefore, w is not an optimal assignment. This allows each sub-problem $X_{w'}$, for which (7) is fulfilled, to be ignored and to be removed from the stack S.

3.5   Algorithm for Solving MCMT Problem

The following Algorithm 1 describes in details the proposed solution of the MCMT problem.

The **while** loop of Algorithm 1 implements *Step 3* of the general structure of the solution. If S has at least one element, then store the top of the stack S in $\{w', B', Bt', k, dt'\}$, and we remove it from the stack with $pop(S)$. Then the body of the loop contains three possibilities.

1. If $dt' > t_0$, then bound is performed, and the algorithm moves to the next iteration of the loop.

Algorithm 1. Solution of the MCMT problem.

function MINCOSTMAXTIME(A, T, n_0)
 $\{r_0, w_0\} \leftarrow \mathcal{H}(A)$
 $t_0 \leftarrow G_T(w_0)$, $S_0 \leftarrow \varnothing$ $\triangleright$ S_0 is a list
 $w \leftarrow \varnothing$, B is a matrix defined with (6)
 $Bt \leftarrow T$, $dt \leftarrow \mathcal{T}(Bt)$
 $X_0 \leftarrow \{w, B, Bt, n, dt\}$, push$(S, X_0)$ $\triangleright$ S is a stack
 while $S \neq \varnothing$ **do**
  $\{w, B, Bt, k, dt\} \leftarrow top(S), pop(S)$
  if $dt \leq t_0$ **then**
   if $k > 2$ **then**
    for $j \leftarrow 1$ to k **do**
     $w_1 \leftarrow w \cup \{B(k+1, j)\}$
     $B_1 \leftarrow [B]_j^1$
     $\{\overline{r}, \widetilde{w}\} \leftarrow \mathcal{H}([B_1]^k)$
     $\overline{w} \leftarrow \{B_1(k, \widetilde{w}(1)), B_1(k, \widetilde{w}(2)), \ldots, B_1(k, \widetilde{w}(k-1))\}$
     $v_1 \leftarrow w_1 \cup \overline{w}$, $r_1 \leftarrow F_A(v_1)$
     if $r_1 = r_0$ **then**
      $t_1 \leftarrow G_T(v_1)$
      if $t_1 < t_0$ **then**
       $t_0 \leftarrow t_1$
       $S_0 \leftarrow \varnothing$
       $Bt_1 \leftarrow [Bt]_j^1$
       $dt_1 \leftarrow \max\{t(w_1), \mathcal{T}(Bt_1)\}$
       $push(S, \{\{w_1, B_1, Bt_1, k-1, dt_1\}\})$
      end if
     end if
    end for
   else
    $V \leftarrow end(w)$
    for $i \leftarrow 1$ to 2 **do**
     $r_1 \leftarrow F_A(V(i))$, $t_1 \leftarrow G_T(V(i))$
     if $r_0 = r_1$ and $t_1 < t_0$ **then**
      $t_0 \leftarrow t_1$, $w_0 \leftarrow V(i)$, $S_0 \leftarrow \{w_0\}$
     else if $r_0 = r_1$ and $t_1 = t_0$ and $|S_0| < n_0$ **then**
      $S_0 \leftarrow S_0 \cup \{V(i)\}$
     end if
    end for
   end if
  end if
 end while
end function

2. If $dt' \leq t_0$ and $k > 2$ the algorithm performs branching of (w', B', Bt', k, dt'), and the resulting sub-problems are pushed into the stack S. If the conditions are met, the current state of t_0 and S_0 are updated.
3. If $dt' \leq t_0$ and $k = 2$, t_0 and S_0 are updated.

After the completion of the **while** loop, the solution of the MCMT problem is the list S_0, with $|S_0|$ being the number of optimal assignments, r_0 stores the minimal cost and t_0 is the minimal possible time.

The correctness of Algorithm 1 follows from the fact that the **while** loop stops after a finite number of iterations. This is so, because the number of sub-problems that can be stored in S is restricted up to a given constant. Besides that, any update of S_0 and t_0 decrements the number of elements in S by 1. The correctness of the branching procedure can be proved by induction using the construction of the sub-problems. The computational complexity of the algorithm is $n_1 O\left(n^4\right)$, where $n_1 = |W|$ is the number of optimal solutions with respect to the cost criterion.

Example 1. Let the matrix A be defined by (12) and the matrix T be defined with (13) given in the appendix of the paper.

We solve Problem 1 for $n_0 = 4$. We calculate that the minimum cost is $r_0 = 218$, the minimum time is $t_0 = 85$ and

$$
\begin{aligned}
S_0 = \{ & (18, 12, 13, 17, 16, 8, 9, 20, 7, 3, 19, 4, 14, 1, 15, 11, 2, 6, 10, 5), \\
& (18, 12, 13, 17, 16, 8, 9, 20, 7, 5, 19, 4, 14, 1, 15, 11, 2, 6, 10, 3), \\
& (18, 12, 13, 17, 16, 8, 9, 20, 10, 3, 19, 4, 14, 1, 15, 11, 2, 6, 7, 5), \\
& (18, 12, 13, 17, 16, 8, 9, 20, 10, 5, 19, 4, 14, 1, 15, 11, 2, 6, 7, 3) \}.
\end{aligned} \tag{8}
$$

Now we solve Problem 1 with the same matrices A and T but for $n = 1025$. As expected, we get a minimum cost of $r_0 = 218$ and a minimum time of $t_0 = 85$. However, the list S_0 has 256 elements. This shows that the number of all optimal plans of Problem 1 is equal to 256.

The analysis of the above solution shows that only 226 bounds on time criterion are performed. At the same time, 2707 iterations of the branching loop are performed. From this observation we can conclude that the time estimates that are used are not always efficient enough. The reason is that the estimate dt does not fully account for the influence of the cost matrix A – a fact that is confirmed by the conducted experiments.

4   List of Solutions of the AP

We select an arbitrary square matrix $A(a_{ij})$ of order n with non-negative elements.

Definition 3. *We shall call the plan $\widetilde{w}$ an **optimal solution of the AP**, when*

$$F_A(\widetilde{w}) \leq F_A(w),$$

for each $w \in P^n$.

Now we can formulate the AP in the following formal way: for an arbitrary square cost matrix A, find an optimal solution $\widetilde{w}$. Based on this formulation, the problem for generation of *Minimum Cost Optimal Solutions List* (MCOSL) is given in Problem 2.

Problem 2 (MCOSL). For an arbitrary square cost matrix A and an arbitrary natural number n_0, generate a list S_0 of optimal solutions of the AP with the following properties.

1. If the AP has more than $n_0 - 1$ optimal solutions, then S_0 contains n_0 elements.
2. If the AP has less than n_0 solutions, then S_0 contains all optimal solutions.

We will solve MCOSL problem following the approach in Sect. 3. In this case, the general form of the approach is as follows.

1. We calculate the elements of the pair $\{r_0, w_0\}$, where $r_0 = \min\limits_{w \in P^n} \{F_A(w)\}$, $w_0 \in P^n$ and $F_A(w_0) = r_0$.
2. We define a list S_0 and a queue S. In the list S_0 we collect the calculated optimal solutions, while in the queue S we place the non-intersecting subtasks, each of them resulting in at least one optimal solution of the initial AP.
3. The list S_0 and the queue S are updated until at least one of the following two conditions are violated:

$$S \neq \varnothing, \tag{9}$$

$$|S_0| + |S| < n_0, \tag{10}$$

where $|\cdot|$ denotes the number of elements in the sequence (list or queue).
4. When the update process stops, there are two possible cases.
   - *Case 1.* $S = \varnothing$. In this case S_0 contains all optimal solutions.
   - *Case 2.* $|S_0| + |S| \geq n_0$. In this case we insert into S_0 the optimal solutions of the sub-problems that are contained in S. The result is a list S_0 of n_0 optimal solutions.

The implementation of the above scheme is given in Algorithm 2.

The correctness of Algorithm 2 can be proved in analogy of the proof of Algorithm 1.

Example 2. We will solve Problem 2 for $n_0 = 4$ and the matrix A, given in (12) given in the paper appendix.

Our implementation of Algorithm 2 calculates that the minimal cost is $r_0 = 218$ and the list of optimal solutions is:

$$
\begin{aligned}
S_0 = \{ & (3, 9, 11, 17, 1, 8, 14, 6, 12, 18, 4, 19, 7, 16, 15, 13, 2, 20, 10, 5), \\
& (3, 12, 11, 17, 1, 8, 9, 20, 7, 5, 4, 19, 14, 16, 15, 13, 2, 6, 10, 18), \\
& (18, 9, 11, 17, 1, 8, 14, 6, 12, 5, 4, 19, 7, 16, 15, 13, 2, 20, 10, 3), \\
& (18, 12, 11, 17, 1, 8, 9, 20, 7, 5, 4, 19, 14, 16, 15, 13, 2, 6, 10, 3) \}.
\end{aligned}
\tag{11}
$$

Algorithm 2. Solution of the MCOSL problem.

---

function MINCOSTLIST(A, n_0)
    $\{r_0, w_0\} \leftarrow \mathcal{H}(A)$
    $w \leftarrow \varnothing$
    B is a matrix defined with (6)
    $X_0 \leftarrow \{w, w_0, B, n\}$,
    enqueue(S, X_0), $S_0 \leftarrow \varnothing$ ▷ S is a queue, S_0 is a list
    while $S \neq \varnothing$ **and** $|S_0| + |S| < n_0$ **do**
        $\{w, v, B, k\} \leftarrow$ front(S), dequeue(S)
        if $k > 2$ **then**
            for $j \leftarrow 1$ to k **do**
                $w_1 \leftarrow w \cup \{B(k+1, j)\}$
                $B_1 \leftarrow [B]_j^1$
                $\{\overline{r}, \overline{w}\} \leftarrow \mathcal{H}([B_1]^k)$
                $\overline{w} \leftarrow \{B_1(k, \overline{w}(1)), \ldots, B_1(k, \overline{w}(k-1))\}$ ▷ original B indexing
                $v_1 \leftarrow w_1 \cup \overline{w}$
                $r_1 \leftarrow F_A(v_1)$
                if $r_1 = r_0$ **then**
                    enqueue(S, $\{w_1, v_1, B_1, k-1\}$)
                end if
            end for
        else
            pushBack(S_0, $\{v\}$)
            if $|S_0| + |S| < n_0$ **then**
                $v_1 \leftarrow v$
                $v_1(n-1) \leftarrow v(n)$
                $v_1(n) \leftarrow v(n-1)$
                if $F_A(v_1) = r_0$ **then**
                    pushBack(S_0, $\{v_1\}$)
                end if
            end if
        end if
    end while
    if $S \neq \varnothing$ **then**
        for $s \leftarrow 1$ to $n_0 - |S_0|$ **do**
            pushBack(S_0, $\{S(s, 2)\}$)
        end for
    end if
    return S_0
end function

Now we solve Problem 2 with the same input matrix A, but for $n_0 = 10^4$. As we can expect, the resulting minimum cost is $r_0 = 218$. However, the list S_0 has 1024 elements. This shows that the number of all optimal solutions of the AP for the matrix A is equal to 1024.

If the matrix A is of 30-th order, and its elements are natural numbers whose values do not exceed 70, then we can expect that the number of optimal solutions is comparable to 10^4.

5 Conclusion

AP is a fundamental problem in the field of operation research. The first known polynomial-time algorithm that solves it is the Hungarian algorithm [15], which is considered as one of the methods that initiate the foundations of the discipline combinatorial optimization [5]. Nowadays, the AP together with its variants like for example quadratic AP [14], and k-assignment problem [8], is a subject of contemporary research with huge significance for many different practical tasks in economics, computer science, machine learning, and many more. Hungarian algorithm itself is investigated and its improvements are looked for in contemporary works (see for example [25]).

Despite its popularity, the vast portion of the existing algorithms are focused on the calculation of a single optimal solution of the AP, and usually the problem of discovering of more than one optimal solution is not considered. We find that methods for generation of a list of optimal solutions for the AP are an important extension of the methods that solve this fundamental task, which is significant for its practical applications.

In this paper we propose a method for composition of a list of selected assignments, that satisfy an additional condition. An important part in our method is given to the procedure $\mathcal{H}$ that implements the Hungarian algorithm. The approach is demonstrated with the solutions of the two problems: MCMT and MCOSL. In the problem MCMT we compose the list of those solutions of AP that are Pareto optimal. In the MCOSL problem an additional condition is the predefined number of elements in the list.

The correctness of the computer program implementation of Algorithm 2 is verified experimentally using matrices of order $n < 8$ for which Problem 2 is feasible to be calculated using other methods. Similarly, the implementation of the solution of Problem 1 is verified using matrices A and T of order $n < 8$, for which brute force techniques can be applied. At the same time, the computational complexity of our implementations is experimentally tested with matrices up to 30-th order (see (12) and (13) in the appendix below).

We have used two different approaches in the implementation of the described algorithms: the symbolic computational system Mathematica [29], and the relatively new programming language for scientific computing Julia [3]. The Mathematica system provides a large set of tools, that are extremely helpful in both implementation and validation steps, while the Julia programming language combines the abilities of dynamic languages together with efficiency, and capability to handle big data inputs. Both implementations are used to verify our experiments and to prove the efficiency of the proposed algorithms.

A   Appendix: Input matrices

$$
\begin{pmatrix}
25 & 25 & 15 & 18 & 25 & 24 & 26 & 42 & 15 & 29 & 25 & 35 & 23 & 19 & 25 & 25 & 25 & 15 & 18 & 25 \\
12 & 11 & 10 & 11 & 20 & 7 & 14 & 16 & 1 & 30 & 25 & 7 & 11 & 21 & 20 & 12 & 11 & 10 & 11 & 20 \\
15 & 8 & 13 & 22 & 15 & 20 & 13 & 15 & 35 & 5 & 1 & 26 & 6 & 16 & 15 & 15 & 8 & 13 & 22 & 15 \\
26 & 5 & 31 & 9 & 23 & 21 & 16 & 25 & 20 & 18 & 18 & 6 & 46 & 25 & 23 & 26 & 5 & 31 & 9 & 23 \\
14 & 35 & 21 & 32 & 27 & 12 & 46 & 27 & 48 & 28 & 5 & 67 & 13 & 23 & 27 & 14 & 35 & 21 & 32 & 27 \\
22 & 23 & 19 & 18 & 19 & 23 & 5 & 5 & 9 & 5 & 19 & 32 & 42 & 32 & 19 & 22 & 23 & 19 & 18 & 19 \\
21 & 12 & 16 & 17 & 21 & 35 & 7 & 26 & 6 & 67 & 32 & 21 & 11 & 15 & 21 & 21 & 12 & 16 & 17 & 21 \\
18 & 21 & 27 & 23 & 18 & 5 & 23 & 65 & 10 & 16 & 67 & 57 & 28 & 32 & 18 & 18 & 21 & 27 & 23 & 18 \\
22 & 20 & 23 & 35 & 24 & 8 & 11 & 25 & 35 & 11 & 21 & 17 & 21 & 21 & 24 & 22 & 20 & 23 & 35 & 24 \\
21 & 17 & 19 & 30 & 19 & 11 & 25 & 11 & 21 & 17 & 21 & 24 & 22 & 24 & 20 & 21 & 17 & 19 & 30 & 19 \\
19 & 26 & 21 & 16 & 21 & 25 & 9 & 12 & 15 & 26 & 14 & 22 & 21 & 18 & 21 & 19 & 26 & 21 & 16 & 21 \\
25 & 24 & 31 & 13 & 16 & 26 & 42 & 15 & 29 & 25 & 35 & 23 & 19 & 25 & 25 & 25 & 24 & 31 & 13 & 16 \\
25 & 22 & 18 & 26 & 25 & 26 & 6 & 16 & 15 & 15 & 8 & 13 & 22 & 15 & 25 & 25 & 22 & 18 & 26 & 25 \\
12 & 32 & 32 & 22 & 23 & 6 & 46 & 25 & 23 & 26 & 5 & 31 & 9 & 23 & 20 & 12 & 32 & 32 & 22 & 23 \\
15 & 25 & 25 & 16 & 25 & 67 & 13 & 23 & 27 & 14 & 35 & 21 & 32 & 27 & 15 & 15 & 25 & 25 & 16 & 25 \\
15 & 8 & 13 & 22 & 15 & 20 & 13 & 15 & 35 & 5 & 1 & 26 & 6 & 16 & 15 & 15 & 8 & 13 & 22 & 15 \\
26 & 5 & 31 & 9 & 23 & 21 & 16 & 25 & 20 & 18 & 18 & 6 & 46 & 25 & 23 & 26 & 5 & 31 & 9 & 23 \\
18 & 21 & 27 & 23 & 18 & 5 & 23 & 65 & 10 & 16 & 67 & 57 & 28 & 32 & 18 & 18 & 21 & 27 & 23 & 18 \\
22 & 20 & 23 & 35 & 24 & 8 & 11 & 25 & 35 & 11 & 21 & 17 & 21 & 21 & 24 & 22 & 20 & 23 & 35 & 24 \\
21 & 17 & 19 & 30 & 19 & 11 & 25 & 11 & 21 & 17 & 21 & 24 & 22 & 24 & 20 & 21 & 17 & 19 & 30 & 19
\end{pmatrix}
\tag{12}
$$

$$\begin{pmatrix}
57\ 56\ 65\ 63\ 65\ 53\ 58\ 44\ 56\ 71\ 70\ 42\ 58\ 72\ 65\ 57\ 56\ 65\ 63\ 65 \\
69\ 69\ 71\ 79\ 57\ 77\ 72\ 55\ 99\ 65\ 52\ 74\ 80\ 69\ 62\ 69\ 69\ 71\ 79\ 62 \\
65\ 73\ 77\ 55\ 69\ 66\ 58\ 85\ 60\ 72\ 80\ 65\ 84\ 66\ 66\ 65\ 73\ 77\ 60\ 66 \\
55\ 85\ 46\ 75\ 63\ 50\ 84\ 70\ 57\ 63\ 73\ 84\ 36\ 56\ 57\ 55\ 85\ 51\ 72\ 57 \\
76\ 42\ 63\ 54\ 44\ 88\ 49\ 50\ 33\ 63\ 85\ 15\ 68\ 57\ 54\ 76\ 47\ 60\ 48\ 54 \\
55\ 61\ 67\ 53\ 81\ 72\ 72\ 76\ 82\ 85\ 63\ 49\ 38\ 49\ 71\ 60\ 58\ 61\ 63\ 71 \\
63\ 74\ 55\ 83\ 74\ 42\ 74\ 65\ 84\ 15\ 49\ 59\ 70\ 75\ 61\ 60\ 68\ 65\ 73\ 56 \\
68\ 50\ 73\ 72\ 59\ 76\ 68\ 25\ 72\ 65\ 13\ 24\ 62\ 50\ 63\ 62\ 60\ 63\ 54\ 66 \\
49\ 80\ 72\ 42\ 57\ 83\ 79\ 57\ 46\ 69\ 60\ 73\ 61\ 60\ 56\ 59\ 70\ 54\ 49\ 62 \\
79\ 78\ 58\ 51\ 72\ 79\ 57\ 70\ 59\ 64\ 69\ 58\ 59\ 56\ 61\ 69\ 60\ 65\ 56\ 52 \\
76\ 51\ 60\ 75\ 69\ 57\ 72\ 68\ 66\ 64\ 68\ 59\ 59\ 63\ 69\ 58\ 58\ 65\ 55\ 79 \\
52\ 57\ 60\ 77\ 66\ 55\ 38\ 66\ 61\ 57\ 46\ 57\ 62\ 65\ 52\ 59\ 62\ 40\ 87\ 79 \\
56\ 69\ 72\ 56\ 56\ 54\ 75\ 74\ 67\ 66\ 72\ 68\ 68\ 62\ 59\ 61\ 49\ 82\ 69\ 52 \\
79\ 58\ 50\ 59\ 57\ 75\ 44\ 57\ 58\ 54\ 76\ 59\ 68\ 61\ 66\ 59\ 68\ 63\ 55\ 58 \\
75\ 57\ 56\ 64\ 56\ 23\ 69\ 58\ 53\ 67\ 55\ 56\ 52\ 59\ 56\ 85\ 70\ 52\ 65\ 66 \\
67\ 73\ 67\ 59\ 75\ 62\ 68\ 65\ 46\ 85\ 76\ 58\ 80\ 55\ 85\ 80\ 69\ 68\ 69\ 75 \\
55\ 75\ 50\ 81\ 59\ 60\ 64\ 56\ 70\ 59\ 66\ 80\ 25\ 75\ 72\ 51\ 76\ 60\ 81\ 59 \\
62\ 60\ 63\ 59\ 63\ 75\ 58\ 25\ 67\ 68\ 19\ 14\ 72\ 63\ 59\ 63\ 70\ 63\ 59\ 63 \\
59\ 70\ 59\ 46\ 56\ 73\ 79\ 52\ 49\ 75\ 50\ 83\ 74\ 56\ 57\ 69\ 70\ 59\ 46\ 56 \\
69\ 65\ 62\ 50\ 62\ 79\ 52\ 73\ 65\ 54\ 79\ 71\ 55\ 57\ 71\ 69\ 65\ 62\ 50\ 62
\end{pmatrix} \tag{13}$$

References

1. Ahuja, R.K., Orlin, J.B., Stein, C., Tarjan, R.E.: Improved algorithms for bipartite network flow. SIAM J. Comput. **23**(5), 906–933 (1994). https://doi.org/10.1137/S0097539791199334

2. Bang-Jensen, J., Gutin, G.Z.: Digraphs Theory Algorithms and Applications. Springer, Berlin (2008). https://doi.org/10.5555/1523254

3. Bezanson, J., Edelman, A., Karpinski, S., Shah, V.B.: Julia: a fresh approach to numerical computing. SIAM Rev. **59**(1), 65–98 (2017). https://doi.org/10.1137/141000671

4. Burkard, R.: Selected topics on assignment problems. Discret. Appl. Math. **123**, 257–302 (2009). https://doi.org/10.1016/S0166-218X(01)00343-2

5. Burkard, R., Dell'Amico, M., Martello, S.: Assignment problems. SIAM, Society for Industrial and Applied Mathematics, University City, Philadelphia (2009). https://doi.org/10.1137/1.9781611972238

6. Diestel, R.: Graph Theory, 5th edn. Springer, Berlin (2017). https://doi.org/10.1007/978-3-662-53622-3

7. Edmonds, J., Karp, R.M.: Theoretical improvements in algorithmic efficiency for network flow problems. J. ACM **19**(2), 248–264 (1972). https://doi.org/10.1145/321694.321699

8. Flezar, K.: A branch-and-bound algorithm for the quadratic multiple knapsack problem. Eur. J. Oper. Res. **298**, 89–98 (2021). https://doi.org/10.1016/j.ejor.2021.06.018

9. Fulkerson, D.R., Glicksberg, I.L., Gross, O.A.: A production line assignment problem. Technical report, RM-1102, The Rand Corporation, Santa Monica, CA (1953)

10. Graham, B.S.: Econometric methods for the analysis of assignment problems in the presence of complementarity and social spillovers. In: Handbook of Social Economics, vol. 1, pp. 965–1052. North-Holland (2011). https://doi.org/10.1016/B978-0-444-53707-2.00002-5

11. Hall, M.: Combinatorial Theory, 2nd edn. Wiley, New York (1998). https://doi.org/10.5555/286075

12. Hopcroft, J.E., Karp, R.M.: An $n^{5/2}$ algorithm for maximum matchings in bipartite graphs. SIAM J. Comput. **2**(4), 225–231 (1973). https://doi.org/10.1137/0202019

13. Horst, R.: Global Optimization: Deterministic Approaches, 2nd edn., pp. 115–178. Springer, Heidelberg (1996). https://doi.org/10.1057/jors.1994.88

14. Karsu, Ö., Azizoglu, M.: An exact algorithm for the minimum squared load assignment problem. Comput. Oper. Res. **106**, 76–90 (2019). https://doi.org/10.1016/j.cor.2019.02.011

15. Kuhn, H.W.: The Hungarian method for the assignment problem. Naval Res. Logistics Q. **2**(1–2), 83–97 (1955). https://doi.org/10.1002/nav.3800020109

16. Kuhn, H.W.: Variants of the Hungarian method for assignment problems. Naval Res. Logistics Q. **3**(4), 253–258 (1956). https://doi.org/10.1002/nav.3800030404

17. Land, A.H., Doig, A.G.: An automatic method of solving discrete programming problems. Econometrica **28**(3), 497–520 (1960). https://doi.org/10.2307/1910129

18. Marinov, M.L., Laskov, L.M.: The travelling salesman problem with the symbolic computational system mathematica. In: Proceedings of the Forty-seven Spring Conference of the Union of Bulgarian Mathematicians, pp. 147–157 (2018)

19. Niebling, J., Eichfelder, G.: Branch-and-bound-based algorithm for nonconvex multiobjective optimization. SIAM J. Optim. **29**(1), 794–821 (2019). https://doi.org/10.1137/18M1169680

20. Orlin, J.B., Ahuja, R.K.: New scaling algorithms for the assignment and minimum mean cycle problems. Math. Program. **54**, 41–56 (1992). https://doi.org/10.1007/BF01586040

21. Padberg, M., Rinaldi, G.: A branch-and-cut algorithm for the resolution of large-scale symmetric traveling salesman problems. IAM Review **33**, 60–100 (1991). https://doi.org/10.1137/1033004

22. Papadimitriou, C.H., Steiglitz, K.: Combinatorial optimization: algorithms and complexity. Dover Books on Computer Science, Prentice-Hall Inc, Hoboken, New Jersey (1982). https://doi.org/10.1109/TASSP.1984.1164450

23. Sarlin, P.E., DeTone, D., Malisiewicz, T., Rabinovich, A.: Superglue: learning feature matching with graph neural networks. In: 2020 IEEE/CVF Conference on Computer Vision and Pattern Recognition (CVPR), pp. 4937–4946 (2020). https://doi.org/10.48550/arXiv.1911.11763

24. Schrijver, A.: A Course in combinatorial optimization. copyright A. Schrijver, CWI, Kruislaan 413, 1098 SJ Amsterdam, The Netherlands and Department of Mathematics, University of Amsterdam, Plantage Muidergracht 24, 1018 TV Amsterdam, The Netherlands (2017). https://homepages.cwi.nl/ lex/files/dict.pdf

25. Shah, K., Reddy, P., Vairamuthu, S.: Improvement in Hungarian algorithm for assignment problem. Adv. Intell. Syst. Comput. **324**, 1–8 (2015). https://doi.org/10.1007/978-81-322-2126-5_1

26. Shen, C.C., Tsai, W.H.: A graph matching approach to optimal task assignment in distributed computing systems using a minimax criterion. IEEE Trans. Comput. **C-34**(3), 197–203 (1985). https://doi.org/10.1109/TC.1985.1676563

27. Shmoys, D.B.: Éva Tardos: an approximation algorithm for the generalized assignment problem. Math. Program. **62**, 461–474 (1993). https://doi.org/10.1007/BF01585178

28. Tomizawa, N.: On some techniques useful for solution of transportation network problems. Networks 1(2), 173–194 (1971). https://doi.org/10.1002/net.3230010206
29. Wolfram, S.: An Elementary Introduction to the Wolfram Language, 2nd edn. Wolfram Media, Incorporated (2017)

Implementation of a CNN for Asterism Classification in Carte du Ciel Astrographic Maps

Lasko M. Laskov$^{(\boxtimes)}$ and Radoslav Radev

Informatics Department, New Bulgarian University, Sofia, Bulgaria
llaskov@nbu.bg

Abstract. Carte du Ciel together with Astrographic Catalogue form a 19th century huge international astronomical project whose goal was to map the stars in the visible sky as faint as 14th magnitude. The result, in the form of astrographic plates and their paper copies – astrographic maps, are stored and investigated in many astronomy institutes worldwide.

The goal of our study is to develop image processing and pattern recognition techniques for automatic extraction of astronomical data from the digitized copies of the astrographic maps. In this paper we present the design and implementation of a convolutional neural network (CNN) for automatic classification of stars images in scanned Carte du Ciel astrographic maps. We do not use any deep learning frameworks to build our model, and we focus on the low-level implementation of the CNN. Also, we provide comparison of our implementation with an implementation based on PyTorch.

Keywords: Deep learning · Convolutional neural network · Astrographic maps

1 Introduction

Carte du Ciel was the major part, along with *Astrographic Catalogue*, of a vast international project that started in 1887 and continued until 1962 in many observatories around the world [5]. The purpose of the project was to create a catalogue of the positions of the stars in the visible sky that are as faint as 11th magnitude. Another goal was to map the relative positions of stars of 14th magnitude and brighter [14].

The data collected was in the form of glass photographic plates taken by the telescopes, called *astrographic plates* [2]. The dimensions of the photographed field was $2° \times 2°$, and their location in the sky were selected in such way, so that the corner of each plate lies at the center of its neighbor [5]. The physical dimensions of the plates were $12\,\text{cm}^2$, and each plate contains triple exposure with an approximate duration 20 min each. The reason for the triple exposure was to

© ICST Institute for Computer Sciences, Social Informatics and Telecommunications Engineering 2023
Published by Springer Nature Switzerland AG 2023. All Rights Reserved
T. Zlateva and G. Tuparov (Eds.): CSECS 2023, LNICST 514, pp. 102–114, 2023.
https://doi.org/10.1007/978-3-031-44668-9_8

be able to distinguish the images of the stars from the images of other types of celestial bodies and different type of noise that can result in the photographic plates (see Fig. 1b).

The *astrographic maps* themself are paper copies that were produced from the astrographic plates using photogravure on copper plates. They represent negative image in which the background in white, and light objects, such as stars, are in black. Each star is represented by a triple image that is called *asterism* by Fresneau [2] (see Fig. 1a).

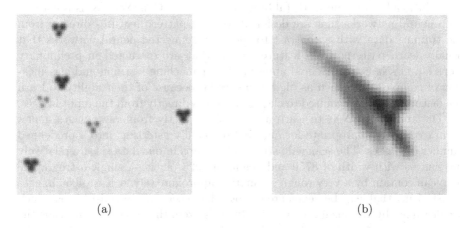

(a)   (b)

Fig. 1. (a) A fragment of an astrographic map containing six asterisms, and (b) an asterism degraded by noise.

Originally, asterisms were used to calculate the exact coordinates of the stars in the astrographic maps. However, they can also contain important information about the star that is represented. A significant difference in the Gaussian distributions of the three images that comprise the asterism can be considered as a proof of an astronomical event, such as stellar explosion, or can be used to conclude that the star is a close binary system variable. Such information can be extremely valuable for the specialists in the field, because of the age of the astrographic plates themself.

The legacy astronomical data is a subject of various research both towards reduction [12,14], and even celestial events detection [2]. More recent works also investigate the digitalization of the Carte du Ciel data and its calibration [9], and search for binary and multiple stars by combining data from Carte du Ciel and Gaia catalogues [10].

The goal of our research is to develop image processing and pattern recognition methods and algorithms that will aid the automatic data extraction from digitized Carte du Ciel astrographic maps [7]. As part of our effort, in this paper we present the design and implementation of a convolutional neural network (CNN) [8] for asterism classification in the scanned Carte du Ciel astrographic maps.

Even though well-known frameworks such as PyTorch and open-source libraries such as TensorFlow (see for example [13]) are commonly adopted in similar researches, an important part of our study is to implement custom framework for machine learning via CNN without the usage of a third-party libraries. However, we have used a PyTorch implementation to compare the results of our CNN implementation.

2   CNN for Asterisms Classification

Convolutional neural network (abbreviated CNN or ConvNet) [8] is a class of deep neural networks that are designed to learn pattern features directly from the training data with a contrast to the fully connected neural networks that usually learn patterns from feature vectors that are extracted in preliminary steps [4]. CNNs are considered appropriate for machine learning and classification of complex data such as digital images [3] because of their ability to learn the features that are required to classify patterns directly from the input images.

The ability of CNNs to learn and classify directly from raw images makes them extremely appropriate for our goal to classify asterisms into a predefined number of classes. The scanned astrographic maps in our data set are relatively big images with width of 8750 and height of 8926 pixels. A single astrographic map can contain by a very rough estimation approximately at least 4056 images of asterisms that can be segmented. Note that there are also asterisms which are degraded by various noise and coordinate system that is contained inside the maps, or are too faint to be detected, and they are not subject of interest for the research, because they cannot be analyzed to extract astronomical data. From this point of view, image preprocessing algorithms applied on asterisms in order to extract feature vectors can be quite expensive.

Apart from the above considerations, a major part of our research is focused on the implementation of the CNN. Although our software uses traditional methods and mechanisms similar to those in well-known machine learning platforms and libraries as PyTorch and TensorFlow [13], it does not use any external libraries to create the classification model. Because of the features of our data, mentioned above, we focus on effectiveness, and for that reason our implementation uses C++ programming language, instead of commonly used systems for technical computing such as Matlab or Mathematica, or popular scripting languages such as Python. Something more, currently our software is able to perform one epoch of training on a dataset of 10^4 normalised grayscale images, 28×28 pixels, tiff format, on a standard personal computer configuration in under two minutes. With this performance and for our experiment, we did not need to add more complexity by implementing GPU acceleration.

2.1   Proposed Network Structure

The CNN proposed in this paper is composed by an input, one or more convolutional layers, a set of fully connected layers, and an output layer (see Fig. 2).

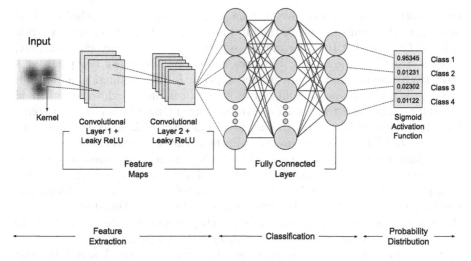

Fig. 2. Topology of the CNN used in our experiment.

Our model allows different number of convolutional layers, and different number and configuration of fully connected layers.

The *input* of the CNN is organized in the form of tensors that store image values [15]. Since a tensor of order K over the field of real numbers $\mathbb{R}$ is denoted

$$\mathcal{T} \in \mathbb{R}^{I_1 \times I_2 \times \ldots \times I_K}, \tag{1}$$

a grayscale image with resolution $N \times M$ can be included in a tensor of second order

$$\mathcal{I} \in \mathbb{R}^{N \times M}. \tag{2}$$

Therefore, the tensor of order 3 that can represent the input of the CNN can be written for L number of input images:

$$\mathcal{A} \in \mathbb{R}^{N \times M \times L}. \tag{3}$$

2.2 Convolutional Layer

A *convolutional layer* performs spatial convolution. Convolution in the spatial domain (image domain) is the sum of products between a digital image f and a filter kernel ω with size $n \times m$ (see [3]):

$$(w \star f)(x, y) = \sum_{s=(1-m)/2}^{(m-1)/2} \sum_{t=(1-n)/2}^{(n-1)/2} \omega(s, t) f(x - s, y - t). \tag{4}$$

On Fig. 2, in the feature extraction section, the convolution is shown using the *receptive field* depicted as a yellow square, where the kernel is the matrix of weights that lies in the neighborhood defined by it. The spatial step with which the receptive field is moved over the image is the *stride*, or in other words it determines the number of pixels the filter moves over the input matrix. A stride value of 1 means that the filter moves over the input image one pixel at a time, while a stride of 2 means that the filter moves over the image two pixels at a time. CNNs use strides that are greater than one for data reduction, and is also used in the process of subsampling or *pooling* that in many architectures is used to achieve invariance to translation. In our current model there is no pooling layer implemented because of the nature of our custom data set *Carte du Ciel Asterism 1)* CDCA1 that we use to train the network (see Sect. 3).

Besides the stride, padding is used by CNN to increase the processing region of the network. In a CNN, a kernel is a filter that moves across an image, scanning each pixel and transforming the data into a smaller or larger format. By adding padding to the image frame, the kernel is provided with additional space to cover the image, which aids in the processing of the image. This allows the CNN to analyze the image more accurately, resulting in better performance.

Our implementation allows multiple convolutional layers, however in most of our experiments we have concluded that two convolutional layers result in better feature extraction and higher accuracy for data that is new for the model. Initially the layer's filter ω is initialised with random coefficients. The convolution process also depends on a set of predefined parameters: image dimensions, ω size n and m, padding, stride, rate of convergence, and bias.

Image dimensions are the image height N and width M, as well as image depth, that in our case is determined by the fact that we use grayscale images with each pixel having an integer value in the closed interval $[0, 255]$.

Kernel size is represented by the dimensions of ω, that are n and m, and by filter repetition and depth.

Padding, which we denote by *pad*, is a single value, representing how many pixels to add on each side of the image. It is used to prevent loss of data around the edges or to enable the usage of larger filters.

Stride, denoted *str*, is also a single value, representing how much the convolutional filter will move on each iteration.

Rate of convergence r_{conv} is a decimal value, representing how quickly the algorithm reaches a solution that we can define as an optimal regarding a given criterion.

Bias b is a decimal value, representing the shift of the output. It is used to shift the activation function result of each neuron in order to clear out any potential offsets.

The convolutional layer has forward and backwards propagation leveraged by the *leaky rectified linear* (Leaky ReLU) [11]:

$$R(z) = \max(\alpha z, z) = \begin{cases} z, & \text{if } z > 0 \\ \alpha z, & \text{otherwise} \end{cases} \tag{5}$$

The first derivative of (5) is then:

$$R'(z) = \begin{cases} 1, & \text{if } z > 0 \\ \alpha, & \text{if } z < 0 \\ \text{indeterminate} & \text{if } z = 0 \end{cases} \tag{6}$$

The constant α determines the slope of the function for negative inputs, and usually $\alpha = 0.01$ or $\alpha = 0.2$. The reason for setting the constant α is to resolve the common problem with the "dying" neurons when the input of the standard rectified linear activation function is a negative number, leading to a zero neuron output.

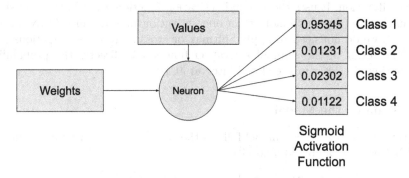

Fig. 3. Scheme of the sigmoid neuron used to build fully connected layers of the CNN.

2.3   Fully Connected Layer

Each fully connected layer l of the CNN is composed by a set of sigmoid neurons, where the ith neuron (Fig. 3) can be represented (see for example [3]

$$z_i(l) = \sum_{j=1}^{s_{l-1}} w_{ij} a_i(l-1) + b_i(l), \tag{7}$$

where s_{l-1} denotes the number of neurons in the previous layer, w_{ij} are the weights, and $b_i(l)$ is the bias weight. $a_i(l) = h(z_i(l))$ defines the output or activation value of the neuron, and in our case the activation function h is the *sigmoid function*:

$$h(z) = \frac{1}{1 + e^{-z}}. \tag{8}$$

Our implementation supports multiple fully connected layers, and for each layer l, it allows the definition of the number of neurons s_l. The hyperparameters that are configurable are: number of input layers, sublayers (hidden layers), number of output classes, bias, adam, and rate of convergence.

The *input layer* is a single number, representing the number of input layers, coming out of the convolutional layer.

The *sublayer* is a vector, representing the topology of the fully connected layer.

The number of output classes is a single number, representing how many output classes are available for the specific dataset. Latter we will show that for our experiments with the MNIST data set [1] it is set to 10, and in our experiments with the asterisms data set, it is set to 4.

The bias is a decimal value, representing the shift of the output.

The *adam* hyperparameter is a boolean value, representing whether to use Adam or SGD as optimization algorithms.

A layer l from the fully-connected section of the CNN calculates class scores for each iteration. It uses the sigmoid activation function given in (8), and since it is uncommon to adopt more than one activation function in a CNN, in our approach we do not need to apply Softmax or cross-entropy loss functions (see [4]). The result of the sigmoid activation function is directly the probability distribution of classes in the closed interval $[0, 1]$.

2.4   Training the Model

The training of the defined model follows the standard algorithm for training of a CNN (see for example [3] and [4]):

1. Input image data in the form of tensor $\mathcal{A}$ defined in (3).
2. Forward pass for each neuron in each feature map.
3. Back propagation for each neuron in each feature map.
4. Weights and bias weight update for each feature map.

A complete run through the entire data set of the above four steps defines one *epoch* of training.

The training algorithm accepts the number of epochs to be performed, logging options and if a validation on each epoch is necessary. During training the parameters of the network are changed in order to get as high accuracy as possible. Validation is usually performed after each epoch with new, unseen data to simulate the testing phase with the weights calculated after each epoch. It gives early warning if the model performs well when faced with new, unseen data, during the validation, the weights are not updated.

Finding the appropriate set of parameters of a neural network that can reduce the cost of the selected cost function that evaluates the performance is a subject of optimization of the training stage. We have implemented two standard optimization algorithms to optimize the process of learning: stochastic gradient descent (SGD), and adaptive moments (Adam) [4].

The SGD algorithm is based on a selection of a relatively small set of random samples that are used to estimate the gradient in each iteration. Then the algorithm follows the gradient downhill.

Adam is an adaptive learning rate optimization algorithm that estimates the gradient based on the first-order, and uncentered second-order moments form the selected samples.

Each epoch loops through all images one by one, forwards it through the layers, calculates the loss, calculates the accuracy and lastly backwards the image through the layers to update the weights.

We adopt *mean squared error* (MSE) loss function

$$MSE = \frac{1}{L} \sum_{i=1}^{L} (y_i - \widehat{y}_i), \tag{9}$$

where L is the number of input images contained in $\mathcal{A}$, y_i is the actual value of the target variable for the ith image, and $\widehat{y}_j$ is the predicted value of the target variable for the ith image. Apparently, the lower the MSE value is, the better performance of the neural network is.

3 CDCA1 and Experiment Results

Table 1. Number of training epochs, training and testing accuracies in percentage achieved with PyTorch and our CNN implementation for both datasets.

	MNIST			CDCA1		
	Epoch	Train	Test	Epoch	Train	Test
PyTorch	5	95.5	95.4	5	74	74
Our library	5	88	83	5	83	73

We have tested our implementation of CNN using two different data set:

1. MNIST data set [1].
2. The first version of our custom Carte du Ciel Asterisms data set (CDCA1).

In both cases we have adopted the CNN architecture that is given in Fig. 2:

1. Two convolutional layers leveraged by the Leaky ReLU function (5).
2. Fully connected layers:
   - the first fully connected layer, composed by 72 sigmoid neurons;
   - the hidden layer, also composed by 72 sigmoid neurons.
3. Output layer that gives the probability for classification in each of the predefined number of classes that determines the number of output neurons.

Also we have compared and verified our implementation by performing the same experiment using an analogous CNN implemented using Python and

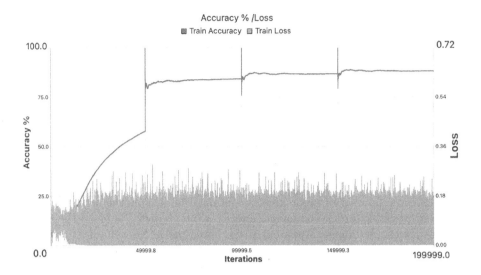

Fig. 4. Train accuracy and train loss of our CNN for the MNIST data set.

PyTorch framework (see Table 1. The main difference between our implementation and PyTorch based implementation is that the latter has also a pooling layer.

We have used the MNIST data set to verify our implementation of CNN prior to our experiments with the asterisms extracted from the Carte du Ciel astrographic maps. The MNIST database contains images of handwritten digits, so the number of output neurons in this case is 10. The dataset consists of 5×10^4 training images and 10^4 testing images, from these 5×10^4 we use 10^4 for validating after the completion of each epoch. However, it should be pointed out that the MNIST dataset is a comprehensive dataset, carefully verified and improved throughout the years of its existence and the images are equally distributed in the all 10 classes. Our CNN reaches 88% accuracy after 5 epoch of training (see Fig. 4).

As expected, for the MNIST data set the PyTorch implementation performs better than the proposed CNN implementation (see Table 1), and the reason for this results is the pooling layer in the PyTorch CNN. However, the experiments with MNIST data set are performed to verify and test the implementation of the proposed software solution.

For the purpose of the experiments with the Carte du Ciel astrographic maps data we have developed the first version of our data set CDCA1 (Carte du Ciel Asterism) that contains segmented images of asterisms from the scanned data. Initially, we have segmented manually more than 1000 asterisms to form the base of the data set. Since this number of input images is quite insufficient to train and test our CNN, we have developed an extra module in our software that generates the CDCA1 by augmenting the base images using the following operations:

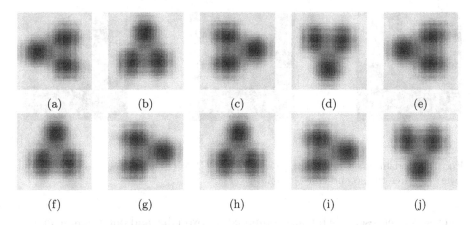

Fig. 5. Transform the original image: (a) rotate by 90°; (b) rotate by 180°; (c) rotate by 270°; (d) horizontal flip; (e) horizontal flip and rotate by 90°; (f) horizontal flip and rotate by 180°; (g) horizontal flip and rotate by 270°; (h) vertical flip; (i) vertical flip and rotate by 90°; (j) vertical flip and rotate by 180°.

- resize images to 28 × 28 pixels;
- normalize images and set all images to grayscale format;
- apply geometrical transformations of rotation, horizontal and vertical flip, and their combinations, given in Fig. 5.

In this way, the resulting CDCA1 dataset consists of more than 14000 asterism images.

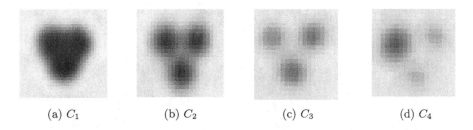

(a) C_1 (b) C_2 (c) C_3 (d) C_4

Fig. 6. The four classes of asterisms in which the CNN classifies data in CDCA1.

We define four classes of asterisms in the dataset CDCA1 (their representatives are given in Fig. 6):

- class C_1 represents asterisms of bright stars whose three images are merged together in a single connected component;
- class C_2 represents the most common case of asterisms composed by three stars images that have relatively equal Gaussian distributions;
- class C_3 represents asterisms composed by two bright and one fainter image;

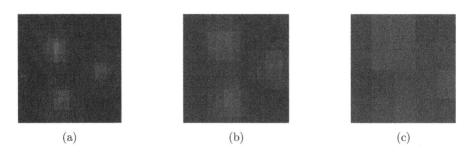

| (a) | (b) | (c) |

Fig. 7. Asterism image heatmap: (a) input of the CNN; (b) after the first convolutional layer; (c) after the second convolutional layer.

– class C_4 represents asterisms composed by two faint and one brighter image.

The CNN achieves 83% accuracy on the CDCA1 dataset after 5 epochs of training (see Fig. 8). During the testing phase, the accuracy reaches 74%. The lower testing accuracy is normal in this case because a single epoch is performed, and the testing data is unknown for the CNN. The result of the convolutional layers is illustrated on Fig. 7, where are given the heatmaps: of the input of the CNN; after the first convolutional layer; and after the second convolutional layer.

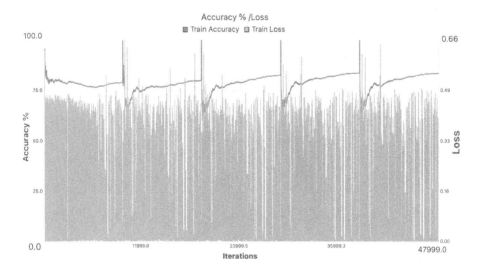

Fig. 8. Train accuracy and train loss of our CNN for the proposed CDCA1 data set.

As it can be seen from the results in Table 1 the performance of the PyTorch implementation and our CNN implementation are extremely close, even though our implementation does not provide a pooling layer. As mentioned above, it can be explained by the nature of the CDCA1 data set, and also by the geometrical distortions that we have applied in order to augment artificially the data set.

4 Conclusion

In this paper we present our implementation of a convolutional neural network (CNN) whose purpose is the automatic classification of asterisms in digitized Carte du Ciel astrographic maps. Our implementation is written in the C++ programming language, and the CNN is implemented without any use of third-party library. The software is tested and verified using the popular MNIST dataset. In order to perform our experiments on the astrographic maps data, we have created our custom CDCA1 dataset, that is composed by manually segmented asterisms, and is augmented using geometrical transformations in order to achieve a number of images that is sufficient to train and test CNN.

The results on CDCA1 show 83% accuracy after 5 epochs of training and 73% accuracy in the testing phase. The lower accuracy during the testing phase can be explained with overfitting that occurs when the model becomes too close to the data point of the training section of the data set. It is a natural result of the augmentation that is used to generate CDCA1. However, these results clearly show that the selected approach is appropriate for the automatic classification of asterisms in the examined data.

As future work, we will implement an option to add a pooling layer to the topology of our CNN. We will also integrate our CNN model with a software for automatic asterisms segmentation from Carte du Ciel astrographic maps [7], which currently is under process of development. The latter will also result in the second version of our dataset CDCA2 that will not involve artificial augmentation, and will contain unique segmented asterisms images. The latter will allow us to perform additional experiments for fine tuning of the CNN hyperparameters.

References

1. Deng, L.: The MNIST database of handwritten digit images for machine learning research [best of the web]. IEEE Signal Process. Mag. **29**(6), 141–142 (2012). https://doi.org/10.1109/MSP.2012.2211477
2. Fresneau, A., Argyle, R.W., Marino, G., Messina, S.: Potential of astrographic plates for stellar flare detection. Astron. J. **121**(1), 517–524 (2001). https://doi.org/10.1002/nav.3800020109
3. Gonzalez, R.C., Woods, R.E.: Digital Image Processing. Pearson, New York (2018)
4. Goodfellow, I., Bengio, Y., Courville, A.: Deep Learning. MIT Press, Cambridge (2016). http://www.deeplearningbook.org
5. Jones, D.: The scientific value of the Carte du Ciel. Astron. Geophys. **41**(5), 5.16–5.20 (2000). https://doi.org/10.1046/j.1468-4004.2000.41516.x
6. Krizhevsky, A., Sutskever, I., E.Hinton, G.: Imagenet classification with deep convolutional neural networks. Commun. ACM **60**(6), 84–90 (2017). https://doi.org/10.1145/3065386
7. Laskov, L.M., Tsvetkov, M.: Data extraction form Carte du Ciel tripple images. Serdica J. Comput. **7**(4), 317–332 (2013)
8. LeCun, Y., Kavukcuoglu, K., Farabet, C.: Convolutional networks and applications in vision. In: Proceedings of 2010 IEEE International Symposium on Circuits and Systems, pp. 253–256 (2010). https://doi.org/10.1109/ISCAS.2010.5537907

9. Lehtinen, K., et al.: Digitization and astrometric calibration of Carte du Ciel photographic plates with Gaia DR1. Astron. Astrophys. **616**, A185 (2018). https://doi.org/10.1051/0004-6361/201832662
10. Lehtinen, K., et al.: Carte du Ciel and Gaia - i. astrometry. Astron. Astrophys. **671**, A16 (2023). https://doi.org/10.1051/0004-6361/202142929
11. Maas, A.L., Hannun, A.Y., Ng, A.Y.: Rectifier nonlinearities improve neural network acoustic models. In: ICML Workshop on Deep Learning for Audio, Speech, and Language Processing, pp. 1–6 (2013)
12. Ortiz-Gil, A., Hiesgen, M., Brosche, P.: A new approach to the reduction of Carte du Ciel plates. Astron. Astrophys. Suppl. Ser. **128**(3), 621–630 (1998). https://doi.org/10.1051/aas:1998168
13. Prakash, K.B., Kanagachidambaresan, G.R. (eds.): Programming with Tensor-Flow. EAI/Springer Innovations in Communication and Computing, Springer Cham (2022). https://doi.org/10.1007/978-3-030-57077-4
14. Urban, S.E.: New reductions of the astrographic catalogue: high accuracy, early epoch positions for proper motion studies. Int. Astron. Union Colloq. **165**, 493–498 (1997). https://doi.org/10.1017/S025292110004700X
15. Vasilescu, M.A.O., Terzopoulos, D.: Multilinear (tensor) image synthesis, analysis, and recognition [exploratory DSP]. IEEE Signal Process. Mag. **24**(6), 118–123 (2007). https://doi.org/10.1109/MSP.2007.906024

Software Engineering

People Make Mistakes – A Survey of Common Causes of Software Defects

Alex Elentukh[✉]

Metropolitan College of Boston University, 1010 Commonwealth Ave, Boston, MA 02215, USA
elentukh@bu.edu

Abstract. Software projects spend a significant effort on fixing defects. In fact, some 'successful' companies are unable to develop new features, since they devote all resources on supporting the multitude of customers and addressing the flow of incoming issues. This justifies the adoption of a well-defined testing and bug fixing process that is tailored for the organizational specifics. The effectiveness of such process drives the effectiveness of the whole organization. Our paper surveys the root causes (RCA/ARCA - Root Cause Analysis and ODC - Orthogonal Defect Classification) of common software defects and makes recommendations based on actual examples. In a context of a public university, the key recommendation is to assure that various angles of a defect prevention and bug fixing processes are explored, as part of a standard computer science curriculum.

Keywords: K.3.2 computer & information science education · software engineering · taxonomy of defects · root cause analysis

1 Introduction

Complexities of finding and fixing software issues are commonly overlooked [1], which results in additional residual defects drifting around a code base [2]. Consider these steps,

Step 1. A Reviewer or Tester finds a defect, then
Step 2. Communicates it to an Author, who
Step 3. Fixes the defect.

If we examine these three steps in detail, an immediate discovery will be that the process is vastly oversimplified. The assumption that an Author successfully fixes only those defects that a Tester reports is distant from reality. Both Author and Reviewer (for a virtue of being human) do err - every step of the way. In fact, a common process usually includes several additional sidekicks, as follows,

- Reviewer imagines an issue, which is not a real defect;
- Reviewer reports a wrong issue, not the one which was discovered;
- Author fixes a different defect, which has never been reported;

T. Zlateva and G. Tuparov (Eds.): CSECS 2023, LNICST 514, pp. 117–133, 2023.
https://doi.org/10.1007/978-3-031-44668-9_9

– And finally (to the surprise of the Data Analyst, (a side-line observer) an undoubtedly improved software emerges from the review and test process.

Pictorial on Fig. 1 reflects the expanded process.

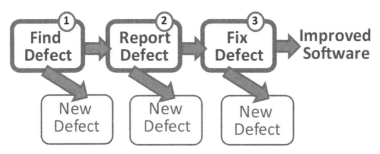

Fig. 1. Complexities of finding and fixing software defects

Question arises as to why the resulting software is still cleaner than the original software. Apparently, in most cases, the number of defects that are being fixed - is greater than the number of new defects that are being introduced.

2 An Example of a Book Review

To illustrate these notions, we consider six actual cases, that are well-known in the industry.

CASE # 1. Pictorial on Fig. 2 shows the front cover of the book published in September 2019. There is an initial copy (or the so-called 'Pre-Publication Draft' marked with a yellow stamp) [3] and Final Version [4] (that is being offered through Amazon, translated into twenty languages and sold over a million copies worldwide). We shall consider an example from initial copy, then the corresponding comment which we provided toward this example, and then the final result. Over three hundred reviewers (including author of this paper) examined the draft and submitted their comments.

Page 128 from Prepublication Draft is shown on Fig. 3.

Page 129 from Prepublication Draft is shown on Fig. 4.

One does not need to be a particularly thorough reviewer to notice that Fig. 9–1 and the top part of Fig. 9–2 – are redundant. However, that was not the comment provided. Here is the exact comment which was communicated, "*Fig. 9–2 at the line 2751 implies that a product could be released, if 'fix rate' is approaching the 'discovery rate'. This is really incorrect. If the 'discovery rate' does not come down, a product should not be shipped, regardless of a 'fix rate'.*"

We should bring about the importance of this comment. Since it attempts to reflect and to correct a common misinterpretation of a real-life situation, "as long as we are able to address *quickly* whatever is coming our way, the product remains in a releasable state". Nothing can be further from the truth. Even though the 'fixing curve' is shifting to the left, the 'discovery rate' will always remain an independent measure, which stands on its own feet; it should never be overlooked.

Fig. 2. The front cover of the book along with its prepublication draft

Consider the Fig. 5 of the Final Version, reflecting the same pages as shown at Fig. 3 and Fig. 4 of the Preproduction Draft. Apparently, the redundant picture has been eliminated; but the comment offered toward this section – was *not* taken.

Why did Reviewer miss the issue with redundant picture? Because Reviewer was preoccupied with a different notion, which is covered in great length in the course they are currently teaching. Why didn't Author take the comment offered by Reviewer? Because Author was preoccupied with the notion of Latent Defects and how to express this notion, assuming the comment does not relate to it. The good news is (as predicted at Fig. 1) that the final version is immensely better than the initial draft.

The biggest surprise of our analysis is that Peer Reviews were missed all together. Reviewer missed it. Author missed it. Writing a comprehensive book that enumerates the key engineering practices and omitting Peer Reviews – seems to be improbable. Although the fact is – Peer Reviews are not covered in the book. One can only speculate about the circumstances of this omission. Particularly considering that Author is a well-recognized expert in Peer Reviews, who went into a great length to publish the book's draft and to air this draft among several hundred reviewers.

What can be a more fitting case study of root causes - but rationing about issues with a book that delves into semantics of software defects. It is worth bringing about the related statistics implied in [5, 6],

– During a peer review, up to twenty percent of all defects are discovered by the Author, due to the stimulation provided by peers.
– There are multiple residue defects that remain undetected, long after a product is shipped.

Such statistics supports the notion that in real scenarios, defects arrive from most unexpected directions. In other words, "even a small ant can bring a large message". Which is opposite to the assumption that defects are exclusively found and reported by professional testers/reviewers and these are the only defects that are being fixed.

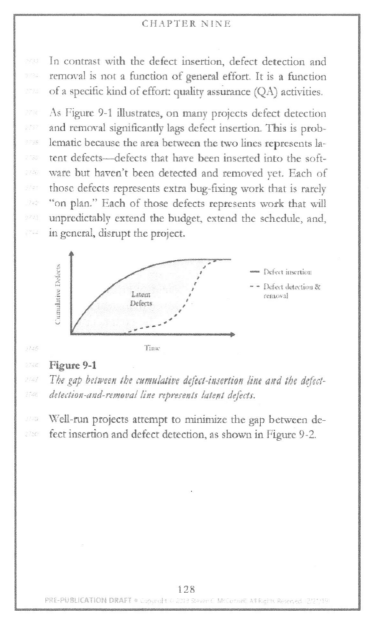

CHAPTER NINE

In contrast with the defect insertion, defect detection and
removal is not a function of general effort. It is a function
of a specific kind of effort: quality assurance (QA) activities.

As Figure 9-1 illustrates, on many projects defect detection
and removal significantly lags defect insertion. This is problematic because the area between the two lines represents latent defects—defects that have been inserted into the software but haven't been detected and removed yet. Each of
those defects represents extra bug-fixing work that is rarely
"on plan." Each of those defects represents work that will
unpredictably extend the budget, extend the schedule, and,
in general, disrupt the project.

Figure 9-1

*The gap between the cumulative defect-insertion line and the defect-
detection-and-removal line represents latent defects.*

Well-run projects attempt to minimize the gap between defect insertion and defect detection, as shown in Figure 9-2.

128

Fig. 3. Example from Preproduction Draft

3   Flukes and Common

Suppose you are adopting a Defect Prevention process in your organization. As a first
step, you need to distinguish common defects and then to assure they are addressed
ahead of all other defects.

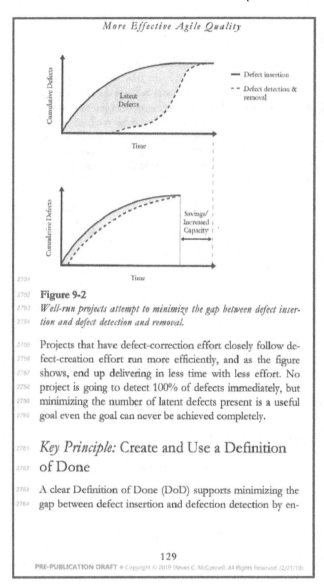

Fig. 4. Example from Preproduction Draft

Consider the following checklist that separates 'common' from other defects, let's call such other defects 'flukes'.

– A defect that manifests itself on ten customers' sites is a 'common' defect
– A defect that causes repeated failure on a single customer site, every ten hours is a 'common' defect
– If ten different types of intermittent failures have the same root-cause, then such a root-cause corresponds to a 'common' defect.

CHAPTER ELEVEN

As the top part of Figure 11-1 illustrates, defect detection and removal significantly lags defect insertion on many projects. This is problematic because the area between the two lines represents latent defects—defects that have been inserted into the software but haven't been detected and removed. Each of those defects represents extra bug-fixing work that is rarely "on plan." Each of those defects represents work that will unpredictably extend the budget, extend the schedule, and, in general, disrupt the project.

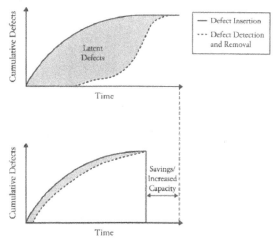

Figure 11-1
The gap between the cumulative defect-insertion line and the defect detection-and-removal line represents latent defects.

Well-run projects minimize the gap between defect insertion and defect detection, as shown in the bottom part of the figure.

156

Fig. 5. Example of Final Version with Comments Addressed

– If ten software engineers, while working independently from each other, inserted the same defect in different parts of code base, such defect is markedly a 'common'.

The purpose of this checklist is to show various angles of common defects. Each of the four points of the checklist can potentially have a corresponding root-cause, as follows,

- User Interface is inconsistent
- Reliability issue, memory leaks
- Design flaw causing a race condition
- Issue with coding standard or operational procedure

Mature organizations have a distinctly different view of software defects, if compared with such a view of immature organizations. For an immature organization, most defects are 'flukes', since their root-causes are hidden. There is an over-abundant flow of defects, and it is impractical to fix all of them, let alone to analyze them. This is contrary to a mature organization, where defects are carefully analyzed and root-causes are eliminated. In other words, mature organizations do not fix defects, they fix root-causes.

The Software Engineering Institute Capability Maturity Model (SEI CMM) [7] includes the process area called Defect Prevention, strategically positioned at the highest Level 5. This process area covers steps for a meticulous investigation of root causes one-defect-at-a-time. It is inappropriate to attempt adopting such process at a lower maturity level, since it would be as 'attempting to drink from a fire hose'.

The ISO 9001:20015 [8], the most generally recognized improvement standard in the world, has one of its six mandatory procedures dedicated to 'preventive action'. The importance of this procedure is emphasized in [9] as an organization without such a procedure documented and used is bound to fail the ISO audit.

4 Taxonomy of Defects as Opportunities

Further we establish several directions toward a systematic analysis of root causes of software defects. It seems counterintuitive to interpret the occurrences of defects as something positive, although this is the only way to focus organizational efforts and to make the best of the situation.

a) Examination of a *repository* of famous defects 'that brought the house down' and 'caused a panic on a street'– should be an imperative part of any training program. Such repository can be a simple extension of a company-wide bug database. Newly-hired engineers should be introduced to both sides of the coin, first, how to do it, and second, an equally important, how *not* to do it. To continue with this concept further, we could not forget the vivid note from a developer, "please do not highlight my defects in the repository; they make me look as an idiot". In fact, overcoming a defensive mentality, creating a safe work place by decriminalizing defects - are the first steps in adopting the repository and administering a company-wide training based on such repository.

b) A comprehensive *regression* suite that is executed all the time; it keeps producing various failures. It also produces a constant flow of opportunities for a team to learn and to improve. To establish such 24X7 regression is easier said than done, since it requires a never-ending support process to address causes of defects.

c) Defects defy logic. They can appear from anywhere. If defects would be logical, it would be very easy to prevent them. A so-called 'fat-finger problem' can be quite persistent and difficult to eliminate, taking into an account its random nature. Chaos Monkey used so successfully by network providers, e.g. Netflix, is the clear proof that *random testing* can be more effective than following some predefined sequence of quasi-logical test steps.

5 Orthogonal Defect Classification

Linking defects with their causes can be an arduous task. Correlation between faults and failures is not trivial, [10], as it depends on multiple factors. Orthogonal Defect Classification (ODC) [11] offers a methodology to redirect the flow of defects into several predefined buckets. Establishing consistent and independent categories is the prudent step in delving into root causes.

It should be noted that dwelling on RCA (Root Cause Analysis) can misguidedly feed its own purpose. Creating a clumsy and bureaucratic RCA process will ultimately deviate from the original goal of avoiding real customer issues. This brings about the ARCA (Lightweight Root Cause Analysis) [10].

It is crucially important to adopt an in-process technique to systematically avoid defects. Still, establishing a *balance* between correction and avoidance – elevates an organization into a steady state and enables it to advance uniformly. One should not give unjust preference to correction or to avoidance. Organizational maturity and business specifics - shall drive this balance. Ram Chillarege, et al. writes in [11] about the gap between statistical defect modeling and qualitative casual analysis. Apparently, such concepts as 'defects semantics' and 'process signature' – can only apply to a context of a mature organization.

Review of voluminous literature on RCA - brings about some interesting research. Andy Ho et al. in [12] describes a linguistic study of some 200,000 problem reports. This inevitably leads to a common language, a lingua franca, an organizational template of how defects should be recorded. James Reason in [13] bridges the disciplinary gulf between psychological theory and reliability engineering. Apparently, mapping such concepts as 'slip' and 'over-confidence' into the parallel universe of coding standards – can produce some invaluable actions.

6 Matching Defect Types with Test Types

Any measurement program, as well as any defect prevention program – are based on an established classification of software defects. Such classification cuts across multiple phases of software process. Ram Chillarege, et al. in [11] speaks volumes about the critical role of ODC.

The common typology of tests includes the following,

- *Usability*. How quickly can a naïve user learn the system?
- *Functional*. Are there any stated requirements that are uncovered by tests?
- *Regression*. Are there any new defects introduced by a software update?
- *Reliability*.
- *Overload*. Is the system exits gracefully from a prohibited state?
- *Performance*. Does response time correspond to the spec?

Each test type has a specific goal. For example, Reliability Test exposes the time-dependent aspect of a system behavior. Hitting a UI button once, could suffice for a Functional Test. Hitting the same button, a thousand times and verifying that memory pool does not leak, constitutes a Reliability Test.

Figure 6 illustrates the classification of defects, that is matched with their corresponding classification of tests.

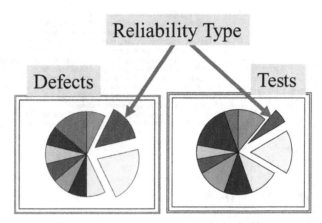

Fig. 6. Matching defect types with test types

Suppose you experience multiple reliability defects. In simplified terms, your system does not stay up and fails frequently. The first direction in investigating the issue is to examine the corresponding Reliability Tests. Looking at a Functional Tests would be a misdirection. Apparently such an investigation is only possible if failures in a defect database, as well as the tests in Quality Center – both have a consistent typology.

Test Types correspond to various *angles* from which a product is examined. Multiple angles (test types) scrutinize the *same* product. The degree of completeness of test coverage is assured by the comprehensive set of test types. Gaps in test types remind a QA Engineer about some tests that could have been missed. Additionally, a great deal of confusion is avoided by prioritizing and focusing the test effort on few selected test types, making sure they do not overlap.

Should note from our experience that Test Management, as an organizational practice, is more mature than Defect Management. An auditor walking into a door is bound to ask about a bug database first. If engineers are not aware of their major defects, this is indicative of some profound organizational issue. On another hand, establishing a consistent Test Management with all its standard templates and training is a significant undertaking. Therefore, when adopting a comprehensive Root Cause Analysis Program, it is logical to start with Defect Management.

7   Integrated Approach Succeed

Here we shall build on the conclusion from the previous section VI. In order to optimize the finding and fixing of software defects, it is prudent to match defect modes with test types. At Fig. 7, Information System Division of NASA, [14] reports the distribution of defects that have been found through a variety of techniques.

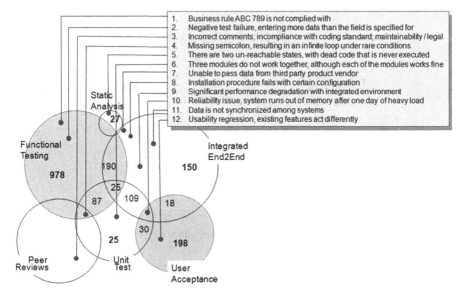

Fig. 7. Integrated Approach to Finding Defects

Here are several general and specific observations.

- There are multiple defects that could only be revealed through a peer review.
- It is overoptimistic to expect finding a reliability issue during a unit test.
- It is far too late to find defects at User Acceptance. One should conduct a detailed root-cause analysis of such defects, so in future to be able identifying similar issues through a different means
- A functional defect found in User Acceptance – should have been found earlier during the functional test.
- Installation defect found in User Acceptance – should have been found by a technical writer during review of the user doc
- Maintainability defect found in Production – should have been found during a code review

In summary, looking at the distribution of defects at Fig. 7, we can arrive at the following conclusions. On one hand, defect modes overlap, as the same defect could be found using several techniques. On another hand, certain techniques are unable to detect certain defect types. For example, a functional test is unable to detect a maintainability defect. Hence, only the *integrated* approach can assure an adequate coverage and succeed in revealing a reasonable number of defects.

8 Defect Cost

When enacting a defect prevention program, many companies prioritize costly failures. [15]. This triggers the whole new set of techniques to monetize the prevention and to convert it into a money-making machine under the umbrella of Cost Avoidance.

Everyone feels in his/her heart that it is cheaper to fix defects early. Question is, "How much cheaper?" In fact, when starting to deal with significant amounts, one should prepare for a clear response.

We shall consider the following example to illustrate the above stated concept. Suppose we deal with an environment of daily software inspections that reveal three major defects per inspection.

Table 1. Calculation of Yearly Expense on Inspections

3	major defects per inspection
1	inspections per day
$200	burden rate
30	effort person/hours per inspection
260	working days in a year
780	major defects in a year
$1,560,000	yearly expense on inspections

Table 1 reflects the scenario of a mid-sized company with a hundred developers. Apparently, the cost of inspections should not be underestimated. It is also a strong recommendation to maintain these numbers for *any* organizational size.

Table 2. Yearly Benefit from Inspections

Cost of a Defect	Yearly Benefit
$200	$ (1,418,400)
$800	$ (993,600)
$5,000	$ 1,980,000
$8,000	$ 4,104,000
$20,000	$ 12,600,000
$50,000	$ 33,840,000

Table 2 shows the calculation of Yearly Benefit as a function of the Cost of a Defect. Table 2 starts with an uncharacteristically-small amount of $200. No company in the world spends so little on fixing a defect in the field. Large companies with millions of live customers - estimate the cost of fixing defects in billions. In fact, looking at the chart at Fig. 8, one can see the benefit from inspections is growing exponentially, after the cost of a defect rolls over a thousand dollars.

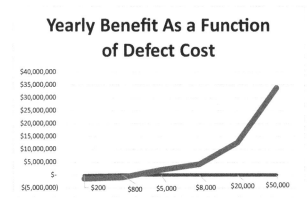

Fig. 8. Yearly benefit from inspections as a function of Defect Cost

Philip Crosby in his classic work [16] titled, "Quality Is Free" establishes that, "systematic drive for quality pays for itself."

Herb Krasner, in [17] writes, "The cost of finding and fixing defects is the largest single expense element in the software lifecycle" estimated at the staggering $1.56 trillion for 2020 in US.

An adoption of a consistent inspection program across a large organization always meets with a natural human resistance. The most common response that a Process Champion hears is that inspections consume too much time. This is contrary to reality (supported by our calculations) – inspections do save time.

9 Holistic Approach

To adopt a consistent practice across an organization, one needs to demonstrate the importance of *every* part of a software process. One way to accomplish this task is to keep performing an on-going Root Cause Analysis and to retain in organizational memory a series of catastrophic failures triggered by skipping each part of the process. In this scenario, RCA is used as a powerful process-adoption tool. To this end, consider the following massively egregious failures. [18, 19].

CASE # 2. Here are quotes from the newspaper covering US Congress investigation into collapse of Health Care Site.

– *"Private contractors in charge of building the federal online health insurance mar-ketplace testified Thursday that the administration went ahead with Oct. 1 launch of HealthCare.gov despite insufficient testing"*
– *"This system just wasn't tested enough," Julie Bataille, director of CMS's office of communications, acknowledged to reporters.*

From reading these quotes, we can attempt to select what most likely went wrong with the site. As a daily event, millions of people jammed into site and eventually brought it down within the course of several morning hours.

a) Incomplete test coverage of original requirements
b) Skill level of test personnel is inadequate
c) Traceability of requirements and tests was not explicitly documented
d) *System limitations due to insufficient design*

The apparent reason for this failure is the point (d), which is contrary to what was originally aired.

CASE # 3. The goal of this analysis is to focus on small software changes that frequently result in uncontrolled ramifications. Consider the following paper quote describing the crash of the New York Stock Exchange.

"…. On Tuesday evening, the NYSE began the rollout of a software release in preparation for the July 11,2015 test of the upcoming SIP timestamp requirement. As a standard NYSE practice, the initial release was deployed on one trading unit. As customers began connecting after 7am on Wednesday morning, there were communication issues between customer gateway and the trading unit with the new release. It was determined that the NYSE and NYSE MKT customer gateways were not loaded with the proper configuration compatible with the new release.…".

Selecting from the list of possible root-causes shall undoubtedly yield the point (d) as a true reason of failure.

a) Requirements
b) Design
c) Test
d) *SCM*

CASE # 4. On Christmas of 2017 South Carolina Lottery sold 70,000 tickets between 5:51 and 7:52 pm. Each ticket gave a purchaser an unfair chance of winning $500. Some folks seized on an opportunity, continued buying tickets and cashed them immediately. Most folks followed the strategy of saving winning tickets for a rainy day. The error-filled tickets totaled for $34 MLN. Tim Madden from state lottery confirmed that they paid $1.7 MLN due to the "programming error of their vendor Intralot" and did not honor any other erroneous tickets. Other officials called the situation a "machine malfunctioning" and "glitch".

Selecting from the following list the most likely cause of a problem - shall yield the point (b).

a) Requirements
b) *Coding*
c) Test
d) SCM

CASE # 5. A well-described case of a brokerage company going bankrupt. On August 1, 2012 Knight Capital lost $440 million, when its trading software went kablooey. As a software engineer inadvertently left a piece of code commented out. Resulting in each transaction missing a fairly small amount. Although the huge volume of a flow of daily trades caused a colossal loss to accumulate very quickly. Within thirty minutes, it was all over, the market maker was out of business and has never recovered.

Apparently, (i) is the most probable root-cause of a problem.

e) Requirements
f) Design
g) Test
h) SCM
i) *Peer Reviews*

CASE # 6. Here is an example of several minor defects that manifested concurrently, causing a catastrophe, because of their compound effect. March 2019, two Boeing 747 Max crashed within a short time span, because of the following,

– faulty hardware sensor at the end of its life
– autopilot (AI system) misbehaved and pushed down the nose of the aircraft
– an urgent software fix was delayed due to some bureaucratic process
– disagree light (feature that is supposed to highlight the variance among sensors) was not installed; this safety feature was marked as optional and sold for $80K
– pilot training did not cover, how to override the misbehavior of an autopilot
– documented procedure was incorrect

Looking at this long list of issues - we arrive at no other conclusion that point (f) is the root cause.

a) Requirements
b) Design
c) Test
d) Documentation
e) Training
f) *Project Management*

Expanding on these far-reaching thoughts, [20, 21], we can confirm that it is insufficient to know a *part* of the process. One must be aware of *all* parts, to comprehend the gist of the *whole*. For example, it is impossible to grow into an expert in Design, while being unaware of Testing. Process components are interdependent; they influence each other. One might assume, "it is enough just to do my job, my little something". But they will be unable to comprehend even a small part, since in-depth angles are bound to be missed.

Figure 9 makes a visual representation of each part of a software process as a sector of a unified circle. As we delved into real-life cases (CASE 2 – 6), it became clear that skipping even a single sector can become a root cause of a profound tragedy.

10   Conclusions

A curriculum of a mature course must follow a clear direction, starting with an introductory material and moving toward more advanced concepts. [22, 23]. A course should 'develop a topic' by showing an explicit path to a learner. To this end, if we divide a

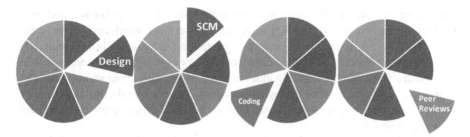

Fig. 9. Mapping catastrophic failures into process components

course into two parts, the first part covers a technique itself, its steps and roles; while the second part delves deeper into the *reasoning* of this approach and its connections to other approaches. In other words, we should divide the scope of a course into WHAT and WHY.

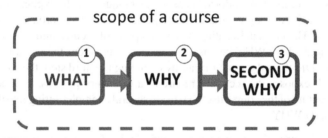

Fig. 10. Scope of the course is divided into WHAT and WHY

For example, the initial WHAT-part covers the software testing technique of *equivalence partitioning* or the peer reviews method of *step-by-step scenarios*. While the second part raises various WHY-questions. Here are several examples of a WHY-question.

– Why – defects tend to cluster
– Why – peer reviews are hugely more effective than personal editing
– Why – Cone of Uncertainty of a test effort is lopsided, as its top part is most commonly missing
– Why - Allpairs combinations reveal the same number of defects as Cartesian reveal
– Why – percent of a project's effort spent on unit test is diminishing, as the size of a project widens
– Why - Sarbanes-Oxley Act (SOX) mandates to separate the test design from test execution
– Why - An organization should keep growing its regression suites
– Why - A unit test should avoid communicating across a network
– Why – A unit test hardy ever goes through a redundancy checks, as a system test does
– Why - Technical debt cannot be addressed with a functional test

During our decade-long practice of teaching courses on quality software engineering – reviewing with students these WHY-questions - proves to be most effective to assure that concepts did sink-in. We orchestrate a certain time pressure, as we ask students to write responses to several dozen WHY-questions in their own words and without a help of ChatGPT. Alternatively, during a verbal questioning, it becomes immediately clear - how fluent our students with these concepts and how comfortable they are discussing them. Such an articulation, reducing ideas to paper - does bring about various additional virtues. Students who thought-through those topics that we covered in the class, students who spent time crafting responses based on their personal experience – are most likely know the subject well.

The topic of our paper is the survey of root causes of various software defects. In a context of a public course (in our case it is the software engineering course) it is important to structure the syllabus in a similar manner, so not to omit the second part, the WHY-part. As in bug fixing, we first observe the manifestation, the *failure*, although we still need to comprehend the *fault* so to correct it and to eliminate the failure. Much like during a university class, we first need to communicate to student *what* needs to be done and then to explain *why* it needs to be done.

Note that it is quite possible to mix-and-match the WHATs and the WHYs. One can very well intertwine the description of steps of a technique with the explanation of reasons it is done that way. Although in our experience, such teaching approach does not prove to be effective. The clear delineation of various parts of a curriculum (showing where WHAT ends and where WHY begins) clarifies and strengthens the overall message.

Figure 10. Develops the topic further by depicting the third step, the so-called SECOND WHY. It exposes the recursive nature of a discovery process, as it points to the deliberate structure of the course itself. Here are several examples fitting into the category of the SECOND WHY.

– Why – Design part of the course is juxtaposed with descriptions of extra-long Black Swan projects that have been halted without their completion
– Why – Peer Reviews part of the course is strategically positioned next to the description of Agile, as the most common software development paradigm
– Why – the description of clustering defects – is positioned within the *equivalence partitioning* chapter of the class

The introduction of the SECOND WHY brings about the concept of never-ending improvement. It motivates one to keep advancing and to keep delving deeper without limitations.

References

1. Jones, C.: Software Engineering Best Practices: Lessons from Successful Projects in the Top Companies. McGraw-Hill Education (2010). A study by a renowned software engineering expert, confirming that bug fixing can consume 30% to 50% of total development effort
2. Coverity Scan: Open Source Report. A survey conducted by the provider of the static analysis tools, found that fixing bugs can consume up to 50% of development time (2012)
3. McConnell, S.: More Effective Agile. Constrrux Press. ISBN: 978–1–7335182–1–5. Prepublication Draft 21-February-2019
4. McConnell, S.: More Effective Agile. Constrrux Press. ISBN: 978–1–7335182–1–5. 01-September-2019

5. IEEE Standard for Software Reviews and Audits, IEEE Std 1028™-2008
6. Wiegers, K.: Peer Reviews in Software. ISBN-13: 978–0201734850
7. SEI CMM version 1.3. https://resources.sei.cmu.edu/library/index.cfm
8. ISO 9001:20015 QMS - Guidelines for Performance Improvements
9. Schmauch, C.H.: ISO 9000 for Software Developers, ASQC Quality Press. ISBN: 0–87389–348–4
10. Lehtinen, T.O.A., Mäntylä, M.V., Vanhanen, J.: Development and evaluation of a lightweight root cause analysis method (ARCA) - field studies at four software companies. Inf. Softw. Technol. **53**(10), 1045–1061 (2011)
11. Chillarege, R., et al.: Orthogonal defect classification - a concept for in-process measurements. IEEE Trans. Softw. Eng. **18**(11) (1992)
12. Ko, A.J., Myers, B.A., Chau, D.H.: A linguistic analysis of how people describe software problems. IEEE Symp. Vis. Lang. Hum.-Centric Comput. (2016)
13. Reason, J.: Human Error. Cambridge University Press, Cambridge (1990)
14. NASA (Information System Division), report from finding software faults through a variety of defect prevention techniques
15. Keshta, I.M.: Software cost estimation approaches: a survey. J. Softw. Eng. Appl. **10**, 824–842 (2017)
16. Crosby, P.: Quality Is Free. McGraw-Hill (1979). For over four decades this book has been an inspiration for numerous improvement efforts
17. Krasner, H.: Cost of Poor Software Quality, Consortium for Information and Software Quality, Report (2021). One might not realize the depth and breadth with which software defects affect all angles of our lives, as shown in this report
18. Paschal, C.A., et al.: Reflections on Software Failure Analysis. CS-SE Conference, Washington, DC, USA (2017)
19. This site documents the variety of actual case studies, www.henricodolfing.com/. Many cases are also covered in the book "The Project Success Model", by Henrico Dolfing available from the same site
20. Carstensen, P., et al.: "Let's Talk About Bugs", Scandinavian Journal of Information Systems. Paper presents the detailed analysis of testing and bug fixing within the context of the Danish conglomerate
21. Elentukh, A., Kanabar, V.: Improving Teaching and Learning Effectiveness of Computer Science Courses – Case Study, CSECS 2019 (2019). This paper summarizes our experience teaching several courses at Metropolitan College of Boston University Computer Science department over five years. A number of innovative teaching techniques are presented in this paper. We specifically address the role of a project archive, when designing a course
22. Hillman, D., Schudy, R., Temkin, A.: Winning Online Instruction. Routledge (2022). The fabric of the book is weaved with the fundamental transformation from synchronous teaching (lectures) into asynchronous teaching (quizzes, assignment, discussions). Such transformation is not perfunctory, as it calls for an extensive discovery
23. Hou, J.: Project and module based teaching and learning. Int. J. Comput. Inf. Eng. **8**(3) 791–796 (2014)

Holistic (Software) Quality Theory.
An Improved Definition and Meta-Model

Dobromir M. Dinev(✉)

New Bulgarian University, Sofia, Bulgaria
dobromir@gmail.com

Abstract. The current article introduces a short historical review of the roots of the holistic (software) quality theory. This review is used both as a presentation of the ground on which the holistic quality has been built upon and correspondingly to introduce a classification of the quality models known today. Since its introduction in 2017, the holistic (software) quality was several times enriched; one such advancement is part of the current work concerning the meta-model used to describe quality itself; thus, better control, management and etc., are achieved.

Keywords: Holistic quality · holistic quality definition · holistic quality meta-model · quality models classification · inherited quality · heuristic quality

1 Historical Roots of the Holistic Approach to (Software) Quality

The quality is deeply rooted in humankind's understanding of the world. Often when the question "What is quality?" is asked, it receives answers depending on the background of the person the question has been asked to. Among the answers, it can be noticed, clearly, the appearance of two words that signify the level of quality itself: "Good" and "Bad". If to be believed, the comprehension of "knowing the good and evil" [1] has been with us from the earliest days of our existence. If not to be believed, we should turn to more trivial things like food, a sense of security, art, etc.; then the first period in the formation of the term quality should be recognised, and its beginning should be referred to as this early moment when humans shaped those ground comprehensions and started distinguishing between the feeling of a secure environment versus the one that is not; furthermore, the situation where there is a "*good* food" and "*bad* food", the "*beautiful*" things verse that are not. Over the time, the humans' organisation became more sophisticated, and the quality started being recognised in the craftsmanship of particular individuals. This encloses the first major period of the term.

In the Roman Republic, those craftsmen gathered in small groups named collegia. The formation of the guilds boosted certain standardisation among the guild members and contributed further "better-quality" goods to be delivered. At the end of the 17th

T. Zlateva and G. Tuparov (Eds.): CSECS 2023, LNICST 514, pp. 134–143, 2023.
https://doi.org/10.1007/978-3-031-44668-9_10

century, the guilds start having the opposite effect on the quality by stopping innovation. Nevertheless, the guilds played their central role in the formation of the first universities centuries ago; for instance, the University of Bologna (established in 1088) [2], and this was leading new ideas to form. Such new ideas from the statistics and economics were at the base of the third period in the quality term to be present. It started with publishing a book that contains a definition of quality. The definition sees quality as an entity having two natures: objective and subjective. [3] The following decades were full of definitions of quality. By Crosby, "quality should be defined as "conformance to requirements" if we are to manage it". [4] Feigenbaum elaborates that the "Quality is customer determination [...] it is based upon customers experience with the product and service, measured against his or her requirements - stated or unstated [...] Product and service quality can be defined as: the total composite product and service characteristics of marketing, engineering, manufacture, through which the product and services in use will meet the expectations of the customer." [5].

The last of the quality fathers' definitions upon which the focus of the current work shall fall is about to be the definition of Juran. The definition has all the features from the previously reviewed. In addition, it has a direct referral to the presence of the defects and the "freedom" from them, stressing that "... it is most convenient to standardise on a short definition of the word quality as "fitness for use" [6].

Despite the first electronic computers being available in the first half of the 20th century, quality was not the focus then. Pieces of evidence that change are given from a conference held by NATO in 1968, where "about fifty experts from all areas concerned with software problems – computer manufacturers, universities, software houses, computer users, etc." [7, 8] gathered to debate topics concerning programming languages, software as a commodity, multiprogramming, time-sharing, and last but not least, the "problems of the large-systems" delivery. That last one relates to the quality and the price paid for achieving it. Such summits ignited a vast development in the quality field (see Fig. 1). In the second half of the 1970s, the first structural software product quality models start being present, for instance, the models of Boehm et al., [9] McCall's model. Richards and Walter [10] further recognised quality as a set of quality characteristics that are decomposable. A popular structural model created in the business was the FURPS model; [11] decomposed the quality into five major characteristics: functionality, usability, reliability, performance, and supportability. The structural software product models are advantageous when quality assurance engineers should model the quality of a particular product, especially when measurable quality goals are set. Nevertheless, the software branch was required to agree upon a standard that might have a broader possibility of being used by the software manufacturers. In December 1991, such an agreement became a fact with the actual issuance of the ISO9126 standard; it resembled many of the characteristics of the previously issued models. The authors of the standard recognise two levels of characteristics: major and sub-characteristics. Functionality, maintainability, usability, efficacy, reliability, and portability are recognised as major software product characteristics. ISO9126 standard is pivotal for the software branch and for the development of the software quality. The additions to the standard made in the following years give birth to the so-called compound models (ISO9126–1, much later ISO/IEC 25010), where not only the software product is in focus but a wider view on the potential impactors (factors) for this quality to be embedded (despite the usability is an early recognised quality characteristic). Another positive impact was the equalisation regarding the terminology used to describe the software quality; furthermore, all this built the solid ground leading for the first attempts to build holistic (software) quality theory to be present, despite some of the broader quality ideas to be available in the first half of the 1980s.

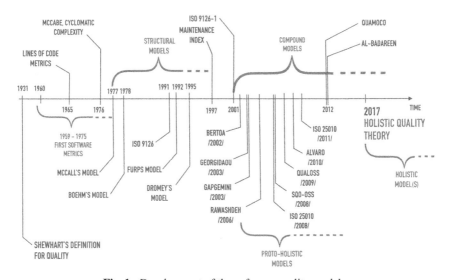

Fig. 1. Development of the software quality models.

At the beginning of the 2000s, a new software delivery business model emerged and became popular. The so-called "out-of-the-box software" or "off-the-shelf software" became an opposing idea to the bespoke. That new business model and technology advance boosted the development of a class of models based on ISO9126 that took some development and software usage specifics into account. The first model from that group was the Bertoa's quality model, which positions the following main characteristics: Functionality, Reliability, Usability, Efficiency, Maintainability, and Portability, but when it comes to the sub-characteristics, although most of them are directly taken from the ISO9126 standard, the sub-characteristics are divided into two major groups reflecting the "runtime" and the overall "lifecycle" of the software product. This is done to firmly settle the idea that the software product should be looked in a different perspective; thus, the software product quality is managed.

The author of the Generic, Multilayered and Customizable Model (or GEQUAMO) [15] was taking the business analysis perspective and fusion it with the quality assurance perspective, from one side and from the other, partially looking for a connection between those two, was introducing the viewpoint of operations as function in the company. The reason for the first relation is related to the apparent fact that each quality characteristic, which should be incorporated into the software product, first needs to be recognised and stated (primarily as a customer or end-user needs). A further important reason for the suggested approach to quality is the managers, developers and end-users by utilising a framework (like the one suggested by the model) to build their own quality model and by assigning a weight to each quality attribute or characteristic of the relative importance of those attributes to be present and later taken into account when the software starts being created.

1.1   The Proto-Holistic (Software) Quality Models

In 1984, Garvin introduced his view on the matter of *"What is quality?"* and *"How is it possible to be defined?"* His understanding entails five possible approaches to defining the term quality. [12, 13] The first approach is the product approach; it looks like the structural product quality models, accumulating additional product characteristics like *durability* and *serviceability*. The *perceived quality* appeared under the product, despite the stand-alone major *user-based* perspective that is entirely related to the customer centricity visible in other quality definitions, for instance, in Crosby's definition. *The manufacturing approach* – gives the engineering perspective to the term quality. Garvin recognises it as the level at which the requirements are fulfilled. The *value-based approach* – adds the critical resource perspective, where time and money are considered. The last approach is the *transcendental approach*. The author believed that the term quality and the quality itself could not be defined precisely. There will always be a part of it that will be left undefined as it is impossible to be presented or represented by any given construct (like the tree structure of characteristics of the structural quality models). Publications like [14, 16] and some holistic quality theory scientific articles prove this statement mostly wrong. Notwithstanding, the model of Garvin should be considered as a proto-holistic quality model since it contains a much broader view of the term quality, not just the product perspective, the manufacturer's perspective, the lack of deficiencies as it is in the definitions of the quality father reviewed above, and it is not that generic as in the definitions of Shewhart and Zeithaml.

Rawashdeh's software product quality model is another instance of a model that focuses on non-bespoke software solutions. [16] The model also continues the tendency of the structural quality models; still, there is a gargantuan difference present on the first level; the model recognises a set of stakeholders at this first level: End-user, Analysts, Quality assurance, Business Owners, and Project manager; and have more than two levels. In the second level, each of those stakeholders' categories is connected with one or a few of the main quality characteristics. On the third and fourth levels, the model is organising the sub-characteristics of the product sub-characteristics and process sub-characteristics streams, positioning in each of them different sub-characteristics in each. Through the four steps, the model introduces a framework for creating customised quality models considering the different perspectives to achieve the accuracy of the quality model; the steps are *Step one*: identification of a small group of high-level quality attributes (characteristics) and utilising the *"devidire et concire"* method to subdivide them into sub-characteristics; *Step two*: distinguishing between external and internal metrics; *Step three*: identification of the user to each quality sub-characteristic (in terms of the model attributes; *Step four*: build the quality model, considering the initially introduced structure of the quality in the ISO9129 and Dormay's quality models.

According to [17, 18], the open-source models regarding the quality became in 2003; all of them are considering the alternative way of creating software opposing the commercial entities' created software. One more common feature can be easily identified across those models. They all thought of specific perspectives related to the open-source community, for instance, but not limited to maturity of the community, serviceability, etc., which is why they should be accepted in this group of quality models.

All proto-holistic (software) quality models share the same feature: they are broadening the views regarding quality. Still, none of them acknowledges and/ or reflects the holistic approach as a philosophy.

2   Classification in the Holistic Context of the (Software) Quality Models

Across the decades, different classifications with the main purpose of categorising the (software) quality models were suggested. The most sound classification related to the software branch is the one published in [19], known as the "Define, Assess, and Predict" classification (DAP). From a holistic point of view, the "Define, Assess, and Predict" classification is a necessary but not enough requirement for a model to be recognised as holistic. The missing additions, recognised for the moment, are from the next perspectives: processes (creation, transformation, etc.), the quality definition that includes the actors in the (software) product ecosystem, and one or few meta-models related to quality being present. This then excludes definitions like Shewhart's and Crosby's or standards such as ISO/IEC 25010. Following this ideology, the models in Fig. 1. (not only) are divided into the next few groups: structural product quality models (MaCall, Boehm, Dormey, OpenBRR, etc.), compound models (Bertoa, Alvaro, Gap Gemini, etc.), proto-holistic models (Garvin, Aaker, QualOSS, etc.) and holistic models (the holistic model suggested since 2017 by the holistic quality theory). To reflect certain settings and advancements in the development of software quality, the proto-holistic models are separated into two main generations: A typical model from generation one is such model that has a structural model that defines the term quality (like in ISO9126, later ISO25010) and there is some additional specific perspective which is considered an important; thus, the quality is achieved. For instance, in Rawashdeh's model, the recognition of the different stakeholders and the process; or in the open-source society models, the place of the open-source society itself is central for providing quality support of the delivered software product (SQO-OSS model).

The members of the second generation of proto-holistic models have in their list of characteristics a clear compliance with the DAP classification, specifically focusing on the prediction word in the abbreviation. Another significant difference between the two generations is the appearance of a meta-model in the second generation that helps to define quality as a term (QUAMOCO).

The holistic quality is compliant with all the characteristics mentioned by the proto-holistic group but also adds the previously mentioned perspectives. (Fig. 2.)

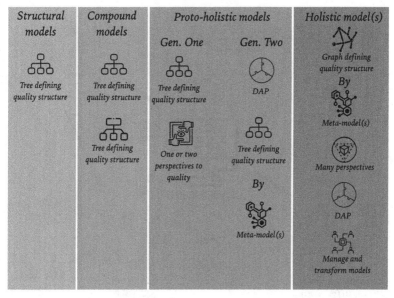

Fig. 2. Summary of the characteristics per category in the suggested classification.

3 The Holistic Definition of Software Quality and the Software Product Ecosystem

The definitions of Crosby and Garvin (reviewed above) introduced a set of stakeholders related to the software product quality; those were: *manufacturing*, the *customer*, *marketing*, and *engineering*. Such entities are recognised in the holistic quality theory as *impactors*.

The stakeholder management introduces a much bigger set of stakeholders, in comparison with the mentioned few, for instance, but not limited to Owners, Investors, Support, Finance, Sales, Government, NPOs/ NGOs, etc. (Fig. 3.) Each of those separate stakeholders can be assigned to a group. Each of those groups has an interest (in some cases legitimate) regarding the manufactured (software) product and the quality of it. This can be used for defining the quality reflecting the holistic philosophy.

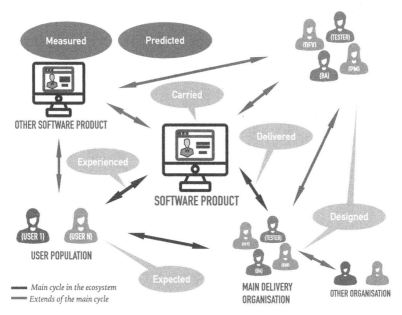

Fig. 3. Major groups of stakeholders in the software product ecosystem.

Utilising the "devidire et concire" principle and in clear desire for the quality later to be managed properly, the term quality is divided into the next seven sub-qualities; this was done reflecting Fig. 3. (Fig. 4):

Carried quality (CaQ) – the quality embedded in manufactured (software) products;

Expected quality (ExQ) – the expected by the users of the (software) product quality, usually in terms of quality components and levels for each component;

Experienced quality (ExpQ) – the quality actually experienced by the users during their use of the (software) product;

Designed quality (DesQ) – the quality that the creator of the (software) product intends to embed in the (software) product itself, i.e. the desired by the creator carried quality. This quality might be equal to none if the creator is not putting any effort into delivering quality;

Delivered quality (DeQ) – the quality that actually reaches the user of the (software) product;

Measured quality (MsQ) – the measured quality of CaQ, ExQ, ExpQ, DesQ, DeQ;

Predicted quality (PrQ) - the predicted levels of CaQ, ExQ, ExpQ, DesQ, DeQ, based on the MsQ.

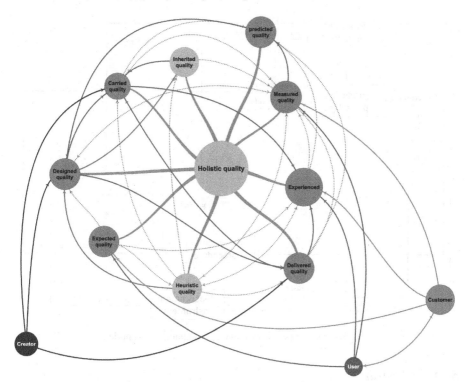

Fig. 4. Major groups in the software product ecosystem.

The additions are the Inherited quality (InhQ) – the quality that is "received" by using another (software) product in the delivery of the creator and Heuristic quality (HeQ) – the quality that is a result of the general rules (heuristics) taken from the use of the (software) product. An instance, from the software delivery branch, is a usability quality component-related heuristic regarding any given web sites stating: that the logo on the main page should not be a link to the same home page.

4 Updated Holistic Quality Meta-model

Following the acknowledgement of [20] for the need for an explicit meta-model to describe the increasingly complex structures of quality models, a meta-model for the software product was introduced. Figure 5 contains the new additions reflecting the management perspective around the quality components by which a proper reflection of the complete (software) product ecosystem can be done.

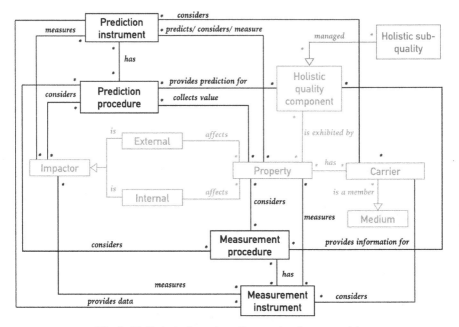

Fig. 5. Holistic (software) quality - updated meta-model.

5 Conclusion

The holistic approach to quality is relatively new happening on the (software) quality (assurance) landscape. The presented addition in the current article cannot be considered a major change to the previously stated theory. Still, the changes enrich the holistic approach making it even more complete. At the same time, it should be remarked that the holistic (software) quality is far from being finished, and the work will continue in the upcoming years.

References

1. The Bible, Genesis ph. 5
2. Rashdall, H.: The Universities of Europe in the Middle Ages, p. 150. Clarendon Press, Salerno, Bologna, Paris (1895)
3. Shewhart, W.A.: Economic Control of Quality of Manufactured Products (1931). Reprint p. 51 (2015)
4. Crosby, P.B.: Quality is Free, the Art of Making Quality Certain (1979). Mentor, ISBN: 978–0451621290
5. Feigenbaum, A.V.: Total Quality Control, p. e4 (2004). ISBN: 978–0070220034
6. M. J. Juran and Frank M. Gryna: Juran's quality control handbook, McGraw-Hill, e4,1988
7. Randell, B.: Software Engineering in 1968, Computing Laboratory – University of Newcastle upon Tyne (1979). p2, p6
8. Naur, P., Randell, B.: Bauer, F.L., Bolliet, L., Helms, H.J. (Eds.): Report on a conference sponsored by the NATO Science Committee, Garmisch, Germany, 7–11 October 1968, p85, p87

9. Boehm, B.W., Brown, J.R., Kaspar, H., Lipow, M., Macleod, G.J., Merrit, M.J.: Characteristics of Software Quality. North-Holland (1978)
10. McCall, J.A., Richards, P.K., Walters, G.F.: Factors in Software Quality, National Technical Information Service (1977)
11. Grady, R.B., Caswell, D.L.: Software Metrics: Establishing a Company-Wide Program. Prentice Hall (1987)
12. Garvin, D.A.: What does "product quality" really mean? Sloan Manage. Rev. **25**, 25–43 (1984)
13. Stylidis, K., Wickman, C., Söderberg, R.: Defining perceived quality in the automotive industry: an engineering approach. Procedia CIRP **36**, 165–170 (2015)
14. Wagner, S., et al.: Operationalised product quality models and assessment: the Quamoco approach. Inf. Softw. Technol. **62**, 101–123 (2015)
15. Georgiadoui, E.: GEQUAMO-a generic, multilayered, customizable software quality model. Softw. Qual. J. **11**(4), 313–323. https://doi.org/10.1023/A:1025817312035
16. Rawashdeh, A., Bassem, M.: A new software quality model for evaluating COTS components. J. Comput. Sci. **2**(4), 373–381 (2006)
17. Adewole, A., Misra, S., Omoregbe, N.: A review of models for evaluating quality in open source software. In: International Conference on Electronic Engineering and Computer Science, IERI Procedia 4, pp. 88–92 (2013)
18. Haaland, K., Groven, A.K., Regnesentral, N., Glott, R., Tannenberg, A.: Free/Libre open source quality models-a comparison between two approaches. In: 4th, 2010 FLOS International Workshop on Free/Libre/Open Source Software, pp. 1–17 (2010)
19. Deissenboeck, F., Juergens, E., Lochmann, K., Wagner, S.: Software quality models: purposes, usage scenarios and requirements. In: Proceedings of the ICSE Workshop on Software Quality, pp. 9–14. IEEE (2009)
20. Kitchenham, B., Linkman, S.G., Pasquini, A., Nanni, V.: The SQUID approach to defining a quality model. Softw. Qual. J. **6**(3), 211–233 (1997). https://doi.org/10.1023/A:101851610 3435

Software Reuse Approach Based on Review and Analysis of Reuse Risks from Projects Uploaded to GitHub

Olena Chebanyuk[1,2]([✉]) [iD]

[1] Department of Informatics, New Bulgarian University, Sofia, Bulgaria
Chebanyuk.olena@gmail.com
[2] Software Engineering Department, National Aviation University, Kyiv, Ukraine

Abstract. Modern and large software systems usually are not developed from scratch. Reuse operations for small modules are not complicated activities. When reuse is organized on level of algorithms or software features, practices of many companies show that reuse procedures are performed on low maturity levels (analysis of software bugs and reuse risks are often performed approximately). According to researches of IBM and many other companies the later you will define any kind of error the more expensive and large scale will be cost of improving your software.

Paper proposes an approach based of reverse engineering activities aimed to estimate reuse risks of existing projects on GitHub before their further reuse. Proposed approach is designed by analysis of typical activities performed in research laboratories of software companies and considers specific of working with GitHub. Model for estimating of reuse risks is proposed. Model covers reuse risks for multilayer applications, but can be extended for other types of projects. Recommendations for developers for extension of the model are outlined.

Keywords: Software Reuse Risks · GitHub · Software Reuse Activities · Software Product Lines · Multi-layered Architecture

1 Introduction

Today development of software projects does not start from scratch. Software development teams expect to reduce development efforts by means of reusing existing software code, interface prototypes, documentation, and other software development artifacts.

From the first look, efforts to adopt architecture and functionality of existing projects to new ones could be estimated as not so difficult. However, in real projects efforts may become so great [1]. Often developer team thinks that the current changes are the last. And then, the procedures of changing are repeated many times. After that new area of adaptation are defined – for example – structure of data sets or necessary interface changing.

© ICST Institute for Computer Sciences, Social Informatics and Telecommunications Engineering 2023
Published by Springer Nature Switzerland AG 2023. All Rights Reserved
T. Zlateva and G. Tuparov (Eds.): CSECS 2023, LNICST 514, pp. 144–155, 2023.
https://doi.org/10.1007/978-3-031-44668-9_11

2   Review of Papers

Approaches that are devoted to software reuse and estimation of reuse risks are developed as two adjacent branches. Summarizing of reuse practices gives a background for development of risks estimation standards and formal approaches of software reuse considering potential development risks.

Paper [2] proposes domain model for considering different reuse risks. It allows to estimate the next factors:

- risk level and its effect on the final subjective and objective project performance;
- the ineffective performance of software projects and the consequential costs
- time overruns,
- missed business prospects;
- errors in software project management activities;
- evaluation and estimation of project performance;
- other related aspects.

It is difficult to use the proposed model because the research questions for validation of the model allowing to estimate different risks were formulated clearly, but answered only partially [2].

Andres Orrego, Tim Menzies, and Oussama El-Rawas have classified reuse activities from different points of view using models COCOMO and COQUALMO. Authors have proposed reuse models and have compared the benefits of software reuse to other activities [3]. Based on this research, project managers have to weigh drawbacks and advantages of software development artifacts reuse. These drawbacks and advantages should be evaluated using results from Software Product Line (SPL) approach practices. They are project-by-project estimation and comparing of reuse tactics with other project development strategies.

Classification of activities is based on ranking and connected with a value of different efforts, schedule, and strategies of using models with competing influences that have not been precisely tuned using local data [3].

Russ Cox has examined the possible negative effects of software reuse. The author has ten years of experience with Google's source code system, which recognizes software dependencies as a first-class reuse problems [4].

Software dependencies are a significant and often overlooked risk. The move to the cheap and granular software reuse has happened so quickly that developers don't yet understand the best practices for choosing and using dependencies properly. The goal is to raise awareness of the danger and encourage further research into possible protections.

The simple models estimating the total cost for reuse can be represented as the sum of the cost of all bad decisions multiplied by the probability of their occurrence:

$$expectedcosts = \sum_{a \in badoutcomes} cost(a) \times probability(a) \tag{1}$$

Conclusions from the Review. Review of the papers shows that investigations in the reuse area deeply focused on some aspects of software reuse. Results often are focused on proposing some models or analytical fundamentals as well as developing common recommendations to answer the question – "How to manage reuse risks?".

From the other side, many efforts and experiments are needed to gather proposed ideas to one complex approach with possibility to organize reuse procedure considering peculiarities of project types, reuse errors and stack of technologies.

It becomes a motivation for author to propose an approach that consider peculiarities of reuse activities for GitHub (because it is a popular software repository) that is used in everyday activities of different stakeholders teams from all over the World.

3   Task and Research Questions

In order to propose the approach for estimation of software reuse risks for GitHub projects it is necessary to solve the next Research Questions (RQs):

RQ1: Investigate typical bugs for GitHub projects with multilayer architecture and summarize, which types of bugs are specific for these projects.

RQ2: Propose a model of reuse risk estimation.

RQ3: Summarize peculiarities for activities, performed in research laboratories, as well as activities aimed to analyze GitHub projects.

RQ4: Propose an approach for estimation of reuse risks for GitHub projects that is based on analysis of source modules semantics, considering specifics of work with GitHub. In order to do this, systematize knowledge about the next aspects from theoretical and practical backgrounds:

RQ4.1: gather and analyze information about the reuse activities from research labs of companies that follow Software Product Lines approach;

RQ4.2: conduct the experimental research, summarizing peculiarities of activities for investigating of different reuse risks of newly downloaded projects. The aim of this research is to define typical bugs for different projects and estimate a dependency between reuse risks, number, and quality of types of bugs for different projects.

4   Gathering of Experimental Data

Aim of this chapter is to define which bugs may be expected in project with multilayer architecture. Projects with multilayer architecture contain three (or more) levels of architecture representation. Examples –web applications (MVC, MVP, MVVM, multilayer applications with monolithic architecture etc.).

The first reuse risk is based on unclear understanding of requirements by all stakeholders.

Consider a part of a requirement specification from a real project (Fig. 1). Text is given without editors' changes.

The first part of specification, marked in yellow and (*), may be understood in different ways by front-end developer, user, tester, and other stakeholders. The seconds part marked in yellow and (**) is an error, because analysis of payment practices for medical services shows that it is necessary to provide payment for current medical service immediately, not later. Grey-marked part contains extra technical detail that is not necessary for user.

As a result of analysis of this requirement specification the first risk is defined.

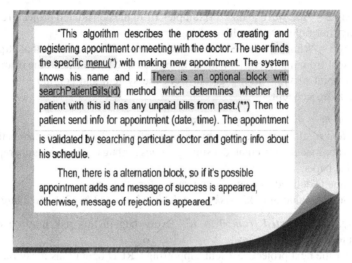

"This algorithm describes the process of creating and registering appointment or meeting with the doctor. The user finds the specific menu(*) with making new appointment. The system knows his name and id. There is an optional block with searchPatientBills(id) method which determines whether the patient with this id has any unpaid bills from past.(**) Then the patient send info for appointment (date, time). The appointment is validated by searching particular doctor and getting info about his schedule.

Then, there is a alternation block, so if it's possible appointment adds and message of success is appeared, otherwise, message of rejection is appeared."

Fig. 1. A fragment of a requirement specification

Risk1 - "Unclear Requirement Specification" and May Be Estimated from 0 to 20. Other risks are defined on the base on analysis of different multilayer application projects. Let's consider results of analysis for different projects.

Project 1: Web-application, which allows to people who have limited vision to book flight tickets.

System goal: possibility to sound text labels and zoom components while booking tickets. Also, possibility to recognize key words using Speech to Text module to perform some part of user scenario. (For example system recognizes a word "reject" and rejects the last booking).

The GitHub project with the closest functionality [5], namely project allowing to book tickets without adaptation needs for weak-eyed people, was investigated. Link to the video, describing project, is represented in [6].

Summary of analysis of bugs, defined in the project.

Project has some testing bugs, namely errors that were not improved during testing. Examples of such bugs are the next: it is impossible to input correct information about child age and cities names by two words. Other errors are related to main functionality of project. One of them is a limited functionality for search and representation of information.

As a result of analysis of bugs for this project the next risk is defined: *Risk2 – "Incorrect input processing".* This risk is based on limiting of some program features because initial information for performing some features is absent. Usually such a risk partially blocks executing of some features of the project.

Bugs that are related to this risk:

– risk 2 bug 1 – *"Incorrect data range".* Examples from the considered project are: there is no possibility to input a child age or input a city name by two words.

- risk 2 bug 2 – *"Interface errors"*. Examples from the considered project: representation only four fields for searching of flights.
- risk 2 bug 3 – *"REST errors"*. Sometimes the source of these errors is that http requests are not sent from interface elements to business logic level. One of the example from the user point of view: user logs out from the system and continues to see pages, specific to his account.

Description of the scheme of risks estimation.

Estimation of all bugs was done by several software development teams the expert evaluations approaches. Calculated resulting values for bugs' estimations are represented below in this paper.

Risk value is defined as a sum of the values for all its bugs.

For example, value of risk2: *risk2 = risk2 bug1 + risk2 bug2 + risk2 bug 3.*

Risk2 May Be Estimated from 0 to 15. Every bug in this risk may be estimated maximum to five points.

Consider the next project "System supporting CRUD operations for library".

The following project from GitHub about this topic was investigated [7]. Link for the video describing project is represented in [8].

As a result of analysis of bugs for this project the next risk is defined:

Risk3 – Resource Missing. Such a risk may be estimated from 0 to 20. Every bug in this risk may be estimated maximum to ten points.This project sometimes has "no database response" situations. This bug is named *"missing database access" (risk 3 bug 1)*. It happens when user can't get access to database (SQL server is not installed when it is needed or there is another business logic error).

Another bug is a *"missing of third-party service" (risk 3 bug 2)*, for example service from some cloud platform is not found.

Consider the next project: Game for study foreign languages.

Game goal: Improve user comprehension. Levels are started from listening words, then sentences, then reading of stories, and writing some words.

The following project from GitHub about this topic was investigated [9]. Link to the video is represented in [10].

During investigation of this project the next testing errors were defined: after switching the task, the window with previous task did not closed. As a result, user may confuse what task need to be completed. Thus, user's score may be calculated in a wrong way.

As a result of analysis of bugs for this project the next risk is defined:

Risk4 – "User Story Error". Such a Risk May Be Estimated from 1 to 5. Usually such a risk may partially confuse user to perform some actions with software.

Consider the next project: Medical system for remote consultations.

System goal: to register a patient and a doctor. Possibility to search doctor and time for appointment to doctor. Doctor can reject or change day or time of appointment. Video conference for appointment. Possibility to send messages and transmit files between doctor and patient. Doctor fills forms with parameters about patient health. System can visualize information about dynamic of patient health.

The next project from GitHub about this topic was investigated [11]. Link to the video is represented in [12].

As a result of analysis of this project the next bugs were defined:

- risk3 bug 1, namely *"missing database access"*. Project depends upon database version. The same bug is met one more time when new information is added or changed. It is implemented as "database updating error".
- risk4, namely *"User story risk"*, is defined. It is represented as unexpected closing of program.

As a result of the analysis of this project new risks and bugs were not defined. Bugs that are repeated will be considered in statistics.

Consider the next project: "Task management system for IT-company with communication module".

System goal: to obtain tasks from the project management, distribute tasks between team members. Possibility to organize meetings, and estimate characteristics of performed tasks (time. Software quality and other parameters). System has a statistics module.

The next project from GitHub about this topic was investigated [13]. Link to the video is represented in [14].

As a result of analysis of this project the next bugs were defined:

- risk2 bug 2, namely *"Interface errors"*. Some elements do not re-drawn correctly when interfaces are changed;
- risk2 bug 3, namely *"REST errors"*. Error of database updating after new information added or changed.
- risk4, namely *"User story risk"*. Sometimes there is an unexpected closing of program.

In such a manner the other projects for different topics were considered.

5   Summarizing of experimental research

Table 1 shows a classification of risks and defined bugs for considered projects. Numeric values of vulnerabilities of the risks and bugs are estimated by experts from different software developers' teams. In order to estimate maximum values of risks (in sentences from previous chapter: "such a risk may be estimated from...") and bugs, from three to five developer teams were involved. Resulting maximum values for bugs are represented in the previous chapter. Table 1 contains concrete values that are based on estimation of defined bugs for described projects.

Due to lack of place in the paper, only unique bugs and risks were described and recorded to video clips. If some risks and bugs were repeated more than one time, they were not being commented and were represented only in the table,

Figure 2 represents the summary of research for different projects. It shows results for fifteen projects with multilayer architecture, some of which were represented in the Table 1.

Table 1. Estimations of reuse risks for different projects

Type of risk and its code	Bugs for this risk and their codes	Names of the projects				
		Weak eyed people	CRUD Library	Game	Medical system	Bug tracing system
R1 Unclear requirement specification	R1_B1 Non correct representation of requirements	1	0	2	8	4
R2 Incorrect input processing	R2_B1 Incorrect data range	3	1	1	5	0
	R2_B2 interface errors	3	2	0	4	3
	R2_B3 REST Errors	4	1	0	5	3
R3 Resource missing	R3_B1 missing database access	0	3	0	7	10
	R3_B2 missing third-party service	4	4	0	2	0
R4 User story error	R4_B1 User is confused what to do	3	1	4	5	1

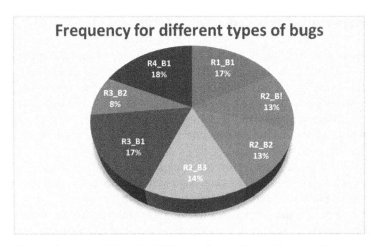

Fig. 2. Summary of bugs for GitHub projects with multilayer architecture.

6 Model for estimating of reuse risks

Every risk is estimated as a sum of values for all its bugs. Denote r_i as the current risk.

$$r_i = \sum_{j=1}^{n} b_j \tag{2}$$

where b_j - value of bug with number j for current risk.

Maximum risk value for project is estimated by the following way:

$$R = \sum_{i=1}^{n} r_j \tag{3}$$

Then the next question becomes actual – "What is the max value of risk from the range $0 \le R \le R_{max}$, where R_{max} is the value when all values of bugs are maximum?".

In order to answer to this question, the same teams of developers have performed the experimental researches. Their tasks were to realize software systems that correspond to system goals descripted for different projects (see chapter 3). Before realization of these projects, the value R for every project was estimated.

The experiment gives the basis for the next conclusion: if the value R for current project is inside of the range $0 \le R \le 0, 25R_{max}$ reuse activities may be performed successfully. One more recommendation was defined from reuse practices that usually successful reuse is done when a new project is developed on the base of one existing project. Link to the video for medical system project that was successfully realized by means of adding functionality is represented in [15].

Conclusion from this chapter. Represented experimental research should help to software teams to understand the background of estimation of reuse risk for unknown projects. Some of risks were analyzed in this chapter. Centrally, other types of risk and bugs, which were not considered here due to of lack of place of the paper, may be added.

It is recommended to use statistical information, represented on Fig. 1, and start to investigate projects from risks that are met more often. When researcher will come.

to the limit $0, 25R_{max}$, the estimation of a project reuse risks should stop.

7 Comparison of peculiarities of reuse activities in research labs and GitHub

The aim of this chapter is to investigate peculiarities of activities performed in research laboratories of different companies and GitHub reuse activities. It will represent a background for proposing an approach for estimation of reuse risks for software projects from GitHub. Table 2 summarizes defined peculiarities.

Table 2. Peculiarities of reuse activities in research laboratories and GitHub repositories.

Approaches that are implemented by research labs when software is prepared for reuse	Approach considering specific of GitHub
Initial data	
More or less structured information about source code from previous projects	GitHub system for searching of information about project using GitHub meta-attributes
Reuse conditions and peculiarities	
Employers work in the same technology stack (or inheritance technology stack) Company follows code quality standards, design patterns, standards for naming of variables, methods, and other approaches [16] Re-user may obtain real information about software (for example through investigating of bug-tracking systems or getting information from company chats) and consider projects details Components for reuse were tested while previous projects were developed [17] Previously developed services are integrated with Infrastructure of the company Projects are implemented following Software Product Line approach [16]	Similar functionality may appear in projects that are realized in different stacks of technologies Re-user may not understand approaches for designing code, comments, interface components and other projects' elements Some of projects may be not finished and functionality may be realized partially Some of projects may depend upon external sources, for example databases or cloud services that are located on customer resources Licensing policies may limit a reuse Sometimes it is no possible to adopt architectural solutions for reuse, for example, when it is necessary to reuse several projects simultaneously

8 Software Reuse Approach Based on Review and Analysis of Reuse Risks From Projects Uploaded to GitHub

The experimental results and the analysis of peculiarities of the activities, performed both in research laboratories and in GitHub, provide a background for designing of the new software reuse approach, allowing to estimate the reuse risks for projects that were uploaded to GitHub. The approach is designed on the base of activities that are performed in research laboratories of software companies. These activities were taken as a basis, because they provide the background to perform reuse operations on higher levels of maturity, as repositories of companies store not only software, but UML diagrams, documentation, and other software development artifacts, allowing to get knowledge about their semantic. Reuse activities are represented in the Table 3.

How to analyze this table?

Activities, mentioned in the middle, are common for both types of reuse.

Activities in left columns are realized in research laboratories. If effective performance of such activities is impossible for GitHub, specific steps for GitHub are represented in the right column. When activities from middle and right column will be read together the reader will receive all steps of the proposed approach.

Table 3. Software reuse approach based on review and analysis of reuse risks from projects uploaded to GitHub

1, Compose of requirement specification
2. Select existing projects with the same functionality
3. Obtain an information about functionality of existing working projects and corresponding documentation (textual description, UML diagrams, licensing policy, screenshots etc.)

3.1.1 Explore bug tracking systems and (or) task management system (Jira or others) for this projects 3.1.2 Get information about frameworks, skipped and improved bugs, software architecture. Unit tests etc	3.1.1 Avoid breaking licensing policies 3.1.2 Explore review of other users

4 Take decision about possibility of reusing of this code in new project [18]

4.1 Investigate the functionality of previous realized systems 4.2 Get information about users' feedback and maintenance activities 4.3 Find view models (front-end elements), unit test and other software development artifacts from other projects for reuse 4.4 Get information about statistic of their reuse	4.1 Perform black-box testing and calculate of value R using (2) and (3) for current project 4.2 Estimate common reuse risk

5. Analyze software architecture 5.1 Verify whether architecture follows SOLID design principles 5.2 Investigate level of dependencies between components 6. Perform other activities of software development lifecycle processes to Implement source code with new functionality

	6.1 Improve the source code of the project, using static code analysis approaches

9 Conclusions

The paper proposes an approach of software projects reuse considering peculiarities of GitHub. Actuality of this approach is approved by fact that GitHub is used by most of software development companies around the World. The proposed approach is based on practices of companies that are performed in research laboratories of great companies (for example IBM, Motorola, Hewlett Packard and many others) [18]. Peculiarity of the proposed approach is that it considers additional steps, allowing to manage reuse risks for unfamiliar projects. These reuse risks were gathered experimentally during analysis of GitHub projects' bugs for projects with multilayer architecture.

Estimation of reuse risks is based on the risk assessment model. Proposed model is flexible and may be extended and reused for different types of projects.

The proposed approach and the model allow to provide a background for raising of maturity level for reuse process, considering peculiarities of reuse activities for projects downloaded from GitHub. The higher maturity levels (fourth and fifth) expect analysis before performing activities, taking conclusions after activities, analyzing mistakes, and considering them in further operations. Performing reuse processes on high maturity level allows to save efforts and resources as well as to avoid situations when reusing may create more problems than advantages.

10   Further Research

It is planned to design the approach of different types of software development artifacts reusing (interface elements, 3D models, software services, and data structures) for multilayer applications.

In order to organize reuse activities it is planned to consider reuse procedures according to layers of multilayer architecture.

For UI and presentation layers, user-friendly and intuitive interfaces may be designed considering factors that influence to human cognitive and emotional abilities [19]. Such interfaces may reduce the next risks: R4 User story error and R2_B2 interface errors.

For business logic layer, collaboration of software services on different cloud platforms (for example Google Cloud Platform and Microsoft Azure) allows "to construct" applications that may help to solve actual tasks from the digital society development, for example, economics or public policy and public administration [20]. Other application of reusing services is education, namely implementing new visualization techniques [21] or development of new algorithms [22]. Reuse of services from reliable cloud platforms may reduce the next risks: R3_B2 missing third-party service.

References

1. Li, D., Tian, P.: Early prediction method of software reliability based on reuse analysis. In 2019 IEEE 4th Advanced Information Technology, Electronic and Automation Con-trol Conference (IAEAC), vol. 1, pp. 545–550. IEEE (2019)
2. Mohammadi, N., Goeke, L., Heisel, M., Surridge, M.: Systematic risk assessment of cloud computing systems using a combined model-based approach. In: Proceedings of the 22nd International Conference on Enterprise Information Systems ICEIS, vol. 2, pp. 53–66 (2020). ISBN: 978-989-758-423-7
3. Orrego, A., Menzies, T., El-Rawas, O.: On the relative merits of software reuse. In: Wang, Q., Garousi, V., Madachy, R., Pfahl, D. (eds) Trustworthy Software Development Processes. ICSP 2009. Lecture Notes in Computer Science, vol. 5543, pp. 186-197. Springer, Berlin, Heidelberg (2009). https://doi.org/10.1007/978-3-642-01680-6_18
4. Cox, R.: Surviving software dependencies: software reuse is finally here but comes with risks. Queue 17(2), 24–47 (2019)
5. NebbAirline GitHub repository https://github.com/Talevska/NebbAirline. Accessed 07 May 2023
6. Lab1_AM https://youtu.be/x6I3drPgM6I. Accessed 07 May 2023
7. Book library repository https://github.com/BnSalahFahmi/book-store. Accessed 07 May 2023
8. Video with bugs of library project https://drive.google.com/drive/folders/1rdHzulQE2UJ4-V6oxS49X9MleD0G2YZC?usp=share_link. Accessed 07 May 2023
9. English study game. https://drive.google.com/file/d/1LhHfuJzhHJ1OWSJxFjwkzdnXcYDJr Q8g/view. Accessed 07 May 2023

10. Game video. https://drive.google.com/drive/folders/1YWSSWEw3wiiq-EY2QbNbXfYQn uPiFY7z?usp=share_link. Accessed 07 May 2023
11. System for rehabilitation. https://github.com/heshanera/HealthPlus. Accessed 07 May 2023
12. Bugs for system HealphPlus. https://drive.google.com/drive/folders/1y8XCFSLoUjpa6e0nR Jtu5jl_hO4hIuXc?usp=share_link. Accessed 07 May 2023
13. Bugtacker. https://github.com/connorleee/BugTracker. Accessed 07 May 2023
14. Video for bug-tracking project. https://drive.google.com/drive/folders/1f6fBZy73-crsofdliy FKKdHg68ZVwrqP?usp=share_link. Accessed 07 May 2023
15. Videos of improvement medical system.https://drive.google.com/drive/folders/1Y0DjzihF o5qmJwAy5toYxIDWj5ARtMSQ?usp=share_link. Accessed 07 May 2023
16. Rajakumari, K.E.: Towards a novel conceptual framework for analyzing code clones to assist in software development and software reuse. In: 2020 4th International Conference on Intelligent Computing and Control Systems (ICICCS), pp. 105–111. IEEE (2020)
17. Griss, M.L.: Software reuse: from library to factory. IBM Syst. J. 32(4), 548-566 (1993). https://doi.org/10.1147/sj.324.0548
18. Dabhade, M., Shivam, S., Manjula, R.: A systematic review of software reuse using domain engineering paradigms. In: Online International Conference on Green Engineering and Technologies (IC-GET). IEEE (2016)
19. Yakovytska, L., Lych, O., Horskyi, O., Khokhlina, O.: Psychological features of emotional stability as a safety factor of air traffic specialists. Transp. Res. Proc. 63, 294–302 (2022). https://doi.org/10.1016/j.trpro.2022.06.016
20. Semenchenko, A., Gurkovskyi, V., Romanenko, Y., Sydorenko, V., Kudrenko, S., Polozhentsev, A.: Ukraine on the road to the european digital market: status and tools for implementing the European digital economy and society index in Ukraine. In: 1st International Workshop on Social Communication and Information Activity in Digital Humanities SCIA-2022, October 20, Lviv, Ukraine, pp. 186–197 (2022)
21. Mavrevski, R., Traykov, M., Trenchev, I.: Interactive approach to learning of sorting algorithms. Int.J. Online Biomed. Eng. (iJOE) 15(08), 120-133 (2019). https://doi.org/10.3991/ijoe.v15i08.10530
22. Mavrevski, R., Traykov, M.: Visualization software for Hydrophobic-polar protein folding model. Sci. Vis. 11(1), 11–19 (2019). https://doi.org/10.26583/sv.11.1.02

Health Informatics

AI-Enabled Infrared Thermography: Machine Learning Approaches in Detecting Peripheral Arterial Disease

Georgi Kostadinov[1,2]([⊠]) [iD]

[1] New Bulgarian University, 21 Montevideo str, 1618 Sofia, Bulgaria
georgi.kostadinov@kelvin.health
[2] Kelvin Health, 47A Cherni Vrah blvd, 1407 Sofia, Bulgaria

Abstract. Peripheral Arterial Disease (PAD) is a common circulatory problem that, if undetected or untreated, can lead to severe health consequences, including amputation. This study presents a novel approach to PAD detection using thermal data collected via a mobile thermal camera, processed, and analysed through various machine learning algorithms. The investigation focused on six machine learning models: Linear Regression, Decision Trees, Random Forest, Neural Network, XGBoost, and LightGBM, and their ability to predict the presence of PAD based on thermal features extracted from different angiosomes of the legs. Each model was trained and validated on a dataset consisting of thermal data from 42 patients, annotated with PAD status based on angiography diagnostics. The performance of each model was evaluated using eight metrics, including accuracy, sensitivity, and specificity. The results indicate that ensemble methods, particularly XGBoost and LightGBM, outperformed the other models with an accuracy of 96.8%. This research demonstrates the potential of thermal imaging coupled with machine learning for the detection of PAD, offering a non-invasive, accessible, and cost-effective diagnostic tool.

Keywords: Peripheral Arterial Disease · Machine Learning · Thermal Imaging · Predictive Models · XGBoost · LightGBM

1 Introduction

1.1 Challenges and Opportunities

Early detection and diagnosis of Peripheral Arterial Disease (PAD) remains a significant challenge in the medical field. Traditional diagnostic methods, often relying on patient-reported symptoms, may not be present until the disease has significantly progressed. However, the inception of modern machine learning (ML) methodologies presents an exciting opportunity to transform PAD diagnostics. Infrared (IR) thermography, a non-invasive tool capable of detecting subtle skin temperature changes, shows promise in detecting PAD [1], but the volume of data generated can be overwhelming.

© ICST Institute for Computer Sciences, Social Informatics and Telecommunications Engineering 2023
Published by Springer Nature Switzerland AG 2023. All Rights Reserved
T. Zlateva and G. Tuparov (Eds.): CSECS 2023, LNICST 514, pp. 159–170, 2023.
https://doi.org/10.1007/978-3-031-44668-9_12

Machine learning comes to the rescue in managing and interpreting this vast data. It can analyse thermal images, identify abnormalities indicative of PAD, and condense the most critical findings into a summarized report, effectively creating a 'synopsis' of a patient's thermal data. This innovative integration of AI and ML with infrared thermography not only increases efficiency but also significantly improves diagnostic accuracy, presenting a new way to revolutionize the early detection of PAD.

1.2 Related Work

The utilization of thermal imaging as a tool for detecting various medical conditions has been extensively studied in recent years [2], with a focus on its potential in diagnosing Peripheral Arterial Disease (PAD) and Diabetic Foot Ulcers (DFUs), given the high rise of patients with these conditions post-COVID.

For instance, in the study by [3], infrared thermography was used to evaluate the severity, functional capacity, and quality of life in patients at high risk for PAD. The study demonstrates the potential of thermography as a non-invasive tool for assessing patients with PAD. Meanwhile, [4] proposed a Support Vector Classification model for PAD identification using features extracted from infrared thermography images.

Various researchers have explored the application of ML techniques in the early diagnosis of DFUs using thermogram images. In a study by [5], asymmetric analysis of temperature features was used for detecting diabetic foot ulcer. The study reported an impressive sensitivity and specificity of 96.5 and 92.41% respectively. Similarly, [6] proposed a machine learning-based model for classifying thermal distribution patterns in the feet of diabetic patients. Several other studies, such as [7, 8], and [9], have further explored the potential of machine learning techniques in interpreting thermogram images for the detection of DFUs.

These studies, however, mostly focus on the detection of foot ulcers in diabetic patients and do not specifically target the detection of PAD. Furthermore, most of the models proposed in these studies, such as Support Vector Machines, are simpler compared to the ensemble and neural network approaches evaluated in this research. This paper also presents a thorough comparison of these machine learning approaches in their ability to detect PAD from thermographic data as well as analysis of four thermal features and their relation to the performance of such models that will help guide further research in the field.

The rest of the paper is structured as follows. Section 2 discusses the proposed work with an overview of the algorithms and metrics used. Section 3 presents the collection, annotation, and processing of the thermal dataset, which forms the basis of this research. Section 4 is explaining the mechanics of the six machine learning (ML) methodologies selected in the presented work, with a specific emphasis on their application in detecting Peripheral Arterial Disease (PAD) through IR thermography data. In Sect. 5, the metrics for the evaluation of the selected methodologies, as well as the results achieved are presented. Finally, in Sect. 6, conclusions are drawn, and the future work is presented.

2 Proposed Work

This paper is an extension of the work presented in [1] by providing a comprehensive overview of the technology and methodologies incorporated within the Artificial Intelligence Supported Infrared Thermography (AISIT) system.

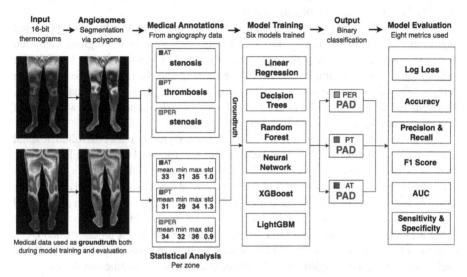

Fig. 1. Proposed work – six models were trained and evaluated by eight metrics in total.

The data acquisition process is detailed, illustrating how the infrared thermographic data is captured, processed, and prepared for further analysis by machine learning models. A discussion on which features are extracted from the thermal images is included.

Moreover, as visualised in **Fig. 1,** six various machine learning (ML) methodologies are explored, ranging from established techniques such as decision tree, random forest, as well as linear regression to more complex methods such as neural networks, XGBoost, and LightGBM. Each of these machine learning techniques is analysed and evaluated based on their ability to accurately identify PAD on IR data. This includes a comparative study detailing the performance metrics for each model, and an analysis on the feature importance used during training.

By offering a more in-depth exploration of the AISIT system from [1] and evaluating various machine learning methodologies, this paper aims to significantly contribute to the ongoing research in the field of PAD detection and diagnostics. Insights from this investigation can potentially drive the development of more accurate and efficient PAD detection systems based on AI and thermography.

3 Dataset

The study utilizes a dataset comprising thermal data from 42 patients, captured via a mobile thermal camera, FLIR One Pro. This dataset is based on the data used in the study in [1]. For each patient, thermal readings were taken from five different angles of the legs—front, back, left, right, and the feet. Additionally, the data collection process includes data from Angiography diagnostics.

The dataset from [1] contains a total of 313 medically and technically annotated angiosome regions of the legs of the 42 patients, with 78% of the regions identified as healthy and 22% - with pathology. Out of these 313 annotated samples, 60% or 188 randomly selected samples were used for training and the rest 125 - for validation purposes. The dataset encompasses a demographic variety [1], with 79% male patients, 21% females, all of Caucasian ethnicity, and a mix of additional factors, with 54% of the patients having diabetes and 76% being smokers.

The data collection process followed a strict medical protocol in a controlled hospital environment, as outlined in [1]. The thermal data was captured using the FLIR mobile thermal camera, taking readings from five different angles of the patient's legs. After that, each angiosome of the leg was manually annotated using the Supervisely[1] software, where polygonal segmentations were used to define each angiosome within the thermal image. Figure 1 demonstrates the process of collecting and annotating data for two angles of the legs – front and back, and three arterial regions, namely, for anterior tibial (AT), posterior tibial (PT), and peroneal (PER) arteries. The same process applies for all five angles and, in total, nine angiosomes of the legs. Each of the angiosome annotations of the legs corresponded with the results from the angiography diagnostics, which categorised each angiosome as healthy, stenosis, or thrombosis. For the purpose of this research, the categories of stenosis and thrombosis were combined into a single category labelled 'PAD,' leaving the healthy category as is.

The raw thermal images were processed into temperature readings using the raw2temp procedure from the R package Thermimage[2]. These temperature readings were subsequently used to extract thermal statistics from each segmented angiosome. Specifically, four thermal features were extracted: mean, minimum, maximum, and standard deviation of the temperature, as also shown on Fig. 1. These features form the basis for training the six ML models used in this study.

4 Machine Learning Methodologies

This section provides an overview of the theoretical foundations and practical implementation details of six machine learning methodologies. These models have been selected due to their ease of implementation, usability, and high interpretability. The emphasis on interpretability is of paramount importance given the context of medical AI systems, where the capability to provide explainable results is crucial. Thus, this section lays the groundwork for the subsequent analysis discussed in this research.

---

[1] Supervisely annotation software – https://supervisely.com.

[2] Thermimage R package - https://cran.r-project.org/web/packages/Thermimage.

4.1 Linear Regression

Linear regression is a fundamental method in statistics and machine learning [10], aiming to forecast a dependent variable based on a set of independent variables. The assumed linear relationship can be represented by the equation:

$$Y = \beta_0 + \beta_1 W_1 + \cdots + \beta_n W_n + \varepsilon \tag{1}$$

Here, Y is the dependent variable, W_1 through W_n are the independent variables, β_0 is the y-intercept, β_1 through β_n are the coefficients quantifying the influence of each W on W, and ε is the random error term. The implementation of the linear regression algorithm was done in the Python[3] programming language using the LinearRegression routines from the library Scikit-learn[4].

In the context of machine learning for Peripheral Arterial Disease (PAD) detection, linear regression can be used to determine the relationship between the four thermal data features (independent variables) and the presence or progression of PAD (dependent variable). The model is trained to minimize the differences between predicted and actual PAD status. Subsequently, it can predict PAD status based on new thermal data inputs.

4.2 Decision Tree

A decision tree [11] has a hierarchical model structure used in decision making and machine learning, consisting of nodes representing features, branches symbolizing decision rules, and leaves indicating outcomes. The root node, positioned at the top, partitions the data based on attribute values. This process runs throughout the tree, leading to a set of decision-making rules.

The decision tree algorithm used in this study is configured with several key parameters. The splitting criterion is set to Gini impurity, which measures the degree of class imbalance at each node. The maximum number of features used for splitting is set to 90% of the total features, while the minimum number of samples required to split a node is set at 30. The tree's maximum depth is limited to 4 to prevent overfitting. The log loss evaluation metric here is used to quantify the difference between predicted probabilities and true class labels. For the technical implementation of the algorithm, the DecisionTreeClassifier routines from the Scikit-learn library were used.

In the context of PAD detection with infrared thermography data, a decision tree can be trained to classify data into 'PAD' and 'healthy' groups based on the thermal features. The model partitions the data based on a series of binary decisions. The path from root to leaf provides a clear set of conditions leading to the prediction, making decision trees particularly interpretable, thus favourable for applications in the medical field.

4.3 Random Forest

A Random Forest [12] is an ensemble learning approach that is essentially a collection of decision trees, each constructed from a different subsample of the training data. The

---

[3] Python programming language - https://python.org.

[4] Scikit-learn Python package - https://scikit-learn.org.

final output of the model is derived by aggregating the predictions from all trees in the ensemble, typically using majority voting for classification tasks or averaging for tasks involving regression.

Using the same parameters as specified in 4.2, each decision tree within the Random Forest is built. The log loss evaluation metric, which quantifies the discrepancy between predicted probabilities and true class labels, is used for assessing the performance during training. The implementation was done using the RandomForestClassifier routines from the Scikit-learn library.

In the context of PAD detection, a Random Forest can utilize the variability in the thermal data features to train a multitude of decision trees. This ensemble approach provides a robust prediction model as it reduces the risk of overfitting seen in single decision trees and increases the generalizability of the model.

4.4   Neural Networks

Artificial neural networks (ANN) are hierarchical structures with layers consisting of nodes called neurons [13]. Each neuron applies a weighted sum to its inputs, the output of which is further calculated using a non-linear function, often referred to as the activation function.

In the presented work, a neural network with two dense, or fully connected, layers are utilized. The first dense layer contains 32 neurons, and the second contains 16. Each neuron in a dense layer is connected to every neuron in the previous layer, and the number of neurons in a layer can be seen as a measure of the layer's complexity or capacity.

The learning rate, a key parameter in training neural networks, is set at 0.05. This parameter determines the size of the steps taken during stochastic gradient descent [14] - the optimization algorithm commonly used to minimize the loss function in neural networks. The ANN architecture and training code was implemented using the PyTorch[5] library.

For the detection of PAD using infrared thermography data, the model is trained on the four thermal features in order to classify the data into the two categories. The log loss evaluation metric was used for minimizing the error rate. Despite its complexity, the neural network can provide a high level of accuracy in predicting PAD status, making it a valuable tool in this application.

4.5   XGBoost

The eXtreme Gradient Boosting (XGBoost) [15] model is a powerful ensemble learning method that leverages the concept of boosting weak learners. It is based on the gradient boosting framework but has been enhanced with a more regularized model formalization to control overfitting and increase performance.

In its essence, XGBoost constructs a strong predictive model, ensemble of multiple weaker predictive models, typically decision trees. Each new tree is grown to correct the residuals (the differences between the predicted and expected results) of the previous trees. The final prediction is calculated as the weighted sum of the predictions made

---

[5] PyTorch deep learning framework - https://pytorch.org.

by all the trees in the ensemble. The objective function of XGBoost that needs to be minimized can be represented as follows:

$$Objective = \sum_{i=1}^{N} \mathcal{L}(y_i, \hat{y}_i) + \sum_{k=1}^{K} \Omega(f_k) \tag{2}$$

where N are the number of data samples, K are the number of decision trees, $\mathcal{L}$ is the loss function that measures the difference between the actual and predicted values, and $\Omega(f_k)$ is the regularization term. The first term encourages the model to fit the data well, while the second term discourages overfitting. In the context of this research, $\mathcal{L}$ is the log loss detailed in the next section. The goal is to predict the probability of the instance being a positive class, which in this context refers to the presence of PAD.

The parameters of the XGBoost model have been tuned to optimize its performance on the specific task of detecting PAD using infrared thermography data. The learning rate is set to 0.075, controlling the shrinkage of the step size used in updates to prevent overfitting. The parameter for maximum depth of a tree is set to 6, balancing the model's complexity and its ability to learn fine-grained patterns. For the implementation of the algorithm, the Python library Xgboost[6] was selected for its ease of use and supported hardware.

XGBoost is a suitable choice for this study given its ability to handle a variety of data types, robustness to outliers, and capability to model complex non-linear relationships, all of which are critical in interpreting infrared thermography data for PAD detection. Its use of gradient boosting framework [15] also offers a robust mechanism for minimizing errors, offering high predictive accuracy.

4.6 LightGBM

LightGBM [16], standing for Light Gradient Boosting Machine, is another gradient boosting framework that employs tree-based methodologies. It is renowned for its speed and efficiency, as well as its suitability for handling large-scale data. LightGBM differs from other tree-based algorithms in its decision-making strategy, opting for a leaf-wise approach over the more conventional level-wise approach. This results in a more complex tree, but it also generally yields lower loss, contributing to better accuracy.

In the context of this project, the LightGBM model is configured for a binary classification task. The parameter for number of leaves, one of the critical parameters for model complexity, is set to 63. The learning rate is set to 0.05. The feature and bagging fraction parameters are both set to 0.9, meaning that 90% of the features and data are used at each iteration, respectively, adding an additional layer of randomness to make the model more robust to overfitting.

The minimum amount of data per leaf is set to 10. This parameter is a regularization measure that prevents the algorithm from creating leaves with fewer than 10 data points, further preventing overfitting. The training process is guided by the log loss metric, similarly to the models before. The implementation was done using the LightGBM[7] software library, maintained by Microsoft.

---

[6] Xgboost Python library - https://xgboost.readthedocs.io/

[7] LightGBM software toolkit - https://github.com/microsoft/LightGBM.

In summary, LightGBM's unique approach to tree building and flexible handling of different types of features, combined with its speed and efficiency, makes it an excellent tool for detecting PAD using infrared thermography data. The selected parameters are specifically aimed at reducing overfitting and achieving high predictive accuracy.

5 Results

5.1 Metrics

To evaluate and quantify the performance of each of the six models and facilitate comparison across them, eight metrics in total are employed. During the training phase, the log loss metric has been selected as the most appropriate for the binary classification task of detecting PAD. For validation purposes, the selected metrics are accuracy, precision, recall, F1 score, Area Under the Receiver Operating Characteristic curve (AUC), as well as sensitivity and specificity. Each of these metrics offers a unique perspective on the performance of the models, capturing different aspects of the prediction results.

Log Loss. The log loss [17] for binary classification problems can be computed as:

$$\mathcal{L} = -\frac{1}{N}\sum\nolimits_{i=1}^{N}\left(y_i\log(\widehat{y_i}) + (1 - y_i)\log(1 - \widehat{y_i})\right) \tag{3}$$

Here, N is the number of samples or instances, y_i is the actual class label (0 or 1 in binary classification) for label i, and $\widehat{y_i}$ is the predicted probability that the sample belongs to a particular class. Due to the logarithmic function, predictions that are close to the true values contribute a small amount to the overall loss, while predictions that are far off contribute significantly more.

Log loss provides a more nuanced view of the performance of a model than metrics like accuracy, as it considers the probability distributions of the predicted probabilities. Furthermore, comparing log loss to other loss metrics such as Mean Squared Error (MSE) and Mean Absolute Error (MAE), it has the advantage of being more sensitive to the confidence of prediction [17], which can be a useful property in binary classification problems. However, it is also more sensitive to outliers and can be more difficult to interpret than some other metrics, like MAE or MSE.

Accuracy, Precision, Recall, F1 Score. These are the basic metrics commonly used in evaluating machine learning tasks [18]. Accuracy represents the ratio of correct predictions from the total number of predictions. While precision is the ratio of the true positive among all positive predictions, providing a measure of the ability to correctly detect cases with PAD, recall is the ratio of the true positive among all actual positive cases, reflecting the model's capacity to detect PAD cases. Finally, the F1 score is the harmonic mean of both precision and recall, making it a unifying metric that balances the two. It offers a more balanced measure when the class distribution is uneven.

AUC. Area under the ROC Curve (AUC) [19] is a robust metric for binary classification problems as it measures the ability to distinguish between the classes at various threshold settings. The ROC curve plots the true positive rates against the false positive rates at multiple thresholds, and AUC measures the entire two-dimensional area underneath this curve. An AUC of 1 signifies a perfect classifier, whereas an AUC of 0.5 speaks for a model equivalent to random guessing.

Sensitivity and Specificity. In the medical field, these are the two most common metrics that evaluate the performance of a binary classification test [20].

Sensitivity measures the ratio of actual positive cases that are correctly identified as such. It is extremely important in the medical field as it gauges the ability to correctly diagnose patients with a particular disease. The higher the sensitivity, the lower the chances of a false negative result. Sensitivity is calculated as follows:

$$Sensitivity = \frac{TP}{TP + FN} \tag{4}$$

Specificity measures the ratio of actual negative cases that are correctly identified. In the medical context, this means the ability to correctly diagnose healthy patients as healthy. High specificity correlates to less false positives, which is important in order to avoid unnecessary treatments or interventions. Specificity is calculated as follows:

$$Specificity = \frac{TN}{TN + FP} \tag{5}$$

In the context of Peripheral Arterial Disease detection, high sensitivity ensures that patients with the disease are identified, reducing the risk of false negatives. This is particularly important in medical conditions where early detection can significantly improve the prognosis. On the other hand, high specificity ensures that healthy individuals are not falsely identified as having the disease, thus avoiding unnecessary further tests or treatments.

5.2 Feature Importance

For each model, a feature importance matrix was generated, revealing important insights about the significance of the four temperature-based features in predicting the presence of Peripheral Arterial Disease. As seen in Fig. 2, the standard deviation of temperature

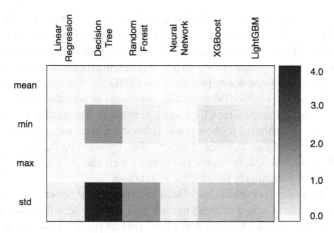

Fig. 2. Feature importance matrix for each model.

consistently emerged as the most influential feature across all machine learning models. This suggests that variation in temperature, rather than just average or extreme values, plays a crucial role in identifying PAD. The minimum temperature was typically the second most important feature, suggesting that the coldest temperature readings may be indicative of compromised blood flow, a characteristic symptom of PAD.

Interestingly, the mean temperature and maximum temperature demonstrated varying levels of importance across different models. While these features held some predictive power in models such as Linear Regression, XGBoost, and LightGBM, they were deemed unimportant by the Decision Trees and Random Forest models. This discrepancy underlines the complexity of PAD detection and the need for a multi-faceted approach.

Overall, these results, underscore the importance of considering the entire range of temperature characteristics - including the mean, extremes, and variability - in the thermographic analysis for PAD detection.

5.3   Performance Analysis

Table 1. Comparative model performance analysis for metrics log loss (Loss), accuracy (Acc.), precision (Pre.), recall (Rec.), F1 score (F1), AUC, sensitivity (Sens.), and specificity (Spec.).

Model	Loss	Acc	Pre	Rec	F1	AUC	Sens	Spec
Linear Regression	0.341	0.873	0.75	1.0	0.588	0.87	0.3	0.981
Decision Trees	0.267	0.873	1.0	1.0	0.512	0.857	0.2	1.0
Random Forest	0.2	0.92	0.667	1.0	0.8	0.977	1.0	0.906
Neural Network	0.358	0.857	0.6	1.0	0.533	0.825	0.3	0.962
XGBoost	0.141	0.968	1.0	1.0	0.909	0.975	1.0	0.962
LightGBM	0.111	0.968	1.0	1.0	0.909	0.985	1.0	0.962

The results of the ML methodologies trained on the thermal data for Peripheral Arterial Disease (PAD) detection are presented in Table 1. Each model was evaluated on all eight metrics. The results obtained from the trained models indicate varying degrees of performance. The performance metrics reveal different aspects of each model's ability to correctly predict the presence or progression of PAD.

Among the models, LightGBM and XGBoost stand out with the lowest log loss and the highest accuracy, precision, recall, F1 score, sensitivity, and specificity. This superior performance can be attributed to their gradient boosting mechanisms, which optimizes the models by iteratively adding weak learners, thereby reducing the bias and variance. Moreover, these models handle feature interactions well and are resistant to overfitting, which makes them particularly suitable for this dataset.

In contrast, Linear Regression and Decision Trees show fewer promising results. The relatively simple structure of these models may struggle with the complex patterns in the thermal data. While Decision Trees have perfect precision, its lower sensitivity indicates its difficulty in detecting true positive PAD cases.

The Random Forest model, an ensemble of Decision Trees, significantly improves the performance over a single Decision Tree, as shown by its lower log loss and higher accuracy, F1 score, and AUC. This improvement underscores the power of ensemble methods in handling complex datasets.

The Neural Network also demonstrates a reasonable performance, although it doesn't outperform LightGBM and XGBoost. This could be due to the relatively simple architecture that was chosen and its hyperparameters or the need for more data to effectively train the network.

These results have several implications for the field. First, they demonstrate the potential of machine learning, particularly advanced gradient boosting models, in detecting PAD using thermal data. This application could significantly enhance early detection and treatment of PAD, thereby improving patient outcomes. Second, these results may guide future research on PAD detection on thermal data, suggesting that focus could be directed towards optimizing models like LightGBM and XGBoost or exploring other complex models, such as deeper neural networks.

6 Conclusions

6.1 Summary

This study presented a comprehensive analysis of six ML models applied to a unique dataset of thermal images from [1] to detect Peripheral Arterial Disease (PAD). The dataset, based on thermal data from 42 patients, was processed and medically annotated, extracting four thermal features from each angiosome region for the training of the models. Importance analysis for each feature was also discussed, that would navigate future research on the topic.

Six models, namely Linear Regression, Decision Trees, Random Forest, Artificial Neural Networks, XGBoost, and LightGBM were trained and evaluated. A variety of metrics, including log loss, accuracy, precision, recall, F1 score, AUC, sensitivity, and specificity were employed to provide a holistic view of the models' performance. The results showed that ensemble models such as XGBoost and LightGBM generally outperformed other models, with LightGBM exhibiting the best overall performance.

6.2 Future Work

While the results of this research are promising, there is always room for growth and further exploration in the field. Future work could include the inclusion of more diverse data, encompassing patients from different ethnic backgrounds, varying age groups, and other lifestyle factors, to increase the generalizability of the models. The exploration of additional thermal features from each angiosome could be further looked into in order to improve the accuracy of the detection models. While six machine learning models were examined in this study, there are numerous other ML models that can be tested, such as convolutional neural networks (CNN), which have shown to perform significantly better in image-based tasks [21]. Lastly, future research could investigate the integration of these models into clinical decision support systems, providing a tool that can aid clinicians in diagnosing PAD. The findings of this study not only contribute to the growing body of research in the field of medically applied thermography and machine learning but also pave the way for future research in this area.

References

1. Stankov, Z., et al.: Infrared thermography—diagnostic method in peripheral artery disease. Arab J. Intervent. Radiol. **7**(S 01), A1217 (2023)
2. Wang, Q., et al.: Infrared thermography for measuring elevated body temperature: clinical accuracy, calibration, and evaluation. Sensors **22**(1) (2022)
3. Huang, C., et al.: The application of infrared thermography in evaluation of patients at high risk for lower extremity peripheral arterial disease. J. Vasc. Surg. **54**(4), 1074–1080 (2011)
4. Padierna, L.C., et al.: Classification method of peripheral arterial disease in patients with type 2 diabetes mellitus by infrared thermography and machine learning. Infrared Phys. Technol. **111**, 103531 (2020)
5. Saminathan, J., et al.: Computer aided detection of diabetic foot ulcer using asymmetry analysis of texture and temperature features. Infrared Phys. Technol. **105**, 103219 (2020)
6. Evangeline, N.C., et al.: Application of non-contact thermography as a screening modality for Diabetic Foot Syndrome – A real time cross sectional research outcome. Biomed. Signal Process. Control **79**, 104054 (2023)
7. Srinivasan, S., et al.: Development of AI classification model for angiosome-wise interpretive substantiation of plantar feet thermal asymmetry in type 2 diabetic subjects using infrared thermograms. J. Therm. Biol **110**, 103370 (2022)
8. Khandakar, A., et al.: A machine learning model for early detection of diabetic foot using thermogram images. Comput. Biol. Med. **137**, 104838 (2021)
9. Maldonado, H., et al.: Automatic detection of risk zones in diabetic foot soles by processing thermographic images taken in an uncontrolled environment. Infrared Phys. Technol. **105**, 103187 (2020)
10. Seber, G.A.F., Lee, A.J.: Linear Regression Analysis, vol. 330. Wiley (2003)
11. Swain, P.H., Hauska, H.: The decision tree classifier: design and potential. IEEE Trans. Geosci. Electron. **15**(3), 142–147 (1977)
12. Breiman, L., et al.: Random forests. Mach. Learn. **45**, 5–32 (2001)
13. Kostadinov, G.: Synopsis of video files using neural networks. In: Proceedings of the 23rd EANN 2022 (2022). https://doi.org/10.1007/978-3-031-08223-8_16
14. Bottou, L.: Large-scale machine learning with stochastic gradient descent. In: Proceedings of COMPSTAT'2010: 19th International Conference on Computational StatisticsParis France, August 22–27, 2010 Keynote, Invited and Contributed Papers. Physica-Verlag HD (2010)
15. Chen, T., et al: Xgboost: extreme gradient boosting. R Package Version 0.4–2 **1**(4), 1–4 (2015)
16. Ke, G., et al: LightGBM: a highly efficient gradient boosting decision tree. Adv. Neural Inf. Process. Syst. **30** (2017)
17. Vovk, V.: The fundamental nature of the log loss function. Fields of Logic and Computation II: Essays Dedicated to Yuri Gurevich on the Occasion of His 75th Birthday, pp. 307–318 (2015)
18. Handelman, G.S., et al.: Peering into the black box of artificial intelligence: evaluation metrics of machine learning methods. Am. J. Roentgenol **212**(1), 38–43 (2019)
19. Hanley, J.A., McNeil, B.J.: The meaning and use of the area under a receiver operating characteristic (ROC) curve. Radiology **143**(1), 29–36 (1982)
20. Sharm, D., Yada, U.B., Sharma, P.: The concept of sensitivity and specificity in relation to two types of errors and its application in medical research. J. Reliabil. Stat. Stud. 53–58 (2009)
21. Li, Z., et al.: A survey of convolutional neural networks: analysis, applications, and prospects. IEEE Trans. Neural Netw. Learn. Syst. (2021)

The Impact of Virtual and Augmented Reality on the Development of Motor Skills and Coordination in Children with Special Educational Needs

Martin Kolev[1], Ivan Trenchev[2] , Metody Traykov[1,3]([✉]) , Radoslav Mavreski[3] ,
and Iliyan Ivanov[3]

[1] New Bulgarian University, Sofia, Bulgaria
`ravenfrost@abv.bg, mtraykov@nbu.bg`
[2] University of Library Studies and Information Technologies, Sofia, Bulgaria
[3] South-West University "Neofit Rilski", Blagoevgrad, Bulgaria
`radoslav_sm@abv.bg, ivanov@swu.bg`

Abstract. This study investigates the impact of virtual reality (VR) and augmented reality (AR) interventions on the development of motor skills and coordination in children with special educational needs (SEN). Utilizing a mixed-methods approach, we employed customized VR/AR activities developed in Unreal Engine and integrated motion tracking technology to create an immersive and engaging environment tailored to the unique needs of the participants.

In this study, we present a methodology for supporting the education of children with SEN using Unreal Engine and NVIDIA VR Funhouse. Our approach focuses on designing immersive and engaging virtual reality (VR) and augmented reality (AR) interventions that target the development of motor skills and coordination in this population. By leveraging the advanced capabilities of Unreal Engine and NVIDIA VR Funhouse, we aim to create customized learning experiences tailored to the unique needs and abilities of children with SEN.

It is important to note that the practical implementation of the research, including participant recruitment, data collection, and analysis, will be conducted in a later stage of the study. The current focus is on developing and refining the methodology and the design of the VR/AR intervention. This groundwork will lay the foundation for future research endeavors, with the ultimate goal of enhancing educational outcomes and the overall well-being of children with SEN.

Keywords: virtual reality · augmented reality · Special Educational Needs · education

1 Introduction

In recent years, virtual and augmented reality (VR/AR) technologies have significantly advanced, offering new possibilities for a variety of applications. One promising area is the enhancement of motor skills and coordination in children with SEN. These children

T. Zlateva and G. Tuparov (Eds.): CSECS 2023, LNICST 514, pp. 171–181, 2023.
https://doi.org/10.1007/978-3-031-44668-9_13

often face unique challenges in developing motor and coordination abilities, which can impact their daily lives and overall well-being. This article aims to explore the potential benefits and applications of VR/AR technologies in supporting the development of these crucial skills in children with SEN. We will discuss the existing research on this topic, review various VR/AR tools and interventions, and consider potential future directions for the field [1–5].

Children with special educational needs often experience difficulties in acquiring and mastering motor skills and coordination. These challenges can arise from a range of conditions, including autism spectrum disorder, cerebral palsy, Down syndrome, and developmental coordination disorder. The development of motor skills and coordination is crucial for these children, as it can significantly impact their ability to perform daily activities, participate in social interactions, and achieve academic success.

Virtual and augmented reality technologies offer immersive and engaging environments that can be tailored to the specific needs and abilities of children with SEN. By simulating real-world scenarios and providing instant feedback, VR/AR can create a safe and controlled space for children to practice and develop their motor skills and coordination. In this section, we will examine how VR/AR can be utilized to support motor skill development, including gamification, adaptive difficulty levels, and personalized interventions [4, 6–12].

Our study will consider various approaches and interventions that have employed VR/AR technologies to improve motor skills and coordination in children with SEN. We will discuss specific tools and methods used. Additionally, we will highlight the challenges and limitations encountered in implementing VR/AR-based interventions, and how researchers and practitioners can address these issues [8, 12–17].

The use of virtual and augmented reality technologies holds great promise in supporting the development of motor skills and coordination for children with special educational needs. By providing immersive, engaging, and personalized experiences [15, 18, 19, 41, 43], VR/AR can give us an innovative and effective means to address the unique challenges faced by these children. Further research and collaboration among researchers, educators, and technology developers will be crucial in maximizing the potential of VR/AR to enhance the lives of children with SEN and their families [19–21].

This research is in the beginning and in this study, we present a technical part of the investigation. The activities mentioned here will be designed in collaboration with special education experts from different universities in Bulgaria to ensure that our approaches were engaging, accessible, and tailored to the unique needs of the participating children.

2   Methodology

To systematically investigate the impact of virtual and augmented reality on the development of motor skills and coordination in children with special educational needs, we will use a mixed-methods approach that incorporates both quantitative and qualitative research methods. This comprehensive methodology will allow us to gain a deeper understanding of the effectiveness and potential limitations of VR/AR interventions [22–35].

Qualitative data from interviews and observations will be transcribed and analyzed using thematic analysis, identifying common themes and patterns related to the children's experiences with the VR/AR intervention [25, 39]. The study will be conducted in accordance with ethical guidelines, ensuring informed consent from the caregivers and assent from the children. Confidentiality and privacy will be maintained throughout the research process, and all data will be securely stored and anonymized.

The technical methodology, which we use in our research, study revolves around the use of Unreal Engine to develop and implement a VR/AR intervention targeting motor skills and coordination in children with special educational needs. In this section, we will describe the specific technical aspects of the study and the process for examining motor skills using the capabilities of Unreal Engine.

Using Unreal Engine, we created a series of customized VR/AR activities that focus on specific motor skills and coordination abilities relevant to our target population. To achieve this, we shall utilize features such as [12–18, 25, 36]:

- Customizable difficulty levels and game mechanics to accommodate different motor abilities. One of the procedures that simplifies the designing of new levels is the reuse of software development artifacts. One of the approaches is described in [49].
- Sensory accommodations, including adjustable visual and auditory settings, to cater to the sensory needs of the participants.
- User-friendly interfaces and clear instructions to create an accessible and comfortable environment.

To effectively analyze and evaluate the motor skills and coordination of the participants within the VR/AR environment, we integrated motion tracking technology into the intervention. This technology allowed us to capture the participants' movements in real-time, providing us with accurate and detailed data on their performance during the VR/AR activities. We used Unreal Engine's compatibility with various motion tracking systems, such as HTC Vive trackers or Oculus sensors, to achieve this [2, 5, 33, 36, 38, 42–48].

Throughout the intervention, which will take place later in the project, we shall collect a range of data to assess the progress of the participants and the effectiveness of the VR/AR activities. This data will include [12, 25, 48]:

- Motion tracking data: By recording the participants' movements during the VR/AR sessions, we will be able to analyze their motor skills and coordination abilities, as well as identify any areas of improvement or difficulty.
- Performance metrics: We will gather data on the performance of the participants in the VR/AR activities, such as task completion time, error rates, and improvement over time. This is going to allow us to evaluate the impact of the intervention on their motor skills development.

Using Unreal Engine's built-in data analysis tools, we can process and analyze the collected data to gain insights into the participants' progress and the effectiveness of the VR/AR intervention [25, 35, 39, 43].

Following the completion of the VR/AR intervention, we will conduct post-intervention assessments using the same standardized tests employed during the pre-intervention phase (e.g., MABC-2, BOT-2). This would allow us to compare the participants' motor skills and coordination abilities before and after the intervention, providing a comprehensive evaluation of their effectiveness [5, 15, 18, 19, 23].

Our technical methodology for studying motor skills using Unreal Engine involves the development of customized VR/AR activities, integration of motion tracking technology, systematic data collection and analysis, and pre- and post-intervention assessments. This approach shall allow us to effectively examine the impact of the VR/AR intervention on the motor skills and coordination of children with special educational needs, providing valuable insights into the potential benefits and limitations of this technology [34–40].

By employing this mixed-methods approach, we aim to provide a comprehensive understanding of the impact of virtual and augmented reality on the development of motor skills and coordination in children with special educational needs, as well as the potential benefits, challenges, and future directions for VR/AR interventions in this context.

3 Result

NVIDIA VR Funhouse is a virtual reality (VR) application that showcases the advanced capabilities of the NVIDIA GameWorks, VRWorks, and PhysX technologies. By leveraging the power of Unreal Engine, a widely-used and versatile game engine, NVIDIA VR Funhouse can be adapted and integrated into our research study to create engaging and immersive VR experiences tailored for children with special educational needs (SEN) [24, 28, 29, 38, 41–48].

To effectively use NVIDIA VR Funhouse for our study, we customized existing mini-games and environments to address the specific motor skills and coordination challenges faced by children with SEN. In order to precise a game scenario, the approach to recovering behavioral UML diagram [50] was used. During reverse engineering activities in order to restore class diagrams structure the approach [51] was used. This involves:

1. Modifying the difficulty levels and game mechanics to accommodate varying levels of motor abilities.
2. Incorporating sensory accommodations, such as customizable visual and auditory settings, to cater to the unique sensory needs of the participants (see Fig. 1).
3. Ensuring that the game environment is accessible, safe, and comfortable for children with SEN, by designing user-friendly interfaces and providing clear instructions.

The customized NVIDIA VR Funhouse mini-games were incorporated into the VR/AR intervention as engaging and interactive activities that target specific motor skills and coordination abilities. For example:

1. A modified version of the "Clown Painter" mini-game is used to practice fine motor skills, such as grasping and controlling a virtual spray paint can, while also working on hand-eye coordination [4, 28, 48].
2. The "Balloon Knight" mini-game is adapted to focus on gross motor skills, like swinging a virtual sword to pop balloons, which could help improve arm movement and spatial awareness (see Fig. 2) [4, 33, 41–44].

During the intervention, participants join these customized VR Fun-house mini-games, with their performance and progress tracked and recorded for subsequent analysis. Using NVIDIA VR Funhouse and Unreal Engine give us several advantages:

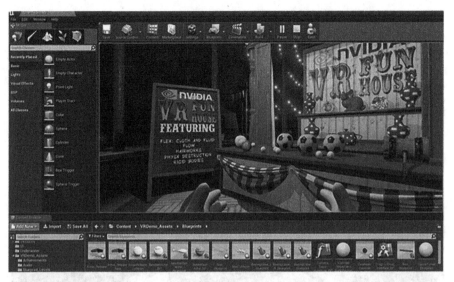

Fig. 1. Created a virtual circus world for children's education in NVIDIA VR Funhouse.

Fig. 2. A child playing in a virtual reality system in NVIDIA VR Funhouse.

1. High-quality graphics and realistic physics simulations create an immersive and engaging environment that can motivate children with SEN to participate in the intervention.
2. The customizable nature of the mini-games allows for personalized experiences tailored to each participant's unique needs and abilities of each participant.
3. Integration with Unreal Engine enables researchers to leverage a vast array of tools and resources, streamlining the development process and facilitating collaboration among developers and researchers.

Using NVIDIA VR Funhouse for Unreal Engine we can harness the power of VR technology to create immersive and engaging experiences that support the development of motor skills and coordination in children with special educational needs (see Fig. 3).

Fig. 3. Management of assets in a virtual reality system

To enhance the effectiveness of the VR/AR intervention, we created a multi-player experience using Unreal Engine's Blueprint system. This allows the child and the therapist (e.g., speech therapist, psychologist) to participate in the same virtual environment simultaneously. By doing this, the therapist can actively guide, support, and assess the child's progress in real-time, promoting a more interactive and collaborative learning experience.

Blueprint is a visual scripting system in Unreal Engine that allows developers to create game logic, interactions, and functionality without the need for traditional programming. To create a multiplayer experience with Blueprint, the following steps will be taken [12, 15, 32–37, 46]:

1. Establish a networked game: We set up a client-server architecture, enabling multiple devices to connect and interact in the same virtual environment. This involves configuring appropriate network settings and replication properties within Blue-print.
2. Create player characters: We designed unique player characters for the child and the therapist, incorporating different avatars, abilities, and interactions to suit their respective roles. These characters can be controlled using the respective input devices (e.g., VR controllers, keyboard/mouse) [1, 15, 19, 48].
3. Develop shared game mechanics: To facilitate meaningful interactions between the child and the therapist, we designed multiplayer game mechanics and activities that promote collaboration and communication. This can include tasks that require teamwork to complete or scenarios where the therapist provides guidance and feedback to the child [15, 18, 23, 33, 36, 48].
4. Implement real-time communication tools: To support effective communication between the child and the therapist, we integrated voice chat or other in-game

communication tools, allowing them to converse and collaborate within the virtual environment.

Integrating a multiplayer experience using Blueprint offers several advantages for our VR/AR intervention:

1. Enhanced engagement: By allowing the child and the therapist to interact in the same virtual environment, the intervention becomes more engaging and motivating, promoting active participation and learning.
2. Real-time guidance and support: The therapist can provide immediate feedback, encouragement, and adjustments to the child's performance, ensuring that the intervention is tailored to the child's needs and progress.
3. Improved assessment and evaluation: The therapist can closely monitor the child's development and engagement in the virtual environment, gaining valuable insights into the effectiveness of the intervention and the child's progress over time.

By incorporating a multiplayer experience using Unreal Engine's Blueprint system, we can create an interactive and collaborative VR/AR intervention that fosters a supportive learning environment for children with special educational needs while providing valuable real-time feedback and guidance from therapists.

4 Conclusion

In conclusion, our research on using virtual reality (VR) and augmented reality (AR) for the development of motor skills and coordination in children with special educational needs (SEN) highlights the potential benefits and challenges of integrating these technologies into educational interventions. By leveraging the advanced capabilities of Unreal Engine and NVIDIA VR Funhouse, we were able to create immersive, engaging, and customizable learning experiences tailored to the unique needs of children with SEN [4, 15, 38].

The preliminary results of our study indicate improvements in motor skills and coordination, as well as high levels of engagement and positive feedback from both participants and their caregivers. This suggests that VR and AR interventions can be effective tools for supporting the education of children with SEN, particularly in the context of motor skills and coordination development.

However, it is essential to acknowledge that this is an emerging field, and further research is needed to fully understand the long-term effects, optimal implementation strategies, and potential limitations of VR and AR interventions in special education. Future studies should consider larger and more diverse samples, as well as explore additional outcome measures and potential applications of these technologies in other areas of education and skill development for children with SEN.

In summary, our research contributes to the growing body of literature on the use of VR and AR in special education, offering valuable insights into the effectiveness and practical considerations of these interventions. As technology continues to advance, is vital for educators, researchers, and practitioners to stay informed and harness the potential of VR and AR to enhance the educational experiences and outcomes for children with special educational needs.

Acknowledgment. These research findings are supported by the National Scientific Research Fund, Project N КП-06-Н67/1.

References

1. Abdelmohsen, M., Arafa, Y.: Training social skills of children with ASD through social virtual robot. In: VR Workshops. IEEE, pp. 314–319 (2021)
2. Ali, N., Ferdig, R.: Why not Virtual Reality?: The Barriers of Using Virtual Reality in Education, pp. 1119–1120 (2002). http://www.editlib.org/f/10946
3. Baroutsis, A., White, S., Ferdinands, E., Goldsmith, W., Lambert, E.: Computational thinking as a foundation for coding: developing student engagement and learning, pp. 10–15 (2019). https://eprints.qut.edu.au/130998/2/130998.pdf; http://purl.org/au-research/grants/arc/
4. Benton, L., Johnson, H.: Widening participation in technology design: a review of the involvement of children with special educational needs and disabilities. Int. J. Child Comput. Interact **3**(4), 23–40 (2015)
5. Bossavit, B., Pina, A.: An interdisciplinary methodology for designing and implementing educational tools for children and youth with special needs. ACM SIGACCESS Access. Comput. **105**, 4–8 (2013)
6. Bryan, S., Campbell, A., Mangina, E.: Scenic spheres - an AR/VR educational game. In: GEM. IEEE, pp. 1–9 (2018)
7. Cai, S., Zhu, G., Wu, Y.-T., Liu, E., Hu, X.: A case study of gesture-based games in enhancing the fine motor skills and recognition of children with autism. Interact. Learn. Environ. **26**, 1039–1052 (2018)
8. Cavanaugh, C., Scheirer, E.: Meeting Needs of Refugee Children and Preservice Teachers through Educational Technology, pp. 698–705 (2007). http://www.editlib.org/f/24627
9. Chan, J., et al.: A systematic review of virtual reality for the assessment of technical skills in neurosurgery. Neurosurgical Focus **51**(2), Article no. E15 (2021). https://doi.org/10.3171/2021.5.focus21210,ISSN 1092–0684
10. Chu, E., Zaman, L.: Exploring alternatives with unreal engine's blueprints visual scripting system. Entertain. Comput. **36**, 100388 (2021). https://doi.org/10.1016/j.entcom.2020.100388
11. Dimitriadi, Y.: Special educational needs and information and communication technology: exploring a model for designing a teacher training course. In: Crawford, C., Davis, N., Price, J., Weber, R., Willis, D. (eds.) SITE 2003--Society for Information Technology & Teacher Education International Conference, pp. 1733–1736. Albuquerque, New Mexico, USA (2003)
12. Dimolareva, M.: Animal-Assisted Interventions in Special Needs Schools: What Works? (2020) https://eprints.lincoln.ac.uk/id/eprint/44792/; https://eprints.lincoln.ac.uk/id/eprint/44792/1/Dimolareva, Mirena - PhD - Psychology.pdf
13. Elwood, S., Zipprich, M.A.: Multimedia ePatternBooks through Mindtool and TypeII Applications. In: Carlsen, R., McFerrin, K., Price, J., Weber, R., Willis, D. (eds.) SITE 2007--Society for Information Technology & Teacher Education International Conference, pp. 1471–1473. San Antonio, Texas, USA (2007)
14. Fröberg, F.: Motorik - Konsekvenser och deras betydelse för idrott och hälsa (2021). http://urn.kb.se/resolve?urn=urn:nbn:se:mau:diva-40677
15. Hatzigiannakoglou, P., Okalidou, A.: Development of an auditory rehabilitation tool for children with cochlear implants through a mobile-based VR and AR serious game. Int. J. Online Biomed. Eng **15**, 81–90 (2019)

16. Hsiao, H.-S., Chen, J.-C.: Using a gesture interactive game-based learning approach to improve preschool children's learning performance and motor skills. Comput. Educ. **95**, 151–162 (2016)
17. Hussain, A., Mkpojiogu, E.O., Okoroafor, P.C.: Assisting children with Autism spectrum disorder with educational mobile apps to acquire language and communication skills: a review. Int. J. Interact. Mob. Technol **15**, 161–170 (2021)
18. Jiang, C., et al.: Co-simulation of the unreal engine and MATLAB/Simulink for automated grain offoading. IFAC-PapersOnLine **55**, 379–384 (2022)
19. John, N., Pop, S., Day, T., Ritsos, P., Headleand, C.: The implementation and validation of a virtual environment for training powered wheelchair manoeuvres. IEEE Trans. Visual Comput. Graphics **24**(5), 1867–1876 (2018)
20. Kauffman, J., Strang, H., Loper, A., Scholars, T.: Using micro-computers to train teachers of the handicapped. Rem. Spec. Educ. **6**(5), 13–17 (1984)
21. Kory-Westlund, J.: Relational AI: creating long-term interpersonal interaction, rapport, and relationships with social robots. Ph.D. Massachusetts Institute of Technology, School of Architecture and Planning (2019). https://hdl.handle.net/1721.1/123627
22. Kosmas, P., Ioannou, A., Retalis, S.: Using embodied learning technology to advance motor performance of children with special educational needs and motor impairments. In: Lavoué, É., Drachsler, H., Verbert, K., Broisin, J., Pérez-Sanagustín, M. (eds.) Data Driven Approaches in Digital Education - 12th European Conference on Technology Enhanced Learning, EC-TEL 2017, pp. 12–15, Tallinn, Estonia, September (2017)
23. Lauer, L., et al.: Investigating the usability of a head-mounted display augmented reality device in elementary school children. Sensors **21**(19), 6623 (2021)
24. Lee-Russell, C.: School partnerships: building a technology rich workforce. In: Proceedings of SITE 2012--Society for Information Technology & Teacher Education International Conference, pp. 3381–3386, Austin, Texas, USA (2012)
25. Lekova, A., Dimitrova, M., Kostova, S., Bouattane, O., Ozaeta, L.: BCI for assessing the emotional and cognitive skills of children with special educational needs. In: Mohajir, M., Achhab, M., Mohajir, B., Jellouli, I., (eds.) 5th IEEE International Congress on Information Science and Technology, pp. 400–403, Marrakech, Morocco (2018)
26. Mårell-Olsson, E., Mejtoft, T., Tovedal, S., Söderström, U.: Opportunities and challenges of using socially intelligent agents: increasing interaction and school participation for children suffering from a long-term illness. Int. J. Inf. Learn. Technol. **38**(4), 393–411 (2021)
27. Messer, D., Thomas, L., Holliman, A., Kucirkova, N.: Evaluating the effectiveness of an educational programming intervention on children's mathematics skills, spatial awareness and working memory. Educ. Inf. Technol. **23**, 2879–2888 (2018)
28. Norte, S.: A Sudoku Game for People with Motor Impairments (2007). http://arxiv.org/abs/0709.1056
29. NVIDIA®. VR Funhouse (2022). https://store.steampowered.com/app/468700/NVIDIA_VR_Funhouse/
30. Papakostas, G., et al.: Estimating children engagement interacting with robots in special education using machine learning. Math. Prob. Eng. **2021**, 1–10 (2021)
31. Pfeffer, K., Wilson, B.: Children's perceptions of dangerous substances. Percept. Mot. Skills **98**(2), 700–710 (2004)
32. Pistoljevic, N., Hulusic, V.: An interactive E-book with an educational game for children with developmental disorders: a pilot user study. In: International Conference on Virtual Worlds and Games for Serious Applications (VS-GAMES) (2017). https://hal.telecom-paris.fr/hal-02288497
33. Ragone, G., Good, J., Howland, K.: How technology applied to music-therapy and sound-based activities addresses motor and social skills in Autistic children. Multimodal Technol. Interact **5**, 11 (2021)

34. Rauschenberger, R., Barakat, B.: Health and safety of VR use by children in an educational use case. In: VR, IEEE, pp. 878–884 (2020)
35. Ricca, A., Chellali, A., Otmane, S.: Influence of hand visualization on tool-based motor skills training in an immersive VR simulator. In: ISMAR, IEEE, pp. 260–268 (2020)
36. Ricca, A., Chellali, A., Otmane, S.: The influence of hand visualization in tool-based motor-skills training, a longitudinal study. In: VR, IEEE, pp. 103–112 (2021)
37. Roby, T. Dehler, C.: What new teachers need to know about technology: a survey and recommendations for educational technologies integration in teacher preparation programs. In: Gibsocn, D., Dodge, B., (eds.) Proceedings of SITE 2010--Society for Information Technology & Teacher Education International Conference, pp. 1806–1813. San Diego, CA, USA (2010)
38. Rodríguez, A., Parra, O., Cañón, N.: AR support system for therapy in 3 to 8-year-old children with altered fine motor skills. Ingénierie des Systèmes d Inf **25**, 405–411 (2020)
39. Senette, C.: Technology-enhanced Programs for Children with Autism: implementing Applied Behavior Analysis Intervention on Mobile Devices. Thesis for: Ph.D. Computer Engineering (2015). https://www.researchgate.net/publication/283497379_Technology-enhanced_Programs_for_Children_with_Autism_implementing_Applied_Behavior_Analysis_Intervention_on_Mobile_Devices
40. Smith, D. Salinas, F.: Effectiveness of multimodality sensory integration and computer applications on motor planning processes of pre-writing and writing skills in children ages 4–7. In: Crawford, C., Davis, N., Price, J., Weber, R., Willis, D. (eds.) Proceedings of SITE 2003--Society for Information Technology & Teacher Education International Conference, p. 3302. Albuquerque, New Mexico, USA (2003)
41. Smyth, K.: Teaching reading comprehension for the development of literacy skills in children with Special Educational Needs (SEN) in mainstream schools: pedagogy, practices and perceptions, April 2021. https://eprints.lincoln.ac.uk/id/eprint/46284/1/KathleenSmyth-PhD (Professional)-Education.pdf
42. Trencheva, M.: Research in the field of finance and accounting training. EDULEARN21, pp. 12399–12406 (2021)
43. Trencheva, M.: Application of information technologies in economics education. INTED2022, pp. 921–926 (2022)
44. Trespalacios, J.: Educational video game design to promote learning and innovation skills: instructional ideas for educators. In P. Resta, P. (ed.) Proceedings of SITE 2012--Society for Information Technology & Teacher Education International Conference, pp. 2640–2645, Austin, Texas, USA (2012)
45. Vernadakis, N., Papastergiou, M., Zetou, E., Antoniou, P.: The impact of an exergame-based intervention on children's fundamental motor skills. Comput. Educ. **83**, 90–102 (2015)
46. Vučković, V., Stanišić, A., Simić, N.: Computer simulation and VR model of the Tesla's Wardenclyffe laboratory. Digital Appl. Archaeol. Cult. Herit. **7**, 42–50 (2017)
47. Wiencke, W.: Effectiveness of quicktime vr as an instructional environment for students with special needs. In Willis, D., Price, J., Davis, N., (eds.) Proceedings of SITE 2002--Society for Information Technology & Teacher Education International Conference, pp. 2281–2284. Nashville, Tennessee, USA (2002)
48. Zarco, L., Siegert, J., Schlegel, T., Bauernhansl, T.: Scope and delimitation of game engine simulations for ultra-flexible production environments. Procedia CIRP **104**, 792–797 (2021)
49. Chebanyuk, O: An approach to class diagram design. In: Proceedings of the 2nd International Conference on Model-Driven Engineering and Software Development (MODELSWARD 2014), pp. 448–453. Scitepres (2014). https://doi.org/10.5220/0004763504480453,ISBN: 978-989-758-007-9

50. Chebanyuk, O: An approach of text to model transformation of software models. in Proceedings of the 13th International Conference on Evaluation of Novel Approaches to Software Engineering, ENASE 2018, pp. 432–439. Scitepress (2018). https://doi.org/10.5220/000680 4504320439,ISBN 978-989-758-300-1

51. Chebanyuk, O: An approach to software assets reusing. In: Zlateva, T., Goleva, R. (eds.) Computer Science and Education in Computer Science. (CSECS 2022). Lecture Notes of the Institute for Computer Sciences, Social Informatics and Telecommunications Engineering, vol 450., pp. 73–83. Springer, Cham (2022). https://doi.org/10.1007/978-3-031-17292-2_6

Deep Learning Models for Vaccinology: Predicting T-cell Epitopes in C57BL/6 Mice

Zitian Zhen[1] ⓘ, Yuhe Wang[1] ⓘ, Derin B. Keskin[1,2] ⓘ, Vladimir Brusic[1,3] ⓘ, Lou Chitkushev[1] ⓘ, and Guang Lan Zhang[1(✉)] ⓘ

[1] Department of Computer Science, Metropolitan College, Boston University, Boston, MA 02215, USA
guanglan@bu.edu
[2] Department of Medical Oncology, Dana-Farber Cancer Institute, Boston, MA 02215, USA
[3] School of Economics, University of Nottingham Ningbo China, Ningbo 315100, China

Abstract. The C57 Black 6 (C57BL/6) mice are one the earliest and most widely used inbred laboratory animals in biomedical research and vaccine development. We propose developing a bioinformatics system for the identification of T-cell epitopes in C57BL/6 mice by integrating multiple contributing factors critical to the antigen processing and recognition pathway. The interaction between peptides and MHC molecules is a highly specific step in the antigen processing pathway and T-cell mediated immunity. As the first step of the project, we built a computational tool for predicting MHC class I binding peptides for the C57BL/6 mice. Utilizing deep learning methods, we trained and rigorously validated the prediction models using naturally eluted MHC ligands. The prediction models are of high accuracy.

Keywords: Bioinformatics System · Deep Learning · Prediction Tool · T-cell Epitope · MHC Binding · C57BL/6 Mice

1 Introduction

The design of vaccines is an intricate, multidimensional task. Because of the growing population and extremely high mobility of the human population, traditional vaccine development technologies are insufficient to address the challenges of pandemics and rapid spread of highly contagious and rapidly mutating viruses. Major challenges are emerging for developing novel vaccines to target pathogens that are difficult to control [1]. Most of newly developed vaccines for protection against COVID-19 are based on vaccine technologies that target antigen-presenting cells that were considered experimental as recently as 2021 [1]. Computational approaches are essential for the rapid development of vaccines because they significantly speed up the vaccine development by rapidly detecting vaccine targets [2]. An effective subunit vaccine must elicit strong immune responses against targets in vaccinated individuals, both B-cell and T-cell responses [3].

Z. Zhen and Y. Wang—These authors contributed equally.

© ICST Institute for Computer Sciences, Social Informatics and Telecommunications Engineering 2023
Published by Springer Nature Switzerland AG 2023. All Rights Reserved
T. Zlateva and G. Tuparov (Eds.): CSECS 2023, LNICST 514, pp. 182–192, 2023.
https://doi.org/10.1007/978-3-031-44668-9_14

The human adaptive immune response, characterized by specificity, involves specialized cells that detect non-self antigens and orchestrate targeted immune reactions [4]. Cytotoxic T cells, a vital component of the adaptive immune system, actively search for short antigenic peptides presented by major histocompatibility complex (MHC) class I molecules. The MHC class I antigen processing pathway involves several key steps: proteins are cleaved into shorter peptides by the proteasome, peptides are translocated into the endoplasmic reticulum (ER) via the transporter associated with antigen processing (TAP), further degradation of peptides may occur in the ER by aminopeptidases, peptides bind MHC molecules, and finally, peptide-MHC complexes are transported to the cell surface for recognition by CD8+T cells [5]. MHC binding is considered the most selective stage in T cell recognition. Peptides presented by MHC and recognized by T cells are referred to as T-cell epitopes. Accurately identifying T cell epitopes speeds up the design and development of epitope-based vaccines [6, 7].

Computational approaches have been successful in designing population-based vaccines by precisely identifying vaccine targets that offer broad protection across population. However, given that COVID-19 is highly contagious and rapidly mutating, there were several practical issues with available vaccines due to viral and host factors [8]: 1) individuals have different immunological profiles, and there will be antigenic mismatch in subpopulations; 2) increased transmissibility reduces vaccine efficiency; and 3) rapid viral mutations make optimal vaccine a moving target. Computational vaccinology needs to address the issues of high host diversity vs. rapid mutation of pathogen, with highly dynamic environment of optimal vaccine targeting. Deep learning has been proposed as an approach for effective vaccine design [9]. It was even suggested that deep learning models cannot be run on personal computers, but they require supercomputing facilities with extensive mass spectrometry support [10, 11]. These approaches are top-down, and they do not resolve the host diversity and target mutability problem. We propose a bottom-up approach whereby deep learning is applicable to individual immunological profiles and the results provide individualized vaccine targets. The trained models then can be used to rapidly assess viral mutations and potential immune escape of viral variants. To explore this goal, we developed a model that targets a specific combination of MHC alleles and, for simplicity, deployed it on a mouse model.

Mouse models are widely utilized in immunological research due to their relatively less complex composition of the immunopeptidome [12]. Studies have shown that vaccines composed of synthetic peptides resembling cancer neoepitopes have resulted in efficient T-cell activities and killed cancer cells in both mouse models and human patients [13–16]. The C57 Black 6 (C57BL/6) mice are one the earliest and most widely used inbred laboratory animals in biomedical research and vaccine development. C57BL/6 mouse expresses two MHC class I alleles, H2-D^b and -K^b [12].

Reverse immunology approaches involve the identification of immune targets through extensive bioinformatics screening of complete pathogenic genomes, followed by experimental validation [17].. Multiple online bioinformatics systems have been developed to predict peptides binding MHC alleles, including H2-D^b and H2-K^b alleles [6, 18, 19]. Many of them were trained mainly based on MHC binding peptides identified using *in vitro* binding assays. MHC-peptide *in vitro* binding assays assess the binding of peptides to specific MHC molecules, a prerequisite for T-cell activation. With technological advancement, liquid chromatography-tandem mass spectrometry (LC-MS/MS) has been employed to physically detect naturally processed and presented peptides on the cell surface [20–22]. We refer to these experimentally determined, naturally processed peptides as eluted ligands. As more and more datasets of eluted ligands are becoming available, this gives us opportunities to build more accurate prediction models using more biologically relevant data while incorporating the antigen processing steps simultaneously [20–23].

Moreover, most existing tools only model a single step in the MHC class I antigen processing pathway, the binding between MHC molecules and peptides. We propose a computational system for the identification of T-cell epitopes in C57BL mice by integrating other contributing factors critical to the antigen processing and recognition pathway, including proteasome cleavage, gene expression, and antigenicity. As the first step, we built a bioinformatics tool that predicts binding peptides of the MHC class I molecules H2-D^b and -K^b, of the C57BL/6 mice. Utilizing deep learning methods, we trained and rigorously validated the prediction models using naturally eluted MHC ligands. The prediction models are of high accuracy. This system is a prototype for exploring personalized targeting of vaccines for highly contagious and rapidly mutating pathogens. Because of high combinatorial complexity of host-pathogen interaction of such viruses, deep learning represents a promising platform for improving personalized vaccine targeting.

2 Materials and Methods

2.1 Data Collection and Transformation

The Immune Epitope Database and Analysis Resource (IEDB) compiles manually curated information on experimentally discovered B Cell and T cell epitopes found on various species, MHC binding peptides, and accompanying experimental settings [24]. Its contents were gathered primarily from literature from 1952 to now. We assembled our training data sets by collecting MHC ligand elution assay data from IEDB and enriched it with information from peptide processing tools [23]. When performing searches in IEDB, the following search criteria were adopted, Epitope: Linear peptide, Assay: MHC ligand, Assay Type: MHC Ligand Elution Assay, Outcome: Positive, and MHC Restriction: H2-D^b (or H2-K^b) protein complex. The search result contained 96,838 assay entries, with 44,565 for H2-D^b and 52,273 for H2-K^b.

We discarded ligands identified only by one positive assay to increase data quality. Ligands with two or more positive assay records were kept in the data sets as MHC binders. Our final dataset included 3,395 H2-D^b ligands and 3,961 H2-K^b ligands of length 8–11. Additional binding peptides were extracted from the NetMHCpan 4.1 training datasets [23]. After comparing the two data sets and removing duplicates, 885 H2-D^b ligands and 1,187 H2-K^b ligands from the NetMHCpan 4.1 dataset were added to the training dataset. Table 1 summarizes the numbers of MHC ligands collected. We also extracted random natural peptides from the NetMHCpan 4.1 datasets to use as non-binders. As the first step, we focused on building prediction models for H2-D^b and -K^b 9-mer ligands.

Table 1. Eluted H2-D^b and H2-K^b ligands collected from IEDB and NetMHCpan 4.1 dataset.

Length	H2-D^b ligands			H2-K^b ligands		
	IEDB	NetMHCpan	Sum	IEDB	NetMHCpan	Sum
8	210	14	224	2411	646	3057
9	**2357**	**585**	**2942**	**1292**	**395**	**1687**
10	481	151	632	175	68	243
11	347	135	482	83	78	161
Sum	3395	885	4280	3961	1187	5148

2.2 The Deep Learning Model

Deep learning, a branch of machine learning, is highly proficient in unveiling patterns from vast, multifaceted labeled data. This proficiency comes from its capacity to model high-level abstractions using architectural constructs known as neural networks [25]. Neural networks consist of interconnected layers, including an input layer, at least one hidden layer, and an output layer. The hidden layers are internal to the network and learn complex features from the inputs, whereas the output layer produces the final predictions. We developed deep neural network (DNN) models with several layers to learn patterns and characteristics within our training data. These layers serve as processing stages - akin to filters - each adding more complexity. We employed the Python Keras library [26] in this study. An Application Programming Interface (API) enables software applications to establish communication and interact with one another. The high-level neural network API of the Keras library can run on top of lower-level libraries like TensorFlow, Theano, or CNTK [25]. Keras provides predefined layers, such as dense (fully connected) layers, convolutional layers, and recurrent layers, which allow for a high degree of flexibility in designing custom neural network architectures. Due to its simplicity and effectiveness, we implemented a sequential model with dense (fully connected) layers using the backpropagation algorithm.

2.3 The Study Design

The overall structure of our study consisted of the following steps:

1. The 9-mer data of both alleles were divided into training and testing datasets using a stratified method to maintain an approximate 80/20 ratio. To ensure reproducibility, we set the random seed to 42. Details of the datasets are shown in Table 2.
2. We encoded each 9-mer ligand in the training data into two NumPy arrays. The first array represents the nine amino acids in the ligand, as shown in Fig. 1. After evaluating several amino acid encoding methods, we selected the one-hot encoding for simplicity and effectiveness [27]. The second array contains a binary label indicating binding (1) or non-binding (0).
3. We then constructed dense neural network models. The final model consists of one input layer and two hidden layers. The first hidden layer contains 128 neurons, and

Table 2. Training and testing datasets for A) H2-D^b and B) H2-K^b. The binder/non-binder ratio is 19/81 and 11/89 for H2-D^b and -K^b training and testing datasets.

Datasets	# of Binders (Percentage)	# of Non-binders (Percentage)	Total
H2-D^b			
Training	2349 (19%)	9992 (81%)	12341
Testing	593 (19%)	2493 (81%)	3086
sum	2942	12485	15427
H2-K^b			
Training	1345 (11%)	10706 (89%)	12051
Testing	342 (11%)	2671 (89%)	3013
sum	1687	13377	15064

	A	C	D	E	F	G	H	I	K	L	M	N	P	Q	R	S	T	V	W	Y
0	1	0	0	0	0	0	0	0	0	0	0	0	0	0	0	0	0	0	0	0
1	1	0	0	0	0	0	0	0	0	0	0	0	0	0	0	0	0	0	0	0
2	0	0	0	0	0	0	0	1	0	0	0	0	0	0	0	0	0	0	0	0
3	0	0	0	0	0	1	0	0	0	0	0	0	0	0	0	0	0	0	0	0
4	0	0	0	0	0	0	0	0	0	0	0	1	0	0	0	0	0	0	0	0
5	0	0	0	0	0	0	0	0	0	0	0	0	0	1	0	0	0	0	0	0
6	0	0	0	0	0	0	0	0	0	1	0	0	0	0	0	0	0	0	0	0
7	0	0	0	0	0	0	0	0	0	0	0	0	0	0	0	0	0	0	0	1
8	0	0	0	0	0	0	0	0	0	0	0	0	0	0	0	0	0	1	0	0

Fig. 1. The array representing the 9-mer peptide, AAIGNQLYV, using One-hot encoding.

the second has 64 neurons with a Leaky ReLU activation function to introduce non-linearity and allow the learning of more complex patterns [28]:

$$LeakyReLU(x) = \begin{cases} x & if \quad x > 0 \\ \alpha x & if \quad x \leq 0 \end{cases} \tag{1}$$

where α is a small positive constant, typically a small fraction. In our model, we set $\alpha = 0.01$ to allow a small gradient for negative values, allowing learning to occur even for negative inputs to avoid the vanishing and exploding gradients problem. The output layer has a sigmoid activation function, guaranteeing that the output is between 0 and 1, making it useful for binary classification [29].

$$Sigmoid(x) = \frac{1}{1 + e^{-2}} \tag{2}$$

MHC binders tend to produce values close to 1(binding), while non-binders tend to yield values close to 0 (non-binding). We compiled this model using the binary cross-entropy loss function [30] since both the sigmoid activation and binary cross-entropy loss functions are constructed for binary classification problems [25].

$$L = -[y * \log(p) + (1 - y) * \log(1 - p)] \tag{3}$$

where y represents the actual class label (either 0 or 1) of the binary classification problem, and p represents the predicted probability of the positive class. The loss function computes the logarithmic loss between p and y. When y is 1, the loss penalizes the model more if it predicts a low probability. When y is 0, the loss penalizes the model more for predicting a high probability for the positive class. The negative sign at the beginning of the equation converted it into a minimization problem. The goal is to minimize this loss function during the training to update the model's parameters and improve its predictive performance.

4. Batch normalization, a technique in deep learning, was applied to improve a neural network's performance. This is achieved by normalizing the mini-batch, and then scaling and shifting the normalized values using learned parameters. Batch normalization stabilizes the distribution of each layer's inputs during training, leading to faster and more stable convergence [31]. After trying various sizes for batch normalization, we chose batch size 32 as it produced the best performance.

5. We also used early stopping, a form of regularization to avoid overfitting [32]. If the model's prediction performance on the validation set does not demonstrate improvement for a predefined number of epochs, the training process stops. We started training by running 100 epochs, and the model stopped in less than 20 epochs. After implementing the early stopping function with hyper-parameter patience being 10, we changed the epoch to 30. We trained the networks with 30 epochs and a batch size 32 and evaluated the model using the testing datasets.

6. We then fine-tuned the hyper-parameters to optimize the performance, including adjusting the number of hidden layers, the size each layer, and the optimizer learning rate. We also tried various activation functions in hidden layers. We defined a callback function, such as Model Checkpoint, to record the best-performing model [25]. This way, we ensured that the best-performing model was recorded during training, which is helpful when trying out multiple sets of parameters and working with large datasets or when training takes a long time. We tried various optimizers and settled on Adam as it produced the best performance (Fig. 2) [33]. In stochastic gradient descent, the learning rate needs to be manually tuned. Adam computes individual learning rates for different parameters, resulting in adaptive learning rates.

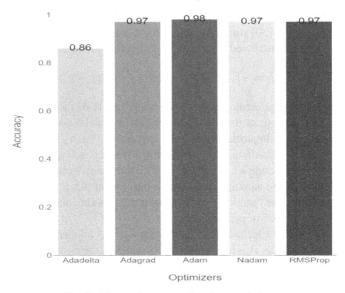

Fig. 2. The performance of various optimizers.

2.4 The Validation Dataset

In 2020, Paul et al. benchmarked the publicly available MHC binding prediction models using a set of H2-D^b and H2-K^b restricted T-cell epitopes derived from the Vaccinia virus (VACV)" [19]. All models demonstrated reasonable prediction performance, and the NetMHCpan-4.0 and MHCflurry, based on deep learning models trained on MHC binding affinity and eluted ligand data, were the top performers among the 17 models evaluated. Many of these models were developed over a decade ago, while NetMHCpan-4.0 and MHCflurry are the newest additions. We validated the developed prediction model using the same published dataset [19]. It contains naturally processed and eluted peptides from VACV-infected mice cells [34]. Out of all LC-MS/MS identified peptides, we filtered out 111 9-mer ligands, 78 for H2-D^b and 33 for H2-K^b. We randomly generated 549 9-mer peptides using the VACV proteomes data and included them as non-binders in the validation dataset.

3   Results

SYFPEITHI is one of the earliest online databases that capture information on MHC binding peptides, MHC binding motifs, and anchor positions et al. [35]. SYFPEITHY motifs were used as a guide for assessing anchor positions in binding peptides. We generated sequence logos using WebLogo [36] based on the 9-mer ligands collected and compared them with binding motifs provided by SYFPEITHI (Fig. 3). Both the H2-D^b binding motifs identify positions 5 and 9 as anchor positions. In addition, the sequence logo showed apparent amino acid selectivity at positions 2 and 3. The H2-K^b binding motifs show high similarity.

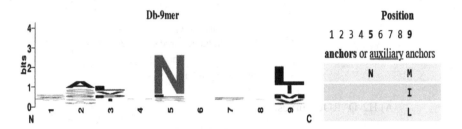

A)   H2-D^b 9-mer binding motifs generated by WebLogo (left) and SYFPEITHI (right).

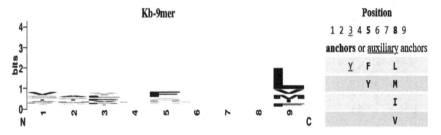

B)   H2-K^b 9-mer binding motifs generated by WebLogo (left) and SYFPEITHI (right).

Fig. 3.   Binding motifs for A) H2-D^b and B) H2-K^b 9-mer peptides.

Our prediction models were trained and tested using the training and testing datasets described in Table 2. The models were validated using the validation dataset. ROC curves (receiver operating characteristic curve) and AUC (area under the ROC) are used to assess the overall prediction performance. As shown in Fig. 4, both models demonstrated high accuracy. The AUC values of the H2-D^b model were 0.98 using the testing data and 0.97 using the validation data. The AUC values of the H2-K^b model were 0.96 using the testing data and 0.92 using the validation data.

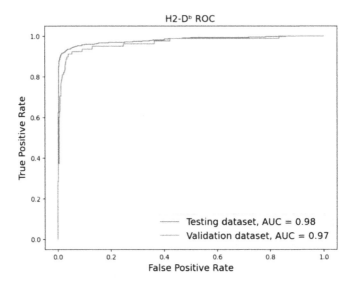

A) H2-D^b ROC curves.

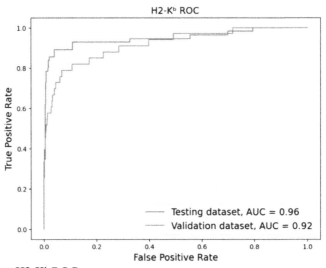

B) H2-K^b ROC curves.

Fig. 4. ROC curves show the performance of the prediction models.

4   Conclusion

Immune-based therapies are revolutionizing cancer care and vaccine development. Most of these therapies are first developed and tested in mice due to their shared mammalian features with humans. Understanding the epitope presentation to the T cells in mice is crucial for analyzing and interpreting these immune therapies. We propose developing a bioinformatics pipeline based on deep learning for *in silico* prediction of T-cell epitopes in C57BL mice. This computational modeling approach integrates peptide binding and antigen processing in one deep learning system. It addresses critical contributing factors to the antigen processing and recognition pathways, including proteasomal cleavage, gene expression, and antigenicity. Here we reported preliminary results on building a prediction tool for peptide binding to $H2-D^b$ and $H2-K^b$ alleles that represent the immunological profile of C57BL/6 mice, a common research model. We trained and rigorously validated dense neural network models using naturally eluted MHC ligands. The prediction models are highly accurate, evidenced by the high AUC values in the testing and validation. We plan to build on this model, incorporate additional tools to develop a highly accurate bioinformatic pipeline for *in silico* prediction of T-cell epitopes in C57BL mice and other mouse models, and extend it to human haplotypes.

References

1. Pollard, A.J., Bijker, E.M.: A guide to vaccinology: from basic principles to new developments. Nat. Rev. Immunol. **21**(2), 83–100 (2021)
2. Osamor, V.C., Ikeakanam, E., Bishung, J., Abiodun, T., Ekpo, R.H.: COVID-19 vaccines: computational tools and development. Inform. Med. Unlocked 101164 (2023)
3. Grødeland, G., Fossum, E., Bogen, B.: Polarizing T and B cell responses by APC-targeted subunit vaccines. Front. Immunol. **6**, 367 (2015)
4. Bonilla, F.A., Oettgen, H.C.: Adaptive immunity. J. Aller. Clin. Immunol. **125**(2), S33–S40 (2010)
5. Shastri, N., Cardinaud, S., Schwab, S.R., Serwold, T., Kunisawa, J.: All the peptides that fit: the beginning, the middle, and the end of the MHC class I antigen-processing pathway. Immunol. Rev. **207**(1), 31–41 (2005)
6. Zhang, G.L., Keskin, B.D., Chitkushev, L.: Extraction of Immune Epitope Information. In: Ranganathan, S., Nakai, K., Schönbach, C., Gribskov, M. (eds.) Encyclopedia of Bioinformatics and Computational Biology, vol. 3, pp. 39–46. Elsevier, Oxford (2019)
7. Brusic, V., Petrovsky, N., Gendel, S.M., Millot, M., Gigonzac, O., Stelman, S.J.: Computational tools for the study of allergens. Allergy **58**(11), 1083–1092 (2003)
8. Tregoning, J.S., Flight, K.E., Higham, S.L., Wang, Z., Pierce, B.F.: Progress of the COVID-19 vaccine effort: viruses, vaccines and variants versus efficacy, effectiveness and escape. Nat. Rev. Immunol. **21**(10), 626–636 (2021)
9. Abbasi, B.A., et al.: Identification of vaccine targets & design of vaccine against SARS-CoV-2 coronavirus using computational and deep learning-based approaches. PeerJ **10**, e13380 (2022)
10. Keshavarzi Arshadi, A., et al.: Artificial intelligence for COVID-19 drug discovery and vaccine development. Front. Artif. Intell. **65** (2020)
11. Bagagir, S.A., Ibrahim, N.K., Bagagir, H.A., Ateeq, R.H.: Covid-19 and artificial intelligence: genome sequencing, drug development and vaccine discovery. J. Infect. Public Health **15**(2), 289–296 (2022)
12. Schuster, H., et al.: A tissue-based draft map of the murine MHC class I immunopeptidome. Sci. Data **5**(1), 1–11 (2018)
13. Banchereau, J., Palucka, K.: Cancer vaccines on the move. Nat. Rev. Clin. Oncol. **15**(1), 9–10 (2018)
14. Sahin, U., Türeci, Ö.: Personalized vaccines for cancer immunotherapy. Science **359**(6382), 1355–1360 (2018)
15. Ott, P.A., et al.: An immunogenic personal neoantigen vaccine for patients with melanoma. Nature **547**(7662), 217–221 (2017)

16. Keskin, D.B., et al.: Neoantigen vaccine generates intratumoral T cell responses in phase Ib glioblastoma trial. Nature **565**(7738), 234–239 (2019)

17. Rappuoli, R., Bottomley, M.J., D'Oro, U., Finco, O., De Gregorio, E.: Reverse vaccinology 2.0: human immunology instructs vaccine antigen design. J. Exp. Med. **213**(4), 469–481 (2016)

18. Zhang, G.L., Sun, J., Chitkushev, L., Brusic, V.: Big data analytics in immunology: a knowledge-based approach. BioMed Res. Int. **2014**, 1–9 (2014)

19. Paul, S., et al.: Benchmarking predictions of MHC class I restricted T cell epitopes in a comprehensively studied model system. PLoS Comput. Biol. **16**(5), e1007757 (2020)

20. Sarkizova, S., et al.: A large peptidome dataset improves HLA class I epitope prediction across most of the human population. Nat. Biotechnol. **38**(2), 199–209 (2020)

21. Abelin, J.G., et al.: Mass spectrometry profiling of HLA-associated peptidomes in mono-allelic cells enables more accurate epitope prediction. Immunity **46**(2), 315–326 (2017)

22. Truex, N.L., et al.: Automated flow synthesis of tumor neoantigen peptides for personalized immunotherapy. Sci. Rep. **10**(1), 723 (2020)

23. Reynisson, B., Alvarez, B., Paul, S., Peters, B., Nielsen, M.: NetMHCpan-4.1 and NetMHCIIpan-4.0: improved predictions of MHC antigen presentation by concurrent motif deconvolution and integration of MS MHC eluted ligand data. Nucleic Acids Res. **48**(W1), W449-W454 (2020)

24. Vita, R., et al.: The immune epitope database (IEDB): 2018 update. Nucleic Acids Res. **47**(D1), D339–D343 (2019)

25. Géron, A.: Hands-On Machine Learning with Scikit-Learn, Keras, and TensorFlow: Concepts, Tools, and Techniques to Build Intelligent Systems, 2nd edn.. O'Reilly Media, (2019)

26. Chollet, F., et al.: (2015). https://github.com/keras-team/keras. Accessed 7 June 2023

27. ElAbd, H., Bromberg, Y., Hoarfrost, A., Lenz, T., Franke, A., Wendorff, M.: Amino acid encoding for deep learning applications. BMC Bioinform. **21**, 1–14 (2020)

28. Maas, A.L., Hannun, A.Y., Ng, A.Y.: Rectifier nonlinearities improve neural network acoustic models. Proc. Icml **30**(1), 3 (2013)

29. Rumelhart, D.E., Hinton, G.E., Williams, R.J.: Learning representations by back-propagating errors. Nature **323**(6088), 533–536 (1986)

30. Topsøe, F.: Bounds for entropy and divergence for distributions over a two-element set. JIPAM. J. Inequal. Pure Appl. Math. **2**(2) (2001)

31. Ioffe, S., Szegedy, C.: Batch normalization: accelerating deep network training by reducing internal covariate shift. In: International Conference on Machine Learning, pp. 448–456 (2015)

32. Yao, Y., Rosasco, L., Caponnetto, A.: On early stopping in gradient descent learning. Constr. Approx. **26**(2), 289–315 (2007)

33. Kingma, D.P., Ba, J.: Adam: a method for stochastic optimization. arXiv preprint arXiv:1412. 6980, (2014)

34. Croft, N.P., et al.: Most viral peptides displayed by class I MHC on infected cells are immunogenic. Proc. Natl. Acad. Sci. **116**(8), 3112–3117 (2019)

35. Schuler, M.M., Nastke, M.D., Stevanović, S.: SYFPEITHI: database for searching and T-cell epitope prediction. Immunoinform.: Predict. Immunogenicity Silico 75–93 (2007)

36. Crooks, G.E., Hon, G., Chandonia, J.M., Brenner, S.E.: WebLogo: a sequence logo generator. Genome Res. **14**(6), 1188–1190 (2004)

Changes in Patterns of Infectivity and Mortality with SARS-CoV-2 Omicron Variant in Bulgaria

Latchezar P. Tomov[1]([⊠]) [iD], Hristina Batselova[2,3] [iD], and Tsvetelina Velikova[4] [iD]

[1] Department of Informatics, New Bulgarian University, 1618 Sofia, Bulgaria
lptomov@nbu.bg
[2] Department of Epidemiology and Disaster Medicine, Medical University, Plovdiv, Bulgaria
dr_batselova@abv.bg
[3] Department of Epidemiology and Disaster Medicine, University Hospital "St George",
6000 Plovdiv, Bulgaria
[4] Medical Faculty, Sofia University St. Kliment Ohridski, 1407 Sofia, Bulgaria
tsvelikova@medfac.mu-sofia.bg

Abstract. We use our previously developed models (branching processes and time series analysis) to track the changes in the spread of the new SARS-COV-2 variant "Omicron" across age groups. We track changes in transmission rates, lethality, and spread between age groups. Omicron was inferred to be less lethal in other studies. We test that by comparing the prediction from our model, which was trained with the data with the previous variants – wild type, alpha and delta variants. We automatically predict new cases by combining the branching process and change point analysis – a reactive approach for precise short-term prediction - the software is installed on the Avitohol supercomputer. We use time series analysis (regression with Arima errors) to predict deaths and to test hypotheses related to the patterns of spread across age groups and the factors that influence it.

Keywords: Branching processes · Arima · Covid-19 · School closures · Lethality

1 Introduction

1.1 Modeling Tools for Covid-19

The classical approach in epidemiology uses deterministic modeling with nonlinear differential equations to test a different hypothesis for certain epidemic after it ends. Usually, it is based on evidence gathered during the different waves related to the incubation period of the pathogen, the basic reproduction number R_0, the mode of transmission, et cetera [1]. With these estimated characteristics, the classical model, such as S-I-R (susceptible-infected-recovered) and its various modifications, such as S-E-I-R (susceptible-exposed-infected-recovered), are set up. Then some simulations are made to compare real-world data with the (usually very noisy). Why simulations? Because these equations are nonlinear and analytical solutions do not exist. In 2014 an exact so-called solution for a simple particular case of the S-I-R model was developed. Still, it

T. Zlateva and G. Tuparov (Eds.): CSECS 2023, LNICST 514, pp. 193–203, 2023.
https://doi.org/10.1007/978-3-031-44668-9_15

involves an integral that can only be solved numerically [2]. These compartmental models have their merit, even though within the deterministic framework, the extinction of a pathogen does not exist. However, they are good as a tool for analysis but have limitations in prediction [3]. Unfortunately, COVID-19 still hasn't ended, and it is not predictable when, how, or if it will end, so post hoc analysis is impossible. New approaches are needed to forecast an ongoing global epidemic in which the main characteristics of the pathogen change rapidly while one dominant variant is replaced by another, and there are no periods with zero new cases, with weak seasonality. Especially a pandemic for which various measures have been taken at various times in various countries to contain cases and, via them – deaths. A new approach, a reactive approach, is needed. We need to be able to forecast for a short-term period without being able to assess precisely the characteristics of tens of different viral variants or be able to predict what the governments and the citizen will do in response to a wave. Thus, we implemented two parallel approaches – one for predicting new cases [4] and one for deaths [5]. The first approach uses a branching process to model the spread and change-point analysis to recalibrate the model automatically from the data with changepoint analysis [6] by estimating the parameters of the whole probability distribution and only then producing a point estimate. The point estimate is made by testing 10 000 different scenarios on a supercomputer in R and calculating the expectation. This is a stochastic approach, which is more suitable for populations that are not very large since the deterministic models are, in a sense, the limit of the stochastics for population tending to infinity. Different stochastic models, such as those described in [7], alleviate some of the difficulties but still lack the ability to adapt to an ongoing epidemic. The second approach uses time series analysis in the form of ARIMA with external regressors with auto.arima() in R [8] to infer the deaths from the new daily cases by age groups with different lags. This model is suitable when the errors of estimation are autocorrelated, which is the case in pandemics with multiple waves. It was created in 2021 for the delta wave and shows two major findings – the exponential distribution of the risk per age up to 70 years and the children (0–19 years) are a major factor in the spread – a key regressor despite their low personal risk.

1.2   Modeling Waves in Bulgaria Prior to the SARS-CoV-2 Omicron Variant

Summary of previous research. Prior to Omicron, Bulgaria had three major waves – the wild type from September 2020 to January 2021, the alpha variant from February 2021 to May 2021 and Delta from July 2021 to January 2022. We estimated the case fatality rate and found that alpha was not significantly more lethal but infected older people and caused more deaths. Delta was substantially more lethal, with 18 000 deaths officially only for Delta and 12 000 from the wild type and the alpha combined. [9]. We were able to estimate the case fatality rate by age groups thanks to access to data for deaths per age group. Our previous paper [5] used a more sophisticated model to predict the total number of weekly deaths from new cases by age group since no data for deaths per age group was accessible at the time. It was an ARIMA model, with added new cases by different age groups and the variants as predictors (the index of the variant as a categorical predictor). It was fitted for the period 6.6.2020–4.11.2021. It worked well for all variants up to and including the Delta variant, which suggests their common nature with the same age groups, and their lags suggest the same mode of transmission and delay between infection and symptom onsets. So, when a novel variant that is significantly different appears, than our model should give predictions for deaths that are incorrect, and the previous regressors would no longer be the optimal ones, with different optimal lags and relative weight of different age groups. In this paper, we extend this model with one more month of Delta wave, which doesn't change its structure or efficiency and try to predict the mixed Delta-Omicron wave after 31.12.2021 that happened in Bulgaria.

2   Modeling the Mixed Omicron-Delta Wave

2.1   Predicting New Daily Cases

We used our mixed model with a branching process and changepoint analysis [4]. We have to note that this model is successfully applied to over 30 different countries from April 2020 up to July 2022, including for Omicron or even for complex mixed waves such as our wave from January 2022 up to March 2022. Results are shown in Figs. 1, 2,

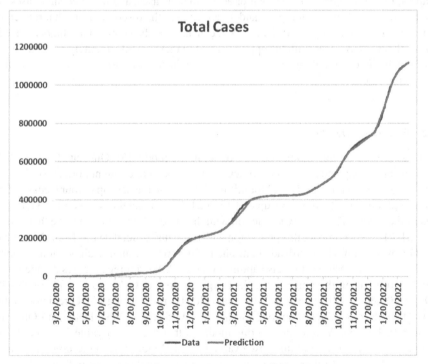

Fig. 1. Prediction for accumulated cases up to 21th of February 2022.

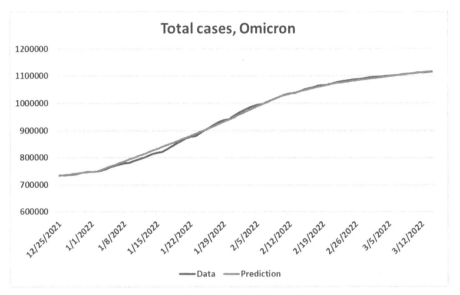

Fig. 2. Prediction for accumulated cases for the mixed Delta-Omicron wave up to 20th of February 2022.

3 and 4. Our model predicts the total or accumulated cases, and the new daily cases are the first finite difference. In Figs. 3 and 4, you can see the discontinuities that reflect the automatically detected regime change. You can also see the significantly higher wave in terms of new daily cases with the appearance of Omicron. Unfortunately, we cannot say how much higher from the new cases are because the testing varies by waves, so further research is needed.

2.2 Predicting Deaths

Here we use our second approach by extending the model [5]. Our data for new daily cases by age group and deaths and comes from the open government portal [10]. It starts on 6.6.2020. The end is 14.3.2022 for this model. We use the data up to four weeks before the end of the pure Delta wave – up to 4.12.2021. We predict the period 4.12–31.12 as a test of the model. Then we try prediction with this model for the mixed wave that started on 1.01.2022. We compare this prediction with the actual official deaths from Omicron to see how well our model is still adequate and if Omicron is similar to all previous variants in characteristics that our models captured very well. We aggregate cases by age group weekly to filter out the noise in the data. Age groups are 0–19, 20–29, 30–39, 40–49, 50–59, 60–69, 70–79, 80–89, and 90+ years old. There is a categorical predictor for the variants with four values. The four variants are Wild type, Alpha, Delta, and Omicron (values 0, 1, 2, 3). A limitation to this model is that we assign value 3 (Omicron) to a wave that starts as a mixture of two variants, and Omicron becomes dominant along the wave. We need further research to predict such complex waves with two different variants.

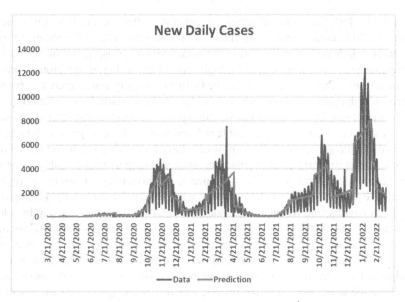

Fig. 3. A derived prediction for new daily cases up to 14th of March 2022.

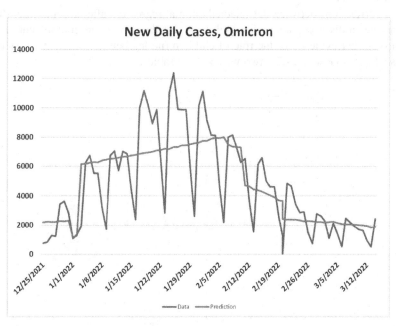

Fig. 4. A derived prediction for new daily cases for the mixed Delta-Omicron wave ip to 14th of March 2022.

In building our model, we follow the same steps as described in our previous publication. [5]. We examine the stationarity with different tests. According to the Augmented

Dickey-Fuller test, the observed series are stationary after second-order differencing. So, our ARIMA model necessarily must include second-order differencing to avoid spurious correlations. We made a principal component analysis, shown in Fig. 5. As in our previous publication, we can see a high level of clustering of age groups into two main directions – 20–49 and 60-, with the 0–19 visibly very much apart and 60–90+. The reason is that, just as in previous waves, the pandemic starts from the children who infect their parents. Our question is why this age group significantly influences overall deaths despite having the lowest possible risk and why we have more considerable lags in our models. People in the age group usually have no children left in the household – 50–59, which in Bulgaria means neither parents nor grandparents are visibly alone with a lower correlation. After various tests we made, we extracted predictor by aggregating different age groups – 0–19 was left that way, while 20–29, 20–30 and 40–49 (the parent group) was aggregated. We also aggregated the "active grandparent" group by adding the somewhat less correlated 50–59 into it – 50–69. By "active grandparent," we mean the usual age at which grandparents can care for children in Bulgaria. However, these categories are mostly based on anecdotal evidence since such research does not exist in Bulgaria. However, this is not relevant to the procedure of building the model per se but only to the interpretation of the results, which may change in the future with new demographic data for the period of the pandemic. Older people above 70 are grouped into one category.

The correlations between the selected optimal regressors after second order difference are generally acceptable, with high value for the parent and grandparent groups, which is further evidence of the role of children (no lag between them also). Here L1 means a lag of one week, L2 – two weeks, etc. (Table 1).

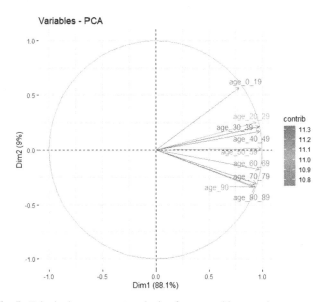

Fig. 5. Principal component analysis of new weekly cases by age groups.

The best model, selected by us and auto.arima(), is ARIMA with second-order differencing and second-order autoregressive terms or ARIMA (2, 2, 0). Its predictive ability is shown in Fig. 6, and its forecasting ability – is in Fig. 7. The parameters of the model and the characteristics of the fit, such as the R squared $-R^2$, the standard error of estimation of the coefficients, the mean squared error (MSE), mean absolute percentage error (MAPE) are shown in Table 2. We can see the high value of R^2, which shows that the model explains more than 97% of the variation and that almost all standard errors of coefficient estimations are at an acceptable level (less than half of the value of the coefficient). There are some interesting things to note about these coefficients. First, the age group 0–19 has a very high coefficient value, noting a high contribution to the deaths, on the same level as the 70 + group. The lowest-risk group is as important as the highest-risk one in predicting deaths for the best model! Our interpretation is in the influence children have on the infection of the parents and grandparents as the main drivers of the pandemic, which is supported for other countries in the latest research [11]. Second, the 70+ group has the lowest or the best ratio of the standard error to coefficient value, which means we are most certainly in that value. This is logical as this is the highest-risk group. The negative coefficients of the autoregressive predictors with one- and two-week lag and the 20–49 group with three weeks lag reflect the nature of the pandemic wave, captured best by compartmental models such as SIR – the idea of the peak of the wave, caused by reaching enough share of people to slow transmission with temporary herd immunity.

Table 1. Correlations between the variables

Variables	0–19 L2	20–49 L1	20–49 L3	50–69 L1	70-plus L0
0–19 L2	1	0.27	−0.36	0.22	0.31
20–49 L1	0.27	1	−0.17	0.87	0.17
20–49 L3	−0.36	−0.17	1	−0.09	−0.15
50–69 L1	0.22	0.87	−0.09	1	0.20
70 + L0	0.31	0.17	−0.15	0.20	1

We tested this model for the rest of the pure Delta wave, and we consider this to be a relatively good forecast, as shown in Fig. 7, including with confidence intervals of 95%.

Predicting SARS-CoV-2 Omicron-Related Deaths
In the case of Bulgaria, we don't have a pure Omicron wave but a mixture of Delta and Omicron variants. This wave, as seen in Fig. 4, was around 10 weeks in length but with very high and early peak around the fourth week, indicating significantly higher effective reproductive and basic reproductive ratios for this variant mixture, mostly due to Omicron. Using our model, we tried to forecast up to the 14th of March, and as it can be seen, the actual deaths were 53% of the predicted ones – something that most probably own to the Omicron. The model underpredicted Delta deaths before Omicron

Table 2. Regression models with ARIMA (2, 2, 0) errors

Model Summary		
	Optimal Model	
Coefficient	Estimate	Standard error
AR1	−0.8119	0.1093
AR2	−0.3899	0.1103
Age 0–19 Lag 2	0.0801	0.0448
Age 20–49 Lag 1	−0.0380	0.0139
Age 20–49 Lag 3	0.0194	0.0054
Age 50–69 Lag 1	0.0803	0.0200
Age 70-plus Lag 0	0.0364	0.0233
Variants [a]	0.7161	34.6957
R^2:	*0.972*	
RMSE:	*55.78*	
Bias:	*−0.97*	
MAPE:	*17.42*	

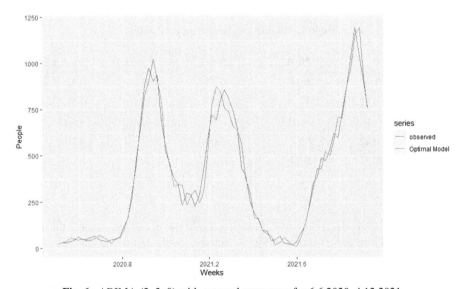

Fig. 6. ARIMA (2, 2, 0) with external regressors for 6.6.2020–4.12.2021.

became dominant in the third week of January 2022. A forecast gets less and less reliable with the extension of the forecasting period, and the uncertainty of how much "milder" Omicron was in that wave is not very low. Still, we consider this enough evidence to

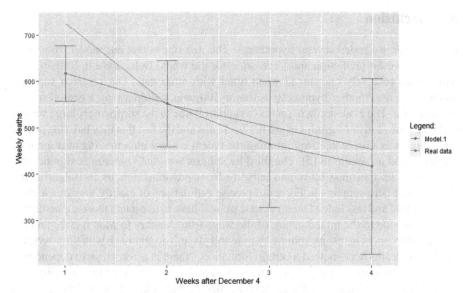

Fig. 7. Prediction for Delta – 4.12.-31.12.2021.

support the more straightforward binary statement that a significant difference exists between deaths from an Omicron and a Delta wave (Fig. 8).

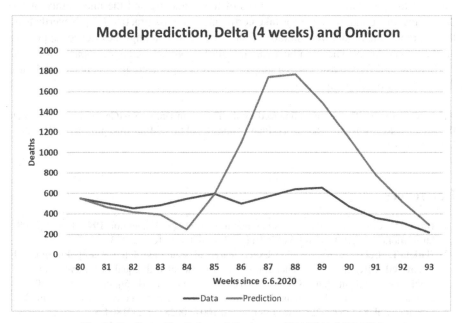

Fig. 8. Prediction for Delta and Omicron –2021/12/4–2022/3/14

3 Conclusion

In this paper, we tested several hypotheses. The first one is that our model from 2021 [5] is suitable for prediction and forecasting for the whole Delta wave in Bulgaria and will remain relatively unchanged when fitted with more data. Our research supports this hypothesis. Another hypothesis is that in Bulgaria, children play a central role in transmission. The evidence here seems to support it due to the surprisingly large weight of the new cases in 0–19 groups in predicting deaths and the fact that they have the largest lag, which was visible just from plotting the recent cases with a moving average with 7 days period as we did in [5]. The third hypothesis was that Omicron is significantly different in its transmissibility and lethality from previous variants in Bulgaria, and the evidence here supports it. For more precise estimations of exactly how much more transmissible and less lethal Omicron was, we will have to use much more sophisticated approaches due to the mixed nature of the wave from January to March 2022 and the various differences in testing volume by time and place. The approach with time-series in predicting deaths here showed a certain limitation – there is autoregressive dependence between cases in one wave and previous waves, and such also exists for mortality. The huge difference in deaths in Bulgaria could also be because, before Omicron, almost 30 000 people died from COVID-19 as an official figure. This is a very high share of the total population of 6.45 million people [12], which limits further deaths since there is an upper limit on the percentage of people that a virus can kill in a limited time frame. An Omicron wave with much lower previous waves would result in many more deaths. Other factors should be taken into account, such as the different vaccination status of the population in various stages of the pandemic and the uncertainty of the data to the anecdotal evidence for fake certificates as mass practice [13]. Nevertheless, this approach and model were suitable to show us some meaningful evidence supporting all three hypotheses. They can be a valuable tool in predicting ongoing pandemics and studying their different aspects as a supplement to stochastic compartmental models and the reactive modeling approach.

Acknowledgment. This study is financed by the European Union-NextGenerationEU, through the National Recovery and Resilience Plan of the Republic of Bulgaria, project № BG-RRP-2.004–0008-C01.

References

1. Brauer, F.: Compartmental models in epidemiology. Math. Epidemiol. **1945**, 19–79 (2008). https://doi.org/10.1007/978-3-540-78911-6_2, PMCID: PMC7122373
2. Harko, T., Lobo, F., Mak, M.K.: Exact analytical solutions of the Susceptible-Infected-Recovered (SIR) epidemic model and of the SIR model with equal death and birth rates. Appl. Math. Comput. **236**, 184–194 (2014). https://doi.org/10.1016/j.amc.2014.03.030
3. Melikechi, O., Young, A.L., Tang, T., et al.: Limits of epidemic prediction using SIR models. J. Math. Biol. **85**, 36 (2022). https://doi.org/10.1007/s00285-022-01804-5
4. Tchorbadjieff, A., Tomov, L.P., Velev, V., Dezhov, G., Manev, V., Mayster, P.: On regime changes of COVID-19 outbreak. J. Appl. Stat. (2023). https://doi.org/10.1080/02664763.2023.2177625

5. Tomov, L., Angelov, S., Tchorbadjieff, A.: Age-specific mortality risk from COVID-19 in Bulgaria. In: Zlateva, T., Goleva, R. (eds.) Computer Science and Education in Computer Science, New Bulgarian University, Sofia, pp. 1–24 (2021)

6. Chen, J., Gupta, A.: On change point detection and estimation. Commun. Stat. Simul. Comput. **30**, 665–697 (2013)

7. Mamis, K., Farazmand, M.: Stochastic compartmental models of the COVID-19 pandemic must have temporally correlated uncertainties. Proc. R. Soc. A.4792022056820220568 (2023). https://doi.org/10.1098/rspa.2022.0568

8. Hyndman, R.J., Khandakar, Y.: Automatic time series forecasting: the forecast package for R. J. Stat. Softw. **26**(3) (2008)

9. Tomov, L., Batselova, H., Velikova, T.V.: Estimating COVID case fatality rate in Bulgaria for 2020–2021. In: Zlateva, T., Goleva, R. (eds.) Computer Science and Education in Computer Science. CSECS 2022. Lecture Notes of the Institute for Computer Sciences, Social Informatics and Telecommunications Engineering, vol 450. Springer, Cham (2022). https://doi.org/10.1007/978-3-031-17292-2_9

10. Bulgarian open data portal. https://data.egov.bg/data/resourceView/e59f95dd-afde-43af-83c8-ea2916badd19. Accessed 10 June 2023

11. Tseng, Y., Olson, K.L., Bloch, D., Mandl, K.D.: Smart Thermometer-based participatory surveillance to discern the role of children in household viral transmission during the COVID-19 pandemic. JAMA Netw. Open **6**(6), e2316190 (2023). https://doi.org/10.1001/jamanetworkopen.2023.16190

12. https://www.bta.bg/en/news/economy/448417-bulgarian-population-numbers-6-447-710-as-at-december-2022-shrinks-by-34-774-pe. Accessed 10 June 2023

13. https://www.rferl.org/a/fake-covid-certificates-romania-bulgaria/31507555.html. Accessed 10 June 2023

Data Representations and Ensemble Deep Learning Networks for Functional Neuroimaging Datasets

Morgan Cambareri[1,2]([✉]) and Farshid Alizadeh-Shabdiz[3]

[1] Biomedical Engineering Department, College of Engineering, Boston University, Boston, MA, USA
mcambareri@mgh.harvard.edu
[2] Center for Neurotechnology and Neurorecovery, Massachusetts General Hospital, Boston, MA, USA
[3] Computer Science Department, MET College, Boston University, Boston, MA, USA

Abstract. This project was designed to test the predictive accuracy of combining two separate data representations of resting state functional magnetic resonance imaging (rs-fMRI) data into an ensemble deep learning architecture. Three main data representations of the same neuroimaging dataset were tested by building associated deep learning architectures and testing their accuracy in predicting if the neuroimaging data originated from healthy controls or from individuals diagnosed with autism spectrum disorder (ASD). The three data representations were 2D correlation matrices derived from time courses extracted from the blood-oxygen-level-dependent (BOLD) signal within the brain, a graph tensor representation of the same connectivity data, and a 3D profile of the posterior cingulate cortex's (PCC) connectivity across the brain. These data representations were fed into a 2D Convolutional Neural Network (2D-CNN), a Graph Convolutional Neural Network (GCN), and a 3D Convolutional Neural Network (3D-CNN) respectively. Finally, the 2D-CNN and the 3D-CNN were chosen to combine into a single ensemble model to test the hypothesis that the combination of two different representations of the same data can improve upon the individual models. This ensemble model performed better than both the 2D-CNN and 3D-CNN models individually when validated using 5-fold cross-validation and 5×2-fold cross validation. However, this improvement was only statistically significant for the comparison with the 3D-CNN model ($p = 0.0224$). This result suggests that using combinations of multiple data representations may improve model accuracy when using functional neuroimaging data in deep learning applications.

Keywords: Functional Neuroimaging · Ensemble Learning · Deep Learning

© ICST Institute for Computer Sciences, Social Informatics and Telecommunications Engineering 2023
Published by Springer Nature Switzerland AG 2023. All Rights Reserved
T. Zlateva and G. Tuparov (Eds.): CSECS 2023, LNICST 514, pp. 204–211, 2023.
https://doi.org/10.1007/978-3-031-44668-9_16

1 Introduction

Deep learning applications for functional neuroimaging datasets, such as resting state functional magnetic resonance imaging (rs-fMRI) data, come with a variety of challenges. These datasets are generally large, have high dimensionality, complex spatiotemporal dynamics, and have a low sample size, which makes training deep learning models more challenging. Despite these challenges deep learning applications for neuroimaging datasets are of great interest in psychiatry and neurology for the potential of these models to identify patient diagnoses, predict prognoses, and individualize treatment [1, 2].

Currently machine learning applications for functional neuroimaging datasets have not demonstrated sufficient accuracy to make their way into clinical practice. To achieve this goal, more research must be done to understand the optimal representations of the input data and model architecture for improving prediction accuracy. Input of the full 4-dimensional rs-FMRI datasets into a deep learning model is not feasible, therefore it is important to find ways to dimensionally reduce these datasets to a more usable format for training while preserving important features.

In this project we investigated three different data representations of resting state functional magnetic resonance imaging (rs-fMRI) data taken from the Autism Brain Imaging Data Exchange (ABIDE) as input into their associated deep learning architectures [3]. We assessed each architecture's accuracy in classifying brain scans into a healthy control (HC) group or an Autism Spectrum Disorder (ASD) group. We then combined two of these models to test the hypothesis that an ensemble deep learning model with inputs from two representations of the same data will result in an overall binary classification accuracy that improves upon the individual models.

2 Methods

2.1 Data Preprocessing

For this analysis the ABIDE I dataset was directly accessed through the Nilearn Python package [4]. The dataset used contains aggregated data from 403 ASD subjects and 468 healthy controls obtained at 16 different scanning sites and was preprocessed using the configurable pipeline for the analysis of connectomes (cpac). Each scan was represented as a 4D dataset (3D volumetric scans with 2 mm^3 isotropic resolution taken every 2 s). The steps taken to ensure clean data included slice timing correction, realignment to correct for motion, and down sampling to 3 mm^3 isotropic resolution. Additional signal cleaning steps like global signal regression, and a low pass filtering of the signal to below 0.1 Hz were also performed. After preprocessing the rs-fMRI data was then transformed into different representations to act as the inputs to three separate deep learning architectures.

2.2 Data Representations

2D - Correlation Matrix Data Representation: For this representation, the data was transformed into 2D correlation matrices as input into a 2D convolutional neural network

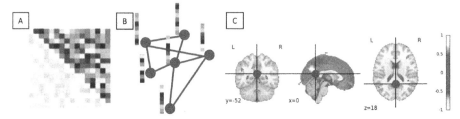

Fig. 1. Data representations of the rs-fMRI data. A) The correlation matrix representation where the brain signals from each ROI are correlated pairwise with all other ROIS to create a 2D correlation matrix of Pearson correlation values from −1 to 1. B) Graph tensor input where each subject scan is represented by a graph composed of edges, nodes and node features. C) A 3D Pearson correlation distribution with the PCC which is known to have altered functional connectivity in individuals with ASD [5].

(CNN) architecture. The 2D correlation matrices are a spatially and temporally simplified form of a rs-fMRI dataset which is created by performing pairwise Pearson correlations for every defined ROI time course (Fig. 1A). This was performed by first obtaining time courses from the resting state volumes using the Harvard oxford probabilistic atlas which defines 48 regions of interest (ROIs) across the cortical surface of the brain [5]. This 2D-CCN was later combined with the 3D-CNN to form an ensemble model.

Graph Tensor Data Representation: In this data representation the previous correlation matrices were converted to a graph data structure which consist of nodes and edges (Fig. 1B). The nodes and edges are defined from the correlation matrix where each ROI in the matrix is represented as a node with the correlation values for that ROI as the node features. The edges (or node connections) were made from the top 15 most correlated values for each node. Each subject's rs-fMRI data was therefore represented by a graph with 48 nodes, each having 47 features and 15 edges. This data was used as input into a graph convolutional network architecture [7].

3D Correlation Distribution Data Representation: For the third data representation the signal within the posterior cingulate cortex (PCC) in the brain was correlated with every other voxel in the volume. This gave us a spatial distribution of the functional connectivity of the PCC in the brain which is known to be altered in individuals with ASD [5] (Fig. 1C). Each dimension in this data (originally $60 \times 72 \times 60$ voxels) was downsampled by two to $30 \times 36 \times 30$ voxels due to memory constraints. This data was used as an input into a 3D-CNN architecture.

3 Results

3.1 2D-CNN Branch Architecture

For this branch the hyperparameters were tuned using the KerasTuner library's random search method. Initial hyperparameter tuning was performed to optimize the number of CNN layers. The architecture that performed the best after 15 epochs was a relatively simple CNN with two 2D-CNN layers with ReLU activation each with 64 filters followed by batch normalization, a max pooling layer and then finally two dense layers with dropout (Fig. 3). The model with the best validation accuracy after 15 epochs had a learning rate of 3.293×10^{-5} with Adam as the chosen optimizer. 5-fold cross validation was performed to test the generalizability of the accuracy. An early stopping callback was added to minimize overfitting. The average accuracy for the 5-fold cross validation was 63.49% with a standard deviation of 1.72% (Fig. 2).

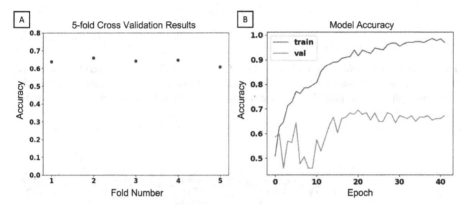

Fig. 2. Validation results of the 2D-CNN architecture. A) 5-fold cross validation accuracy across all folds. B) An example accuracy curve from one of the 5-fold cross validation iterations with early stopping. The average accuracy was found to be 63.49% with a standard deviation of 1.72%.

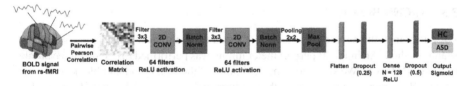

Fig. 3. 2D-CNN Architecture

3.2 GCN Branch Architecture

5-fold cross validation was used to choose the hyperparameters that had the best validation accuracy across all folds. From this tuning an architecture was chosen with 3 graph convolutional layers, each with ReLU activation and 64 layers followed by 2 dense layers both with ReLU activation and a final output layer with sigmoid activation (Fig. 5). Adam was chosen as the optimizer with a batch size of 150 samples and 0.0050 as the learning rate. These were all chosen by individually tuning the parameters in the architecture to achieve the highest validation accuracy. The average accuracy was found to be 60.30% with a standard deviation of 1.90% (Fig. 4).

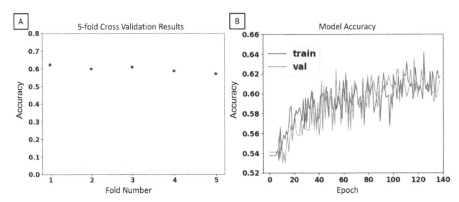

Fig. 4. 5-Fold cross validation results from the GCN model. A) The accuracy results from each of the 5-fold cross validations. B) An example accuracy curve from one of the 5-fold cross validation iterations with early stopping. The average accuracy across all folds was 60.30% with a standard deviation of 1.90%.

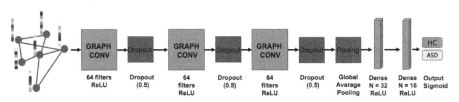

Fig. 5. Graph Convolutional Network Architecture

3.3 3D-CNN Branch

For this branch the hyperparameters were tuned using the KerasTuner library's random search method. An initial hyperparameter tuning was performed to decide on the number of 3D-CNN layers. We structured the beginning of the CNN model in blocks consisting of two 3D convolutional layers with 64 filters and $3 \times 3 \times 3$ kernels, followed by a MaxPool 3D layer and batch normalization. These blocks were followed by a flattening layer, 2 dense layers with ReLU activation functions, dropout, and a final sigmoid output layer (Fig. 7). Initial tuning was performed to choose the optimal number of CNN blocks and the type of optimizer based on validation accuracy of the model after 10 epochs. The model with the highest accuracy contained 1 block with stochastic gradient descent accelerated with Nesterov. Hyperparameter tuning continued for choosing the optimal learning rate, number of filters in the convolution blocks, the type of activation functions for CNN layers, dense layers, and the number of neurons in the dense layers. The final hyperparameters chosen were 15 filters for the first CNN block with ReLU activation, followed by a second CNN layer with 50 filters and ReLU activation. The dense layers contained 960 neurons and 630 neurons each with Tanh activation functions. The optimal learning rate was found to be 3.019×10^{-5}. 5-fold cross validation with early stopping was then performed to measure the final accuracy. The final 5-fold cross validation average accuracy was 57.06% with a standard deviation of 2.91% (Fig. 6).

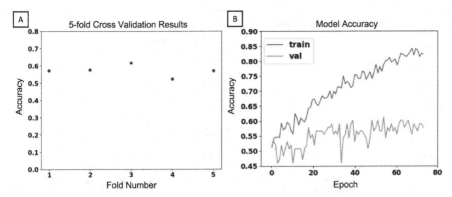

Fig. 6. 5-Fold Cross Validation Results from final 3D-CNN Branch. A) The accuracy results from each of the 5-fold cross validation iterations. B) An example accuracy curve from one of the 5-fold cross validation iterations with early stopping. The average accuracy across all folds was 57.06% with a standard deviation of 2.91%.

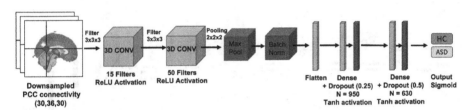

Fig. 7. 3D-CNN Architecture

3.4 Ensemble Architecture

Finally, the two CNN branches (2DCNN+3DCNN) were used to create an ensemble neural network which concatenated the outputs of the two models and added two dense layers before the final output layer. For each branch the hyperparameters were consistent with the original models, however the optimizer chosen was Adam and the learning rate was averaged between the two previous values (3.156×10^{-5}). 5-fold cross validation was run on a random sampling of the original data. The average final validation accuracy on all 5 folds was found to be to be 64.63% with a standard deviation of 1.62% (Figs. 8 and 9).

3.5 5 × 2-Fold Cross Validation

To test the significance between the ensemble learning model and the two original CNN models, a modified t-test was used to compare the accuracies of the models' 5 × 2-fold cross validation results [8]. Accuracies for each fold were acquired across the 2D-CNN, 3D-CNN and ensemble CNN models, and a modified student t-test was performed. The ensemble method outperformed the 2D-CNN model and the 3D-CNN model. However, only the comparison with the 3D-CNN model attained statistical significance. The 5 × 2-fold mean accuracies for the models were 61.66% with SD of 3.05% for the ensemble

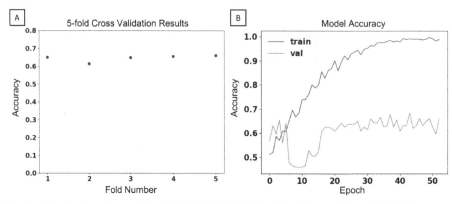

Fig. 8. Results from the combined 2DCNN+3DCNN combined ensemble model. A) Accuracy results from each of the 5-fold cross validations. B) An example accuracy curve from one of the 5-fold cross validation iterations with early stopping. The average accuracy across all folds was found to be 64.63% with a standard deviation of 1.62%.

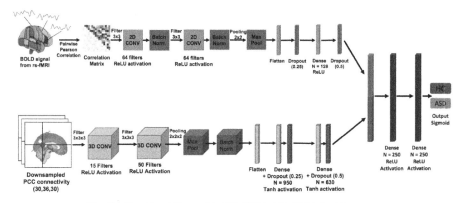

Fig. 9. Combined Ensemble 2D-CNN+3D-CNN Architecture

CNN model, 59.18% with an SD of 3.47% for the 2D-CNN model, and 54.54% with an SD of 2.10%. There was no significant difference between the 2D-CNN and the ensemble model accuracies (p = 0.747). There was a significant improvement between the 3D-CNN and ensemble model accuracies (p = 0.0224).

4   Conclusion

The performance of the ensemble model shows an increase over the two individual models when 5-fold cross validation and 5×2-fold cross validation was performed. This improvement is statistically significant when comparing this model to the individual 3D-CNN model (p = 0.0224), but not to the 2D-CNN model (P = 0.747). The improvement in performance of this ensemble learning model suggests that including multiple representations of functional neuroimaging may increase the information that the model can learn from. The non-significant result could be due to the low predictive accuracy of the 3D-CNN branch, which may add limited predictive power to the ensemble model. The PCC connectivity data for this stream was downsampled, possibly eliminating some key features which reduced the accuracy. Further optimization of the preprocessing steps, the ROIs chosen for time course selection, and seed region selections for the 3D connectivity data would likely improve model quality. It may be easier to see improvements in an ensemble model with higher accuracy in both branches.

It is important to emphasize that the accuracies of the individual models reported here do not support the idea that one data representation is better than the others. The data types themselves contain different information, and the quality of information they contain is dependent upon how they are represented. For example, the correlation matrices were created using the Harvard-Oxford cortical atlas, therefore the matrix would contain different information if time courses were extracted from ROIs defined in a different atlas. The 3D-PCC connectivity data was only generated using one seed area; other seed areas might prove more useful, but they were not tested for this project. Therefore, a direct comparison of the three data types is not possible to determine based on the scope of this project.

References

1. Smucny, J., Shi, G., Davidson, I.: Deep learning in neuroimaging: overcoming challenges with emerging approaches. Front. Psych. **13**, 912600 (2022)
2. Vieira, S., Pinaya, W.H., Mechelli, A.: Using deep learning to investigate the neuroimaging correlates of psychiatric and neurological disorders: methods and applications. Neurosci. Biobehav. Rev. **74**(Pt A), 58–75 (2017)
3. Craddock, C., et al.: The neuro bureau preprocessing initiative: open sharing of preprocessed neuroimaging data and derivatives. Neuroinformatics **7**, 5 (2013)
4. Nilearn Library (2010–2022) GitHub Repository. http://nilearn.github.io/stable/auto_exam ples/index.html. Accessed 20 June 2023
5. Hull, J.V., Dokovna, L.B., Jacokes, Z.J., Torgerson, C.M., Irimia, A., Van Horn, J.D.: Resting-state functional connectivity in autism spectrum disorders: a review. Front. Psych. **7**, 205 (2017)
6. Rushmore, R.J., Bouix, S., Kubicki, M., Rathi, Y., Yeterian, E., Makris, N.: HOA2.0-ComPaRe: a next generation harvard-oxford atlas comparative parcellation reasoning method for human and macaque individual brain parcellation and atlases of the cerebral cortex. Front. Neuroanat. **16**, 1035420 (2022)
7. CSIRO's Data61, StellarGraph Machine Learning Library GitHub Repository (2018). https://github.com/stellargraph/stellargraph. Accessed 20 June 2023
8. Dieterich, T.G.: Approximate statistical tests for comparing supervised classification learning algorithms. Neural Comput. **10**, 1895–1923 (1998)

Computer Architecture and Networks

A Methodology for Engineering Design and Simulation of a Satellite Horn Antenna

Yoana Ivanova[✉] and Georgi Petrov

New Bulgarian University, 21 Montevideo Str., 1618 Sofia, Bulgaria
{yivanova,gpetrov}@nbu.bg

Abstract. This empirical research described in the paper aims to present applications of integrated technology solutions based on 3D modeling and simulation methods in satellite communications. The concept of the study is expressed in the proposed methodology related to conducting tests in several simulation environments in order to design functional prototypes. One of the main scientific and applied contributions of this methodology is considered to be the use of a 3D author's model of a pyramidal horn antenna for satellite communication.

In satellite communications and microwave applications, pyramidal horn antennas are used because of their UHF and SHF operational frequency ranges between 300 MHz and 30 GHz. They can be used as irradiators in lenticular and mirror antennas as well as an active element in dish antennas because they represent radiating structures built as extensions of standard rectangular waveguides in order to improve their directivity. The main requirements for an optimal system are maximum directivity and a minimum width of the radiation pattern, which is a graphical representation by a 2D or 3D diagram of the distribution of radiated energy into space, which is functionally dependent on the direction.

The assessment and analysis of the obtained results show that the simulation data of the preliminary tests is correct, which means that the 3D object is modeled precisely, verified and validated according to all requirements in the selected simulation systems.

Keywords: 3D and simulation modeling · 3D printing · satellite horn antenna

1 Introduction

Nowadays, antennas are mainly designed using electromagnetic 3D simulators, which provide an environment where a simulation 3D model of the antenna can be created in great detail and tested. In the antenna design process can be applied numerical techniques for electromagnetic analysis which are different compared to analytical ones as they are classified into integral methods (method of moments), differential methods (methods of finite differences and elements) and optical methods. *"The numerical simulation is performed in 3 steps: pre-processing, processing, and post-processing"* [1]. For example, the FDTD (Finite-Difference Time Domain) is a method of finite differences characterized by its capabilities for modeling nano-scale optical devices.

© ICST Institute for Computer Sciences, Social Informatics and Telecommunications Engineering 2023
Published by Springer Nature Switzerland AG 2023. All Rights Reserved
T. Zlateva and G. Tuparov (Eds.): CSECS 2023, LNICST 514, pp. 215–232, 2023.
https://doi.org/10.1007/978-3-031-44668-9_18

Therefore, the objective of the present research is to upgrade a previous author's experimental study (2004) realized by the software for horn and reflector analysis (Sabor). The basic scenario is realized by a parabolic mirror with a diameter between 50 and 100 cm irradiated by a planar antenna at a frequency of 2.45 GHz. The generated value of the gain is 33 dB. It should be noted that microstrip patches are planar structures which are used in microwave and radio frequency range.

The update of prior work is necessary due to some limitations of microstrip patches compared to other antenna types. For instance, they have a lesser gain than parabolic reflector antennas and are susceptible to interference from nearby objects and changes in the dielectric substrate's characteristics. Pyramidal horn antennas provide higher gain, better directivity, and a wider bandwidth. It is significant to note that pyramidal horn antennas have lower sidelobes, which means that interference from undesirable directions can be effectively reduced. Therefore, the primary focus of this study is on the modeling and simulation of pyramidal horn antennas.

Practically, the essence of the methodology proposed in the article is shown in Fig. 1 and presented in Sects. 2 and 3. In Sect. 2, the main concept of the current experiment is described. It is realized by using an engineering 3D model of a pyramidal horn antenna with dimensions generated in a Horn Antenna Calculator [2] and visualized by using an Easy RF Calculator that generates a horn antenna radiation pattern at the selected frequency [3]. The simulation study continues with a verification of the 3D model in the simulation product CST Studio Suite 2022. The implementation of the modeling process in Autodesk 123D Design is described in Sect. 3.

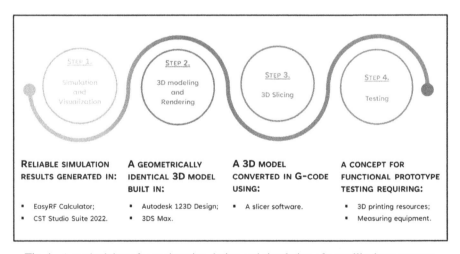

Fig. 1. A methodology for engineering design and simulation of a satellite horn antenna.

2 Simulations of the Radiation Pattern of the Pyramidal Horn Antenna

2.1 Calculating a Pyramidal Horn Antenna

There are different types of rectangular horn antennas depending on the direction of flaring [4].

- *sectoral horn antennas* – they are characterized by one-directional flaring. *"If this flaring is in the direction of an electrical vector, it is called a sectoral E-plane horn antenna, and if the flaring is in the direction of a magnetic vector, then it is called a sectoral H-plane horn antenna"*.
- *pyramidal horn antennas* – its *"flaring is done in the electrical as well as magnetic vector of the rectangular waveguide"*. One of the main characteristics of these antennas is the emitting opening called aperture (A), which must meet the requirement of being at least twice as large as the waveguide. The formulas for the A_E (L_E - slant length of the side in the E-field direction) and A_H (L_H - the slant length of the side in the H-field direction) are [5]:

$$A_E = \sqrt{2\lambda L_E} \tag{1}$$

$$A_H = \sqrt{3\lambda L_H}. \tag{2}$$

The effective aperture A_{Eff} depends on the optimal gain G, as follows:

$$A_{Eff} = \frac{G\lambda^2}{4\pi} \tag{3}$$

Due to these specifics, it is necessary to make some assumptions before starting the simulation study:

- *in the simulation environment, the antenna can be considered as an ideal lossless device, which means that the gain (G) is equal to the directivity (Dir., D);*
- *in a physical environment G < D.*

Table 1 includes the results generated by the calculators used. In Figs. 2, 3, and 4, screenshots from EasyRF Calculator for the three selected frequencies are shown. The reference planes for linearly polarized antennas, E-plane (the electric field) and H-plane (the magnetizing field) are orthogonal to each other: Phi = 90° (E-plane) and Phi = 0° (H-plane). Unlike the strongest "mainlobe" in the center, "sidelobes" can radiate in other directions, which is not desirable [6]. The electric field vector can be denoted by E_y and is drawn in red, while the magnetic field vectors H_x and H_z are drawn, respectively, in blue and green.

Table 1. A comparison of the results generated in the Horn Antenna and EasyRF Calculators.

Antennas	f, GHz	AxB, mm	G, dBi Horn Antenna Calculator	D, dBi EasyRF Calculator
A_1	8	61.5×41	12	19.56
A_2	4	123×82	12	13.80
A_3	2	246×164	12	7.98

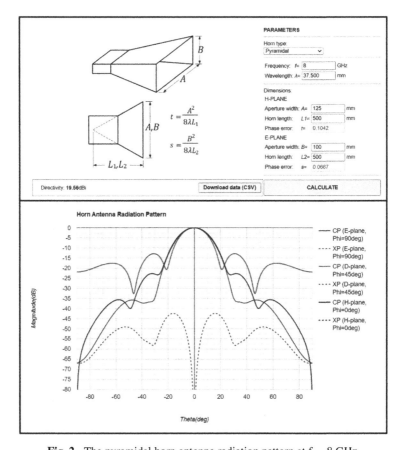

Fig. 2. The pyramidal horn antenna radiation pattern at f = 8 GHz.

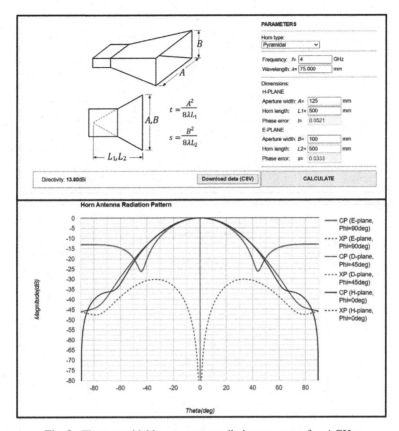

Fig. 3. The pyramidal horn antenna radiation pattern at f = 4 GHz.

Actually, the FDTD method solves Maxwell's equations at discrete points on a mesh in time and space to simulate wave propagation. It *"computes E and H at grid points spaced Δx, Δy, and Δz apart, with E and H interlaced in all three spatial dimensions. FDTD includes the effects of scattering, transmission, reflection, absorption, etc."* [7, 8]. The Maxwell – Heaviside equations represent differential equations that are expressed mathematically as follows:

$$\nabla \cdot D = \rho_v \tag{4}$$

$$\nabla \cdot B = 0 \tag{5}$$

$$\nabla \times E = -\frac{\partial B}{\partial t} \tag{6}$$

$$\nabla \times H = j + \frac{\partial D}{\partial t} \tag{7}$$

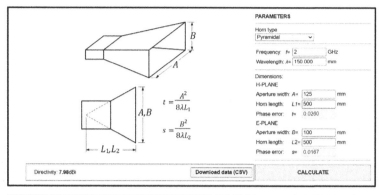

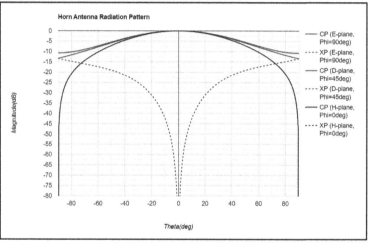

Fig. 4. The pyramidal horn antenna radiation pattern at f = 2 GHz.

In the Eqs. 4 and 5 are accepted the following designations:

- *electric flux density (D) – the propagation of the electric field (E) through a medium with permittivity (ε):*

$$D = \varepsilon E \tag{8}$$

- *magnetic flux density (B) - the propagation of the magnetic field (H) through a medium with permeability (μ):*

$$B = \mu H \tag{9}$$

- *charge density (ρv) describes the distribution of the charge within the medium.*
- *current density (j) - describes the distribution of current within the medium.*

After applying the curl operator to both sides of Eq. 6, the obtained result is as follows:

$$\nabla \cdot \nabla \times E = -\nabla \frac{\partial \times B}{\partial t} \tag{10}$$

$$\nabla^2 E = -\nabla \frac{\partial \times \mu H}{\partial t}$$ (11)

$$\nabla \times H = j + \frac{\partial D}{\partial t} = j + \frac{\partial \varepsilon E}{\partial t}$$ (12)

$$\nabla^2 E = \frac{\mu \varepsilon \partial^2 E}{\partial t^2}$$ (13)

$$\nabla^2 E = \frac{\partial^2 E}{\partial x^2} + \frac{\partial^2 E}{\partial y^2} + \frac{\partial^2 E}{\partial y^2}$$ (14)

Obviously, the percentage error is smallest for A_2 – 13% assuming the true value is generated in the EasyRF Calculator and 15% otherwise. It is calculated by the following formula:

$$\text{Error} = \frac{V_o - V_t}{V_t},$$ (15)

where *Error* is the percentage error, V_o is the observed value, and V_t is the true value.

2.2 A Verification of the Simulation 3D Model of a Pyramidal Horn Antenna

As it can be seen in Table 2, the values of the gain in the EasyRF Calculator are about 1.5 times higher compared to those generated in CST Studio Suite 2022. In Fig. 5 and 6 the farfield radiation patterns at 4 and 2 GHz are shown. The farfield radiation directivity diagrams at 8, 4, and 2 GHz are shown respectively in Figs. 7, 8, and 9 depending on the angle "Phi" that measures the angular distance to the x-axis in the lateral plane, while the angle "Theta" measures the angular distance from the pole that is situated in the z-direction. These angles are defined in the "Spherical Coordinate System", which means that "for a Cartesian vector (x, y, z) of length r, the angles can be obtained by the following relations [9]:

$$\varphi = arctan\frac{y}{x}$$ (16)

$$\theta = arccos\frac{z}{r}$$ (17)

Table 2. A comparison of the results generated in EasyRF Calculator and CST Studio Suite.

Antennas	f, GHz	A × B, mm	D, dBi EasyRF Calculator	D, dBi CST Studio Suite
A_1	8	61.5 × 41	19.56	12.51
A_2	4	123 × 82	13.80	7.825
A_3	2	246 × 164	7.98	5.399

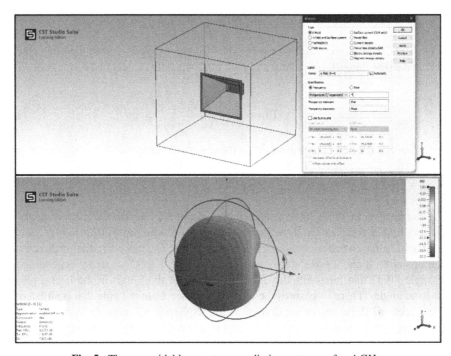

Fig. 5. The pyramidal horn antenna radiation pattern at f = 4 GHz.

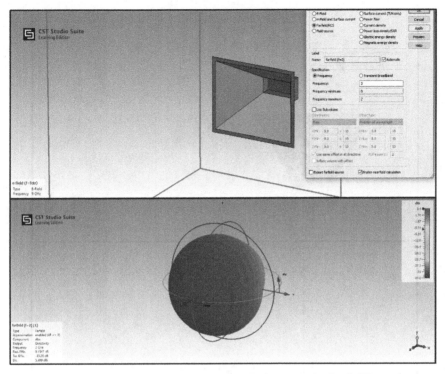

Fig. 6. The pyramidal horn antenna radiation pattern at f = 2 GHz.

2.3 Assessment and Analysis of the Simulation Results

In order to evaluate and analyze the simulation results, directivity diagrams and radiation patterns from previous studies by author[1] *("Excitation sources of a mirror antenna for wireless Internet", 2004)* are applied for comparison to illustrate the progress of the visualizations of the simulation results (Figs. 10 and 11). It can be concluded that, despite the high quality of the 3D visualizations generated in Zeland IE3D and Sabor, the possibility to import a 3D model of a radio engineering device into the simulation environment is an advantage in terms of clarity.

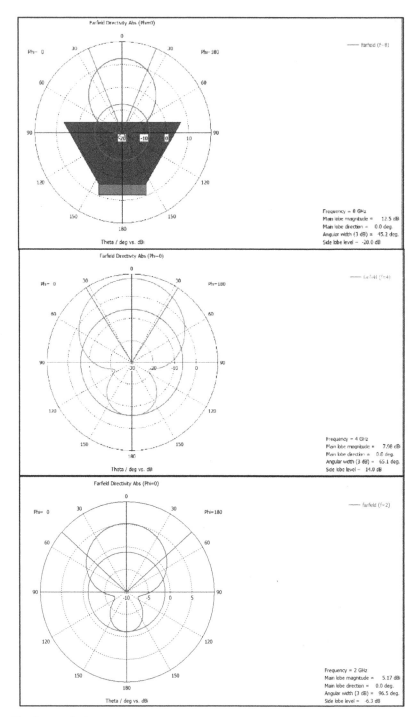

Fig. 7. The farfield radiation directivity diagrams at Phi = 0° and f = 8, 4, and 2 GHz.

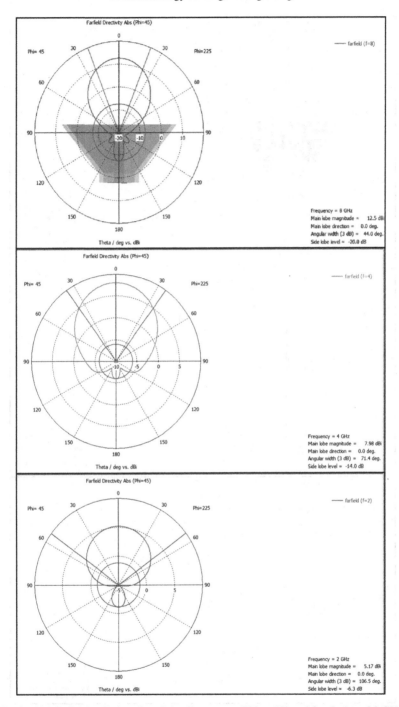

Fig. 8. The farfield radiation directivity diagrams at Phi = 45° and f = 8, 4, and 2 GHz.

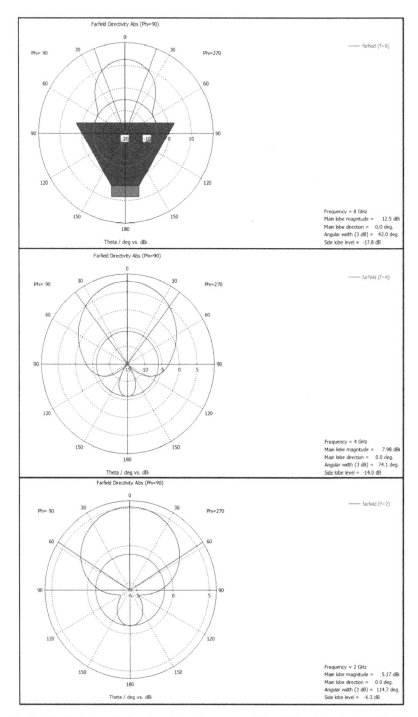

Fig. 9. The farfield radiation directivity diagrams at Phi $= 90°$ and f $= 8$, 4, and 2 GHz.

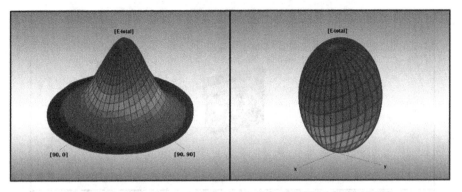

Fig. 10. Radiation patterns generated in Zeland IE3D at f = 2.45 GHz

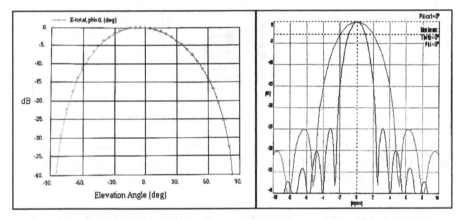

Fig. 11. Directivity diagrams generated in Zeland IE3D and Sabor at f = 2.45 GHz

3 3D Modeling of a Functional Prototype of a Pyramidal Horn Antenna

3.1 3D Modeling Methods

The author's 3D model is created by the method of solid modeling following the steps and by the tools in Table 3 using software for engineering modeling Autodesk 123D Design, with the dimensions generated in the Horn Antenna Calculator at 8 GHz simulated and visualized using a "macros" 3D model in CST Studio Suite 2022 as it is described in Sect. 2. Some examples of 3D visualizations generated in the simulator are shown in Fig. 12 to illustrate the advantage of using 3D computer graphics in engineering and science in order to achieve greater clarity and informativeness of output data.

Actually, 3D models can be imported into simulation environments for conducting additional tests for the purposes of a detailed comparison analysis with the results obtained in item 2.2 of Sect. 2. In regard to practical 3D modeling, the first algorithm is recommended as more direct, while the second could be determined as more complex

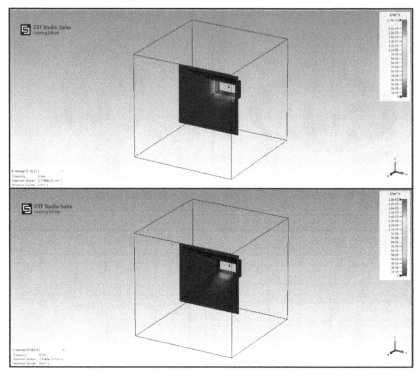

Fig. 12. Visualizations using a 3D model of a pyramidal horn antenna in CST Studio Suite 2022 at f = 8 GHz: e-energy; h-energy.

but suitable for some particular situations of difficulties related to possible input parameter limitations of some tools like "Shell", which defines the thickness of the antenna's wall.

Table 3. Algorithms for 3D modeling of a pyramidal horn antenna in Autodesk 123D Design.

Solid Modeling	Groups of Tools	3D Modeling Algorithm
Method 1	Construct, Modify, Transform	Primitive Box > Smart Scale > Sketch: Rectangle > Transform: Measure > Transform: Align > Construct: Loft > Modify: Shell
Method 2	Construct, Modify, Combine, Transform	Primitive Box > Smart Scale > Transform: Align > Clone > Combine: Subtract > Tweak > Sketch: Rectangle > Construct: Extrude > Delete

Rendered images of the model with a different metal material applied in Autodesk 123D Design and 3DS Max are shown in Fig. 13 to compare the level of visual realism. In fact, the main advantage of Autodesk 123D Design is the capability for precise engineering modeling, while the quality of visualization looks high in 3DS Max.

3.2   A Concept for Testing 3D Printed Functional Prototypes of a Satellite Horn Antenna

The model of a pyramidal horn antenna can be 3D printed and used for testing using conventional and compatible physical devices. Before the printing process, the model must be sliced in a slicer software like PrusaSlicer, Lychee, Cura, XYZ Print, etc. Regardless of the printing technology (FDM - Fused Deposition Modeling used for 0.9–2.4 GHz, SLS- Selective Laser Sintering for frequencies above 1.3 GHz), in all cases, additional manual processing of the final products is required, considering smoothing the working surfaces of the antennas or additional varnishing of the products with a UV protective layer. Both types of materials require coating the working surfaces and all contact interface areas with a metallized layer of silver zinc paint or by vacuum metallizing the products.

The use of semi-transparent materials allows the creation of multi-colored products that can be used in teaching students, thus making it possible to see the working surfaces and elements of the antenna inside, even making a gradual colorization of the working surfaces show the intensity of the electromagnetic fields (EMF) inside the antenna. The proposed methodology can be applied not only to antennas but also to the production of larger microwave systems using waveguides with very complex architectures.

It should be noted that applications of such systems must be used carefully because 3D printed technology using different types of plastics can reduce the lifecycle of systems because of material degradation over time, deformations because of higher working temperatures, and sudden failures of components because of lower temperatures. The superiority achieved by this technology is mainly associated with the possibility to make spare parts or to design and test highly complex waveguide systems, as well as the lower price of the final product compared to classic metallic products. Particular attention should be paid to the creation of products that are designed to fly or work in vacuum space due to the presence of voids and microcracks.

Autodesk 123D Design   3DS Max

Fig. 13. Rendered images of the 3D model of a pyramidal horn antenna with a metal material applied.

4 Conclusion

In conclusion, it can be summarized that the completion of all the steps in the proposed methodology ensures reliable results and qualitative visualizations in simulation environments, while the 3D modeling products provide highly realistic rendering and can be combined successfully to achieve professional results. The contemporary design with CAD/CAM and 3D printing of radio engineering devices is a high-tech area providing innovative technologies that contribute to serial machine production at the stages of precise engineering modeling, manufacturing, and testing functional prototypes.

This research can be continued by 3D printing the model from different materials (PLA and PETG) after a pre-printing preparation. In addition, the proper selection of 3D printing resources (filaments and 3D printers) is important to improve the quality of the functional prototypes, which can be used to conduct experimental research with measuring physical devices [10]. Conducting experiments in laboratory conditions can be not only very effective and productive but also related to methods for the investigation of EMF [11, 12] as well as innovative solutions for the prevention of electromagnetic radiation from mobile radio transmitting stations [13] and gamming attacks.

References

1. Dankov, P.: Anteni za mobilni i satelitni komunikatsii, prilozhenia za ustanovyavane na mestopolozhenie, GPS-sistemi. In: Conference: Lyatno uchilishte za uchiteli "Fizika za i sas smartfon", 11–15 yuli, FzF na SU "Sv. Kliment Ohridski", Sofia (2016)
2. Kustarev, V.: Horn Antenna online calculator, (2015–2022). https://3g-aerial.ben/online-cal culations/antenna-calculations/horn-antenna-online-calculator. Accessed 15 May 2023
3. EasyRF. https://hornantennacalculator.blogspot.com/p/calculator.html. Accessed 15 May 2023
4. Meena, M., Prakash, V.: Simulation results of rectangular horn antenna. Int. J. Eng. Technol. 3(1), 171–179 (2018)
5. Electronics Notes. Microwave Horn Antenna Theory. https://www.electronics-notes.com/art icles/antennas-propagation/horn-antenna/theory-equations.php. Accessed 21 May 2023
6. Dankov, P.: Microwave measurement of electrical fields in different media – principles, methods and instrumentation. J. Phys: Conf. Ser. **516**(1), 012001 (2014)
7. David, D.S.K., Jeong, Y., Wu, Y.C., Ham, S.: An analytical antenna modeling of electromagnetic wave propagation in inhomogeneous media using FDTD: a comprehensive study. Sensors 23(8), 3896 (2023). https://doi.org/10.3390/s23083896
8. SYNOPSYS, Finite-Difference Time-Domain Method. https://www.synopsys.com/glossary/ what-is-fdtd.html#C. Accessed 21 May 2023
9. Farfield Calculation Overview. https://space.mit.edu/RADIO/CST_online/mergedProjects/ 3D/special_postpr/special_postpr_pp_farfield.htm
10. Pasarelski R., Pasarelska, T.: Metodika za izsledvane i analiz na radiotehnicheski prametri na universalni mobilni telekomunikatsionni sistemi, Sbornik nauchni trudove ot godishna nauchna konferentsia s mezhdunarodno uchastie na natsionalen voenen universitet "Vasil Levski" – Veliko Tarnovo (2013)
11. Stancheva, A., Tzvetkov, P., Mihova, P.: International research projects - justification for introduction of lower exposure limits for EMF with low intensity, CD "Godishnik, tom 1" 2014. Departament Zdraveopazvane i sotsialna rabota, NBU, Sofia (2014). ISSN 1313-7875

12. Stancheva, A., Pasarelski, R., Kadrev, V.: Metodi za namalyavane na radiosmushteniyata v LTE mrezhi. Sbornik dokladi ot godishna universitetska nauchna konferentsia, pp. 670–677, Natsionalen voenen universitet "Vasil Levski", V.Tarnovo (2017). ISSN 2367-7481

13. Pasarelski, R., Stancheva, A., Tsvetkov, P.: Mehanizmi za preventsia ot elektromagnitno izlachvane ot mobilni radiopredavatelni stantsii. In: Sbornik dokladi na XXVI Mezhdunaroden nauchen simpozium s mezhdunarodno uchastie „Metrologia i metrologichno osiguryavane2016, Sozopol, Bulgaria, pp. 383–392 (2016). ISSN 1313-9126

Optimized FPGA Implementation of an Artificial Neural Network Using a Single Neuron

Yassen Gorbounov[1]([✉]) [iD] and Hao Chen[2] [iD]

[1] New Bulgarian University and MGU "St. Ivan Rilsky", Sofia, Bulgaria
ygorbounov@nbu.bg
[2] China University of Mining and Technology, Xuzhou 221000, People's Republic of China
hchen@cumt.edu.cn

Abstract. Since its emergence in the early 1940s as a connectionist approximation of the functioning of neurons in the brain, artificial neural networks have undergone significant development. The trend of increasing complexity is steadily exponential and includes an ever-increasing variety of models. This is due on the one hand to the achievements in microelectronics, and on the other to the growing interest and development of the mathematical apparatus in the field of artificial intelligence. It can be assumed however that overcomplicating the structure of the artificial neural network is no guarantee of success. Following this reasoning, the paper proposes a continuation of the author's previous research to create an optimized neural network designed for use on resource-constrained hardware. The new solution aims to present a design procedure for building neural networks using only a single hardware neuron by using context switching and time multiplexing by the aid of an FPGA device. This would lead to significant reduction in computational requirements and the possibility of creating small but very efficient artificial neural networks.

Keywords: Artificial Neural Network · Contextual Switching · Hardware Acceleration · FPGA · Optimization

1 Motivation

The study of the principles and working patterns of the nervous system of living organisms has a long history. The first attempts to recreate it with technical means date back to the early 1940s, when the neurophysiologist Warren McCulloch, and the mathematician Walter Pitts published a research on possible working model of the neuron [17]. Their point of view has been oriented toward the use of electronic circuits to model simple neural networks. In general, the modeling of artificial neural networks (ANN) aims at not only recreating the basic functionality of the neural cell alone but also mimicking intelligence at the biological level by simulating the neurophysiology of the brain. The ultimate goal is to achieve such a mechanism of information processing, which is as close

© ICST Institute for Computer Sciences, Social Informatics and Telecommunications Engineering 2023
Published by Springer Nature Switzerland AG 2023. All Rights Reserved
T. Zlateva and G. Tuparov (Eds.): CSECS 2023, LNICST 514, pp. 233–246, 2023.
https://doi.org/10.1007/978-3-031-44668-9_19

as possible to the processes taking place in a set of multi-connected neurons, and then make all this work in a hardware computation device. Thus the information processing is parallel and distributed among multiple simple, interconnected elements. In theory, a single nonlinear layer with a very large number of neurons can learn arbitrary relations between the input and the output of that layer. Increasing the number of layers and the ways their individual nodes (neurons) are interconnected, may lead to an even more efficient learning process [16]. ANNs are capable of solving a large variety of linear and nonlinear problems, so in a more general mathematical sense, neural networks are considered by [23] as a universal approximator. The final objective of these models is to create a technical device capable of learning and making decisions similar to the human brain and at the same time outperforming its speed of data processing.

A consistent overview of the major ANN topologies, taxonomy, and chronological development is provided by the members of the Asimov Institute [16]. Without claiming to be exhaustive, in Table 1 are outlined the major milestones in the development of ANN [3, 18, 25, 29].

Table 1. Key milestones in the evolution of the ANN development.

Year	Authors	Achievement
1943	W. McCulloch, W. Pitts	Modeled a simple NN with electronic circuits [17]
1949	D. O'Hebb	The learning hypothesis of biological neurons – Hebbian Learning [9]
1957	F. Rosenblatt	Perceptron, the oldest ANN model still in use today [27]
1959	B. Widrow, M. Hoff	(Multiple) ADAptive LINear Elements – ADALINE, MADALINE [34]
1969	M. Minsky, S. Pappert	Demonstrate the impossibility for a single-layer perceptron to learn an XOR function [19]
1974	P. Werbos	Backpropagation – backward propagation algorithm of errors propagation working back from output nodes to input nodes [33]
1982	J. Hopfield	Hopfield network. A content-addressable model for understanding human memory [10]
1998	LeCun	Convolutional Neural Network (ConvNet, CNN). A class of ANN mostly applied for image analysis. It uses the convolution instead of matrix multiplication [15]
1985–2006	Various scientists	Boltzmann Machine (Ackley), Autoencoder (Rumelhart), Multilayer Perception (Rumelhart, Hinton, Williams), Recurrent Neural Network (Jordan), Restricted Boltzmann Machine (Smolensky), LeNet (LeCun), Long short-term Memory LSTM (Hochreiter, Schmidhuber), Deep Belief network (Hinton)
2005	F. Scarselli, S. Yong, M. Gori, M. Hagenbuchner, A. Tsoi, M. Maggini	Graph Neural Network (GNN). A class of ANN for processing data that are given as graphs [28, 35]
2012	A. Krizhevsky	AleXNET. It is the first fast GPU-implementation of a CNN [14]

(continued)

Table 1. (*continued*)

Year	Authors	Achievement
2014	I. Goodfellow	Generative Adversarial Networks (GNN). ML framework with two NN where one agent's gain is another agent's loss [6, 32]
2020	OpenAI	Generative Pre-trained Transformer 3 (GPT-3), a deep learning model to produce human-like text [1]

It can be seen from this table that the diversity and the capabilities of ANNs are constantly rising all along with the increase of their complexity. There are authors however that claim that "fewer neurons are needed as experience is gained". Such an observation has been made by the renowned professor of molecular and cell biology at the University of California, Berkeley, Walter Freeman, who is among the founders of computational neuroscience, where mathematics is employed to study brain dynamics. He concludes that "after sniffing again and again it appears that only a few neurons are sufficient", and "animals and humans can perceive same information for things like odour, but require different amount of neurons – flies have 100 000 neurons while human brain has billions" [4]. McCulloch and Pitts with their cybernetic neuron model [17], and Karl Pribram [24] with his studies on brain dynamics, have strongly impacted Freeman's scientific thought. This interpretation differs from theories in neuroscience, which aim to collect data from as many neurons as possible, which can then be analyzed offline to improve understanding of the brain's information processing [13].

Apart from the main task of solving the function approximation, object recognition, or decision-making problem, ANNs nowadays face the need to overcome the problem of saving power. The latter is obvious, since the number of neurons in the mathematical model, the topological complexity, and therefore the required computation resources, are growing at breakneck speed. In [36] a very important observation is made, namely, the fact that a considerable amount of arithmetic operations in ANN do repeat many times, so in order to decrease the energy consumption redundant computations can be eliminated. The authors of that study called their model CORN (COmputation Reuse-aware Neural network accelerator) and proposed the neurons to share their computation results. Another study [20] discusses a multiplexing technique called DataMUX which allows ANN to analyze multiple data streams in nearly simultaneous manner by multiplexing the inputs and the outputs. In this study, the software approach has been taken as the experimental platform and no hardware implementations have been attempted. A recent paper in Nature Communications [30] discusses the possibility to build a deep neural network using a single neuron. The architecture proposed by the authors is named "folded-in-time DNN (Fit-DNN)" and uses multiple time-delayed feedback loops to model the so called delay dynamical system, again by software means. In fact, to date, the design and implementation of neural networks using high-performance hardware is gaining a lot of speed [21, 22, 26, 33]. However, the trend of increasing complexity, and therefore increasing the cost of computing power, continues to be sustainable.

In the present research, an attempt is made to go even further by allowing the entire artificial neural network to be implemented using a single hardware neuron. For neural networks with a smaller number of layers and up to a few tens of neurons, this approach can be very efficient and quite sufficient to solve the entire task. For more complex neural networks such as deep neural networks (DNN), convolutional neural networks (CNN), graph neural networks (GNN), etc., this approach can aid in combining a network built using a single hardware neuron and time-multiplexed computations [7] for modeling of one layer or one node in a graph respectively, and next context-switching of the weight matrices and the activation function matrices. The latter can lead to a reduction in the total number of network layers, a significant reduction in hardware resources, and hence strongly decreased energy consumption. This suggests the possibility of creating more affordable, smarter, and energy-efficient devices that employ space-constrained hardware, without making a compromise with the performance.

The remainder of this work is organized as follows: At first in chapter "Hardware model of the artificial neuron," it is described the hardware principle that lies behind the implementation of the artificial neuron. Discussed are its building blocks and the quantization problem. In chapter "The single-layer artificial neural network" the context switching organization proposed in the previous work of the authors [7] is reintroduced as it can aid in understanding the approach presented in the next chapter "The single hardware-neuron network". Directions for future improvement are given in chapter "Future work". The chapter "Conclusions" summarizes the results.

2 Hardware Model of the Artificial Neuron

In living organisms, the nervous system is made up of nerve cells called neurons, which are their basic structural units. An abstract model of the living neural cell together with its analogical mathematical model is depicted in Fig. 1. It puts together the biological terms (A), the corresponding mathematical abstract counterparts (B), and the basic task that is performed in the process of converting the input to output (C). In the biological cell, the entry points of the neuron are the nerve endings obtained from the branching of axons that come from other nerve cells, each end being connected by a dendrite. The point of connection is called a synapse. In reality, the neuron endings and dendrites do not touch but are located at a very small distance (50 to 200 angstroms), which is called the synaptic gap. Dendrites come together in bundles, which are their connection to the cell body, called the soma. The output of the soma is a filamentous outgrowth called an axon. It serves to carry electrical energy to the dendrites of another neuron. The condition for the occurrence of an electrical potential depends on the sum of the magnitudes of the stimulating effects that the neuron receives through its inputs. When sufficiently large input stimuli are received, the neuron is activated and generates (fires) an output signal with constant amplitude and variable frequency, i.e. the neuron acts as a threshold function with saturation. This corresponds to a decision making. The high speed of information processing in the biological nervous system is due to the high number of neurons (about 10^{12} in mammals, about 10^7 in reptiles, and about 10^5 in flies), and their complex multi-connected topology, which has dynamic behavior.

The mathematical model is much more simple but clearly reflects the main components in the living cell. Each synaptic connection consists of a multiplier that computes the product of a given input with a weight which purpose is to model the strength of

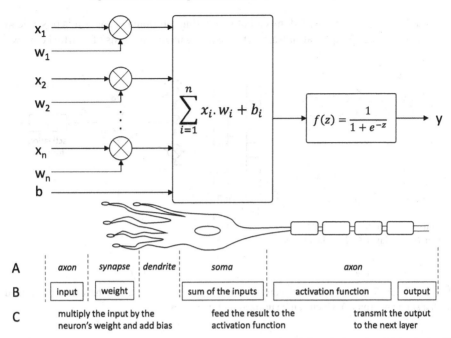

Fig. 1. A model of the artificial neuron along with a functional description: A – biological cell parts description, B – mathematical abstraction equivalent, and C – functions.

the synaptic link. Technically the weights are organized in matrix form and contain the knowledge of the neural network. Their negative or positive values are obtained during the learning process which consists of strengthening or weakening the connections between neurons. The products along with a tuning parameter called the bias, are fed to the cell body which sums them up and feeds the result to the activation function. The latter models the behavior of the axon and may take various predefined implementation forms. It determines the relationship between the neurons of the consecutive layers.

The following conclusions can be drawn from the presented model: (a) the inputs are high-dimensional; (b) the outputs are multidimensional; (c) multiple multipliers are required; (d) one multi-input adder is required; (e) the activation function can be of different types depending on the layer.

In multilayer neural networks, the listed structural elements are multiplied by the number of neurons and can occupy significant hardware resources. Additionally, calculations are performed using signed floating-point arithmetic. When building artificial neural networks using a purely hardware approach, programmable logic circuits of the Field Programmable Gate Array (FPGA) type are most often used. On the one hand, they offer an extremely high level of parallelism and great flexibility, but on the other hand, they do not have built-in floating-point units (FPU) so they do not support the floating-point (FP) standard IEEE-75 [11].

Everything said above leads to the conclusion that instead of having multiple repeating nodes, it is possible to build a single one as shown in Fig. 2. Following the principles of modularity and regularity [8] instead of generating multiple instances it is possible to use a surrounding (peripheral) infrastructure and organize it in terms of a virtual context.

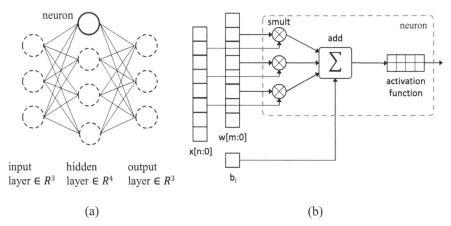

Fig. 2. The artificial neural network consists of multiple repeating nodes (a) that can be substituted with a single neuron (b) which can be utilized multiple times.

Given the three-layer, 7-neuron network from Fig. 2 (not counting the input layer as it just forms the inputs), the processing effort can be computed as 21 multiplications, 28 additions and 7 activations. The numbers for a single neuron unit are seven times less.

The weight matrices (knowledge), the bias (corrective factor that shifts the activation function across the plane), and the activation function (decision making), are structured as arrays. In order to reduce the memory consumption, it is suitable to reduce the precision and process the numbers in signed fixed-point arithmetic [5]. This process in called quantization and can be easily done by performing the shift operation to upscale and downscale the FP number. In [2, 12] it is stated that 8-bit integer multiplies can consume 6X less energy and occupy 6X less area than IEEE 754 16-bit floating-point multiplies, and the advantage for integer addition is improved 13 times in terms of energy and 38 times in terms of area. A transition from 32-bit to 8-bit arithmetic would reduce the model size by a factor of 4, and so there will be a significant reduction in memory. The IEEE 754 standard specifies the 32-bit single precision numbers as a binary number (N_{FP32}) with three fields, namely the sign bit, 8 bits for the exponent (E-127) and 23 bits for the mantissa (M) (1). The exponent is a biased 8-bit unsigned integer, ranging from -126 to $+127$. This is due to the fact that special numbers are represented with -127 (all 0s) and $+128$ (all 1s).

$$N_{FP32} = \pm M.b^{E-127} = (-1)^{b_{31}}.2^{(E-127)}.\left(1 + \sum_{i=1}^{23} b_{23-i}.2^{-i}\right) \tag{1}$$

Generally, the quantized 8-bit number N_{q8} can be obtained from the 32-bit IEEE 754 binary number N_{FP32} as shown in Fig. 3 by following (2):

$$N_{q8} = rnd\left(\frac{N_{FP32}}{2.max(abs(N_{FP32}))/256}\right) \tag{2}$$

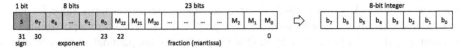

Fig. 3. IEEE 754 single precision floating point

The denominator is the scaling factor that maps the floating-point dynamic-range to the range $[-128, 127]$, and *rnd* is a rounding function. A possible drawback is that the ANN can lose accuracy because information precision is poorer but, depending on loss factor, the quantized ANN can in fact result in a very minimal loss. This comes at the price of improved latency, memory usage, and power.

3 The Single-Layer Artificial Neural Network

The concept of the single-layer artificial neural network is depicted in Fig. 4.

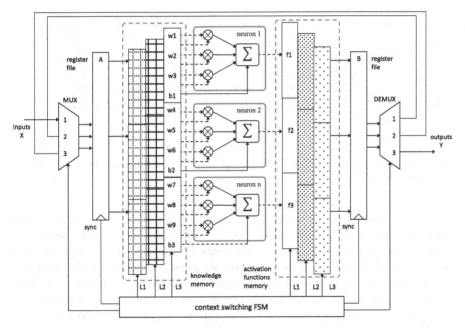

Fig. 4. The single-layer context-switching ANN structure

In a previous research of the authors [7] is has been discussed a model of an artificial neural network with a single hardware layer of processing units. As can be seen from Fig. 2, the ANN consists of a number of repeating structures – neurons, arranged in layers. Each layer is dependent on the data from another layer (in most topologies this is the previous layer). That means instead of multiplying the processing units it is convenient to multiply only the weights, biases and activation functions matrices, and keep the number of neurons equal to their number in the largest layer since for the unused nodes the matrices will be zeroed. The proposed approach offers a possibility to perform pipelining of the computation chain by switching the parameters set (context) over time. The increase in the processing time between layers is near to zero. The model is simplified and the example has a maximum of three neurons in a layer but it can be easily expanded to more neurons. The vectors of the real inputs and the ones of the subsequent layer outputs are multiplexed and stored one at a time in the input register file (A) which serves the purpose of synchronizing the data transfer. Their values enter the neurons together with the vectors of the knowledge base – the memory arrays that contain weights and biases for the layers L1, L2 and L3. After the data are being processed, the individual neuron firing decision is made based on the associated activation function. Finally, the outputs are stored in another register file (B) and are distributed next with the aid of the output demultiplexer.

The synchronization process is managed by the context-switching finite state machine (FSM) whose directed graph, states encoding, transition, and output tables are given in Fig. 5.

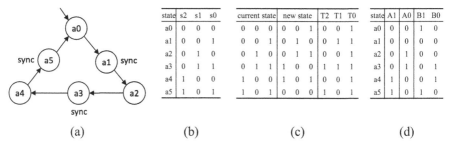

state	s2	s1	s0
a0	0	0	0
a1	0	0	1
a2	0	1	0
a3	0	1	1
a4	1	0	0
a5	1	0	1

current state			new state			T2	T1	T0
0	0	0	0	0	1	0	0	1
0	0	1	0	1	0	0	1	1
0	1	0	0	1	1	0	0	1
0	1	1	1	0	0	1	1	1
1	0	0	1	0	1	0	0	1
1	0	1	0	0	0	1	0	1

state	A1	A0	B1	B0
a0	0	0	1	0
a1	0	0	0	0
a2	0	1	0	0
a3	0	1	0	1
a4	1	0	0	1
a5	1	0	1	0

(a)   (b)   (c)   (d)

Fig. 5. The context-switching FSM directed graph (a), states encoding (b), state transitions (c), and outputs table (d)

This finite state machine works as a simple counter if taking states a0, a2, and a4 (even states) and as a data transfer synchronizer if taking states a1, a3, and a5 (odd states). The counter functionality takes its outputs directly from the state register and is connected to selector inputs of the input multiplexer and the output demultiplexer. The outputs table (Fig. 5(d) is divided in two halves – the A-side determines the *sync* signal for the input register file and other input-related tasks, while the B-side determines the *sync* signal for the output register file and controls the output data distribution.

The schematic diagram of the synthesized finite state machine device with the aid of T-type flip-flops is shown in Fig. 6. It is in fact a parallel synchronous counter with associated outputs decoding logic. The FSM is of a deterministic synchronous Moore-type. The parallel implementation guarantees that there will be no cumulative delay in the signal propagation chain.

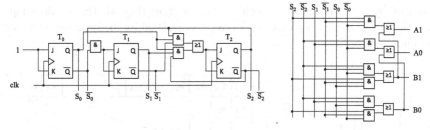

Fig. 6. The synthesized finite state machine (left) and the outputs generation (right)

The general mathematical form of the elaborated single layer neural network is (3).

$$
\begin{pmatrix} h_{k1} \\ h_{k2} \\ \vdots \\ h_{kn} \end{pmatrix} = \begin{pmatrix} w_{i1k1} & w_{i2k1} & \cdots & w_{imk1} \\ w_{i1k2} & w_{i2k2} & \cdots & w_{imk2} \\ \vdots & \vdots & \vdots & \vdots \\ w_{i1kn} & w_{i2kn} & \cdots & w_{imkn} \end{pmatrix} \begin{pmatrix} h_{i1} \\ h_{i2} \\ \vdots \\ h_{in} \end{pmatrix} + \begin{pmatrix} b_{k1} \\ b_{k2} \\ \vdots \\ b_{kn} \end{pmatrix}
$$
$$
= \begin{pmatrix} w_{i1k1}.h_{i1} + w_{i2k1}.h_{i2} + \cdots + w_{imk1}.h_{im} + b_{k1} \\ w_{i1k2}.h_{i1} + w_{i2k2}.h_{i2} + \cdots + w_{imk2}.h_{im} + b_{k2} \\ \vdots \\ w_{i1kn}.h_{i1} + w_{i2kn}.h_{i2} + \cdots + w_{imkn}.h_{im} + b_{km} \end{pmatrix}
\tag{3}
$$

In this equation h is the single neuron, w is one of the weights, k is the index for next and i is the index for the previous layer of the network. As it can be seen weight and bias matrices can easily fit in two- and single-dimensional arrays respectively. A linear data structure memory array is very convenient for storing the matrices.

4   The Single Hardware-Neuron Network

The artificial neural network discussed above contains a single layer in which computations are performed in parallel. There are no dependencies between individual neurons of this layer. It is therefore possible, at the cost of a small delay, to use a single neuron to perform computations with data sequentially fed to it. For this purpose, it is necessary to add a second state machine to time multiplex the weights coefficients and bias of the neuron's inputs, as well as the activation functions and the final result of its output. The presentation of all the data remains unchanged, in matrix form.

The weights that are associated with each input constitute a multidimensional array. In this array elements in each row correspond to the weights of the respected neuron, the elements in each column are associated with the equally numbered inputs and the depth of the array corresponds to the different layers. The multidimensional array can be transformed into a two-dimensional one as shown in Fig. 7. That means it can fit into a memory and be manipulated using simple addressing arithmetic.

After this step, the array takes the form of the one shown in Fig. 8 which represents an unfolded-in-time structure. This allows the inputs to be multiplexed with the aid of the finite state machine. Each row in this array corresponds to a network layer, and is controlled by the layer context-switching state machine (Fig. 4). The multiplexing of the weights groups and biases for a neuron is controlled by the time-unfolding state machine.

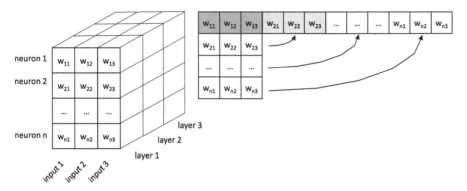

Fig. 7. The three-dimensional array can be converted into a two-dimensional one.

neuron 1			neuron 2			neuron 3				neuron n			
w^1_{11}	w^1_{12}	w^1_{13}	w^1_{21}	w^1_{22}	w^1_{23}	w^1_{31}	w^1_{32}	w^1_{33}	...	w^1_{n1}	w^1_{n2}	w^1_{n3}	layer 1
w^2_{11}	w^2_{12}	w^2_{13}	w^2_{21}	w^2_{22}	w^2_{23}	w^2_{31}	w^2_{32}	w^2_{33}	...	w^2_{n1}	w^2_{n2}	w^2_{n3}	layer 2
...	...	...	...	...	...	...	...	...	...				...
w^k_{11}	w^k_{12}	w^k_{13}	w^k_{21}	w^k_{22}	w^k_{23}	w^k_{31}	w^k_{32}	w^k_{33}	...	w^k_{n1}	w^k_{n2}	w^k_{n3}	layer k
time 1			time 2			time 3				time n			

time →

Fig. 8. The two-dimensional representation of the time multiplexed weights matrix. The superscript denotes layer number.

The proposed single hardware neuron architecture is depicted in Fig. 9. There is a single processing unit that involves several multiplications (three in the example) and a single summation at a time. The performance of execution of these operations is dependent on the type of the microarchitecture implementation. The algorithms can be highly optimized for speed, occupied space or power efficiency. The proposed structure also significantly reduces the memory space that is required by the activation function compared with the method proposed in [7]. Moreover, based on the principles of regularity and modularity, the activation function can be implemented in various ways and new functions can be added without needing a redesign of the rest of the circuit. For instance, it is possible to implement the activation function as a look-up table (LUT) which is very fast but not always precise. Or it can be implemented by using some special algorithm such as CORDIC (COordinate Rotation DIgital Computer) or the partial linear approximation of a nonlinear function (PLAN) where the exponent and division are replaced with shift and add operations.

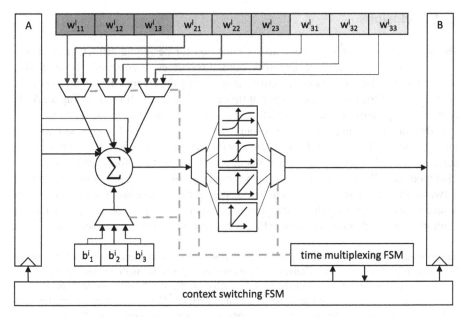

Fig. 9. The single hardware-neuron network

The single hardware-neuron network effectively combines the context switching approach proposed in [7] with the newly proposed time multiplexing mechanism. This suggests that the neural network built using this method will require many times less computing power and energy. A similar structure could be multiplied so that several completely independent artificial neural networks run simultaneously on a single FPGA device which may find myriads of applications in technical fields such as machine learning, robotics and many others.

5 Future Work

The early stage of the present research suggests a huge amount of future work aimed at verifying real networks built in the proposed way, as well as finding new high-performance application areas. It is planned to carry out experiments on the application of the artificial neural network with a single hardware neuron in tasks of functional approximation, simple pattern recognition, and machine learning through the construction of multilayer neural networks. A good candidate where the proposed approach can find a real application, are Graph Neural Networks (GNN), where machine learning algorithms can make useful predictions at the level of nodes, edges, or entire graphs. An irrevocable future task is to conduct a comparative analysis and performance benchmarking with other networks built in a classical way with multiple neurons. The expectations are that the qualities of the proposed network with a single hardware neuron will exceed the indicators of performance, energy efficiency, and area of occupied computing resources, achieved by mass-developed conventional methods.

6 Conclusions

The article presents an innovative author's method for designing artificial neural networks intended for use on devices with limited resources. It combines the switching context methodology for resource sharing, proposed by the authors in previous research, with a novel approach that uses time multiplexing. The latter allows building an ANN using a single hardware neuron which leads to a significant reduction of the processing effort and achieving even better resource utilization. Despite being in an early and immature stage, the suggested design strategy provides a viable mathematical model that deserves to be developed further and opens a quite broad field for scientific research. This method will allow for the design and implementation of highly optimized neural networks that can fit in resource-constrained digital hardware while keeping the performance metrics high. Hopefully, the proposed research will provide research ideas for committed researchers in the field of FPGA-based neural network acceleration.

Acknowledgments. The research paper is written in relation with the agreements between the New Bulgarian University, the China University of Mining and Technology, and the University of Mining and Geology "St. Ivan Rilski" on the subjects "Research and improvement of nodes and elements of the control of mechatronic systems" (MEMF-175/10.05.2023), "Joint Research and Development of key technologies for autonomous control systems", and "Construction of International Joint Laboratory for new energy power generation and electric vehicles".

References

1. Brown, T., Mann, B., Ryder, N., et al.: Language models are few-shot learners. OpenAI (2020). https://doi.org/10.48550/arXiv.2005.14165
2. Dally, W.: High performance hardware for machine learning, cadence ENN summit. NVIDIA Corporation, Stanford University (2016)
3. Eberhart, R., Dobbins, R.: Early neural network development history: the age of Camelot. IEEE Eng. Med. Biol. Mag. **9**(3), 15–18 (1990). https://doi.org/10.1109/51.59207
4. Freeman, W.: Mass Action in the Nervous System. Academic Press (2012). ISBN-13 978-0124120471
5. Gholami, A., Kim, S., Dong, Z.: A survey of quantization methods for efficient neural network inference. In: Low-Power Computer Vision: Improving the Efficiency of Artificial Intelligence (2012). https://doi.org/10.48550/arXiv.2103.13630
6. Goodfellow, I., Pouget-Abadie, J., Mirza, M. et al.: Generative adversarial nets (2014). arXiv: 1406.2661 [stat.ML], https://doi.org/10.48550/arXiv.1406.2661
7. Gorbounov, Y., Chen, H.: Context-switching neural node for constrained-space hardware. In: Zlateva, T., Goleva, R. (eds.) CSECS 2022. Lecture Notes of the Institute for Computer Sciences, Social Informatics and Telecommunications Engineering, vol. 450, pp. 45–59. Springer, Cham (2022). https://doi.org/10.1007/978-3-031-17292-2_4
8. Harris, D., Harris, S.: Digital Design and Computer Architecture, 2edn. Morgan Kaufmann, Elsevier (2013). ISBN 978-0-12-394424-5
9. Hebb, D.: The Organization of Behavior: A Neuropsychological Theory. Willey, USA (1949)
10. Hopfield, J.: Neural networks and physical systems with emergent collective computational abilities. Proc. Natl. Acad. Sci. **79**(8), 2554–2558 (1982). https://doi.org/10.1073/pnas.79.8.2554

11. IEEE Std 754-2019, IEEE Computer Society. 2019. IEEE Standard for Floating-Point Arithmetic IEEE STD 754-2019, pp. 1-84, ISBN 978-1-5044-5924-2
12. Jouppi, N., Young, C., Patil, N., et al.: In-datacenter performance analysis of a tensor processing unit. In: 44th International Symposium on Computer Architecture (ISCA) (2017). https://doi.org/10.48550/arXiv.1704.04760
13. Kay, L.: How brains create the world: the dynamical legacy of walter J Freeman in olfactory system physiology. Chaos Complex Lett. **11**(1), 41–47 (2017). PMID: 30686946; PMCID: PMC6344053
14. Krizhevsky, A., Sutskever, I., Hinton, G.: ImageNet classification with deep convolutional neural networks. In: Advances in Neural Information Processing Systems, vol. 25, no. 2 (2012). https://doi.org/10.1145/3065386
15. LeCun, Y., Bottou, L., Bengio, Y., et al.: Gradient-based learning applied to document recognition. Proc. IEEE **86**(11), 2278–2323 (1998). https://doi.org/10.1109/5.726791
16. Leijnen, S., Veen, F.: The neural network zoo. In: Conference Theoretical Information Studies, Proceedings, vol. 47, no. 9 (2020). https://doi.org/10.3390/proceedings47010009
17. McCulloch, W., Pitts, W.: A logical calculus of the ideas immanent in nervous activity. Bull. Mathe. Biophys. **5**, 115–133 (1943). https://doi.org/10.1007/BF02478259
18. Medium, Brief History of Neural Networks by Strachnyi, K. https://medium.com/analytics-vidhya/brief-history-of-neural-networks-44c2bf72eec. Accessed 21 Mar 2023
19. Minsky, M., Papert, S.: Perceptrons: An Introduction to Computational Geometry. MIT Press (1969). ISBN 0 262 13043 2
20. Murahari, V., Jimenez, C., Yang, R., et al.: DataMUX: data multiplexing for neural networks. In: 36th Conference on Neural Information Processing Systems (2022). https://doi.org/10.48550/arXiv.2202.09318
21. Nurvitadhi, E., Sheffield, D., Sim, J.: Accelerating binarized neural networks: comparison of FPGA, CPU, GPU, and ASIC. In: International Conference on Field-Programmable Technology, Xi'an, China, pp. 77–84 (2016). https://doi.org/10.1109/FPT.2016.7929192
22. Omondi, A.R., Rajapakse, J.C., Bajger, M.: FPGA Neurocomputers. In: Omondi, A.R., Rajapakse, J.C. (eds.) FPGA Implementations of Neural Networks, pp. 1–37. Springer, Boston (2006). https://doi.org/10.1007/0-387-28487-7_1. ISBN-10 0-387-28485-0
23. Poggio, T., Girosi, F.: Networks for approximation and learning. Proc. IEEE **78**(9), 1481–1497 (1990)
24. Pribram, K.: The neurophysiology of remembering. Sci. Am. **220**(1), 73–86 (1969). https://doi.org/10.1038/scientificamerican0169-73
25. Puttagunta, M., Ravi, S.: Medical image analysis based on deep learning approach. Multimed. Tools Appl. (2020). https://doi.org/10.1007/s11042-021-10707-4
26. Ray, P.: A review on TinyML: state-of-the-art and prospects. J. King Saud Univ. – Comput. Inf. Sci. **34**(4), 1595–1623 (2022), https://doi.org/10.1016/j.jksuci.2021.11.019
27. Rosenblatt, F.: The Perceptron - a perceiving and recognizing automaton. Report 85-460-1. Cornell Aeronautical Laboratory (1957)
28. Scarselli, F., Yong, S., Gori, M., et al.: Graph neural networks for ranking web pages. In: IEEE/WIC/ACM International Conference on Web Intelligence (WI 2005) (2005). https://doi.org/10.1109/WI.2005.67
29. Schmidhuber, J.: Deep learning in neural networks: an overview. Neural Netw. **61**, 85–117 (2015). https://doi.org/10.1016/j.neunet.2014.09.003
30. Stelzer, F., Röhm, A., Vicente, R., et al.: Deep neural networks using a single neuron: folded-in-time architecture using feedback-modulated delay loops. Nat. Commun. **12**, 5164 (2021). https://doi.org/10.1038/s41467-021-25427-4
31. Wang, C., Luo, Z.: A review of the optimal design of neural keywords: deep learning; deep neural network; FPGA; optimization; hardware acceleration Networks Based on FPGA. Appl. Sci. **12**, 10771 (2022). https://doi.org/10.3390/app122110771

32. Wang, Z., She, Q., Ward, T.: Generative Adversarial networks in computer vision: a survey and taxonomy. ACM Comput. Surv. (2020). ISSN 0360-0300
33. Werbos, P.: Beyond regression: new tools for prediction and analysis in the behavioral sciences. Ph.D. thesis, Committee on Applied Mathematics, Harvard University (1974)
34. Widrow, B., Hoff, M.: Adaptive switching circuits. In: IRE WESCON Convention Record, New York, pp. 96–104 (1960). https://doi.org/10.7551/mitpress/4943.003.0012
35. Wu, L., Cui, P., Pei, J., et al.: Graph Neural Networks: Foundations, Frontiers, and Applications. Springer, Heidelberg (2022). https://doi.org/10.1007/978-981-16-6054-2. ISBN 978-9811660535
36. Yasoubi, A., Hojabr, R., Modarressi, M.: Power-efficient accelerator design for neural networks using computation reuse. IEEE Comput. Archit. Lett. **16**(1), 72–75 (2017). https://doi.org/10.1109/LCA.2016.2521654. ISSN 1556-6056

An Approach to Environmental Study from Observations and Sensing Towards a Digital Twin

Rossitza Goleva[1]($\boxtimes$) (iD), Alexandar Savov[2], Vasko Tomanov[3], Valentin Monov[3],
Zhivka Koleva[2], Radosveta Sokullu[4] (iD), Hristina Kostadinova[1], Svetoslav Mihaylov[5],
and Nuno Garcia[6] (iD)

[1] New Bulgarian University, Montevideo Str. 21, Sofia, Bulgaria
rgoleva@gmail.com
[2] Comicon Ltd., Sofia, Bulgaria
{savov,koleva}@comicon.bg
[3] B2N Ltd., London, UK
vt@b2net.net
[4] Ege University, Izmir, Turkey
radosveta.sokullu@ege.edu.tr
[5] Consultant, Sofia, Bulgaria
[6] Computer Science Department of the University of Beira Interior, Covilhã, Portugal
ngarcia@di.ubi.pt

Abstract. Long-term well-living is highly correlated to the level of environmental studies. Arctic ice melting, global warming, storms, and forest fires occur more and more often. In the process of digitalization of life, a new technology of digital twins is becoming appropriate for better studies and prediction of disasters. Many papers and projects have been focused on wildfires last decade and some of them present the idea of forest fire simulation. In this work, we present an IoT-cloud-digital twin solution where a new sensor for environment sensing is developed, integrated with the drone observations of the area, and feeding the database on the server locally and in the cloud with fresh data from the observation. All data collected in real-time, near-real-time, and non-real-time feed a digital twin model where the fires are simulated. The unique combination of real data and simulated data in the virtual environment allows better prediction of disasters, coordination in prevention procedures, and clear analyses of the risk for the environment and citizens.

Keywords: Sensors · Digital Twins · Data Sharing · Edge · Dew · Fog · Cloud Computing Technologies · Risk Analyses · Disaster Prediction

1 Introduction

Last decade digital twin technology is becoming more and more important for different industrial sectors. It was proven to be helpful in production management and failures [1], autonomous robots [2] where intensive standardization is taking place [3]. International

T. Zlateva and G. Tuparov (Eds.): CSECS 2023, LNICST 514, pp. 247–262, 2023.
https://doi.org/10.1007/978-3-031-44668-9_20

Standard Organization (ISO) [4] and IBM [5] are among the leaders in this process. While applying digital twin technology the systems need to be sustainable, scalable, and interoperable, open to be fed with fresh and historical data, and be expanded with new features and functionalities [6]. The accuracy of the models, real data, and simulated data implemented in digital twins is a matter of intensive analysis because of the reflection to risk evaluation and preventive measures of nature and citizens [7].

Digital twins are successfully implemented in intelligent transportation systems [8]. Smart home and smart office solutions [9] are very promising implementation places for the technology as well as the energy sector [10]. The domain-driven approach is demonstrated in [11].

Forests and other wooded land cover over 43.52% of the EU's land space, with about 16 million private forest owners. Also, 40% of forests are publicly owned. In recent years large pieces of forests have been destroyed by fires, due to climate changes. Fire-fighting teams must be aware of the possibility of fire occurrence and spread, to act immediately in case of real crises. The best solutions used so far with thermal cameras on towers can only detect forest fires and cannot be used in rugged and uneven terrains, such as most forests.

According to data on wildfires by EFFIS [40] over 400000 ha of natural areas have burnt in the EU for the first 10 months of 2020, despite the use of the available technological means like fire monitoring towers. EFFIS graphics show a constant increase in the number of fires and burned areas during the last years. But "healthy and resilient forests are a key part of efforts to combat the negative impacts of climate change. Studies have shown trees can reduce temperatures by 9 degrees and energy costs by $7.8 billion a year".

The social impact of the solution includes:

– more saved human lives and health of firefighters and affected people, also saving of flora and fauna in wild areas
– reduction of materials and finance needed for the fire fighting and further recovery
– reduced carbon emissions.

The work objective is to develop a new solution for forest fire monitoring, based on a drone-sensor system, that can be applied to all types of surfaces including rugged and uneven ones.

In our work, we present the architecture and idea of digital twin implementation in forest fires. The work is inspired by the environmental problem raised recently thanks to the wildfires and the necessity to look for solutions for risk management and preventive measures of authorities.

The paper is organized as follows. We define the architecture of the platform at the beginning and continue with the presentation of its parts. Sensors, drones, traveling schedules, and the communication protocol are defined next. In the end, we present services and numerical results.

2   Literature Review and Problem Definition

The creation of a digital twin of the area where wildfire is expected faces multiple challenges. The first question is which areas are more vulnerable to the fires. The authorities in every country in the world create a so-called risk map for the fires and this information is shared with the Emergency Response Coordination Centre [12] and World Health Organization [13]. This study is based on observed fires and historical data from satellites.

Our work proposes a way to build and define the main functions of a digital twin of the areas that are at risk for wildfires. The solution could be used in the short term and be developed in the medium and long term. The idea is to warn citizens and authorities about the risk well in advance and try to localize the source as early as possible. This might be the way to save resources and prevent the environment. Areas protected by Natura 2000, national parks, agriculture crops, and areas with historical significance are also a matter of special interest.

Many papers last years have been published in digital twin development. Basic guidelines on how to correlate real-time data and other data models in the digital copy are presented in [14]. Problems in digital twin development and continuous exploitation are highlighted in [15]. Detailed surveys on technologies and future trends are published by Mihai et al. in [16]. Technology such as FIWARE has a feature to coordinate open data with digital twins [17]. Correlation between Industry 5.0, Society 5.0, and 5G/ 6G networks could be seen in [18]. A serious survey on digital twin implementation for edge solutions is presented in [19]. Implementation with drones could be seen in [20]. Implementation in the metro transport management using a digital twin is shown in [21]. The smart city digital twin idea is presented in [22]. Special attention to security issues is published in [23]. A digital twin of ocean observations and specific implementation in the Baltic Sea is shown in [24]. Many challenges in preparing and exploiting a digital twin in the long term are published in [25].

Most of the wildfire solutions and especially predictions are based on the implementation of Machine Learning and Neural Networks algorithms [26–28]. Correlation with vegetation process similar to the proposed here solution is done in [29]. Special attention is paid to the wildfires spreading [30]. Wildfire path prediction is important for forest fire authorities while planning their activities and evacuating citizens [31].

There are two solutions for wildfire digital twins in [32] and [33]. The first one implements machine-to-machine technologies for interaction between field devices and the digital twin. The work of Sanchez-Guzman in [33] models burning times estimates.

Sensor network implementation for wildfire detection is shown in [34]. Image processing techniques implemented on astronomical images are shown in [35]. Software asset reuse that is important in digital twin technology is seen in [36, 37].

In our work, we present a new forest fire sensor that could be fixed on the trees or flown on a drone. The drone carries the controller that collects near-real-time data from sensors. All data are transferred to the local server and the cloud where the service and the digital twin are fed. Further on by implementing Chandler Burning Index, using real data and historical data, data from other sources such as the predicted risk level of wildfire is analyzed precisely and appropriate alarms are raised to the authorities. The work is supported by projects UFO (emerging indUstries new value chains boosted by small Flying Objects) and 4F (Flying Forest Fires Fighting) [38, 39] where multiple flying object solutions could be seen.

3 Flying Forest Fires Fighting Architecture

The architecture of the 4F platform including the digital twin is presented in Fig. 1. It includes a typical Internet of Things (IoT) solution developed and implemented in the forest. Services for real data monitoring that could be run locally on a server and in the cloud are created. The right part of the picture demonstrates the digital twin structure that is fed by real data from the deployed infrastructure and simulates the rest of the parameters necessary for the simulation of the real environment and the implementation of additional algorithms for risk analyses and disaster prediction.

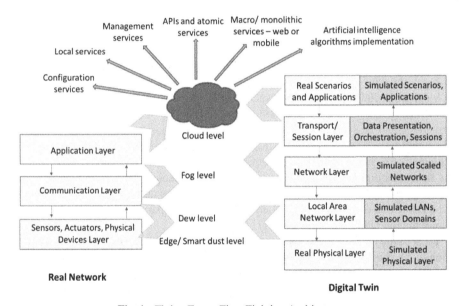

Fig. 1. Flying Forest Fires Fighting Architecture.

The left part of the model has only three layers that are typical for IoT solutions. The right part has 5 layers and every layer is divided into two different sections, one for the real network mirror copy and one for the simulated copy of the network. There are no rules on how to coordinate the real and simulated networks together yet and in our solution we implemented well-known technologies for network simulations from phone and computer networks where the event-driven model is run in different time scales and estimation of the parameters is based on the independent samples of events and the law of large numbers.

The simulated part is developed after a careful study of the nature of the model parameters. It implements different distributions for different types of events. Transitional and steady-state states of the digital twin model are analyzed to allow estimation of events such as the probability of the biomass to fire, estimated time for the biomass to burn, the way and the rate at which the fire might be spread, the correlation between the rate of the wind and the fire spreading pattern in specific forest area, the correlation between the temperature and humidity predictions and fire spreading in short-term, etc.

Where the physical platform is distributed the digital twins of different regions could be centralized or distributed by implementing known cloud/ fog/ dew/ edge computing technologies. This will help the process of enhancements with Machine Learning algorithms, atomic and monolithic services, different APIs, managed services, and many other additional functions.

When developed the model of the forest could be enhanced further with more precise instruments to reach better accuracy in preventing measures. Furthermore, the model could be easily reused in different regions implementing similar sensors or being part of another digital twin for estimation of another disaster such as floods for example.

Digital Twin could become an interesting place for the training of firemen and citizens, especially children and senior adults. The prevention services developed on top of the model may have a high social impact.

4 Drone-Based Sensors

The objective to create a new sensor and to integrate the existing ones into the solution is to perform Earth observation for detection and measurement purposes, before, during, and after a forest fire. Consequently measurements:

– before the fire are useful for risk analyses and prevention
– during the fire are implemented for fire spread analyses, resource damages analyses, and fighting activities planning
– after the fire are important for restoration activities and monitoring as well as for better prevention planning.

Measured parameters are related to climate changes and their level of correlation to the forest fire management parameters and procedures. The solution consists of:

– sensors for measuring soil (or biomass) moisture and temperature, installed in forests (Fig. 2 and Fig. 3)
– sensors for measuring air temperature, humidity, and particle matter mounted on a drone (Fig. 4)
– communication gateway mounted on a drone

Technical challenges solved during the development of the solution are:

A. Selection of microcontroller of the latest generation LoRa (Low Range) radio modules with minimal energy consumption. A study has been conducted on the latest developments of radio modules that implement the latest generation of SX1262 LoRa transmitter, created by the patent holder Semtech Corporation.
B. Minimal energy consumption for measurement and communication. Three models of LoRa radio modules are studied and tested in different operating modes.
C. Optimal use of the capacity of the power supply battery. A battery with optimal characteristics is selected, as well as a low-dropout voltage regulator.

Fig. 2. Soil moisture and humidity sensor

Fig. 3. Air moisture, humidity, and temperature sensor.

Fig. 4. The drone carries sensors and a gateway.

D. Ensured communication exchange between a sensor and a gateway at a certain drone flight speed. A basic algorithm has been developed, that guarantees data communication exchange between the sensor and the gateway in a minimal time slot window.

E. Integrating an antenna with an optimal radiation pattern. Seven types of LoRa antennas have been tested. The selected antenna, that is implemented in the sensor, provides the best communication connection with the gateway on the drone, regardless of the direction of the drone's flight.

F. Measurement of moisture and temperature of soil and biomass at optimal accuracy/energy consumption ratio.

The sensor for Moisture&Temperature (M&T) measuring supports communication according to a Low Power Wide Area Network (LPWAN) protocol and has a probe for soil moisture and T(temperature) measuring.

Contemporary sensors are implemented in the forest that do not require a change of batteries for the lifetime of the sensor.

Because the M&T sensors are spread in a broad range in the forest, the gateways for data collection could not be stationary. This is the reason to propose a gateway that could fly on a drone and collect data from sensors under the flying schedule and routes.

Climate parameters are not changing in real-time and this allows monitoring of the sensor data in non-real-time, i.e. in intervals from hours to days. Drones also could not fly in all conditions.

To avoid missing data, the M&T sensors take measurements periodically and record the average, maximal, and minimal values in buffers for the last 10 days and the last 10 weeks. When a drone appears, the sensors send the buffered data.

The 4F drone-based sensor system is applicable for all types of terrains, incl. rugged and uneven ones, and at the prevention, detection, and restoration phases of wildfires. Our approach is to collect, process, and analyze information from sensors located in forests and on the drone to predict and detect forest fires, as well as to monitor the recovery after fires (Fig. 5).

The main technological challenges are:

– Moisture measurements
– Network planning including drone flight plan and schedule
– Data analyses and risk management using Machine Learning to avoid false alarms.

The focus of the innovation is to use a wireless LPWAN sensor network, where the central communication device called "gateway" is installed on a drone.

If the gateway is located on the Earth's surface, then communication between it and the sensors might be impossible due to the presence of rocks, uneven terrain, and dense foliage, which prevent the propagation of radio waves in the horizontal direction. But if the gateway rises in height, then it can collect data from all sensors within a radius of several kilometers.

The second problem solved is the communication between the gateway and the software IoT platform that collects data from the sensors. Most often, the land surface in forests lacks coverage with 3G/4G/5G communication networks. But when the drone rises above the ground and flies over a wide area, it can get good coverage of the 3G/4G/5G network and transmit the collected data to the IoT platform (Fig. 6).

The innovation is aimed at applying existing technology in a new area, i.e. application of a wireless LPWAN sensor network for the phases of prevention, detection, and restoration of forest fires.

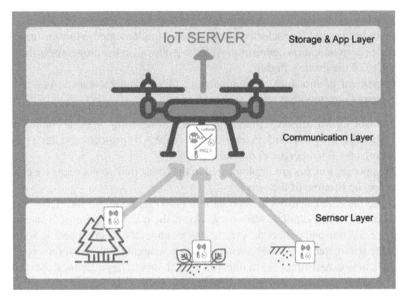

Fig. 5. Collection of data.

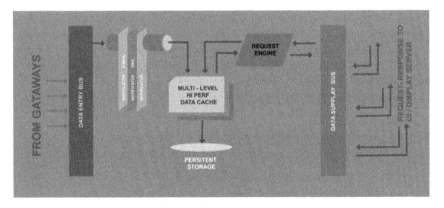

Fig. 6. Gateway structure.

The experiments are organized by:

- semi-professional drone, providing the necessary flight time and power supply for the installed gateway and sensors
- one communication gateway mounted on the drone with the capacity to collect and keep sensors' data from many measuring flights
- set of sensors for measuring temperature, humidity, and particle matters mounted on the drone
- several sensors for measuring soil (or biomass) moisture and temperature, installed in a forest

The monitored forest is flown around periodically. The collected data is processed, visualized, and analyzed. Selection of the most suitable LPWAN technology, radio frequency, modules, sensors, communication devices, and a drone for the experiments is done.

After-fire monitoring is useful for the correct recovery of damaged areas and for further prevention. The data gathered by the drone is collected to the special data matrix and is a matter of further analysis (Fig. 7). The data is also visualized on the map of the area that is under observation (Fig. 8).

Fig. 7. Mission Data Matrix.

5   Communication Protocol

Successful experiments have been carried through multiple configurations and preliminary results have been obtained to prove the vitality of the solution. The first thing to define was the structure of the payload of the LoRa messages exchanged. Three types of messages are implemented (Figs. 9 and 10):

– DATA
– POLL
– ACK

For every sensor, the DATA message carries message type, sensor number, timestamp, soil moisture, soil temperature, air temperature, air relative humidity, and battery voltage including the data from sensors from the last 15 days. The total payload length is 72 bytes.

POOL message has only 7 or 3 bytes depending on the presence of the timestamp in the payload including also sensor identifier and message type. It is intended to ask for data from the sensor.

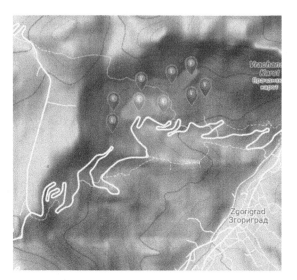

Fig. 8. Map of the area under observation.

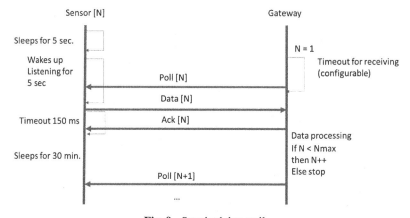

Fig. 9. Standard data poll.

The standard implementation of the LoRa protocol is shown in Fig. 9. The version with data repetition is drawn in Fig. 10. The timeout for receiving data at the gateway could be changed. Every gateway knows all assigned own sensor identifiers and is pooling them one by one. The schedule for pooling could be changed in specific implementations.

6   4F Services

The collected data needs to be not only stored but also analyzed to enable the creation of services and appropriate alarms to the authorities related to the levels of risk of forest fires, detected fires, and the way Nature is restored from fire. This data needs to be also visualized and correlated to the previously defined reference levels and values of wildfire

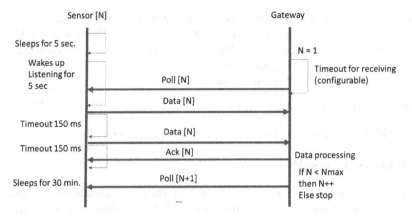

Fig. 10. Data poll with repetition.

management. Data correlation, and data visualization in different scales are supported by the IoT software (Fig. 11). The 4F solution allows the development of new services for fire brigades, citizens, and other stakeholders. Alarms and reports are generated.

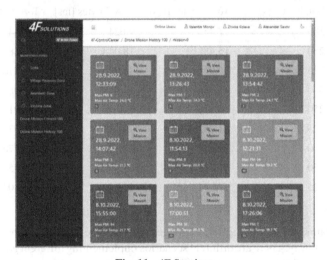

Fig. 11. 4F Services.

The presented service is made out of the near-real-time data collected from the sensors. However, additional data could be implemented and additional simulation modules could be developed in the scope of the local services and digital twin of the area under observation. Configuration and managed services are developed and not included in this paper.

The IoT software platform has functionality for data gathering into the database, map visualization, measurements report, alarms, and reference values for the alarms from sensors. The work is intended for forest fire risk analyses and management at the prevention, detection, and restoration phases. There are many various ways to estimate the fire danger. One of the fastest and easiest is the Chandler Burning Index (CBI). It uses air temperature and relative humidity. That number received is correlated to the Fire Danger severity measured in percentages.

The calculation is based on the following formula

$$CBI = (((110 - 1.373 * RH) - 0.54 * (10.20 - T)) * \left(124 * 10^{-0.0142*RH}\right)))/60,$$

where RH is humidity in %, and T is temperature in degrees Celsius.

7 Numerical Results

The presented numerical results show only the information necessary for protocol configuration between the gateway and the sensors (Table 1). There is a high correlation between the bandwidth, Spread Factor (SF), number of bytes to transmit, and Time on the Air (ToA). The values for the timeouts in the protocol are selected to succeed the transmission without any problems.

Table 1. Time on air of messages

No	SF	Bandwidth [kHz]	ToA 3 bytes [ms]	ToA 7 bytes [ms]	ToA 72 bytes [ms]
1	SF7	500	7,744	9,024	33,344
2	SF7	250	15,488	18,048	66,688
3	SF7	125	30,976	36,096	133,376
4	SF8	500	15,488	18,048	59,008
5	SF8	250	30,976	36,096	118,016
6	SF8	125	61,952	72,192	236,032
7	SF9	500	25,856	30,976	107,776
8	SF9	250	51,712	61,952	215,552
9	SF9	125	103,424	123,904	431,104

The transmission time of big data messages will limit the number of sensors assigned to the given gateway. There are different scenarios implementing different gateway flying schedules with different sets of sensors. The mapping between the flying plans and sensor network scaling and scenarios implemented are under intensive analysis.

8 Conclusions and Future Work Plans

This work presents an idea of how to build a digital twin of the areas at risk of wildfires. The intention is to define with more precision how Nature could be prevented, how the citizens and local resources could be prevented, and how the local authorities could react in the prevention, detection, and restoration phases of the fires. The platform proposed is open for data and function enhancements. The experiments conducted show the way the data starts from the sensors and goes to the cloud and digital twin.

Potential customers of the 4F solution could be addressed such as:

- Public authorities to assure better protection and reaction to forest fires
- Private forest owners
- Commercial companies who want to install the proposed solution.
- European and national programs for environmental protection

We also work on expanding the 4F solution for alternative applications like agriculture, flood management, draughts management, pipeline inspection, border security, and many others.

Acknowledgments. This work is developed under the support of multiple projects:

- 2021- 2022 Flying Forest Fires Fighting (4F), EU project, "Emerging industries new value chains boosted by small Flying Objects" (UFO), financed by the INNOSUP component of the HORIZON 2020 programme of the European Commission under Grant Agreement 873411, https://eic.ec.europa.eu/news/ufo-emerging-industries-new-value-chains-boosted-small-flying-objects-2022-02-22_en.

- 2022 - 2023 Prototype Design of the LoRa® Repeater for Unified Signals and Channel Selection Management (LIOREPLICON), National Innovation Fund, Bulgaria.

- 2020–2021 Research and Development of Prototype of Multifunctional IIo LPWAN Communication Model for Wireless Data Transmission of Ecological Parameters Using Sensors – TeleEco, National Innovation Fund, Bulgaria.

References

1. Feng, H., Gomes, C., Thule, C., Lausdahl, K., Losifidis, A., Larsen, P.G.: Introduction to digital twin engineering. In: Proceedings of the 2021 Annual Modeling and Simulation Conference, ANNSIM 2021, pp. 1–12 (2021). https://doi.org/10.23919/ANNSIM52504.2021.9552135

2. Lumer-Klabbers, G., Hausted, J.O., Kvistgaard, J.L., Macedo, H.D., Frasheri, M., Larsen, P.G.: Towards a digital twin framework for autonomous robots. In: Proceedings - 2021 IEEE 45th Annual Computers, Software, and Applications Conference, COMPSAC 2021, pp. 1254–1259 (2021). https://doi.org/10.1109/COMPSAC51774.2021

3. Ferko, E., Bucaioni, A., Pelliccione, P., Behnam, M.: Standardisation in digital twin architectures in manufacturing. In: 2023 IEEE 20th International Conference on Software Architecture (ICSA), pp. 70–81 (2023). doi:https://doi.org/10.1109/ICSA56044.2023.00015

4. ISO International Standard ISO 23247. Automation systems and integration—Digital twin framework for manufacturing—Part 1: Overview and general principles. International Organization for Standardization (2021)

5. Stanford-Clark, B.A., Frank-schultz, E., Harris, M.: Ibm. What are digital twins? (2019). https://developer.ibm.com/articles/what-are-digital-twins/

6. Goleva, R., Mihaylov, S.: European catalogue of ICT water standards and specifications. Shaping Europe's digital future, REPORT/STUDY, Team responsible, Smart Mobility and Living (Unit H.5), Directorate-General for Communications Networks, Content and Technology, pp. 1–128 European Commis. Brussels (2020). https://ec.europa.eu/digital-single-market/en/news/european-catalogue-ict-water-standards-and-specifications

7. Corradini, F., Fedeli, A., Polini, A., Re, B.: Towards a digital twin modelling notation. In: Proceedings of the 2022 IEEE International Conference on Dependable, Autonomic and Secure Computing, International Conference on Pervasive Intelligence and Computing, International

Conference on Cloud and Big Data Computing, International Conference on Cyber Science and Technology Congress, DASC/PiCom/CBDCom/CyberSciTech 2022, Falerna, Italy, pp. 1–6. IEEE (2022). https://doi.org/10.1109/DASC/PiCom/CBDCom/Cy55231.2022.992 7827, https://ieeexplore.ieee.org/document/9927827/

8. Bao, L., Wang, Q., Jiang, Y.: Review of digital twin for intelligent transportation system. In: 2021 International Conference on Information Control, Electrical Engineering and Rail Transit (ICEERT), pp. 309–315. IEEE (2021). https://doi.org/10.1109/ICEERT53919.2021. 00064, https://ieeexplore.ieee.org/document/9666030/

9. Xiao, Y., Jia, Y., Hu, Q., Cheng, X., Gong, B., Yu, J.: CommandFence: a novel digital-twin-based preventive framework for securing smart home systems. IEEE Trans Dependable Secur Comput. **20**(3), 2450–2465 (2023). https://doi.org/10.1109/TDSC.2022.3184185

10. Han, J., Hong, Q., Syed, M.H., Khan, M.A.U., Yang, G., et al.: Cloud-edge hosted digital twins for coordinated control of distributed energy resources. IEEE Trans. Cloud Comput. (2022). https://doi.org/10.1109/TCC.2022.3191837

11. MacIas, A., Navarro, E., Cuesta, C.E., Zdun, U.: Architecting digital twins using a domain-driven design-based approach*. In: Proceedings - IEEE 20th International Conference on Software Architecture, ICSA 2023, pp. 153–163 (2023). https://doi.org/10.1109/ICSA56044. 2023

12. Emergency Response Coordination Centre (2023). https://erccportal.jrc.ec.europa.eu/#/echo-flash-items/latest

13. World health organization (2023). https://www.who.int/health-topics/wildfires?gclid=Cjw KCAjwgqejBhBAEiwAuWHioF1_L2QMeX6vGUf-6FRtzgiUoM4k95nuJxSIO9QHTY6 FdParLTIrzRoCGZQQAvD_BwE#tab=tab_1

14. Piroumian, V.: Making digital twins work. Comput. (Long Beach Calif.) **56**(1), 42–51 (2023). https://doi.org/10.1109/MC.2022.3206101

15. Faraboschi, P., Frachtenberg, E., Laplante, P., Milojicic, D., Saracco, R.: Digital transformation: lights and shadows. Comput. (Long Beach Calif.) **56**(4), 123–130 (2023). https://doi. org/10.1109/MC.2023.3241726

16. Mihai, S., Yaqoob, M., Hung, D.V., Davis, W., Towakel, P., Raza, M., et al.: Digital twins: a survey on enabling technologies, challenges, trends and future prospects. IEEE Commun. Surv. Tutor. **24**(4), 2255–2291 (2022). https://doi.org/10.1109/COMST.2022.3208773

17. Conde, J., Munoz-Arcentales, A., Alonso, A., Huecas, G., Salvachua, J.: Collaboration of digital twins through linked open data: architecture with FIWARE as enabling technology. IT Prof. **24**(6), 41–46 (2022). https://doi.org/10.1109/MITP.2022.3224826

18. Maier, M., Ebrahimzadeh, A., Beniiche, A., Rostami, S.: The art of 6G (TAO 6G): how to wire society 5.0 [invited]. J. Opt. Commun. Netw. **14**(2), A101–A112 (2022). https://doi.org/ 10.1364/JOCN.438522

19. Tang, F., Chen, X., Rodrigues, T.K., Zhao, M., Kato, N.: Survey on digital twin edge networks (DITEN) toward 6G. IEEE Open J. Commun. Soc. **3**, 1360–1381 (2022). https://doi.org/10. 1109/OJCOMS.2022.3197811

20. Lian, S., Zhang, H., Sun, W., Zhang, Y.: Lightweight digital twin and federated learning with distributed incentive in air-ground 6G networks. In: IEEE Vehicular Technology Conference, vol. 2022-June (2022). https://doi.org/10.1109/VTC2022-Spring54318.2022.9860796

21. Wang, X., Song, H., Zha, W., Li, J., Dong, H.: Digital twin based validation platform for smart metro scenarios. In: Proceedings of the 2021 IEEE 1st International Conference on Digital Twins Parallel Intelligence, DTPI 2021, pp. 386–389 (2021). https://doi.org/10.1109/ DTPI52967.2021.9540161

22. Mylonas, G., Kalogeras, A., Kalogeras, G., Anagnostopoulos, C., Alexakos, C., Munoz, L.: Digital twins from smart manufacturing to smart cities: a survey. IEEE Access **9**, 143222–143249 (2021). https://doi.org/10.1109/ACCESS.2021.3120843

23. Xu, Q., Ali, S., Yue, T.: Digital twin-based anomaly detection in cyber-physical systems. In: Proceedings - 2021 IEEE 14th International Conference on Software Testing, Verification and Validation, ICST 2021, pp. 205–216 (2021). https://doi.org/10.1109/ICST49551.2021.00031

24. Barbie, A., Pech, N., Hasselbring, W., Flogel, S., Wenzhofer, F., Walter, M., et al.: Developing an underwater network of ocean observation systems with digital twin prototypes - a field report from the baltic sea. IEEE Internet Comput. **26**(3), 33–42 (2022). https://doi.org/10.1109/MIC.2021.3065245

25. Masaracchia, A., Sharma, V., Canberk, B., Dobre, O.A., Duong, T.Q.: Digital twin for 6G: taxonomy, research challenges, and the road ahead. IEEE Open J. Commun. Soc. **3**, 2137–2150 (2022). https://doi.org/10.1109/OJCOMS.2022.3219015

26. Spiller, D., Amici, S., Ansalone, L.: Transfer learning analysis for wildfire segmentation using PRISMA hyperspectral imagery and convolutional neural networks. In: Work Hyperspectral Image Signal Process Evolution in Remote Sensing, vol. 2022-September (2022). https://doi.org/10.1109/WHISPERS56178.2022.9955054

27. Mahdi, A.S., Mahmood, S.A.: Analysis of deep learning methods for early wildfire detection systems: review. In: IICETA 2022 - 5th International Conference on Engineering Technology and its Application, pp. 271–276 (2022). https://doi.org/10.1109/IICETA54559.2022.9888515

28. Wang, Z., He, B., Lai, X.: Balanced random forest model is more suitable for wildfire risk assessment. In: International Geoscience Remote Sensing Symposium, vol. 2022-July, pp. 3596–3599 (2022). https://doi.org/10.1109/IGARSS46834.2022.9883573

29. Zhang, J.: Using a decomposing method to analyze the spatial-temporal relationship between vegetation drought and wildfire in California. In: International Geoscience Remote Sensing Symposium, vol. 2022-July, pp. 5728–5731 (2022). https://doi.org/10.1109/IGARSS46834.2022.9883888

30. Huot, F., Hu, R.L., Goyal, N., Sankar, T., Ihme, M., Chen, Y.F.: Next day wildfire spread: a machine learning dataset to predict wildfire spreading from remote-sensing data. IEEE Trans. Geosci. Remote Sens. **60** (2022). https://doi.org/10.1109/TGRS.2022.3192974

31. Makhaba, M., Winberg, S.: Wildfire path prediction spread using machine learning. In: International Conference on Electrical, Computer and Energy Technologies, ICECET 2022 (2022). https://doi.org/10.1109/ICECET55527.2022.9872974

32. Hyeong-Su, K., Jin-Woo, K., Yun, S., Kim, W.T.: A novel wildfire digital-twin framework using interactive wildfire spread simulator. In: International Conference on Ubiquitous Future Networks, ICUFN, vol. 2019-July, pp. 636–638 (2019). https://doi.org/10.1109/ICUFN.2019.8806107

33. Sanchez-Guzman, G., Velasquez, W., Alvarez-Alvarado, M.S.: Modeling a simulated forest to get burning times of tree species using a digital twin. In: 2022 IEEE 12th Annual Computing and Communication Workshop and Conference, CCWC 2022, pp. 639–643 (2022). https://doi.org/10.1109/CCWC54503.2022.9720768

34. Peinl, P., Goleva, R., Ackoski, J.: Advanced system for the prevention and early detection of forest fires (ASPires). Proceedings of the ACM Symposium on Applied Computing, pp. 1200–1203 (2020). https://doi.org/10.1145/3341105.3374052

35. Laskov, L.M.: Methods for document image de-warping. Astron. Astrophys. Trans. **30**(4), 511–522 (2018)

36. Chebanyuk, O.: An approach to software assets reusing. In: Zlateva, T., Goleva, R. (eds.) CSECS 2022. Lecture Notes of the Institute for Computer Sciences, Social Informatics and Telecommunications Engineering, vol. 450, pp. 73–83. Springer, Cham (2022). https://doi.org/10.1007/978-3-031-17292-2_6

37. Chebanyuk, O.V., Palahin, O.V., Markov, K.K.: Domain engineering approach of software requirement analysis. In: CEUR Workshop Proceedings, vol. 2866, pp. 164–73 (2020). ISSN 1613-0073
38. UFO: emerging indUstries new value chains boosted by small Flying Objects (2022). https://eic.ec.europa.eu/news/ufo-emerging-industries-new-value-chains-boosted-small-flying-objects-2022-02-22
39. Flying Forest Fires Fighting (4F) Project. https://comicon.bg/en/
40. European Forest Fire Information System (2023). https://effis.jrc.ec.europa.eu/

Business Informatics

The Application of Data Analytics for Understanding Patterns of Mergers and Acquisitions and CEO Characteristics in and between Crisis Times

Kathleen Park[1]([✉]), Eugene Pinsky[2], Noor Kaiser[2], Akhil Subramani[2], and Yue Ying[1]

[1] Administrative Sciences Department, Metropolitan College, Boston University, Boston, MA 02215, USA
kmparque@bu.edu
[2] Computer Science Department, Metropolitan College, Boston University, Boston, MA 02215, USA
epinsky@bu.edu

Abstract. We examine patterns and dynamics of M&A occurrence with attention to three crises or instances of economic disruption—the dot.com bubble, the global financial crisis, and, for future evaluation, the covid-19 global pandemic—while also taking potential CEO demographic (e.g., age) and outcome (e.g., compensation) factors into consideration. Specifically, we examine the frequency, size, and characteristics of M&A transactions across different industries, and we analyze the age, gender, education, experience, and compensation of CEOs across various industries. Drawing on the SDC Platinum and BoardEx databases, we examine US M&A valued over 250 million USD in the 11 global industry classification standard (GICS) sectors from 1999–2018 for n = 14,405 M&A and n = 20,745 CEOs. Using clustering analysis, we define groupings of patterns of M&A transactions before and after the global financial crisis (circa 2008–2009) to show that M&A decreased and then resumed across sectors, although to different degrees for each sector. Using both clustering and PCA, we determine groupings of CEO characteristics before and after the global financial crisis, demonstrating variation in selected demographics of individuals leading organizations before and after that crisis. In addition, initial analysis of our CEO-level data indicates merging to be a predominantly male CEO-driven activity with inferred egoistic, reputational, and power rewards as well as longer-term wealth-building effects, as direct non-contingent compensation does not markedly change for CEOs in the aggregate before and after M&A.

Keywords: Mergers and acquisitions · CEOs · Crises · M&A motivations · M&A outcomes

T. Zlateva and G. Tuparov (Eds.): CSECS 2023, LNICST 514, pp. 265–280, 2023.
https://doi.org/10.1007/978-3-031-44668-9_21

1 Introduction

Mergers and acquisitions (M&A) are a common strategy for companies looking to enter new markets, grow, and gain competitive advantage [24]. However, these transactions can be complex and risky [21], and their success depends on various factors such as market conditions, industry trends, integration of the firms [6], and the characteristics of the companies and leaders involved [12]. With the increasing availability of data and advanced analytics tools, researchers and practitioners have turned to data analytics to explore M&A activities and identify crisis-delimited patterns in their frequency, size, and success [16]. This paper contributes to the literature by applying data analytics to M&A and CEO activity patterns.

CEOs are key decision-makers in organizations [14] and their characteristics [23] and interests [26] can have a significant impact on M&A outcomes [28]. We have therefore also turned to data analytics to explore characteristics of CEOs involved in M&A in various industries [2]. By analyzing these characteristics, we aim to identify patterns and trends that may have implications for firm leaders as well as policymakers and regulators [22].

The question of the optimal conditions for a firm in choosing to merge or not merge with another firm has been intensively debated for decades [8]. The question has arisen most proximately in relation to intermittent yet unpredictable crises such as bubbles, crashes, and large-scale health concerns, often creating additional uncertainty [25] and constraints in merging [3]. In evaluating the context of M&A occurrence in and between crisis times, some scholars have pointed to institutional-level economic and market robustness factors as preeminent [11], while other scholars have identified corporate governance [4] and CEO-level factors with respect to demographic background, motivations, and anticipated financial reward outcomes as strongly driving decisions to merge or not [10, 18]. Previous studies have not adequately addressed that each cycle of economic downturn and recovery has both commonalities and differences that can considered as external drivers of market forces alongside internal (to the firm) demographic, motivational, and reward drivers at the CEO level [20]. There are many external and internal drivers that can impact M&A transactions [13]. However, a polarized consideration of external and internal drivers has created a conundrum. Isolating the economic and market circumstances from the dynamics at the leadership level inside the firm and not looking at each economic downturn and recovery as both unique and convergent with previous such incidents has led to a gap in the completeness of our understanding around the catalysts of M&A and the firm-, industry- and CEO-level consequences observed around the occurrence of these transactions.

In essence, we argue that both economic and market forces [7] and CEO level factors [19] should be taken into consideration in better comprehending merging. By exploring the convergence of economic and market factors alongside CEO demographic background, motivational [26] and reward factors [10], our research reinforces the importance of studying firms in conjunction with their leaders [5] and sheds light on the neglected issue of the previously perhaps excessive partitioning of M&A contributing factors into external and internal domains.

We can regard economic bubbles, international financial turmoil, and global pandemics as instances of environmental or external factors. Specifically, we concentrate on the global financial crisis (GFC) as a type of external factor, and we explore its influence on different industries toward establishing commonalities or differences in impact on M&A volume and valuation across broad industry sectors. We also explore the GFC impact on the internal factor of CEO characteristics such as age, income, and nationality among the types of large US firms experiencing M&A activity before and after the crisis. We therefore examine the following research questions:

(1) What are the impacts of market conditions and economic circumstances on the volume and valuation of M&A deals by sector, 1999–2018, before and after the global financial crisis (before and after 2008)?
(2) What are any discernible patterns in CEO demographic characteristics before and after the global financial crisis?
(3) What implications can be drawn for the projected impact of the global pandemic, beginning in 2019, on M&A occurrence?

It is possible that different industry sectors—being subject to difference balances of regulatory, market and technological pressures as well as to different vicissitudes in leadership styles and transitions—could experience different combinations of internal and external drivers of M&A. For instance, the technology sector could be more influenced by external factors, such as the level of competition and the pace of technological change. The financial sector, subject to perhaps more intense regulatory scrutiny and statutory oversight, could be more influenced by internal factors, such as the leadership desire for reputational or wealth enhancement via improving financial performance. Alternatively, in a sector such as healthcare, external factors such as regulatory changes and technological advancements could be the primary drivers of M&A activity, while internal factors such as leadership interest in achieving economies of scale and expanding market share could also be important.

2 Data Analysis and Visualization

2.1 Data

We collected data from SDC Platinum and BoardEx for firms and CEOs. Based on the intersection of specialized sources, we developed two customized datasets:

1. M&A: We obtained all M&A transactions from 1999–2018 with a deal size greater than or equal to 250 million USD. We limited both acquirer and target companies by restricting the time range and minimum deal value [15], and we similarly used a filter to obtain only US acquiring and target companies. We subsequently grouped all transactions from finer-grained sub-industries into broader industry categorization, according to the Global Industry Classification Standard (GICS) system. This system decreased our industry sector categorization, enabling clearer data visualizations later in our analysis. Furthermore, we intentionally excluded all deals from the legal sector, as M&A are highly regulated in this field and are not very reflective of the market environment.

2. CEOs and related corporate governance structure: Based on data from the SDC Platinum and BoardEx databases, we examine US M&A valued over 250 million USD in the 11 global industry classification standard (GICS) sectors from 1999–2018 for n = 14,405 M&A and n = 20,745 CEOs.

We now provide visualization and analysis with respect to the research questions.

2.2 Visualization and Statistics

For the first part, we view our data from a higher level to have a general understanding of M&A activity in the time frames we are evaluating. We find a distribution of transaction frequencies across different sectors. Industries with high M&A frequencies include financials (Fig. 1), consumer discretionary, industrials (Fig. 2) and utilities (Fig. 3). As these industries experienced more robust M&A activity, we examined them more closely in the relevant time ranges. Additionally, we note that all sectors experienced fluctuating volume and valuation in M&A activity from 1999-2018. The intermittent declines and rebounds correspond to the two major economic shocks of the time: the high-tech, dot.com meltdown around 2001 and the global financial crisis 2008-2009. Reduced rates of M&A activity occur in the approximately one to three years following the economic and market shock. The patterns in each sector may appear roughly similar in upswings, downturns, and recovery around each shock, but our later analysis with percentile clustering reveals a more detailed distinction and grouping in the patterns of M&A activity and resilience in the financials, consumer discretionary, utilities and industrials sectors previously mentioned.

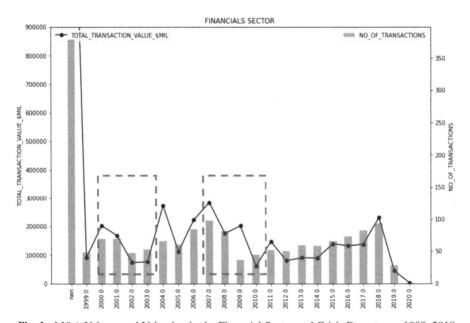

Fig. 1. M&A Volume and Valuation in the Financial Sector and Crisis Downturns, 1998–2018

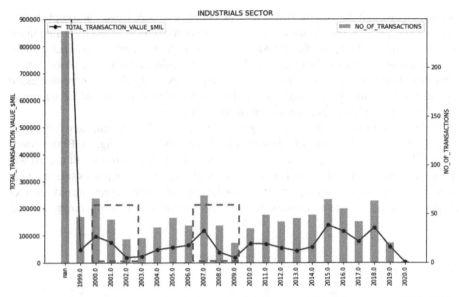

Fig. 2. M&A Volume and Valuation in the Industrial Sector and Crisis Downturns, 1998–2018

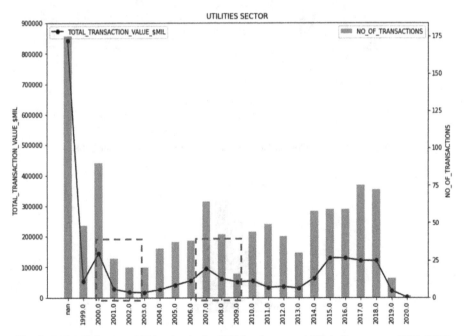

Fig. 3. M&A Volume and Valuation in the Utilities Sector and Crisis Downturns, 1998–2018

In the percentile groupings (Appendix A), we notice variations by specific sector when comparing before and after the GFC. The financial sector takes a dominant position, leading in the both the volume (number) and valuation of M&A deals accomplished in any time period. Conversely, the real estate sector is consistently absent from among the high-value deals. However, after 2008 a shift occurs, with more high-value M&A deals in the "essentials" sectors of healthcare, industrials, and utilities. We further observe more diversity in industry among low-value transactions, possibly due to more distressed acquisitions of smaller companies facing dissolution, as well as some M&A occurring most likely to optimize resource allocation and market share.

From the CEOs data, the average age of CEOs increased two years across different sectors (Fig. 4) when comparing before (Fig. 5) and after 2008 (Fig. 6). Both periods show CEO age hovering around the high-50s, but all sectors show a slight age growth after the financial crisis (Fig. 7). This increase could result from companies seeking more senior candidates for the management team or the original members growing older. Either hypothesis suggests a more conservative and risk-averse attitude from companies after the crisis.

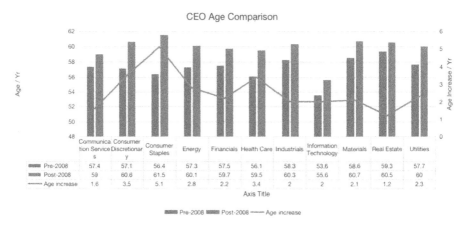

CEO Age Comparison

	Communication Services	Consumer Discretionary	Consumer Staples	Energy	Financials	Health Care	Industrials	Information Technology	Materials	Real Estate	Utilities
Pre-2008	57.4	57.1	56.4	57.3	57.5	56.1	58.3	53.6	58.6	59.3	57.7
Post-2008	59	60.6	61.5	60.1	59.7	59.5	60.3	55.6	60.7	60.5	60
Age increase	1.6	3.5	5.1	2.8	2.2	3.4	2	2	2.1	1.2	2.3

Axis Title

Pre-2008   Post-2008   Age increase

Fig. 4. CEO Age Comparisons by Sector and Before and After 2008

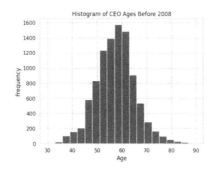

Histogram of CEO Ages Before 2008

Fig. 5. CEO Age Distribution Before 2008

The role of CEO appears to be heavily dominated by US nationals before 2008 and even more so after (Fig. 8). The nationality status could be skewed in favor of US citizens

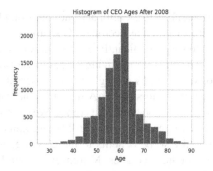

Fig. 6. CEO Age Distribution After 2008

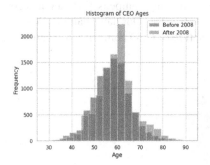

Fig. 7. CEO Age Distributions Shift Before and After 2008

because this dataset is focused on companies based in or associated with the US in some capacity. Furthermore, the top three nationalities are Anglo (US, Canada, and UK). This too makes intuitive sense as this is fairly evident in the real world.

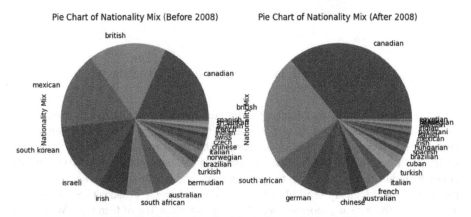

Fig. 8. CEO Nationality Mix Before and After 2008

Additionally, we draw attention to preliminary findings around CEO salaries and corporate governance structure variation by sector. CEO salaries, bonuses, and total wealth accumulation do not seem to vary significantly between CEOs who are and are not active in M&A. CEO salaries in our dataset remain high regardless of strategic innovations or variations in frequency or value of M&A (Fig. 9). This observation suggests that salary and wealth are not primary motivators of M&A for CEOs, at least in comparing CEOs leading M&A transactions before and after crisis times. We cannot directly measure personal or positional power increases, which may still be relevant as motivators for CEOs pursuing M&A. There could also be benefits to the CEO dealmakers such as receiving reputational boosts or media accolades. Moreover, we are here directly assessing CEO base salary, which is often the lowest portion of the total compensation or wealth accumulation. Bonuses, stock options, grants, severance, golden parachutes, and other firms of contingent or incentivizing compensation can also come into play and are not reflected in the present observations. Our data analytics in Sect. 3.2 take greater account of the multidimensional nature of CEO compensation and wealth accumulation.

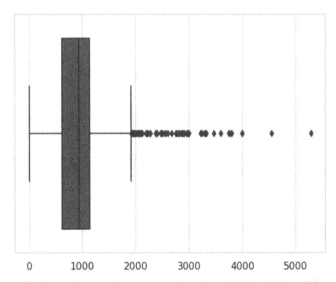

Fig. 9. CEO annual base salary dispersion in USD millions 000

CEOs are not the sole decision makers for pursuing M&A, as such high-level strategic decisions must also be supported by the board of directors. The CEO, chairperson, and other board members are three vital parts within the corporate governance structure of the firm. Interestingly, we find that the number of directors on the board varies considerably by industry (Fig. 10), with technology firms leading the way. In this case we use the finer grained industry level classifications rather than the broader GISC sectors to disaggregate the data at a more nuanced level of understanding of firm type. Within the tech world, the software and computer services firms have the largest number of directors, perhaps because of a greater interest for involvement or a greater need for oversight given the increased popularity and rapid growth of these firms within the specified time. Pharmaceuticals and biotechnology firms are a close second.

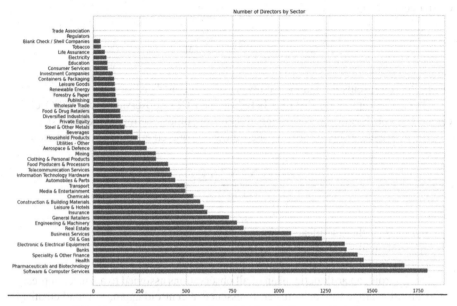

Fig. 10. Distribution of the size of the board directors by industry

3 Clustering and PCA

Clustering allocates data with similar characteristics into groups. Principal components analysis (PCA) reduces the features or dimensions of the dataset, while k-means clustering allocates the observations into groups by applying a distance metric. We divided the data into groups based on similarities in the data. Using a standard k-means clustering, we grouped M&A deals into k groups. We evaluated the centroids as arithmetic means of all the data points assigned to a cluster. Centroids represent typical members of the cluster.

3.1 Cluster Trajectories

Our clustering analysis allocates observations of CEO characteristics into groups according to similarities in the characteristics. We do a standard k-means clustering to assign CEOs into k groups. The k-means algorithm typically iterates until the inter-cluster distance for each observation is less than the intra-cluster distance, with more specialized methods now available for minimizing the sum of the squared distance from each observation to a cluster, when different clusters have different value or cost [27].

Starting from $X = \{x_1, x_2, x_3......x_n\}$ observations and $V = \{v_1, v_2, v_3........v_n\}$ cluster centers, the algorithm proceeds as follows: first, randomly choose c centers. Then, determine the distance between each CEO observation (also known as a data point) and cluster center. Next assign the observation to the cluster center whose distance from that center is the minimum of all the cluster centers. Subsequently, recalculate the new cluster center using:

$$v_i = (1 \backslash c_i) \sum_{j=1}^{c_i} x_i$$

where, 'c_i' represents the number of observations in the ith cluster.

Then, re-compute the distance between each CEO observation and CEO cluster center. If no observation was reassigned then stop, otherwise repeat the third step.

The above algorithm minimizes the following squared error objective function:

$$J(V) = \sum_{i=1}^{c} \sum_{j=1}^{c_j} \left(\|x_i - v_j\| \right)^2$$

where,

'$\|x_i - v_j\|$' is the Euclidean distance between x_i and v_j.

'c_i' is the number of observations in the ith cluster.

'c' is the number of cluster centers [17].

The centroid, an arithmetic mean of all observations assigned to a cluster, represents an idealized average for each cluster. In essence, a centroid captures a mathematically typical member of its cluster, although that member may not exist in reality. Our clustering analysis grouped CEOs based on characteristics such as gender, age, salary, bonus, and total compensation and wealth accumulation. In this graph, it is evident that cluster 2 is entirely separate from clusters 0, 1 and 3, whereas there is some overlap in clusters 3 and 1, and clusters 1 and 0, respectively. It is of value to note that in addition to cluster 2 being far apart from the other three clusters, the points within cluster 2 are far apart from one another as well as demonstrated by the one outlier in cluster 2.

3.2 PCA Dimensions

PCA involves a data matrix $\mathbf{Z}$, accompanied by a metric matrix $\mathbf{I}_p$ defined in $\mathbb{R}^p$, and another metric $\mathbf{N}_p$ defined in $\mathbb{R}^n$ (generally $\mathbf{N} = (1/n)\mathbf{I}_n$). The PCA process reduces a dataset from numerous dimensions into fewer, more parsimonious dimensions representing linear (re)combinations of variables from the original dimensions. The matrix $\mathbf{Z}$ can be defined as follows:

- supposing a normalized PCA: $\mathbf{Z} = \mathbf{XS}^{-1}$, where $\mathbf{S}$ is the diagonal matrix of standard deviations.
- supposing a non-normalized PCA: $\mathbf{Z} = \mathbf{X}$.

The fit in $\mathbb{R}^p$ has to do with: $\mathbf{Z}^T\mathbf{NZu} = \lambda u$, with $\mathbf{u}^T\mathbf{u} = 1$.

The fit in $\mathbb{R}^n$ has to do with: $\mathbf{N}^{\frac{1}{2}}\mathbf{ZZ}^T\mathbf{N}^{\frac{1}{2}}v = \lambda v$, with $\mathbf{v}^T\mathbf{v} = 1$.

The transition relations can be written as:

$$\mathbf{u} = \frac{1}{\sqrt{\lambda}}\mathbf{Z}^T\mathbf{N}^{\frac{1}{2}}\mathbf{v}$$

$$\mathbf{v} = \frac{1}{\sqrt{\lambda}}\mathbf{N}^{\frac{1}{2}}\mathbf{Zu}$$

The symmetric matrix intended to be diagonalized is $\mathbf{Z^T NZ}$. This matrix accords with the correlations matrix for a normalized (rescaled to the properties of a normal distribution with $\mu = 1$ and $\sigma = 1$) PCA, or with a covariance matrix, for a non-normalized PCA [9].

PC1 and PC2 are the first and second principal components, respectively, obtained from PCA on our dataset (Fig. 11). As noted, PCA is a technique used to reduce the dimensionality of a dataset by finding the directions of maximum variance in the data and projecting the data onto a new coordinate system along these directions. In our analysis, PCA was used to reduce the original dataset with eight features (gender, nationality mix, sector, age, salary, bonus, total salary + bonus, and total wealth) into a two-dimensional dataset represented by PC1 and PC2.

PC1 and PC2 are linear combinations of the original features that account for the largest amount of variance in the data. Therefore, PC1 and PC2 are new variables that summarize the information contained in the original features. The scatter plot shows the data points in this new two-dimensional space, where the x-axis is PC1 and the y-axis is PC2. The silhouette score for the hierarchical clustering is 0.3229. The silhouette metric captures how well the data points have been clustered, with a range of possible values $(-1,1)$ and values greater than 1 representing a good capture.

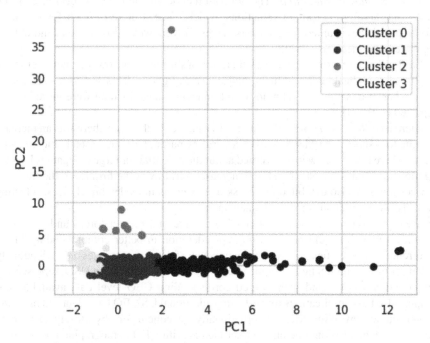

Fig. 11. PCA Hierarchical Clustering Results on CEO Characteristics

The values of PC1 and PC2 tell you how similar yet different CEOs are in terms of the variables included in the analysis. CEOs who have similar values on PC1 and PC2 are more similar to each other in terms of their characteristics, while CEOs who have different values on PC1 and PC2 are more dissimilar.

In the context of this analysis, clustering the CEOs based on their values on PC1 and PC2 allows us to identify groups of CEOs who have similar characteristics. By analyzing the differences between these groups, we can gain insights into the characteristics that distinguish successful CEOs from less successful ones.

4 Conclusion

In this paper, we have analyzed external and internal drivers of mergers and acquisitions (M&A) in the pre-pandemic decades of 1999-2018, as part of understanding strategic innovations in intercorporate combinations and variations in volume and valuation of mergers and acquisitions in and between crisis times.

The global financial crisis (GFC) in 2008-2009, like the dot.com bubble before it, had significant impacts on mergers and acquisitions (M&A) in several ways:

Decreased Deal Activity: Similar to the dot.com bubble bursting, the GFC led to a significant decrease in M&A activity as companies were hesitant to engage in transactions during times of uncertainty and economic instability. This led to a decrease in the number of deals as well as the overall value of transactions.

Lower Company Valuations: The dot.com meltdown and the GFC decreased stock prices and therefore corporate valuations, which made it more difficult for sellers to get the prices they wanted for their businesses. Buyers were also cautious and able to negotiate better deals as a result.

Shift in Focus: During both crises, there was a shift in focus towards more defensive sectors such as healthcare, utilities, and consumer goods. This led to a decrease in the number of deals in the technology and financial sectors, which were more heavily impacted by the crises.

Increased Regulatory Scrutiny: In the aftermath of both crises, there was an increase in regulatory scrutiny of M&A deals. The scrutiny particularly increased in the financial sector, where regulators were concerned about the potential for large companies becoming too big to fail. Consistent with the increased scrutiny at the firm level, the financial services industry also exhibited more risk-aversiveness in leadership choices, selecting typically older candidates for top management.

We have argued that both "external" economic and market forces and "internal" CEO level factors should be taken into consideration in better comprehending M&A occurrence and outcomes. As our present universe of data encompasses only US publicly traded acquirers and US targets, with M&A valued over 250 million USD, representing the 11 GICS sectors, and with limited corresponding CEO level data available, our findings also have implications for collecting additional US CEO level data and pursuing further studies involving M&A internationally. In conclusion, by closely examining the convergence of economic and market factors with CEO demographic background, motivational and reward factors, our research emphasizes the importance of studying firms in conjunction with their leaders and sheds light on the neglected issue of the previously excessive partitioning of M&A contributing factors into external and internal domains.

Our analysis uncovered patterns in M&A varying by the 11 global industry classification standard (GICS) sectors and by cycles of economic downturn and recovery. Using clustering analysis on M&A from SDC Platinum, with transactions valued over 250 million USD with publicly-traded US acquiring firms and publicly-traded or privately held US target firms, we determine similarities and differences in M&A activity by GICS sector and across economic eras. The economic cycles include two major market shocks: the high-tech dot.com meltdown around 2001 and the global financial crisis in 2008-2009. We find that the distributions of M&A by GICS sectors can be grouped into three major patterns, reflecting upsurges, downturns, and resilience for recovery even following major market upheavals. Additionally, combining CEO-level data from BoardEx with firm-level SDC Platinum transactions, we have preliminary findings regarding CEO demographic background and reward drivers of M&A transactions. We focus on the period before covid-19, and implications of our research are to consider the impact of the covid-19 pandemic on current and future M&A activity in various regions of the world [1], given current circumstances of global economic retrenchment and the associated decline in M&A. These findings and methods can be generalized into questions on other aspects of M&A as well. We aim to address such questions in our subsequent research.

Acknowledgements. The authors thank Kathleen Berger of the Pardee Library Information Services, Frederick S. Pardee Management Library, Boston University and James Zeitler of the Baker Library Research Services, Harvard Business School, Harvard University, for their respective assistance with the data collection. We deeply thank the Office of the Dean, the Department of Administrative Sciences, and the Department of Computer Science at Boston University Metropolitan College for their support.

Appendix A: M&A Frequency by GISC Sector Before and After 2008

Here are comparisons of percentile groupings by quartiles of M&A frequency and value for various GISC sectors before and after 2008:

1. Pre 2008:

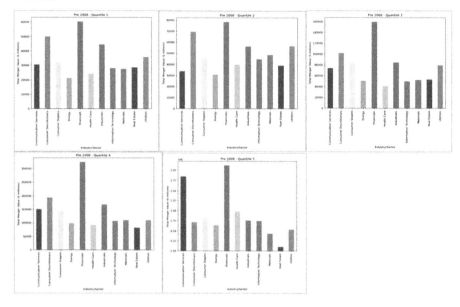

2. Post 2008:

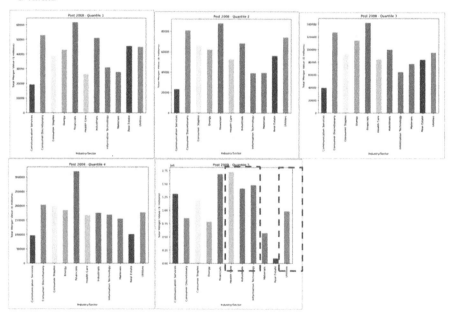

References

1. Ahern, K.R., Daminelli, D., Fracassi, C.: Lost in translation? The effect of cultural values on mergers around the world. J. Financ. Econ. **117**(1), 165–189 (2015). https://doi.org/10.1016/j.jfineco.2012.08.006

2. Arsini, L., Straccamore, M., Zaccaria, A.: Prediction and visualization of mergers and acquisitions using economic complexity. PLoS ONE **18**(4), e0283217 (2023). https://doi.org/10.1371/journal.pone.0283217

3. Balogh, A., Creedy, U., Wright, D.: Time to acquire: regulatory burden and M&A activity. Int. Rev. Financ. Anal. **82**, 102047 (2022). https://doi.org/10.1016/j.irfa.2022.102047

4. Bebchuck, L.A.: The myth of the shareholder franchise. Va. Law Rev. **93**(3), 675–732 (2007)

5. Bhuyan, M.N.H., Subedi, M., Akter, M.: CEO-friendly boards and seasoned equity offerings. J. Behav. Exp. Finan. **36**, 100761 (2022). https://doi.org/10.1016/j.jbef.2022.100761

6. Brueller, N.N., Carmeli, A., Markman, G.D.: Linking merger and acquisition strategies to postmerger integration: a configurational perspective of human resource management. J. Manag. **44**(5), 1793–1818 (2018). https://doi.org/10.1177/0149206315626270

7. Croci, E., et al.: The role of corporate political strategies in M&As. J. Corp. Finan. **43**, 260–287 (2017). https://doi.org/10.1016/j.jcorpfin.2017.01.009

8. Cumming, D., et al.: Mergers and acquisitions research in finance and accounting: past, present, and future. European Financial Management. In Press, pp. 1– 41 (2023). https://doi.org/10.1111/eufm.12417

9. Ding, C., He, X.: K-means clustering via principal component analysis. In: Proceedings of the 21st International Conference on Machine Learning. Association for Computing Machinery, Banff, Alberta, Canada, p. 29 (2004)

10. Elnahas, A.M., Kim, D.: CEO political ideology and mergers and acquisitions decisions. J. Corp. Finan. **45**, 162–175 (2017). https://doi.org/10.1016/j.jcorpfin.2017.04.013

11. Ferreira, M.P., dos Reis, N.R., Pinto, C.F.: Three decades of strategic management research on M&As: citations, co-citations, and topics. Glob. Econ. Manage. Rev. **21**(1), 13–24 (2016). https://doi.org/10.1016/j.gemrev.2015.12.002

12. Fralich, R., Bitektine, A.: "Invincibles" and "invisibles": CEO status and the 'Matthew effect' in strategic decision-making. Long Range Plan. **53**(3), 101887 (2020). https://doi.org/10.1016/j.lrp.2019.05.007

13. Guidi, M., et al.: Spreading the sin: an empirical assessment from corporate takeovers. Int. Rev. Financ. Anal. **71**, 101535 (2020). https://doi.org/10.1016/j.irfa.2020.101535

14. Holm, H.J., Nee, V., Opper, S.: Strategic decisions: behavioral differences between CEOs and others. Exp. Econ. **23**(1), 154–180 (2020). https://doi.org/10.1007/s10683-019-09604-3

15. Hussain, T., et al.: Powerful bidders and value creation in M&As. Int. Rev. Financ. Anal. **81**, 102076 (2022). https://doi.org/10.1016/j.irfa.2022.102076

16. Jiang, T.: Using machine learning to analyze merger activity [Brief Research Report]. Front. Appl. Math. Statist. **7**, 649501 (2021). https://doi.org/10.3389/fams.2021.649501

17. Kanungo, T., et al.: A local search approximation algorithm for k-means clustering. Comput. Geom. **28**(2), 89–112 (2004). https://doi.org/10.1016/j.comgeo.2004.03.003

18. Leung, H., Tse, J., Westerholm, P.J.: CEO traders and corporate acquisitions. J. Corp. Finan. **54**, 107–127 (2019). https://doi.org/10.1016/j.jcorpfin.2017.09.013

19. Markoczy, L., Kolev, K.D., Qian, C.: Trade-off among stakeholders: CEO political orientation and corporate social irresponsibility. Long Range Plan. **56**(2), 102273 (2023). https://doi.org/10.1016/j.lrp.2022.102273

20. Moeller, S.B., Schlingemann, F.P., Stulz, R.M.: Wealth destruction on a massive scale? A study of acquiring-firm returns in the recent merger wave. J. Finan. **60**(2), 757–782 (2005). https://doi.org/10.1111/j.1540-6261.2005.00745.x

21. Ott, C.: The risks of mergers and acquisitions—analyzing the incentives for risk reporting in item 1A of 10-K filings. J. Bus. Res. **106**, 158–181 (2020). https://doi.org/10.1016/j.jbusres.2019.08.028

22. Petridis, K., et al.: A Support Vector Machine model for classification of efficiency: an application to M&A. Res. Int. Bus. Financ. **61**, 101633 (2022). https://doi.org/10.1016/j.ribaf.2022.101633

23. Plaksina, Y., Gallagher, L., Dowling, M.: CEO social status and M&A decision making. Int. Rev. Financ. Anal. **64**, 282–300 (2019). https://doi.org/10.1016/j.irfa.2019.06.006

24. Seth, S.: The 5 biggest acquisitions in history: deals worth over $100 billion each. Investopedia (2020). https://www.investopedia.com/investing/biggest-acquisitions-in-history/

25. Simpson, J.J., Sariol, M.: Uncertainty, entrepreneurial orientation, and the pursuit of M&A: managing the unpredictable. J. Bus. Res. **142**, 423–434 (2022). https://doi.org/10.1016/j.jbusres.2022.01.006

26. Wulf, J.: Do CEOs in mergers trade power for premium? Evidence from 'mergers of equals.' J. Law Econ. Organ. **20**(1), 60–101 (2004)

27. Zhang, Z., et al.: Improved approximation algorithms for solving the squared metric k-facility location problem. Theoret. Comput. Sci. **942**, 107–122 (2023). https://doi.org/10.1016/j.tcs.2022.11.027

28. Zhou, L., et al.: Celebrity CEOs and corporate investment: a psychological contract perspective. Int. Rev. Financ. Anal. **87**, 102636 (2023). https://doi.org/10.1016/j.irfa.2023.102636

Interdependencies Between Cryptocurrency Markets, Precious Metals and Energy Resources

Ivan Rusevski[1]([✉])[ID], Ana Todorovska[1][ID], Irena Vodenska[3][ID],
Ljubomir Chitkushev[2][ID], and Dimitar Trajanov[1,2][ID]

[1] Faculty of Computer Science and Engineering, Ss. Cyril and Methodius
University in Skopje, Skopje, Republic of North Macedonia
{ivan.rusevski,ana.todorovska,dimitar.trajanov}@finki.ukim.mk

[2] Computer Science Department, Metropolitan College, Boston University,
Boston, MA, USA
{lou,dtrajano}@bu.edu

[3] Administrative Sciences Department, Financial Management,
Metropolitan College, Boston University, Boston, MA, USA
vodenska@bu.edu

Abstract. In a rapidly changing world where no market or economy is secure, interconnectivity is becoming a key feature of almost all social and economic systems. As a brand-new digital asset, cryptocurrencies are quickly taking over the world economy. Cryptocurrencies are becoming alternative investments as a store of value compared to precious metals. The purpose of this study is to examine the connections between cryptocurrencies, precious metals, and energy resources using structured numerical data. To achieve this goal, two approaches are employed to create networks that reveal relationships between cryptocurrencies (Bitcoin, Ethereum, Cardano, Chainlink, Litecoin, Stellar, and Ripple), precious metals (Gold, Silver, and Platinum), and energy resources (Oil and Natural Gas) based on their daily prices and returns. The interdependence of the networks is further examined to reveal similarities between the created networks. The proposed methodology facilitates an understanding of the dynamics of cryptocurrency markets, the factors that influence them, and the potential for future research to expand and include additional cryptocurrencies.

Keywords: Cryptocurrencies · Precious metals · Energy resources · Interdependence · Networks

1 Introduction

Globalization has a tremendous impact on the structure of the financial markets and the development of the economy in our interconnected world. The swift

© ICST Institute for Computer Sciences, Social Informatics and Telecommunications Engineering 2023
Published by Springer Nature Switzerland AG 2023. All Rights Reserved
T. Zlateva and G. Tuparov (Eds.): CSECS 2023, LNICST 514, pp. 281–292, 2023.
https://doi.org/10.1007/978-3-031-44668-9_22

development of progressive technologies has brought about significant changes in various industries and society as a whole. These technologies have the potential to improve efficiency, productivity, and decision-making, thereby contributing to economic growth. One such advancement is the emergence of digital currencies, particularly cryptocurrencies. Cryptocurrencies are a type of digital currency that utilizes cryptography for security. They are decentralized, meaning they are not under the control of any government or financial institution. The most well-known digital currency is Bitcoin, but there are many others like Ethereum, Litecoin, and Ripple. Cryptocurrencies have gained popularity due to their potential for fast and cheap transactions, as well as their ability to operate outside of traditional financial systems. These days, cryptocurrencies are a crucial component of the world financial system [1].

Interdependencies between cryptocurrencies have been analyzed to understand better the dynamics in the cryptocurrency markets and the different processes that influence their performance [2]. To examine the interconnectivity of cryptocurrencies and potential price shifts due to such influence, centrality measures have been calculated to extract insights from cryptocurrency networks [3]. Researchers investigated the impact of stock market indexes S&P500 and Dow Jones on the prices of eighteen major cryptocurrencies, utilizing the cutting-edge time series prediction library (XGBoost) to develop daily price prediction models for all cryptocurrencies [4]. Another study seeks to explore the relationships between cryptocurrencies and traditional financial markets, analyzing connectivity networks of seven cryptocurrencies and seven conventional economic indicators using an explainable AI model that learns asset dependencies and presents them in a human-understandable format [5]. The relationship between Bitcoin's power consumption and the market is the target of a study that finds a relationship between Bitcoin's power consumption and its daily returns as well as trading volume. Bitcoin's second crash also causes a high correlation with electricity consumption [6]. Investing in Bitcoin compared to gold as a hedge against oil-related uncertainties caused by the COVID-19 pandemic has found gold to act as an increasingly weak diversifier as the pandemic intensifies [7]. Another study researches tail spillover effects between cryptocurrencies and uncertainty in the gold, oil, and stock markets using a cross-quantile approach. They preview that cryptocurrency and traditional markets are inconsiderably connected under normal conditions [8]. The negative consequences of cryptocurrencies' high-power energy consumption on the environment and sustainability have piqued the curiosity of a wide number of regulators and market actors. One study employs a network method to examine the interdependence between clean energy, green markets, and cryptocurrency [9]. Another study will use three machine learning models to investigate the effect of cryptocurrencies and the US dollar in predicting oil prices before and during the COVID-19 outbreak. Support vector machines, Multilayer Perceptron Neural Networks, and Generalized Regression Neural Networks are all examples of neural networks [10].Interdependence about information among multiple commodities such as energy, metals and agricultural commodities, and cryptocurrencies have been examined using a time-varying entropy-based approach, minimum spanning tree, and various centrality measures [11].

This paper expands on earlier studies by integrating traditional commodities and the growing cryptocurrency market.

2   Data

We have chosen the seven cryptocurrencies with the highest market capitalization from the more than 22,000 listed on Coinmarketcap[1]. Additionally, we select three of the most popular precious metals and two publicly traded energy resources. We then retrieve historical prices for each asset from the resources Yahoo Finance[2] and Investing[3] We gather data for the time period between November 2019 to November 2022, a period of high volatility and price swings.

2.1   Cryptocurrencies

We select seven cryptocurrencies based on relevance and largest market capitalization over the years: Bitcoin, Ethereum, Cardano, Ripple, Litecoin, Chainlink, and Stellar. For every cryptocurrency, the price dataset includes the date, open and close prices, high and low prices, volume and adjusted closing price.

2.2   Precious Metals and Energy Resources

The three most popular and most traded precious metals we select are Gold, Silver, and Platinum. Additionally, we choose to use Crude Oil and Natural Gas, two publicly traded energy resources, due to their significant economic impact. For each precious metal and energy resource, the historical price dataset includes the date, open price, high and low prices, close price, adjusted closing price, and volume.

3   Methodology

Our research models the relationships between cryptocurrencies, precious metals, and energy resources using a correlation-based approach [12].To uncover correlations between cryptocurrencies, precious metals, and energy resources, we employ Pearson's correlation coefficient as a starting point. Pearson's correlation coefficient is a descriptive statistic that summarizes the characteristics of the dataset. It describes the strength and direction of the linear relationship between two quantitative variables.

---

[1] https://coinmarketcap.com/.
[2] https://finance.yahoo.com/.
[3] https://www.investing.com/.

3.1   Daily Price Correlations

We first use daily prices to obtain time series of daily prices for cryptocurrencies, precious metals, and energy resources by taking the last price at the close of the trading market. As cryptocurrencies are traded 24/7, we take the last price at 11:59 p.m. UTC. However, precious metals and energy resources are not traded on weekends and certain holidays, so we use the previous day's price for days when the market is closed, and no price data is available. This ensures that we have datasets of identical size for all cryptocurrencies, precious metals, and energy resources so that we can accordingly calculate daily correlations. We use these daily correlations to create the first three networks: a network created using cryptocurrency prices, a network created using precious metals and energy resources prices, and a network created using cryptocurrency, precious metals, and energy resources prices.

3.2   Daily Return Correlations

Second, we use daily returns to obtain time series of daily returns correlations for cryptocurrencies, precious metals, and energy resources. The daily return is a measure of the percentage change in the value of an investment or portfolio over the course of a day. It represents the gain or loss in the value of an economic asset as a result of changes in market conditions, economic events, or other factors that may affect the asset's performance. This metric can be calculated if the price of a certain economic asset within a given time period is known. The daily return is calculated as the difference between the current price of the asset and its price on the previous day, divided by the value on the previous day. To obtain the percentage of the daily return, the required result should be multiplied by one hundred as shown in the following Eq. 1.

$$Daily\ Return = (\frac{current\ day\ closing\ price - previous\ day\ closing\ price}{prior\ day\ closing\ price}) * 100 \tag{1}$$

For example, if an asset has a positive daily return of 1%, it means that its value has increased by 1% from the previous day's closing price. Daily return is used to assess short-term performance and provide insight into the volatility and risk of an investment. To calculate daily returns, we use the daily price time series data. We then calculate the Pearson correlation coefficient using the daily return time series to obtain daily return correlations. Based on these correlations, we create networks for cryptocurrencies, precious metals, and energy resources.

3.3   Centrality Measures

Centrality measures in network theory are quantitative metrics used to assess the importance or influence of nodes within a network. These measures aim to identify nodes that play crucial roles in terms of their position, connectivity, or control within the network. For this research we use the following measures: eigenvector centrality, node strength, and closeness centrality.

Eigenvector centrality takes into account both the number and quality of a node's connections. It assigns higher centrality to nodes that are connected to other highly central nodes. This measure captures the idea that the importance of a node is determined by the importance of its neighbors.

In network theory, node strength refers to a measure of the total strength or importance of a node in a weighted network. Node strength is calculated by summing the weights of all the edges connected to a specific node. It provides a quantitative measure of the overall influence or significance of a node in the network based on the total weight of its connections.

Closeness centrality measures how close a node is to all other nodes in the network. It calculates the average shortest path length between a node and all other nodes in the network. Nodes with higher closeness centrality are more central as they can reach other nodes more quickly.

4 Results

In our research, we study the intra and inter-dependencies of cryptocurrencies and precious metals, and energy resources, however, we pay special attention to the links between different types of economic assets. We use the strongest 1/2 of all links to create networks based on correlations between assets of the same type, however, we use the strongest 1/3 of all links when creating networks based on correlations between assets of different types.

4.1 Networks Created Using Daily Price Correlations

First, we study the cryptocurrency network generated using daily price correlations, shown in Fig. 1. This network shows the interdependence between cryptocurrencies with respect to their price.

We observe that Bitcoin is the most influential cryptocurrency, with four strong links, followed by Ethereum, Litecoin, Chainlink, and Stellar, which have three strong links each. The strongest connection in this network is between Litecoin and Stellar, with a value of 0.96.

Next, we observe the network of precious metals and energy resources generated using daily price correlations, shown in Fig. 2. This network only shows the interdependence between precious metals and energy resources with respect to this data.

We see that Platinum is the most influential among precious metals and energy resources, with the highest number of strong links, 3 in total, followed by Gold and Silver, with two strong links each. The strongest relationship is between Oil and Gas, with a value of 0.84.

Figure 3 shows the network of cryptocurrencies, precious metals, and energy resources created using daily price correlations. This network shows the interdependence between cryptocurrencies and precious metals, and energy resources in terms of their price.

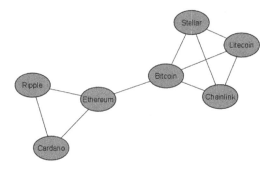

Fig. 1. Network showing one-half of the strongest network links based on cryptocurrency daily price correlations.

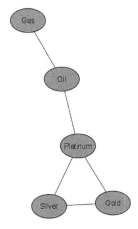

Fig. 2. Network showing one-half of the strongest network links based on precious metals and energy resources daily price correlations.

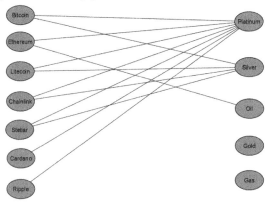

Fig. 3. Network showing one-third of the strongest network links based on cryptocurrency, precious metals and energy resources daily price correlations.

We find that Platinum has the highest degree of the node (7), followed by Silver which has the degree of the node (3). Cryptocurrencies in this network all have low node degrees. The strongest link in this network is between Stellar and Platinum, with a value of 0.72.

Table 1 shows the centrality measures for the network of cryptocurrencies, precious metals, and energy resources created using daily price correlations. The eigenvector centrality is highest for Platinum with a value of 0.46, followed by Silver with a value of 0.41, and Bitcoin with a value of 0.3. All other cryptocurrencies have similar values for this measure ranging between 0.24–0.27, while Gold and Gas have the lowest with 0.18 and 0.16. The node strength measure is highest for Platinum with a value of 4.33, Silver with a value of 3.82,2, and Oil with a value of 2.48. Among cryptocurrencies, the values are similar and range between 1.75–1.9, with the exception of Bitcoin and Ethereum, which have values of 2.3 and 2.26, respectively. The closeness centrality measure is highest for Platinum with a value of 4.83, for Stellar cryptocurrencies with a value of 4.55, followed by Chainlink, Litecoin, and Bitcoin with values of 4.32, 4.28, and 4.23, respectively. From the data, we can notice that Platinum has the strongest influence. Cryptocurrencies are not as influential, with the exception of Stellar, which exhibits high closeness centrality.

4.2 Networks Created Using Daily Return Correlations

Figure 4 shows the cryptocurrency network created using daily return correlations. This network shows the interdependence between cryptocurrencies in terms of this variable. We see that Ethereum, Cardano, and Litecoin are the most influential cryptocurrencies, with four strong links each, followed by Chainlink, with three strong links. The strongest connection in this network is between Ethereum and Litecoin, with a value of 0.82.

The network of precious metals and energy resources created using daily return correlations is shown in Fig. 5. This network only shows the interdependence between precious metals and energy resources with respect to this variable. From this network, we can conclude that Platinum is the most influential among precious metals and energy resources, with a total of 4 strong links, followed by Gold and Silver, with two strong links each. In this network, the closest connection is between Silver and Gold, with a value of 0.77.

Figure 6 shows the network of cryptocurrencies, precious metals, and energy resources created using daily return correlations. The network displays the interdependence between cryptocurrencies and precious metals, and energy resources in terms of this variable. We can notice that Platinum has the highest node degree (5), followed by Silver and Bitcoin, which has the node degree (4). The strongest link in this network is between Litecoin and Silver, with a value of 0.1.

Table 2 shows the details of centrality measures for the nodes of this network. The eigenvector centrality is highest for Silver with a value of 0.45, followed by Platinum with a value of 0.41, and Bitcoin with a value of 0.37, and Litecoin with a value of 0.34. All other cryptocurrencies have values for this measure ranging between 0.15–0.3. The measure for node strength is highest for Silver

Table 1. Centrality measures for the network based on cryptocurrency, precious metals and energy resources daily prices.

Asset	eigenvector centrality	node strength	closeness centrality
Bitcoin	0.3	2.3	4.23
Cardano	0.25	1.9	3.07
Stellar	0.27	1.87	4.55
Ripple	0.24	1.84	3
Chainlink	0.27	1.87	4.32
Litecoin	0.26	1.75	4.28
Ethereum	0.27	2.26	3.14
Gas	0.16	1.46	2.01
Oil	0.26	2.48	2.75
Gold	0.18	1.69	1.91
Silver	0.41	3.82	3.72
Platinum	0.46	4.33	4.83

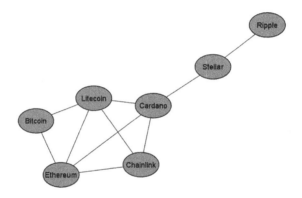

Fig. 4. Network showing one-half of the strongest network links based on cryptocurrency daily price correlations.

with a value of 0.47, Platinum with a value of 0.45, and Oil with a value of 0.31. Among cryptocurrencies, the values range between 0.11–0.28, with the exception of Bitcoin, which has a value of 0.34. The measure of closeness centrality is highest for Silver, with a value of 21.29, and Platinum, with a value of 19.1, among cryptocurrencies Bitcoin, with a value of 20.43, followed by Litecoin, with a value of 20.21. The other cryptocurrencies have a value between 11.22–15.9. From the data, we can notice that Silver has the strongest influence. Cryptocurrencies are not as influential, with the exception of Bitcoin, which exhibits high closeness centrality.

Fig. 5. Network showing one-half of the strongest network links based on precious metals and energy resources daily return correlations.

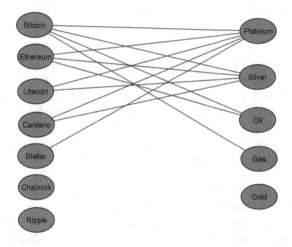

Fig. 6. Network showing one-third of the strongest network links based on cryptocurrency, precious metals and energy resources daily return correlations.

5 Discussion

Our research provides an analysis approach for dependencies between cryptocurrencies and some precious metals and energy resources. The methodology we apply is based on organized numerical data that is freely available to the public collected on a daily basis. We calculate correlations based on daily prices and daily returns using this data. Then we investigate the relationships between seven cryptocurrencies (Bitcoin, Stellar, Cardano, Litecoin, Chainlink, Ethereum, and Ripple), three precious metals (Gold, Silver, and Platinum), and two energy resources (Gas and Oil), both based on their daily prices and daily returns. We

Table 2. Centrality measures for the network based on cryptocurrency, precious metals and energy resources daily returns.

Asset	eigenvector centrality	node strength	closeness centrality
Bitcoin	0.37	0.34	20.43
Cardano	0.26	0.22	14.02
Stellar	0.15	0.11	11.33
Ripple	0.17	0.14	11.22
Chainlink	0.2	0.16	12.01
Litecoin	0.34	0.28	20.21
Ethereum	0.3	0.27	15.9
Gas	0.15	0.14	11.6
Oil	0.29	0.31	14.04
Gold	0.17	0.16	11.11
Silver	0.45	0.47	21.29
Platinum	0.41	0.45	19.1

create networks using the correlations to gain insight into the interdependencies between cryptocurrencies, precious metals, and energy resources. Our results show that when daily price correlations are used, Platinum stands out with the strongest measures of centrality out of the precious metals, followed by Silver which has higher degrees compared to cryptocurrencies, which do not appear to be as central, except for Stellar, showing a strong closeness centrality. When we analyze the correlations of daily returns, our results show that Silver has the strongest measures of centrality, followed by Platinum which has higher degrees compared to cryptocurrencies, with the exception of Bitcoin, which stands out with the strongest measures of centrality among cryptocurrencies. In addition, energy resources, oil, and gas, show a very low correlation with cryptocurrencies and precious metals, with the exception of Bitcoin and Ethereum, with which they have a medium correlation, which may be due to different market dynamics and influence.

Based on the results we obtained, it is evident that there is a strong correlation between precious metals and cryptocurrencies. This can be attributed to the strategy adopted by both individual and corporate investors to diversify their investment portfolios by including speculative and risky investments in cryptocurrencies, which have the potential for significant returns. Cryptocurrencies are often considered an alternative investment opportunity and are compared to precious metals in this context. In contrast, precious metals have a long history as a store of value and a hedge against inflation and economic uncertainty. They are frequently utilized as a safe haven asset during periods of market volatility and geopolitical instability.

Both cryptocurrencies and precious metals have limitations of use, although these limitations differ in nature. While cryptocurrencies can be used to buy

goods and services from merchants who accept them as payment, their acceptance is still limited compared to traditional forms of payment like cash or
credit cards. Precious metals have been traditionally used as a store of value
and a means of exchange, but they have limited use in day-to-day transactions.
They are not easily divisible, and their physical nature makes them difficult to
transport and store securely. Overall, depending on the specific needs and circumstances of the users, both cryptocurrencies and precious metals have their
limitations and benefits.

6   Conclusion

In this paper, we present a methodology for analyzing the connections between
cryptocurrencies, precious metals, and energy resources based on publicly available datasets of structured data. We create and analyze networks of seven
cryptocurrencies (Bitcoin, Cardano, Ripple, Stellar, Chainlink, Ethereum, and
Litecoin), three precious metals (Gold, Silver, and Platinum), and two energy
resources (Oil and Gas) using a correlation of their prices and daily returns data.

The results of this paper show that by looking only at the cryptocurrency
market, we can not pick a single main driver that moves the market. However,
when we look at precious metals and energy resources alone, the main driver
is definitely Platinum. In addition, when we cross-reference the cryptocurrency,
precious metal, and energy resource markets, it is interesting to note that Platinum is highly correlated with all cryptocurrencies.

While cryptocurrency markets are new and unpredictable, they are positioned to integrate into the traditional financial system through growing usage
of blockchain technology or by providing alternative payment methods in order
to create a unified global currency. The relationship between cryptocurrency
markets and precious metals, oil, and gas markets is not direct and can be considered to be not significant.

While all of these markets can be affected by global economic and geopolitical
factors, they have different underlying drivers and face different challenges. For
instance, the value of precious metals can be influenced by factors such as central
bank policy, while the price of oil and gas is largely driven by supply and demand
dynamics. The value of cryptocurrencies, on the other hand, is driven by factors
such as investor sentiment and adoption. However, in some cases, changes in the
value of cryptocurrencies, precious metals, oil, and gas can have an impact on
the other market, but this is not always the case. It is important to keep in mind
that markets are very dynamic, and correlations can change over time.

The methodology we show in this paper is a basis for understanding the
complex world of cryptocurrencies and traditional markets, including precious
metals and energy resources, as well as a stimulus for further research in this
area. Our methodology is scalable and may be developed to incorporate a greater
number of cryptocurrencies and other traditional economic indicators, as well as
to cover a larger time period. We hope that our research will contribute to greater
understanding of various financial markets and the influence of major events,
taking into consideration both traditional and innovative emerging markets.

References

1. Monia, M.: "Cryptocurrency." Ekonomika - Journal for Economic Theory and Practice and Social Issues, 105–122 (2018)
2. Todorovska, A., et al.: Analysis of cryptocurrency interdependencies. In: Proceedings of Blockchain in Kyoto, vol. 2021, no. BCK21, p. 011004 (2021)
3. Peshov, H., et al.: Using centrality measures to extract knowledge from cryptocurrencies' interdependencies networks. In: Zdravkova, K., Basnarkov, L. (eds.) ICT Innovations 2022. Reshaping the Future Towards a New Normal, vol. 1740, pp. 76–90. Springer, Cham (2023). https://doi.org/10.1007/978-3-031-22792-9_7
4. Gorast, A.: The influence of stock market indexes (S&P500 and Dow Jones) on cryptocurrencies prices (2022)
5. Todorovska, A., et al.: Interdependency between Classical Economic Indicators and Crypto-Markets Available at SSRN 4196995
6. Huynh, A.N.Q., Duong, D., Burggraf, T., Luong, H.T.T., Bui, N.H.: Energy consumption and Bitcoin market. Asia-Pac. Finan. Markets **29**(1), 79–93 (2022)
7. Ren, X., Wang, R., Duan, K., Chen, J.: Dynamics of the sheltering role of Bitcoin against crude oil market crash with varying severity of the COVID-19: a comparison with gold. Res. Int. Bus. Financ. **62**, 101672 (2022)
8. Mensi, W., Gubareva, M., Ko, H.U., Vo, X.V., Kang, S.H.: Tail spillover effects between cryptocurrencies and uncertainty in the gold, oil, and stock markets. Finan. Innovation **9**(1), 1–27 (2023)
9. Arfaoui, N., Naeem, M.A., Boubaker, S., Mirza, N., Karim, S.: Interdependence of clean energy and green markets with cryptocurrencies. Energy Econ. **120**, 106584 (2023)
10. Ibrahim, B.A., Elamer, A.A., Abdou, H.A.: The role of cryptocurrencies in predicting oil prices pre and during COVID-19 pandemic using machine learning. Ann. Oper. Res. 1–44 (2022)
11. Ji, Q., Bouri, E., Roubaud, D., Kristoufek, L.: Information interdependence among energy, cryptocurrency and major commodity markets. Energy Econ. **81**, 1042–1055 (2019)
12. Ho, K.H., Chiu, W.H., Li, C.: A network analysis of the cryptocurrency market. In: 2020 IEEE Symposium Series on Computational Intelligence (SSCI), pp. 2178–2185. IEEE (2020)

Exploring Banking Stability Through Diverse Parameters and Mathematical Models

Miglena Trencheva[(⊠)] [ID]

South-West University "Neofit Rilski", Blagoevgrad, Bulgaria
megy_tr2001@swu.bg

Abstract. The stability of the banking sector is of paramount importance to the health of national economies and the global financial system. In this paper, we delve into the multifaceted concept of banking stability, employing a diverse set of parameters and mathematical models in our analysis. Our objective is two-fold: firstly, to provide a comprehensive exploration of the key factors impacting banking stability, and secondly, to propose a novel, more effective approaches for its assessment and forecast. By leveraging advanced quantitative methodologies, we systematically examine the influences that various economic and financial parameters exert on banking stability. Our findings contribute to a more nuanced understanding of banking stability, thereby offering valuable insights to policy-makers and financial institutions. Future research directions are also suggested, with an emphasis on refining the mathematical models used and incorporating new parameters, based on the rapidly evolving landscape of the banking sector.

Keywords: Banking Stability · Diverse Parameters · Mathematical Models · global financial system

1 Introduction

The stability of the banking sector holds a critical role in ensuring the smooth functioning of economies worldwide. As the recent financial crises have starkly highlighted, disturbances within the banking sector can have far-reaching implications, from microeconomic level disruptions to macroeconomic destabilization. As such, a comprehensive understanding of the dynamics and influences underpinning banking stability is a priority for policymakers, regulators, and financial institutions alike [1–7, 12].

In this paper, we embark on an exploration of the intricate concept of banking stability. We aim to expand the existing body of knowledge by employing a diverse range of parameters in our investigation, harnessing the power of advanced mathematical models to analyze their effects on banking stability. The parameters we consider encompass a broad spectrum, including but not limited to macroeconomic indicators, bank-specific characteristics, and wider financial market conditions [5–10].

Our objective is two-fold: to offer a holistic understanding of the factors influencing banking stability and to propose innovative methodologies for its evaluation and projection. We strive to not only identify the key determinants of banking stability but also to

© ICST Institute for Computer Sciences, Social Informatics and Telecommunications Engineering 2023
Published by Springer Nature Switzerland AG 2023. All Rights Reserved
T. Zlateva and G. Tuparov (Eds.): CSECS 2023, LNICST 514, pp. 293–304, 2023.
https://doi.org/10.1007/978-3-031-44668-9_23

forecast future trends, thereby enabling preemptive measures to ensure banking sector resilience.

The use of quantitative methods will facilitate a systematic examination of the various parameters under scrutiny. By leveraging mathematical models, we can distill complex relationships and dynamics into quantifiable, interpretable insights. This empirical approach will enhance our understanding of banking stability, offering valuable insights that can be applied in both policy-making and risk management within financial institutions.

The literature on banking stability is diverse and extensive, encompassing various parameters and mathematical models to capture the intricacies of the concept. This section critically reviews the existing body of work, shedding light on the evolution of thought in this area and identifying gaps that our study aims to fill [7, 11–15].

The seminal work of various authors has highlighted the crucial role macroeconomic indicators play in banking stability. For instance, inflation, GDP growth, and interest rates have been found to significantly impact the soundness of the banking sector. However, the interplay between these indicators and banking stability is complex and often contingent upon the specific context of each economy, calling for further research in this area [16–21].

Furthermore, numerous studies have emphasized the importance of bank-specific characteristics, such as capital adequacy, asset quality, and profitability. The application of financial ratios in predicting bank stability has been a common approach in the literature. However, the dynamic nature of the banking industry necessitates continual validation of these ratios and the exploration of potential new indicators [15–18].

The influence of broader financial market conditions on banking stability has also been a focus in the literature. Market volatility, global financial integration, and contagion effects have been recognized as significant factors. Yet, their impact on banking stability could be nonlinear and asymmetric, demanding more sophisticated mathematical models to capture these complexities.

Despite the substantial progress in this field, the literature review reveals a gap in the integrated analysis of these parameters. Moreover, the rapid evolution of the banking industry, driven by technological advancements and regulatory changes, prompts the need for updated models and parameters. Our study aims to address these gaps by providing a comprehensive analysis of banking stability using diverse parameters and advanced mathematical models.

The article "Changes in the rules of the banking union"[1] by Consilium discusses changes in the rules of the European Union's banking union. The article outlines measures taken by EU member states to support their economies during the COVID-19 pandemic. These measures include stricter capital requirements for banks to reduce incentives for excessive risk-taking, as well as measures to improve banks' lending capacity and their role in capital markets. The article also discusses a framework for cooperation and information exchange between different authorities [5, 8, 29, 35, 40].

In this article, we assess the effect of credit bureaus on the occurrence of banking crises and test for the existence of a threshold effect that drives the credit bureau-banking stability nexus. We use data from 32 countries for a period from 2004 to 2016. [5, 12, 18, 34, 38]. One of the aims of our research is to find the existence of a nonlinear relationship

---

[1] https://www.consilium.europa.eu/en/policies/banking-union/

between private and public credit bureaus and banking stability. Also, we will try to find a correlation between the number of credit bureaus and banking instability [24, 35–40].

Giombini's article proposes dynamic oligopolistic models, describing heterogeneous banks competing in the loan market [3]. The authors consider two boundedly rational banks. Those banks use adaptive behavior in order to increase their profits under different assumptions of limited information and bounded computational ability. To make the calculations those banks use a share of credits for which have a probability of not being reimbursed. [12, 25, 34–38].

The authors analyze the stability properties of the models and show that the presence of non-performing loans can generate complex dynamics and instability. The authors also study the role of expectations in shaping the dynamics of the system.

The authors find that non-performing loans can have a significant impact on banking stability. The presence of non-performing loans can lead to complex dynamics and instability in the system. Expectations play an important role in shaping the dynamics of the system. The authors show that different expectations can lead to different outcomes in terms of banking stability [21–26].

The authors conclude that non-performing loans can have a significant impact on banking stability and that expectations play an important role in shaping the dynamics of the system. The authors suggest that further research is needed to better understand the complex dynamics generated by non-performing loans and expectations [34–38].

Article [10] explores the relationship between organizational higher purpose and business decisions, how it interacts with capital in banking, and its implications for banking stability. The authors develop a simple theoretical model that provides an economic rationale for the results [32–40]. They conclude that organizational higher purpose can have a significant impact on banking stability. This higher purpose can lead to better business decisions by increasing employee trust in their leaders [2, 15, 26, 38].

2 Methodology

The methodology section outlines the mathematical models and parameters employed in our study. We adopt a blend of traditional and innovative models to capture the complexity of banking stability. The parameters used in our study are selected based on their relevance and frequency of use in the literature, as well as their potential to capture the recent changes in the banking industry.

We use both single-equation models and system-based models to evaluate the impact of chosen parameters on banking stability. Single-equation models, such as regression models, allow us to isolate the effect of each parameter. In contrast, system-based models, like vector autoregression (VAR), enable us to capture the interdependencies between different parameters [1–5, 22–24].

Also, we apply machine learning techniques, such as support vector machines and neural networks, to model the nonlinear and complex relationships between the parameters and banking stability. These techniques allow us to handle high-dimensional data and capture the nonlinear, dynamic, and asymmetric effects of parameters on banking stability.

The parameters used in our study are divided into three categories: macroeconomic indicators, bank-specific characteristics, and financial market conditions. Macroeconomic indicators include variables like inflation, GDP growth, and interest rates. Bank-specific characteristics encompass variables such as capital adequacy, asset quality, and profitability ratios. Financial market conditions incorporate indicators like market volatility and global financial integration measures [15–18].

The general form of our model of individual returnable assets is:

$$R_{t+1} = \mu_{t+1} + \sigma_{t+1}z_{t+1}, \quad cz_{t+1} \sim i.i.d.D(0, 1) \tag{1}$$

where:

- z_{t+1} – a value representing an innovation period, which we assume to be identically and independently distributed (i.i.d.);
- $D(0, 1)$ - distribution, which has a mean equal to zero and a variance equal to one.
- μ_{t+1} - conditional mean return ($E_t[R_{t+1}]$);
- σ_{t+1}^2 - conditional variance ($E_t[R_{t+1} - \mu_{t+1}]^2$) [5, 28].

It is not easy to find a clear connection between the conditional mean and assuming a zero return for the mean, which might indeed be the most reasonable choice when managing risk [20, 21, 39].

Let's consider the Morgan Risk Metrics model for dynamic volatility. This model calculates tomorrow's volatility (time $t + 1$) at time t:

$$\sigma_{t+1}^2 = 0.94\sigma_t^2 + 0.06R_t^2 \tag{2}$$

At $t = 0$, the volatility σ_0^2 can be a sample variance for available past data [5, 15, 38].

Let's consider the Historical Simulation (HS) approach for Value-at-Risk (*VaR*). Let's say today is day t and we have a portfolio of n assets. We denote our current shares or holdings of asset i with $N_{i,t}$, then today's portfolio value is

$$V_{PF,t} = \sum_{i=1}^{n} N_{i,t}S_{i,t} \tag{3}$$

Using the past asset prices for today's firm portfolio, we can compute the old value of a 'pseudo' portfolio. The 'pseudo' portfolio is the portfolio that we will obtain if we use today's portfolio at that time. For example,

$$V_{PF,t-1} = \sum_{i=1}^{n} N_{i,t}S_{i,t-1}. \tag{4}$$

Now, we can define the pseudo-logarithmic return as follow:

$$R_{PF,t} = \ln\left(\frac{V_{PF,t}}{V_{PF,t-1}}\right). \tag{5}$$

Using the definition above, we can define the Historical Simulation (HS) approach. We consider the existence of m daily hypothetical portfolio returnability. The formula to compute the value uses the portfolio's assets (past prices) and portfolio weights (today's values): $\left\{R_{PF,t+1-\tau}\right\}_{\tau=1}^{m}$.

The HS technique assumes that the distribution of tomorrow's portfolio return, $R_{PF,t+1}$, will be approximated to the empirical distribution of the past m observations, $\left\{R_{PF,t+1-\tau}\right\}_{\tau=1}^{m}$. In other words, the distribution of $R_{PF,t+1}$ is captured by the histogram of $\left\{R_{PF,t+1-\tau}\right\}_{\tau=1}^{m}$. The variable VaR with range size p is computed as the $100p\%$ quantile of the past portfolio return sequence [2, 15, 35–40]. Therefore,

$$VaR_{t+1}^{P} = -Percentile\left(\left\{R_{PF,t+1-\tau}\right\}_{\tau=1}^{m}\right). \qquad (6)$$

In this way, we simply sort the returns $\left\{R_{PF,t+1-\tau}\right\}_{\tau=1}^{m}$ n ascending order and choose VaR_{t+1}^{P} to be such a number that only $100p\%$ of the observations are smaller than VaR_{t+1}^{P}. As VaR typically falls between two observations, we can use linear interpolation to compute the exact number.

3 Findings and Discussion

Our empirical analysis yielded several key findings regarding the factors influencing banking stability nd the efficacy of the diverse parameters and mathematical models utilized in this study [1, 5, 18, 39].

1. Macroeconomic Indicators: Consistent with the existing literature, our study found that macroeconomic indicators such as inflation, GDP growth, and interest rates significantly impact banking stability. Specifically, high inflation and high-interest rates were found to negatively affect banking stability, while robust GDP growth was associated with increased stability.
2. Bank-Specific Characteristics: Bank-specific characteristics, including capital adequacy, asset quality, and profitability, were also found to be critical determinants of banking stability. Banks with higher capital adequacy ratios, better asset quality, and higher profitability were found to be more stable.
3. Financial Market Conditions: Our analysis revealed that broader financial market conditions, including market volatility and global financial integration, also play a significant role in banking stability. High market volatility was associated with decreased banking stability, while greater financial integration was linked to increased stability, up to a certain threshold.
4. Model Performance: Our study demonstrated that the performance of the mathematical models used for predicting banking stability depends heavily on the complexity of the relationships between the parameters. Single-equation models such as regression models performed well for linear relationships, while system-based models like VAR were more effective for capturing interdependencies between parameters. Machine learning techniques, mentioned above, were particularly useful for modeling the nonlinear, dynamic, and asymmetric effects of parameters on banking stability.
5. Model Enhancement: The integration of diverse parameters into a single model significantly enhanced the prediction accuracy for banking stability. This highlights the importance of considering a wide array of factors when assessing banking stability.

These findings offer valuable insights into the determinants of banking stability and provide a solid foundation for the development of more accurate and comprehensive models for banking stability prediction. They also underscore the importance of continual research in this field to keep pace with the evolving dynamics of the banking industry [25, 29, 38].

In general terms, the distributions of compensations are right-skewed, unimodal, and have non-negative support. Therefore, they approximately have the form of a gamma distribution. To achieve greater flexibility, we allow a shift over the distance x_0. Hence, we approximate the cumulative distribution (cd) function for S to the cd function for $Z + X_0$, where $Z \sim$ gamma (α, β) [25, 28, 39] (Table 1).

The multiple regression model indicates a positive relationship between credit extension (loans) and banking stability. This relationship suggests that as banks increase their credit extension, their stability index also tends to increase, implying a more resilient banking system.

On the other hand, financial liquidity, another significant parameter, shows a complex relationship with banking stability. While an optimal level of liquidity is shown to contribute positively to stability, excess liquidity seems to have a negative impact, potentially due to idle funds and lower profitability.

Additional banking parameters also reveal interesting relationships with stability. Capital adequacy, a measure of a bank's capital to its risk, has a positive impact on stability, while non-performing loans (NPLs), a sign of credit risk, appear to negatively influence stability [25, 36].

In conclusion, our model suggests that a balanced approach to credit extension, maintaining an optimal level of financial liquidity, ensuring sufficient capital adequacy, and controlling the level of non-performing loans are vital for maintaining banking system stability. Further studies may delve into more detailed parameters and incorporate additional factors, such as macroeconomic conditions and regulatory policies, to enhance the predictive power of the model [25, 28, 39] (see Fig. 1).

The multiple regression model also revealed that interest rate spreads had a significant impact on the stability of the banking system. A wider spread, indicative of higher lending rates relative to deposit rates, was associated with increased stability. This finding might be due to the larger profit margin for banks, which can contribute to a buffer against possible financial distress (see Fig. 2).

Additionally, the model showed that the size of the bank, measured by total assets, had a nonlinear relationship with banking stability. Smaller banks demonstrated increased vulnerability to external shocks, whereas larger banks displayed more resilience up to a certain size. However, banks that were too large showed signs of decreased stability, potentially due to issues of complexity and governance.

The role of diversification in a bank's portfolio was also examined. Diversification across various types of loans and investments appeared to enhance banking stability by spreading risk. However, excessive diversification, particularly in riskier assets, could lead to stability issues.

Table 1. The most commonly used discrete and continuous distributions

Distribution	Density and support	Moments and invariants	Mgf
Binormal (n, p) $(0 < p < 1, n \in \mathbb{N})$	$\binom{n}{x} p^x (1-p)^{n-x}$, $x = 0, 1, \ldots, n$	$E = np$, $Var = np(1-p)$, $\gamma = \frac{np(1-p)(1-2p)}{\sigma^3}$	$\left(1 - p + pe^t\right)^n$
Bernoulli (p)	$\equiv$ Binomial $(1, p)$		
Poisson (λ) $(\lambda > 0)$	$e^{-\lambda} \frac{\lambda^x}{x!}, x = 0, 1, \ldots$	$E = Var = \lambda, \gamma = 1/\sqrt{\lambda}$, $\kappa_j = \lambda, j = 1, 2, \ldots$	$exp\left[\lambda\left(e^t - 1\right)\right]$
Negative binomial (r, p) $(r > 0, 0 < p < 1)$	$\binom{r+x-1}{x} p^r (1-p)^x$ $x = 0, 1, 2, \ldots$	$E = r(1-p)/p$, $Var = E/p$, $\gamma = (2-p)/p\sigma$	$\left(\frac{p}{1-(1-p)e^t}\right)^r$
Geometrically (p)	$\equiv$ Negative binomial $(1, p)$		
Monotonous (a, b) $(a < b)$	$\frac{1}{b-a}; a < x < b$	$E = (a+b)/2$, $Var = (b-a)^2/12$, $\gamma = 0$	$\frac{e^{bt} - e^{at}}{(b-a)t}$
$N\left(\mu, \sigma^2\right)$ $(\sigma > 0)$	$\frac{1}{\sigma\sqrt{2\pi}} exp \frac{-(x+\mu)^2}{2\sigma^2}$	$E = \mu$, $Var = \sigma^2, \gamma = 0$ $(\kappa = 0, j \geq 3)$	$exp\left(\mu t + \frac{1}{2}\sigma^2 t^2\right)$
Gama (α, β) $(\alpha, \beta > 0)$	$\frac{\beta^\alpha}{\Gamma(\alpha)} x^{\alpha-1} e^{-\beta x}, x > 0$	$E = \alpha/\beta$, $Var = \alpha/\beta^2$, $\gamma = 2/\sqrt{\alpha}$	$\left(\frac{\beta}{\beta-t}\right)^\alpha (t < \beta)$
Exponential (β)	$\equiv$ gamma $(1, \beta)$		
$\chi^2(k)(k \in \mathbb{N})$	$\equiv$ gamma$(k/2, 1/2)$		
Beta (a, b) $(a > 0, b > 0)$	$\frac{x^{a-1}(1-x)^{b-1}}{B(a,b)}$, $0 < x < 1$	$E = \frac{a}{a+b}$, $Var = \frac{E(1-E)}{a+b+1}$	

(continued)

Table 1. (*continued*)

Distribution	Density and support	Moments and invariants	*Mgf*
Log-normal (μ, σ^2) $(\sigma > 0)$	$\frac{1}{x\sigma\sqrt{2\pi}}exp\frac{-(\log x-\mu)^2}{2\sigma^2}$, $x < 0$	$E = e^{\mu+\sigma^2/2}$, $Var = e^{2\mu+2\sigma^2} - e^{2\mu+\sigma^2}$, $\gamma = c^3 + 3c, where c^2 = Var/E^2$	
Pareto (α, x_0) $(\alpha, x_0 > 0)$	$\frac{\alpha x_0^{\alpha}}{x^{\alpha+1}}$, $x > x_0$	$E = \frac{\alpha x_0}{\alpha-1}$, $Var = \frac{\alpha x_0^2}{(\alpha-1)^2(\alpha-2)}$	

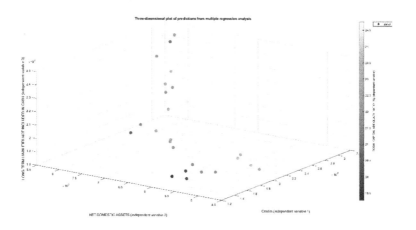

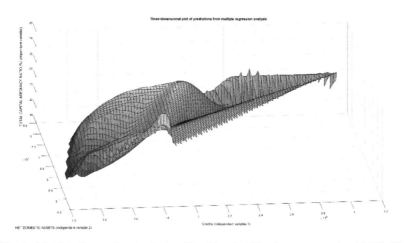

Fig. 1. Multiple Regression Analysis of Banking Stability Parameters using MATLAB

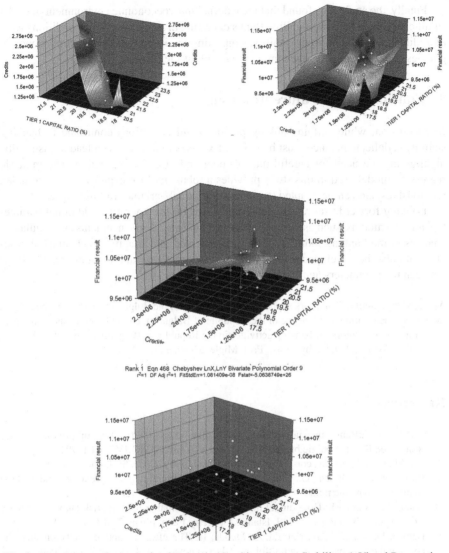

Rank 1 Eqn 468 Chebyshev LnX,LnY Bivariate Polynomial Order 9
r²=1 DF Adj r²=1 FitStdErr=1.081409e-08 Fstat=-5.0638749e+26

Fig. 2. Non-Parametric Analysis of Bulgarian Banking System Stability: A Visual Perspective

Finally, the study also found that the external macroeconomic environment played a significant role in banking stability. Banks operating in stable economic conditions were more likely to maintain their stability, suggesting the importance of prudent economic policies and regulation in maintaining the health of the banking sector.

4 Conclusion and Future Research

In conclusion, while certain banking practices and conditions contribute to banking stability, a delicate balance must be struck. Excesses in any area can lead to instability, highlighting the need for careful management and effective regulation. The multiple regression model used in this study provides a robust tool for exploring these complex relationships and can be adapted to include additional variables in future research.

Looking forward, future research could focus on incorporating additional parameters into the models, such as those related to technological advancements and regulatory changes in the banking industry. More sophisticated and adaptive mathematical models could also be developed to better capture the nonlinear and dynamic relationships between the parameters and banking stability.

Acknowledgements. This work supported by the project of the Bulgarian National Science Fund (Ministry of Education and Science of the Republic of Bulgaria), entitled: "Analysis of the main indicators and regulators for banking activities in the Republic of Bulgaria", contract № КП-06-M35/3 from 30.12.2019, led by Assist. Prof. Miglena Trencheva.

References

1. Albulescu, C.:Bank financial stability, bank valuation and international oil prices: evidence from listed Russian public banks. https://doi.org/10.48550/ARXIV.2004.12791
2. Ali, M.: Credit bureaus, corruption and banking stability. Econ. Syst. **46**(3), 1–8 (2022)
3. Bacchiocchi, A., Bischi, G., Giombini, G.: Non-performing loans, expectations and banking stability: a dynamic model. Chaos Solitons Fractals **157**, 1–14 (2022)
4. Banna, H., Alam, M.: Does digital financial inclusion matter for bank risk-taking? Evidence from the dual-banking system. J. Islamic Monetary Econ. Finan. **7**, 401–430 (2021)
5. Banwo, O., Caccioli, F., Harrald, P., Medda, F.: The effect of heterogeneity on financial contagion due to overlapping portfolios. Adv. Complex Syst. **19**(8), 1650016 (2016)
6. Bindseil, U., Lanari, E.: Fire sales, the LOLR and bank runs with continuous asset liquidity. https://doi.org/10.48550/ARXIV.2010.11030
7. Birch, A., Aste, T.: Systemic losses due to counter party risk in a stylized banking system. J. Stat. Phys. **156**, 998–1024 (2014)
8. Bownik, M., Johnson, B., McCreary-Ellis, S.: Stability of iterated dyadic filter banks. https://doi.org/10.48550/ARXIV.2212.10709
9. Buljan, A., Deskar-Skrbic, M., Dumicic, M.: What drives banks' appetite for sovereign debt in CEE countries? Public Sect. Econ. **44**, 179–201 (2020)
10. Bunderson, S., Thakor, A.: Higher purpose, banking and stability. J. Bank. Finan. **140**, 1–13 (2022)
11. Caccioli, F., Catanach, T., Farmer, J.: Heterogeneity, correlations and financial contagion. https://doi.org/10.48550/ARXIV.1109.1213

12. Cannas, A., et al.: Implications of storing urinary DNA from different populations for molecular analyses. PLoS ONE **4**, e6985 (2009)
13. Carmona, R., Fouque, J.-P., Sun, L.-H.: Mean field games and systemic risk. https://doi.org/10.48550/ARXIV.1308.2172
14. Chaum, D., Grothoff, C., Moser, T.: How to issue a central bank digital currency. doi:https://doi.org/10.48550/ARXIV.2103.00254
15. Coelho, N., Gonçalves, S., Romano, A.: Endemic plant species conservation: biotechnological approaches. Plants **9**(3), 345 (2020)
16. Erçen, H.İ, Özdeşer, H., Türsoy, T.: The impact of macroeconomic sustainability on exchange rate: hybrid machine-learning approach. Sustainability **14**, 1–19 (2022)
17. Feinstein, Z.: Harry Potter and the Goblin Bank of Gringotts. https://doi.org/10.48550/ARXIV.1703.10469
18. Ghosh, S.: Financial inclusion and banking stability: does interest rate repression matter? Financ. Res. Lett. **50**, 1–8 (2022)
19. Hanley, B.: The impact of LIBOR linked borrowing to cover venture bank investment loans creates a new systemic risk. https://doi.org/10.48550/ARXIV.1809.01987
20. Hassanzadeh, S., Mashayekhi, B.: A conceptual model for the reasons and circumstance of earnings management in Iranian Banks. Acc. Auditing Rev. **26**(3), 371–393 (2019)
21. Hossain, M., Ahamed, F.: Comprehensive analysis on determinants of bank profitability in Bangladesh. https://doi.org/10.48550/ARXIV.2105.14198
22. Ibrahim, M.: A comparative study of financial performance between conventional and Islamic banking in United Arab Emirates. Int. J. Econ. Financ. **5**, 868–874 (2015)
23. Ichiba, T., Ludkovski, M., Sarantsev, A.: Dynamic contagion in a banking system with births and defaults. https://doi.org/10.48550/ARXIV.1807.09897
24. Kabundi, A., Simone, F.: Euro area banking and monetary policy shocks in the QE era. J. Financ. Stab. **63**, 1–27 (2022)
25. Kaliyev, K., Nurmakhanova, M.: Bank risk evaluation through z-score measure and its effect on financial health of the industry of transitional economy of Kazakhstan. Хабаршысы. Экономика сериясы **133**, 40–50 (2020)
26. Laurent, A., et al.: Optimized manufacture of lyophilized dermal fibroblasts for next-generation off-the-shelf progenitor biological bandages in topical post-burn regenerative medicine. Biomedicines **9**, 2–33 (2021)
27. Lavreniuk, V., Shevchuk, V.: The nature and assessment of systemic risk in terms of liquidity of the banking system. Probl. Ekonomiki **4**, 213–222 (2016)
28. Lipton, A.: Modern monetary circuit theory, stability of interconnected banking network, and balance sheet optimization for individual banks. https://doi.org/10.48550/ARXIV.1510.07608
29. Mahmutoğlu, M., Ardor, H.: The effects of the macroprudential policies on Turkish banking sector. İşletme Araştırmaları Dergisi **11**, 2371–2383 (2019)
30. Mousavi, S., Mackay, R., Tucker, A.: Contagion and stability in financial networks. https://doi.org/10.48550/ARXIV.1603.04099
31. Neuberger, D., Rissi, R.: Macroprudential banking regulation: does one size fit all? J. Banking Financ. Econ. **2014**, 5–28 (2014)
32. Niţescu, D., Florin Alexandru, D., Ciurel, A.: Banking sector and bank liquidity – key actors within financial crises? Theor. Appl. Econ. **27**, 147–168 (2020)
33. Novickytė, L.: Banking consolidation process and impact to financial stability. Mokslas: Lietuvos Ateitis **2**(2), 62–68 (2010)
34. Papp, P., Wattenhofer, R.: Sequential defaulting in financial networks. https://doi.org/10.48550/ARXIV.2011.10485
35. Scalas, E.: Basel II for physicists: a discussion paper. https://doi.org/10.48550/ARXIV.COND-MAT/0501320

36. Smaga, P., Wiliński, M., Ochnicki, P., Arendarski, P., Gubiec, T.: Can banks default overnight? Modeling endogenous contagion on O/N interbank market. https://doi.org/10.48550/ARXIV.1603.05142

37. Sumarti, N., Gunadi, I.: Reserve requirement analysis using a dynamical system of a bank based on Monti-Klein model of bank's profit function. https://doi.org/10.48550/ARXIV.1306.0468

38. Tengstrand, S.N., Tomaszewski, P., Borg, M., Jabangwe, R.: Challenges of adopting SAFe in the banking industry – a study two years after its introduction. https://doi.org/10.48550/ARXIV.2104.13992

39. Vanka, S., Dehghani, M., Prabhu, K., Aravind, R.: A class of multi-channel cosine modulated IIR filter banks. https://doi.org/10.48550/ARXIV.CS/0702100

40. Zvonova, E.: Current problems of public debt and sovereign defaults to the EU countries. Финансы: теория и практика **20**, 105–117 (2017)

An Integrated Framework for Assessing Data and Business Analytics Skills for the Job Market

Krystie Dickson[(✉)] and Vladimir Zlatev

Department of Administrative Sciences, Applied Business Analytics Program, Boston University Metropolitan College, Boston, MA 02215, USA
krystied@bu.edu
https://www.bu.edu/met/faculty

Abstract. We present a framework for integrating academic programs and students' preparation for the job market. A graduate program's curricula, especially in data and business analytics, should prepare students for landing their dream job and prepare them to excel in their desired roles and grow within the company. Our approach is to assist our students in (i) their active participation in charting a course for their career and (ii) becoming a competitive force within the market based on knowledge gained in the program. The Applied Business Analytics program at Boston University Metropolitan College has created a competitive curriculum that shapes students into leaders by assessing the marketplace's needs (a function of its environment) and preparing our students to become lifelong learners, thereby creating their competitive advantage.

The model we've created contains three key areas, (i) the academic program and the valuation of its quality through skill development, (ii) the evaluation of the job market as a subset of the macro environment, (iii) the active preparation of students in our consultation service offerings to become competitive players in the job market. We introduce the complex nature of this model by discussing the various tools offered to our students, our approach for conducting job market assessments, and the framework for creating diagnostic tools for skills assessment.

Keywords: skills development · skills assessment · student employability · industry assessment · career planning · competitive landscape analysis · knowledge competence · business analytics curriculum · job placement

1 Introduction

Two key differentiators of the Applied Business Analytics (ABA) graduate degree program are (i) the competitive landscape analysis of our graduate program, as presented during the 16th CSECS Conference on Computer Science and Education in Computer Science (CSECS) [4], and (ii) the ABA Graduates' Employability Support service, as presented during the 18th EAI International Conference on CSECS [1]. In the ABA program, we are constantly searching for ways to support our students in their journey of landing their 'dream job'. Our competitive landscape analysis program helps us ascertain

© ICST Institute for Computer Sciences, Social Informatics and Telecommunications Engineering 2023
Published by Springer Nature Switzerland AG 2023. All Rights Reserved
T. Zlateva and G. Tuparov (Eds.): CSECS 2023, LNICST 514, pp. 305–320, 2023.
https://doi.org/10.1007/978-3-031-44668-9_24

the strength of the degree program compared to the top universities in the U.S. offering a master's degree in business analytics. Our employability support service model helps students prepare to enter the job market by creating their ePortfolio, an online web application demonstrating their skills, experience, and the application of their abilities to utilize data in solving the problems that companies face. The employability service model also helps students better understand the job market, including companies and industries hiring talents matching our students' skills. Lastly, this model allows students to prepare for their technical interviews, a key component to successfully hiring talent within analytics.

Our next focus in this series of analyses we've conducted is to ensure that we are equipping our students with the knowledge to be successful within the job market. This knowledge will land them a job aligned with their career aspirations and help them succeed to become significant contributors to the company's overall success. We now present our methodology for advancing our program at a course level that meets the demands of the job market and beyond.

2 Methodology

Our ongoing research in student employability has been a rewarding experience as students have benefitted from the critical services offered in the ABA@BU Graduates Employability Service Model [1]. Since its publication, a website has been created to store all our service materials and resources needed for students to land their dream job [2]. To continuously refine this model, we are now taking a high-level view of the integrations between the academic programs, positions to be filled in the job market, and student's ability and preparedness to demonstrate that they are the right fit for various roles within the marketplace. We present a three-step approach for curriculum improvement by adding skillsets required by selected industries. Our first step focuses on completing an industry assessment to gain a deeper understanding of the job roles and the top skills needed for an applicant to be considered and successfully chosen for the role. The second step involves an assessment of the current state of a degree program's curriculum, specifically focusing on each course within the program to understand its learning objectives and skills outcomes clearly. Here we are determining the gap between the current course curricula and the industry's requirements. The third step focuses on additional diagnostic testing upon nearing the completion of the program so that students can demonstrate the broad range of skills developed across key areas or pillars of a degree program. The following are the details of our approach:

2.1 Diagnostic Assessment of an Academic Program's Quality Through Skill Development

For an academic program to be deemed a success, constant evaluation is required. These programs must be designed in such a manner that they equip students with the skills necessary to secure roles within the industry and also to train students to become lifelong learners. From this perspective, programs must conduct thorough assessments of the needs of the industry and incorporate this information into the design, development, or enhancements of the program's curriculum. The critical thing to mention here is that the program is on a continuous loop of valuation, enhancement, and development. We aim to assess the program's current state, one course at a time, and make improvements based on the industry's needs, as visualized in Fig. 1 below.

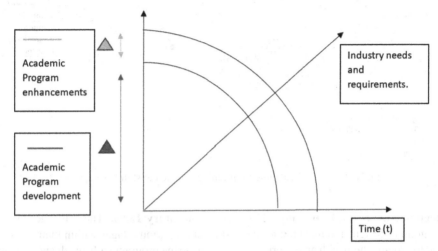

Fig. 1. Diagram representing the enhancements of academic programs based on the increasing needs of the industry as a function of time.

By applying tools like the ABA@BU Competitive analysis framework [4], we can quantitatively assess the program's strength based on key differentiating factors like program rankings, delivery format, tuition, and total credits. In addition to this approach, we would like to propose a diagnostic assessment tool to determine the fit between the academic program's offerings and the needs of the Industry. It requires a thorough review and valuation of the skills offered through individual courses and the skills to be gained through the completion of industry-relevant certifications. For each class, it is essential to determine the skills offered and difficulty level ranging from beginner to advanced. In addition, it is crucial to identify industry-relevant certifications and skills gained through completing these certifications that can complement the student's learning. Through the combination of the skills earned in the degree program and the skills offered through the completion of the relevant industry certifications, students will now have a competitive advantage within the job market as their skills demonstrate that they can meet job performance standards and also the ability to grow within the role and take on additional challenges which then leads to a rewarding career. To further explore this approach, we will discuss the development of the academic program to offer skills at the beginner's, intermediate and advanced levels and skills obtained through industry certifications. Figure 2 represents our approach to skill development by segmenting our audience into various groups and designing content that will meet or surpass each group's needs, ensuring that they are a successful fit for specific roles within the job market.

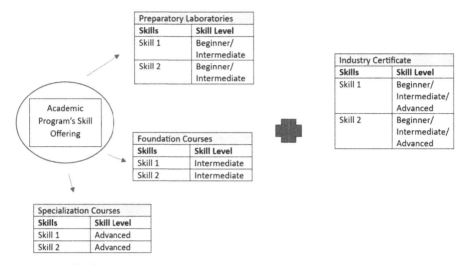

Fig. 2. The ABA Academic Program's Approach to skill development.

Beginner-Level Skill Offerings Through Preparatory Labs. The ABA academic program is designed to meet the needs of students at various stages within their careers and to provide them with an opportunity to complete the program with an advanced level of command of the industry-required skills. There is a unique challenge posed to us as we received interest in the program from five categories of individuals:

o With less than two years of working experience
o With 2–5 years of working experience
o With more than five years of work experience
o With no experience who just graduated with a bachelor's degree
o Individuals who are switching careers

We have aimed to design and develop a program to meet the needs of these varying groups keeping in mind the rapid advancement of the Industry as a result of the advancements made in the technological landscape, thereby increasing the complexities of problems within the Industry and the need for capable individuals to solve these challenges. The program starts by introducing all students to what we call preparatory laboratories. These laboratories are designed to provide foundational knowledge to develop missing skills in the programming languages R, Python, SQL, and software applications such as Microsoft Excel, Microsoft Power B.I., and more. For the groups of persons with more than two years of working experience, these laboratories serve as a refresher to help prepare these students for the next stage, obtaining intermediate-level skill development through our program's foundational courses.

Intermediate-Level Skill Offerings Through Foundation Courses. Once students have completed the preparatory labs, the next stage of skill development, the intermediate level, can be obtained through the completion of several of our foundation courses. Students will learn in-depth knowledge and applications of the statistical language, R, with applications to real-world datasets.

Advanced Level Skill Offerings Through Specialization Courses. The specialization and elective courses provide students with advanced knowledge in R, Python, SQL, and various visualization tools, for example, Microsoft Power B.I., Tableau, and Google Data Studio (Looker).

These three levels of the program's courses provide students with the skills needed to be successful in the job market. As the business analytics field is highly competitive, the program aims to provide students with a competitive edge by completing in-demand course certifications. The certifications allow students to learn and test their skill levels and demonstrate to potential employers that they can solve challenging problems.

Increasing Student Competitiveness in the Industry Through the Completion of Industry-Relevant Certifications. Our goal is to enable our students to become competitive applicants within the Industry by completing industry-relevant certifications. Potential employers widely accept these certifications as evidence that the applicant is dedicated to the field and has the aptitude for learning and contributing to the organization's success and, in turn, personal growth.

2.2 Job Market Assessment

The job market assessment aims to determine the critical skills needed for a job seeker to succeed in the field of analytics. It is essential for academic programs to stay abreast of the changing needs of the Industry and to incorporate in their program's curricula the skills needed to become successful within the selected field. There are several ways in which programs can obtain this information. One is collecting data from various job sites, compiled through manual or automated efforts like web scraping. Our approach is to gain support from companies like Lightcast [5], which delivers job market data with the option for clients to design and develop their reports to understand the job market's needs thoroughly. Figure 3 displays our approach to assessing the job market.

The first step seeks to identify the occupational category under which the particular course's skills generally fall and is part of the Standard Occupational Classification (SOC) Code system, which the U.S. Bureau of Labor Statistics uses to group workers into various categories [3]. To determine key employment statistics, we are focusing on the following areas: (i) the total unique job postings, (ii) the total number of employers in search of talent, (iii) the median salary, (iv) a summary of the popular job titles for that category determined by the number of postings per job title, (v) a summary of the top cities with job postings for that category or group and, (vi) a summary of the top industries. This valuation gives us a high-level view of the demand for talent for each occupational category. The second stage requires a deep dive into this data to understand the demand and supply of the necessary top skills for the overall occupational category and top job titles, see Fig. 4.

We identify the top software, specialized skills, and top qualifications in demand for the occupational category. For each of the three elements in the skills identification chart, we conduct an additional evaluation to determine the supply/ demand ratio by identifying the percentage of job postings that required a specific skill, the rate of job applicants that possessed the talent, and the computation of the supply/ demand ratio.

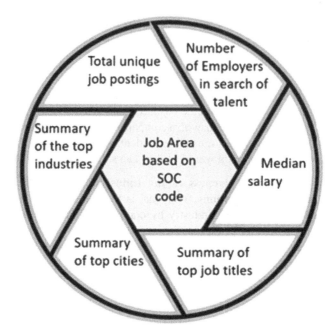

Fig. 3. The ABA Academic Program's Approach to the Assessment of the Job Market.

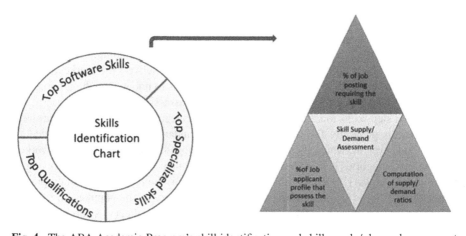

Fig. 4. The ABA Academic Program's skill identification and skill supply/ demand assessment approach.

These results will provide an idea of what is needed within the market and whether this demand is covered.

2.3   Determination of the Presence of In-Demand Skills Within the Course Curriculum at a Beginner, Intermediate, or Advanced Level

The next step would be to perform a gap analysis to address whether the required skills in the skills identification chart exist within the course curriculum, and if it exists within the curriculum, at what level it exists: beginners, intermediate, or advanced. It concludes by altering the learning objectives within the course curriculum to include the newly required skill.

2.4   Students' Preparation to Enter the Workforce

Throughout the degree program, we've prepared students to gain skills in the field of business analytics at beginner, intermediate, and advanced levels. Before completing the program, students should test their knowledge through participation in our Employability Services, Service 3 – preparation for Technical Interview Simulations. Our faculty designed and developed this diagnostic approach to test students' technical competency based on the top skills needed in business analytics: SQL, R, Python, and Microsoft Excel ([2] section Instructions for the ABA Program's Technical Interviews). In collaboration with our technical services team, we created the technical infrastructure to support this simulation environment through the Blackboard Learning Management System, where we can store a test bank of questions across the significant analytics programming languages, including software applications like Microsoft Excel and the accompanying datasets that students are required to utilize for solving the questions or business problems presented.

Students are required to register for these sessions. Upon successful registration, students will receive instructions on how to proceed with their technical interviews. On the day of the technical interview, students choose one offered by the system topic. A question from our test bank is then displayed randomly to the student, upon which the student has forty-five minutes to solve the problem. Students will then have 15 min to complete a presentation deck demonstrating their approach to solving the problem and the results obtained. They present in front of a panel of faculty members who will ask probing questions and provide feedback for improvement.

3   Applications of the Methodology

The presented methodology demonstrated our approach to enhancing a program's curriculum and its relations to preparing students for the job market. We will illustrate this approach by applying this methodology to one of the program's specialization courses, Web Analytics for Business.

3.1   Market Assessment for the Field of Web Analytics

Based on reports generated from Lightcast for the period January 2020 to April 2022, related to SOC code 13–1161, Market Research Analyst and Marketing Specialists, there were over 527,357 unique job postings within the U.S. a resounding 36% of all job postings within the U.S. over 107,746 employers were competing for talent within this field (appendix 2, industry statistics). Massachusetts ranked 7th within the U.S. with 17,388 job posts, with California ranking at 1 with 88,263 job posts (appendix 3, state statistics).

Based on the job postings, a few of the relevant job titles we've seen are Marketing Analysts, Digital Marketing Consultants, Social Media Specialists, Search Engine Optimization Specialists, Marketing Coordinators, Digital Marketing Consultants, Web Marketing Managers, Business Intelligence Analysts and more (appendix 4, top job titles).

From the job postings, the top software skills required were Microsoft Excel, Microsoft Office, Microsoft PowerPoint, and Google Analytics (appendix 5, top software skills). More than 60,756 job postings require the following skills: Google Analytics, Microsoft PowerPoint, Microsoft Office, and Microsoft Excel (appendix 6, a dashboard summarizing the critical data).

For the role of Marketing Analyst, there's a slight difference in the required skills; for example, we now see the inclusion of SQL, Dashboard, and Business Intelligence Software like Tableau and Python (appendix 7, job posts and top software skills required for Marketing Analysts). Based on this assessment, the skills in demand in the industry are Microsoft Excel, Microsoft Office, Microsoft PowerPoint, Google Analytics, SQL, Dashboard, and Business Intelligence Software like Tableau and Python (Fig. 5).

Fig. 5. Skills needed for a successful career in Web Analytics.

3.2 Incorporating Industry Skills into Curriculum Design and Enhancement for Specialization Course Web Analytics for Business

Incorporation of Industry Skills into the Curriculum. Having this knowledge of the skills that are in – demand within the market, for our students to be competitive and receive top positions, we incorporated these skills into the design enhancement of the curriculum. At the preparatory lab level, students are required to complete AD100, which covers the skill areas of Microsoft Excel and Microsoft Office. PY100 prepares students for basic or beginner knowledge in Python, covering the concepts needed to familiarize them with the programming language and its components. Our program's foundation course equips students with the knowledge of presenting findings of the analysis performed and utilizing tools like Microsoft PowerPoint. It also exposes students to using visualization software like Microsoft Power B.I. The program covers several learning objectives described below at the specialization course level, Web Analytics (See Table 1). For the first learning objective, exposure to data collection principles and techniques, students are given hands-on experience in collecting external data. These data do not exist within the company through practices like web scraping, a valuable skill needed in developing competitive intelligence reports. Students are then exposed to knowledge of advanced techniques like Text Mining and Sentiment Analysis to uncover patterns and more profound meaning within the data collected. In internal data collection, students are exposed to understanding customer behavior on a website and introduced to tools like Google Analytics, one of the job market's most sought-after tools in the field of Digital Marketing, Market Research Analysts, and Marketing Analysts. The second learning objective focuses on Data Storage, Analysis, and Visualization. Students gain hands-on experience designing and developing relational database management systems to store structured data collected from various sources.

Students then utilize Structures Query Language (SQL) to create and query the database and extract data to create visualizations using Python or R. The third learning objective focuses on data analysis for the performance of communication channels like email marketing, Social Media Analytics, and Mobile Analytics. Students are introduced to marketing campaigns like MailChimp, Constant Contact to distribute and monitor the performance of marketing campaigns. Google Analytics for Firebase is also introduced as an opportunity to track the performance of mobile applications to determine revenue earned through the application, number of downloads, number of uninstalls and number of application crashes, to name a few. The final Learning Objective looks at the Applications of topics in Web Analytics. This area focuses allowing students to gain the experience of designing websites while providing consideration for the analysis of web traffic data. This means that students are designing these websites intending to collect and measurement of customer behavior data. Students are then exposed to the strategies used to generate traffic to their websites, and they begin measuring customer data. Visualization tools like Google Data Studio are then used to create visualizations demonstrating various key performance indicators for the business. Students are then introduced to conducting experiments, more specifically A/B testing, informing the changes to be made on their websites. The idea here is that before an actual change is made, let's run a test to determine customer's acceptance of this change before we finalize the change on a website.

Table 1. Web Analytics learning objectives and skills offered.

Learning Objectives	Sub Areas	Software Skills	Specialized Skills
Data Collection	External Data Collection - Web Scraping	Python	Text Mining, Sentiment Analysis
	Internal Data Collection - Customer Behavior Data	Google Analytics	Google Analytics
Data Storage, Analysis and Visualization	Relational Database Design & Development	SQL	Database design
	Database Queries	SQL	
	Query result extraction & visualization	SQL, Python	
Marketing Communication Analytics	Email Marketing— Campaign Design & Execution & Analysis	Google Analytics, MailChimp, Constant Contact	Email Marketing
	Social Media Analytics		Social Media Analytics
	Mobile Application Analytics	Google Analytics for Firebase	
Applications of topics in Web Analytics	Web Design & Development	Blogger, Google Sites, Wix, Squarespace	Web Design & Development
	Web Traffic Analysis	Google Analytics	Google Analytics
	Dashboard Design & Development	Google Data Studio	Google Data Studio
	Web Experimentation	Google Optimize	A/9 Testing
	Presentation of Findings and recommendations	Microsoft Power Point	

Increasing Student Competitiveness in the Industry Through Completing Industry-Relevant Certifications for Top Required Skill, Google Analytics. As part of the Web Analytics course requirements, students must complete several courses from the Google Analytics Academy platform. The first certification is the Google Analytics for Beginners certification, which covers several introductory topics on becoming familiarized with the Google Analytics interface, including creating an account, exploring the interface and the various reports established to understand user behavior, and more. The second required certification, Advanced Google Analytics, exposes students to advanced topics like creating custom metrics, reports, dimensions, and more. As these courses are based on the Google Analytics Universal Analytics property, which will be retired by Google on June 30th, students will be asked to complete the Google Analytics Certification, which will test their skills in setting up a Google Analytics 4 property identification for websites and using the new interface to gain insights into user behavior.

4 Conclusion and What's Next

The next step in this assessment is to develop a dashboard displaying the data for all the critical areas of our proposed framework, especially for the job market assessment. Here we would like the dashboard to show the occupational category related to a specific course, the top statistics on the job market, and a deep dive into the skills by completing the skill identification chart and computing the skill/ demand ratios, and also refining the course curriculum to match the latest trend in the data.

So far, we've completed the skills assessment on a high level. Our next step is to repeat the process by focusing on the skill identification chart for the top job titles in the SOC 13-1161 Marketing Research Analysts and Marketing Specialists occupational job category.

Appendix 1: Instructions for the ABA Program's Technical Interviews

Session #1: Testing your technical skills in Python & SQL for Business Analytics Applications.

Availability: Item is available, but some students or groups may not have access.

Enabled: Adaptive Release, Statistics Tracking

Welcome to the Technical Interviews on testing your knowledge in Python and SQL

We are pleased to have you join us and wish you a successful learning experience upon the completion of this interview. During this interview, you will be provided with questions to be solved using either SQL or Python.

The aim of this event is to provide you with an opportunity to apply the skills and techniques learned in your ABA program to solve problems in a time sensitive, interview-style environment.

The following are the rules for partaking in this event:

1. The first step is to register for a Technical Interview. On the left-hand menu bar, select the *Technical Interview: Sessions Registration* link.
2. On the day of your Technical Interview, go to the **MET Applied Business Analytics Programs** blackboard site and on the left-hand menu bar, select *Technical Interview: Sessions*
3. Promptly at 2:00 pm ET, you will be provided with a list of topics to choose from and these topics will be displayed below. Examples of topics can include (but not limited to) Regression Analysis, Sentiment Analysis, Clustering and much more. Please select **ONE** topic.
4. A question and dataset will then be provided, and you have a total of 45 minutes to complete this exercise.
5. At 2:45 pm, you'll have 15 minutes to complete a presentation deck to demonstrate your findings. Submit your presentation deck at the end of the 15-minute timer.
6. You cannot submit anything after 3:00 pm. At 3:00 pm, you will be invited by the moderators to present the **solutions you submitted** and the interpretation of the results within 5 minutes. You will have another 10 minutes for Q&A.
7. At 3:00 pm – 5:00 pm ET, you will have your live presentations. You will present your findings to a panel of professors, and they will provide you with feedback on your performance and also recommendations for improvement. For the presentation of your findings, please go to the *Zoom Employability Consultations* room in the MET Applied Business Analytics Programs blackboard site.

Session #1: Technical Interview Date

The Technical Interviews for session 1, Python and SQL is offered on Friday 10th February 2023, 2:00 pm – 5:00 pm ET.

Tools Needed for Session #1 Topics

1) For all Python questions, please use Jupyter Notebook to write all your codes and run all outputs.
2) You can download Anaconda from the link below, and after installation, you can use the embedded Jupyter notebook. https://www.anaconda.com/
3) However, if you are using Win 11 system (which is known as very incompatible with many software), you can use the online version of Jupyter Notebook from the link here: https://jupyter.org/try-jupyter/retro/notebooks/?path=notebooks/Intro.ipynb
4) All submissions for Python questions should be a Jupyter Notebook file (.ipynb file), or a pdf file printed out from the notebook. Please include all your codes and outputs in your submissions.
5) For all SQL questions, all you need to do is to write the queries and explain your logic during the presentation. You can submit a text file, or a word file, as long as it can be opened and reviewed by all operating systems.

Appendix 2: Job Posting Data for Marketing Research Analyst and Marketing Analyst

Job Postings Overview

527,357	107,746
Unique Postings @	Employers Competing @
1.48M Total Postings	1.42M Total Employers

29 Days	3 : 1
Median Posting Duration @	Posting Intensity @
Regional Average: 28 Days	Regional Average: 3 : 1

Appendix 3: Job Posting by State

State Name	∨ Unique Postings from Jan 2020 - Apr 2022
California	88,263
Texas	47,079
New York	38,523
Florida	35,751
Illinois	24,658
Georgia	17,453
Massachusetts	17,388
North Carolina	16,740
Colorado	16,186
Ohio	15,947

Appendix 4: Job Titles

Job Title	Total/Unique (Jan 2020 - Apr 2022)	Posting Intensity	Median Posting Duration
Marketing Coordinators	98,333 / 37,068	3 : 1	30 days
Marketing Specialists	60,660 / 23,565	3 : 1	28 days
Marketing Assistants	52,910 / 17,268	3 : 1	29 days
Digital Marketing Specialists	44,374 / 16,741	3 : 1	27 days
Social Media Managers	43,676 / 14,107	3 : 1	31 days
Marketing Associates	32,302 / 11,175	3 : 1	30 days
Social Media Specialists	33,612 / 9,686	3 : 1	27 days
Social Media Coordinators	24,379 / 7,754	3 : 1	28 days
Marketing Analysts	17,439 / 7,151	2 : 1	26 days
Email Marketing Specialists	34,467 / 5,721	6 : 1	28 days

Appendix 5: Top Software Skills

Skills	Postings	% of Total Postings	Profiles	% of Total Profiles
Microsoft Excel	106,351	20%	128,064	17%
Microsoft Office	84,558	16%	137,844	18%
Microsoft PowerPoint	81,635	15%	97,685	13%
Google Analytics	60,756	12%	31,454	4%
Instagram	54,500	10%	19,315	3%
Adobe Photoshop	43,397	8%	40,906	5%
Salesforce	40,644	8%	23,955	3%
Microsoft Outlook	35,664	7%	19,864	3%
HyperText Markup Language (HTML)	35,418	7%	20,720	3%
Adobe Creative Suite	30,112	6%	18,584	2%

Appendix 6: Dashboard Displaying Top Software Skills

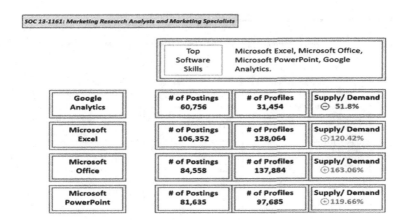

Appendix 7: Dashboard Displaying Top Specialized Skills

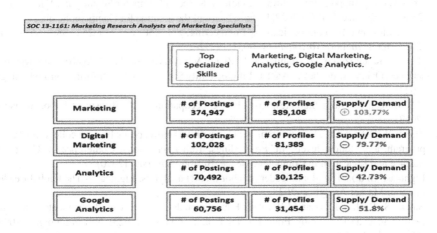

Appendix 8: Industry Analysis Dashboard

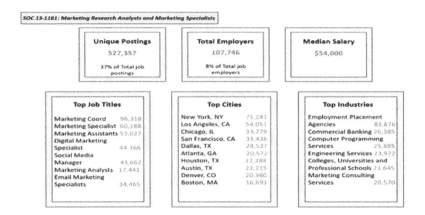

References

1. Dickson, K., Khan, M., Zlatev, V.: ABA@BU program competitiveness and ABA graduates employability support. In: Zlateva, T., Goleva, R. (eds.) Computer Science and Education in Computer Science. CSECS 2022. Lecture Notes of the Institute for Computer Sciences, Social Informatics and Telecommunications Engineering, vol. 450, pp. 245–262. Springer, Cham (2022). https://doi.org/10.1007/978-3-031-17292-2_20
2. Dickson, K., Graziano, M., Riauwindu, P., Zlatev, V.: Overview on the ABA@BU employability services. Overview on the ABA@BU Employability Services---MET Information Technology (2023)
3. U.S. Bureau of Labor Statistics: List of SOC occupations. U.S. Bureau of Labor Statistics (2023)
4. Zlatev, V., Dickson, K., Doddavaram, R.: Competitive landscape analysis on college, academic program, and student levels. In: Proceedings, 16th International Conference on Computer Science and Education in Computer Science. Boston University (2020)
5. Lightcast. (n.d.).: The global leader in labor market analytics. Lightcast - The Global Leader in Labor Market Analytics (2023)
6. Batool, S., Rashid, J., Nisar, M.W., et al.: Educational data mining to predict students' academic performance: a survey study. Educ. Inf. Technol. **28**, 905–971 (2023). https://doi.org/10.1007/s10639-022-11152-y
7. Zhao, X., Cox, A.: International study and graduate employability: employer, teacher and student perspectives. In: Singh, J.K.N., Latiner Raby, R., Bista, K. (eds) International Student Employability. Knowledge Studies in Higher Education, vol. 12, pp. 203–216. Springer, Cham (2022). https://doi.org/10.1007/978-3-031-33254-8_13

Assessing the Resilience of the Banking System in the Republic of Bulgaria Using Mathematical Models

Metodi Traykov[1]([✉]) [iD] and Miglena Trencheva[2] [iD]

[1] New Bulgarian University, Sofia, Bulgaria
mtraykov@nbu.bg
[2] South-West University "Neofit Rilski", Blagoevgrad, Bulgaria
megy_tr2001@swu.bg

Abstract. This paper provides an in-depth evaluation of the resilience and stability of the banking system in the Republic of Bulgaria, utilizing innovative mathematical models for analysis. The study focuses on the period from 2016 to 2022, a time characterized by significant economic and financial fluctuations worldwide.

The research presents a rigorous assessment of the Bulgarian banking system's stability, emphasizing the application of mathematical models including stress testing, factor analysis, and stochastic modeling. These models are employed to evaluate the systemic risk factors and determine the banking system's resilience under various stress scenarios.

Our findings reveal that the Bulgarian banking system demonstrates notable resilience despite the challenging economic conditions. We attribute this robustness primarily to effective regulatory measures, responsible banking practices, and the system's inherent structural strengths.

Nonetheless, the study also identifies potential vulnerabilities and provides strategic recommendations for further bolstering the system's resilience. This research has significant implications for banking regulators, financial institutions, and policymakers, contributing to a more comprehensive understanding of the banking system's resilience, thereby informing future regulatory and policy decisions.

Keywords: Banking System · Mathematical Models · resilience · Stability

1 Introduction

Capital adequacy is a key characteristic of the banking system because it gives investors and depositors confidence in the "safety and stability" of the banking system. Also, capital adequacy is important because the changes in the levels of capital adequacy act as a "brake" or "accelerator" for economic growth. The establishment of banking supervision ensures that the banks have adequate capital for their transaction matures.

© ICST Institute for Computer Sciences, Social Informatics and Telecommunications Engineering 2023
Published by Springer Nature Switzerland AG 2023. All Rights Reserved
T. Zlateva and G. Tuparov (Eds.): CSECS 2023, LNICST 514, pp. 321–331, 2023.
https://doi.org/10.1007/978-3-031-44668-9_25

Increasing the minimum capital threshold will guarantee that the banks will have more capital for their deposits, but this will slow the economy by limiting the volume of lending by banks. Decreasing the regulatory minimum capital will make the banks more competitive by using more aggressive lending, but it will decrease the overall confidence in the banking system's ability to withstand potential business cycle downturns [1–5].

In a fractional banking system, banks are required to keep a small portion of every borrowed lev on hand. This basic characteristic of the "fractional banking system" is known as the multiplier effect. In other words, the initial deposit creates many investments and loans. Determining capital levels in the banking system is analogous to using the gas pedal or brake in a car; increasing capital levels will lead to increased security at the expense of slowing economic activity. So, raising or lowering interest rates (or manipulating foreign exchange rates between currencies) affects the level of economic activity and decreases or increases the level of business and household economic growth in the economy as a whole [3, 5].

To achieve the "safety and stability" standards in the U.S., banks follow the CAMEL standard which has two main aspects:

1. An assessment of the banking experts using five key aspects of banking conditions and operations:
- Capital adequacy;
- Asset quality;
- Management;
- Earnings;
- Liquidity;
2. A grade (based on a scale of 1 to 5) of banking stability and conditions according to mentioned above categories.

In addition, the Federal Reserve uses a complex rating system to evaluate banks by the following elements: earnings (E), subsidiary companies (P), bank subsidiaries (B), capital adequacy (consolidated), and other (non-bank) subsidiaries (O).

Banks are very flexible companies and they aim to maximize their profits using financial innovations. They adapt deposits and loans to the needs of firms and households. Competitiveness in deposits from customers requires paying the highest interest rate for a given maturity, and competitiveness in lending requires providing credit with the lowest interest rates [6].

The main focus of the article is on the interaction between the concepts of global financial stability and economic competitiveness. Also, we will consider the role of the Basel Agreement in harmonizing global standards and capital adequacy in the banking industry.

Capital adequacy management is a direct tool. The regulation of capital, by its nature, benefits some banks while reducing the competitiveness of others. The issues here pertain to the comparison between small banks and those involved with small businesses, mortgages, and consumers and corporations. However, the "harmonization" of international regulations lacks a clear academic thesis: regulating capital in the banking system is similar to regulating the economic activity in an individual economy. As a result of the global financial crisis (GFC), we already know that regulating the capital adequacy of banks is not sufficient to ensure their safety, and stability [7–10].

The Basel process is an essential and constructive element in achieving global financial stability, especially after the abandonment of the Bretton Woods system and the increasing deregulation of international capital flows. The agreements have contributed to the stability of the international banking system. Also, they have participated in the market to create financial risks in new markets and avoid regulations [11].

The Basel Agreement is often used in managing the global financial system and coordinating efforts necessary to achieve global financial stability between Ministries of Finance, central banks, and regulators. The Basel Agreement essentially represents a series of documents that are constantly under review. The first agreements and basic principles were established on the principle of the "home country". The second set of documents relates to the harmonization of national standards for maintaining adequate capital in the banking sector [12–15].

Numerous violations have been established, some of which are given to national regulations by the "Right of Discretion", to apply regulatory regulation or even to ignore it [16, 17].

2 Methodology

Mark Flannery says "There is a balancing act that politicians must perform between creating a truly safe system and maintaining its applicability. If you restrict banks too much, financial activity will decrease or shift to non-bank institutions, rendering the rules ineffective". Mark Flannery has been tracking Basel regulations for two decades. He is a professor at the University of Florida in Gainesville.

In order to meet the needs of clients, banks adapt financial products or create entirely new financial instruments. Financial regulators need to be informed about such activities to assess whether new or modified guidelines and regulations will ensure standards of stability and safety. Banks develop financial instruments to trade on private interbank markets or public exchanges. They respond to competitive challenges and invest all the funds they control by reducing the amount of money held unused and required to be held in reserve, as per the requirements of banking regulators [18–20].

Bank competition is a process of reducing the advantages of business competitors (or increasing one's advantages) at the global, national, or local level. In the banking sector, increasing someone's competitiveness also affects the attractiveness of the bank as a target for acquisition. Other appropriate terms are "pro-competitive" and "anti-competitive" [21–26].

Let's say that we are an investor faced with a stream of known future obligations. We want to own a portfolio of bonds through which we can meet these obligations. We would like to do this at minimal costs, but we also want to own a portfolio that is unlikely to encounter problems in case of changes in interest rates. Let's have one obligation L, which must be paid over the last 5 years. If we can find safe zero-coupon bonds with a 5-year maturity with a face value of F, we can simply buy L/F bonds. In this case, we have two options, namely to face reinvestment risk (If the maturity of the bonds <5 years), and to face interest rate risk (if the maturity of the bonds >five years). The perfect case for us is to find a zero-coupon bond that has a maturity equal to the date of each obligation. Unfortunately, this is impossible, and we need to find another way to protect our bond portfolio. A possible solution is immunization.

Let $P(\lambda)$ be a function that gives us a relation between the price of the bond and the yield.

Given a stream of cash flows at times $t_0, t_1, \ldots, t_n$, then the duration of the stream can be define as follow:

$$D = \frac{PV(t_0)t_0 + PV(t_1)t_1 + PV(t_2)t_2 + \cdots + PV(t_n)t_n}{PV}, \tag{1}$$

where [27, 28]:

- PV – the value of the entire stream;
- $PV(t_i)$ - the cash flow at a time $i = 0, 1, \ldots, n$.

The duration appears as a weighted average of the times of the cash flows. The duration of a zero-coupon bond is the time to maturity. Using the yield as a discount rate to calculate the present values in a general bond, we will obtain Macaulay duration:

$$D = \frac{\sum_{k=1}^{n} \frac{k}{m} \frac{c_k}{(1+\lambda/m)^k}}{\sum_{k=1}^{n} \frac{c_k}{(1+\lambda/m)^k}}, \tag{2}$$

where m is coupon payments per year. In order to understand why the duration is useful, we must calculate the derivative of the price concerning the yield [28]:

$$\frac{dP}{d\lambda} = \frac{d}{d\lambda}\left(\sum_{k=1}^{n} \frac{c_k}{(1+\lambda/m)^k}\right) = \sum_{k=1}^{n} c_k \frac{d}{d\lambda}\left[\frac{1}{(1+\lambda/m)^k}\right]$$
$$= -\sum_{k=1}^{n} \frac{k}{m} \frac{c_k}{(1+\lambda/m)^{k+1}}. \tag{3}$$

If the modified duration (D_m) is $D/(1+\lambda/m)$, then

$$\frac{dP}{d\lambda} = -D_M. \tag{4}$$

The D_m is related to the slope of the curve, representing the yield. To obtain this curve we must use the prices at a given point in time. In our context, this is the price elasticity of the bond concerning changes in yield. In this case, we can use a first-order approximation:

$$\delta P \approx -D_m P \delta \lambda. \tag{5}$$

We can get an even better approximation with the help of a second-order approximation [28–30]. This is done by defining convexity:

$$C = \frac{1}{P} \frac{d^2P}{d\lambda^2}. \tag{6}$$

So, we have

$$C = \frac{1}{P\left(1+\frac{\lambda}{m}\right)^2} \sum_{k=1}^{n} \frac{k(k+1)}{m^2} \frac{c_k}{\left(1+\frac{\lambda}{m}\right)^k} \tag{7}$$

The unit of measure for convexity is time squared. Here the slower decrease in value when the required return increases is represented by greater convexity. Also, if the required return decreases, then the greater convexity means a faster increase in the corresponding value. So, the second-order approximation is based on both convexity and duration:

$$\delta P \approx -D_M P \delta\lambda + \frac{PC}{2}(\delta\lambda)^2. \tag{8}$$

If the yield is the same for all bonds, it can be shown that the duration of the portfolio is simply the weighted average of all durations [25–31].

3 Result

Due to the complexity of portfolios held by financial institutions, standardized methods for measuring the risk to which a bank may be exposed are necessary, especially for those banks that play major roles in the financial markets. Complex financial instruments such as options, and swaps, as well as various types of structured loans, collateralized mortgage obligations (CMOs), and collateralized debt obligations (CDOs), are required. The different asset classes within a portfolio have different risk evaluation methods, and combining these risks in a meaningful way can be challenging (see Fig. 1, 2 and 3). It is natural to determine firm-wide risk using the distribution of potential losses at a fixed future moment (each unit within a financial institution contributes to profit or loss). This will give us a meaningful measure of firm-wide risk, which provides the value of the risk.

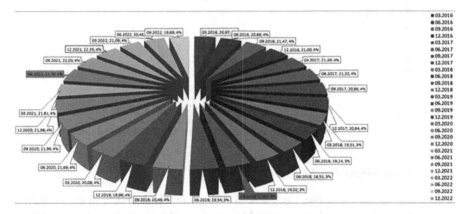

Fig. 1. Base Tier 1 Equity Ratio (%) In First Group

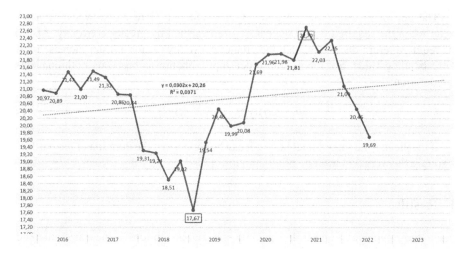

Fig. 2. The estimated value for the ratio of the basic equity of Tier 1 (%) for the end of 2023 is 21.23.

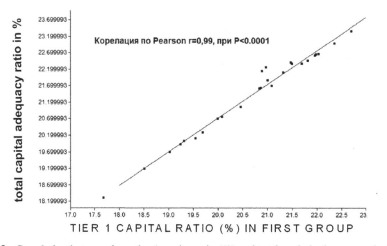

Fig. 3. Correlation between base tier 1 equity ratio (%) and total capital adequacy ratio (%)

3.1 Multiple Regression Analysis

A model ($z = f(x, y)$) of the dependence of Financial result (*FR*, z in the model) on Credits (*Cr*, x in the model) and receivables from the non-governmental sector (*RNS*, y in the model) was found:

A model ($z = f(x, y)$) of the dependence of Fixed Capital (*CS*, z in the model) on Credits (*Cr*, x in the model) and receivables from the non-governmental sector (*RNS*, y in the model) was found:

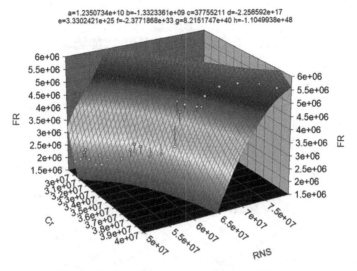

Fig. 4. Model of the dependence on Financial result

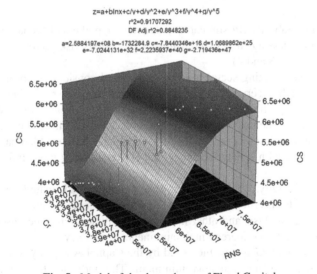

z=a+blnx+c/y+d/y^2+e/y^3+f/y^4+g/y^5
r^2=0.91707292
DF Adj r^2=0.8848235

a=2.5884197e+08 b=-1732284.9 c=-7.8440346e+16 d=1.0689862e+25
e=-7.0244131e+32 f=2.2235937e+40 g=-2.719436e+47

Fig. 5. Model of the dependence of Fixed Capital

A model $(z = f(x, y))$ of the dependence of capital and reserves (*CandR*, z in the model) on Credits (*Cr*, x in the model) and receivables from the non-governmental sector (RNS, y in the model) was found:

The banking system of the Republic of Bulgaria has demonstrated a notable degree of resilience in the past eight years. Systemic stability has been a critical focus, considering the interconnected nature of financial institutions and their collective exposure to market risk. The application of regression analysis and stress testing has been instrumental in

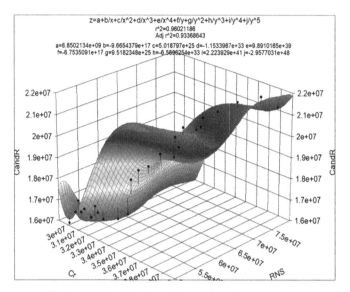

Fig. 6. Model of the dependence of capital and reserves

quantifying this stability. By simulating numerous hypothetical scenarios, these tools have helped in assessing the potential impact of various risk factors on the banking sector (see Fig. 1, 2, 3 and 4).

The Bulgarian banking sector has also showcased considerable progress in credit management, which is a crucial aspect of banking stability. The ratio of non-performing loans has seen a significant reduction, reflecting the effectiveness of credit risk management strategies. The use of credit scoring models and machine learning algorithms has been instrumental in this regard. These technologies have enabled banks to predict borrower behavior with greater accuracy, thereby facilitating more informed lending decisions.

In terms of liquidity, Bulgarian banks have maintained adequate levels of financial reserves. This factor is crucial for ensuring that banks can meet their short-term obligations. Time series analysis and other mathematical models have been used to forecast future liquidity needs and thereby maintain financial solvency.

Moreover, capital adequacy, measured by the Capital Adequacy Ratio (CAR), has remained well above the regulatory minimum. This indicates that Bulgarian banks possess sufficient capital to absorb a reasonable amount of losses before becoming insolvent.

In conclusion, the Bulgarian banking system has demonstrated commendable stability over the past eight years, as evidenced by robust systemic stability, effective credit management, adequate liquidity, and high capital adequacy. These factors, combined with the innovative use of mathematical models and techniques, suggest a positive trajectory for the Bulgarian banking sector moving forward.

It is important to differentiate the Capital Adequacy Requirement (CAR), and the Capital Reserve Requirements (CRR) of a bank. CAR represents how banks should manage their capital or how they should finance themselves, particularly in terms of the mix between debt and equity on their balance sheets. CRR represents the minimum reserve that each bank must hold (see Fig. 4 and Fig. 5).

The mandatory minimum reserves, or liquidity requirements, represent a small portion of the deposits that need to be held in highly liquid forms, such as cash. The cash reserve ratio is the ratio of reserves in the form of physical cash, precious metals, or government notes. Here we want to note that liquid securities enable banks to adjust their portfolio by holding government securities at any time without affecting profitability (see Fig. 6).

These two concepts are often opposing. Capital requirements are a ratio of assets to certain types of liabilities or capital. On the other hand, reserve requirements are a ratio of certain obligations held against certain types of assets.

Our regression model confirms that the Modigliani-Miller theorem is valid for the banking sector in the US, as more leverage leads to an increase in the beta coefficient of the banking system. To see the link between the capital asset pricing model and the Modigliani-Miller theorem, we would need to trace this effect using the required return on equity. We may achieve this using our regression model:

$$\text{Cost of Equity} = \text{Risk - Free Rate} + \beta\text{equity} * \text{Market Risk Premium}$$

$$\text{Cost of Equity} = \text{Risk - Free Rate} + (\beta 2 * \text{leverage}) * \text{Market Risk Premium}$$

3.2 Conclusion

Our study shows that an increase in dividend payout symbolizes a decrease in firms' cost of potential loss in capital markets and thus increases investor confidence in the firm. As a result, the dividend payout ratio should have a positive relationship with leverage. The dividend payout in relation to the pecking order theory is considered related to the financial deficit. This means that an increase in paid dividends is due to the greater need for external financing. Following the pecking order theory, debt financing is first in line to meet these needs, and therefore the level of leverage increases.

Acknowledgements. This work supported by the project of the Bulgarian National Science Fund (Ministry of Education and Science of the Republic of Bulgaria), entitled: "Analysis of the main indicators and regulators for banking activities in the Republic of Bulgaria", contract № КП-06-М35/3 from 30.12.2019, led by Assist. Prof. Miglena Trencheva.

References

1. Abogun, S., Olaniyi, T., Ijaiya, M., Fagbemi, T.: Earnings persistence of Nigerian listed banks. J. Siasat Bisnis **24**(2), 168–178 (2020)
2. Astuti, Y.: Analisis CAR dan ISR terhadap ROA Perbankan Syariah yang Terdaftar di JII Periode 2015–2019. Mabsya **3**, 116–127 (2021)

3. Aswal, D., Sharma, D.: Determinants of stock prices of the banking sector with reference to private sector banks. Analele Universității Constantin Brâncuşi din Târgu Jiu : Seria Economie **5**, 5–14 (2020)
4. Scherer, B., Martin, D.: Modern Portfolio Optimization with NuOPT™, S-PLUS®, and S+Bayes™. Springer, New York (2005). https://doi.org/10.1007/978-0-387-27586-4
5. Djuraidah, A., Silvianti, P., Yaman, A.: Analisis Risiko Operasional Bank XXX dengan Metode Teori Nilai Ekstrim. Statistika **11**(2), 115–126 (2011)
6. Filip, B.: A comparative analysis on banking systems' profitability between western European and cee countries. J. Public Adm. Finan. Law **5**, 168–181 (2016)
7. Gîrlea, M.: Modelul de business bancar: tendinţe actuale. Studia Universitatis Moldaviae: Stiinte Exacte si Economice. Studia universitatis moldaviae **2**(102), 102–107 (2017)
8. Hartono, A.: Пengukuran kinerja keuangan dengan metode eagles (Studi Kasus Pada Bank BUMN Yang Listing Di BEI Tahun 2011–2013). Ekuilibrium: J. Ilmiah Bidan Ilmu Ekonomi **10**, 55–68 (2016)
9. Horbachov, P., Makarichev, A.: Estimation of delay on signalized intersections of urban streets with a three-phase signal. Avtomobil'nyj Transport (Har'kov) **44**, 30–39 (2019)
10. Isayas, Y.: Determinants of banks' profitability: empirical evidence from banks in Ethiopia. Cogent Econ. Finan. **10**, 2031433 (2022)
11. Kartal, M.: Yeniden Yapılandırma Çalışmalarının Bankacılık Sektörünün Gelişimine Etkileri: Türkiye İncelemesi (effects of restructuring efforts to the development of banking sector: Turkey examination). İşletme Araştırmaları Dergisi **11**, 3172–3189 (2019)
12. Katranzhy, L., Podskrebko, O., Krasko, V.: Modelling the dynamics of the adequacy of bank's regulatory capital. Baltic J. Econ. Stud. **4**, 188–194 (2018)
13. Klepczarek, E.: Determinants of European banks' capital adequacy. Comp. Econ. Res. **18**, 81–98 (2015)
14. Kozarević, E., Polić, N., Perić, A.: Financial system development progress in western Balkans. Banks Bank Syst. **12**, 7–19 (2017)
15. Hall, M.: Implementation of the BIS "rules" on capital adequacy assessment. A comparative study of the approaches adopted in the UK, the USA and Japan. PSL Q. Rev. **45**, (2013)
16. Minasyan, V.: New ways to measure catastrophic financial risks: "VaR to the power of t" Measures and How to Calculate Them. Финансы: теория и практика **24**, 92–109 (2020)
17. Taleb, N.: Dynamic Hedging: Managing Vanilla and Exotic Options. Wiley, New York (1996)
18. Nguyen, V., Liu, D.: The impact of ownership structure on Vietnamese commercial banks' profitability. Int. J. Econ. Financ. Issues **10**(3), 187–194 (2020)
19. Noreen, U., Alamdar, F., Tariq, T.: Capital buffers and bank risk: empirical study of adjustment of Pakistani banks. Int. J. Econ. Financ. Issues **6**, 1798–1806 (2016)
20. Pambuko, Z., Pramesti, D.: The effectiveness of bank aceh syariah conversion decisions. Economica: J. Ekon. Islam **11**, 1–23 (2020)
21. Pantos, S.: Designing stress tests for UK fast-growing firms and Fintech. Risks **11**(2), 1–22 (2023)
22. Rebonato, R.: Interest-Rate Option Model, 2nd edn. Wiley, Chichester (2000)
23. Rebonato, R.: Modern Pricing of Interest-Rate Derivatives: The LIBOR Market Model and Beyond. Princeton University Press, Princeton (2002)
24. Rahman, M., Chowdhury, A., Mouri, D.: Relationship between risk-taking, capital regulation and bank performance: empirical evidence from Bangladesh. Eurasian J. Bus. Econ. **11**, 29–57 (2018)
25. Ranka, M., Milica, N., Marijana, L.: Relationship between macroeconomic aggregates and bank performance. Megatrend Revija **13**, 131–146 (2016)
26. Rehman, Z., Muhammad, N., Sarwar, B., Raz, M.: Impact of risk management strategies on the credit risk faced by commercial banks of Balochistan. Financ. Innov. **5**, 1–13 (2019)

27. Rosawati, Y., Pinem, D.: Pengaruh dana pihak ketiga, permodalan, aktiva produktif dan likuiditas terhadap jumlah penyaluran kredit perbankan. Ekon. dan Bisnis **4**, 157–172 (2017)
28. Shreve, S.: Stochastic Calculus for Finance, vol. I & II. Springer, New York (2003). https://doi.org/10.1007/978-0-387-22527-2
29. Sundaresan, S.: Fixed Income Markets and Their Derivatives. South Western College Publishing, Cincinnati (1997)
30. Setiawan, R., Putri, N., Rachmansyah, A.: Determinant net interest margin pada bank perkreditan rakyat indonesia. J. Riset Bisnis dan Manajemen **12**, 1–9 (2019)
31. Susila, G.: Pengaruh kualitas aktiva produktif, capital adequacy ratio, dan loan to deposit ratio terhadap profitabilitas pada lembaga perkreditan desa. J. Ilmu Sosial dan Humaniora **6**, 108–114 (2017)
32. Sutrisno, S.: Risiko, Efisiensi dan Kinerja pada Bank Konvensional di Indonesia. J. Ilmiah Akuntansi dan Bisnis, 111–116 (2017)
33. Visita, L.: The effect of inflation, profit-loss sharing loan, and capital adequacy towards performance of Indonesian Islamic banks. DIJB (Diponegoro Int. J. Bus.) **2**, 57–63 (2019)
34. Wang, S., Liu, Q., Yuksel, S., Dincer, H.: Hesitant linguistic term sets-based hybrid analysis for renewable energy investments. IEEE Access **7**, 114223–114235 (2019)
35. Yehorycheva, S., Kolodiziev, O., Prasolova, S.: Actual problems of the capital stability management in the Ukraine's banking system. Banks Bank Syst. **12**, 60–67 (2017)

Education in Computer Science

The Ecosystem of Computer Science Education in Bulgarian Primary School – State of the Art

Georgi Tuparov[1]([✉]) [iD] and Daniela Tuparova[2] [iD]

[1] New Bulgarian University, 21 Montevideo bld., 1618 Sofia, Bulgaria
gtuparov@nbu.bg
[2] Neofit Rilski South-West University, 66 Ivan Mihailov Str, 2700 Blagoevgrad, Bulgaria
ddureva@swu.bg

Abstract. Nowadays, many countries have started developing and implementing new curricula in the area of Computer Science (CS) as core or elective school subjects in different school levels. In Bulgaria a "Computer Modeling" course was introduced in 2016 for primary school in third and fourth grades (9–10-year-old). The new subject is directed towards basic concepts in Computer Science and programming in block-based environment.

This new school subject was (and partially continues to be) a challenge for all stakeholders in the educational area. Initially, it was a problem to provide enough prepared teachers and appropriate educational resources. Moreover, there are a lot of didactical problems such as the proper presentation of many abstract concepts in CS. In addition, the syllabi set relations to the mathematical concepts studied in the next grades such as negative numbers, coordinates, angles' metrics, random numbers.

In the paper the components of the ecosystem of CS education in Bulgarian primary schools are presented. The syllabi, teacher training issues, educational institutions efforts and overall challenges are discussed. A crucial component in the successful implementation of the subject - teachers' qualification, their experience, and competencies, is identified.

Keywords: Computer Science Education · Primary School · Challenges · Curricula · Educational Ecosystem · Bulgaria

1 Introduction

The digital transformation in the most sectors of society requires people with high levels of digital competence. The society needs not only people who are users of digital devices, nowadays we need people with strong algorithmic and computational thinking, people who will add value to the development of IT industry. Nowadays, many countries have started developing and implementing new curricula in the area of Computer Science (CS) as core or elective school subjects in different school levels [1–4].

The standards for computer science education, including primary school and even kindergarten level, have been developed in different countries e.g. United States (CSTA

T. Zlateva and G. Tuparov (Eds.): CSECS 2023, LNICST 514, pp. 335–346, 2023.
https://doi.org/10.1007/978-3-031-44668-9_26

Standard) [5], United Kingdom (CAS - Computing at School), Australia, New Zealand, Israel [6], EU countries [7], Germany [8].

In Bulgaria, the CS area school subjects have different names, mainly according to topics included, i.e. "Informatics", "Information Technologies", and "Computer modeling". Traditionally, "Informatics" subject includes topics about algorithms and computer programming. Courses in "Information Technologies" are focused on the use of different technologies in daily life – word processing, spreadsheets, presentation, Internet services, hardware etc. Computer modeling was introduced in 2016 as new core subject for Bulgarian primary school students in 3rd and 4th grade (9–10-year-old) and teaching started in 2018/2019 school year. The new subject is directed towards basic concepts in computer science and programming in block-based environment.

The focus of the paper are the main components of the educational ecosystem in computer science education in Bulgarian primary schools and challenges rising in the process of implementation of computer science subject at the primary school level. Successful implementation of any course in schools, especially computer science subject, depends on the educational ecosystem.

The paper is organized in three chapters: Overview of computer science education in Bulgaria, Educational ecosystem in computer science education in primary schools and Challenges in teaching computer science in primary schools in Bulgaria.

2 Overview of Computer Science Education in Bulgaria

2.1 Educational System in Bulgaria

The school education in Bulgaria [9] is obligatory from the first grade (age of seven) till tenth grade (age of 16). Schools can be municipal, state, private, or religious. Also, the schools are specialized or non-specialized. According to the stage or level of education, non-specialized schools are:

- "primary (I to IV grade);
- main (I to VII grade);
- high schools (VIII to XII grade);
- united (I to X grade);
- secondary (I to XII grade)" [9].

2.2 History of Computer Science Education in Bulgaria

Teaching in Computer Science in Bulgaria started at the end of the 1960s years [10] and beginning of 1970s years as courses in Mathematical high schools. The CS area school subjects in Bulgaria have different names, mainly according to topics included, i.e. "Informatics", "Information Technologies", and "Computer Modeling". Traditionally, "Informatics" subject includes topics about algorithms and computer programming. Courses in "Information Technologies" are focused on the use of different technologies in daily life – word processing, spreadsheets, presentation, Internet services, hardware etc.

In the frame of the experimental curricula developed by the Problem Group of Education at Bulgarian Academy of Science from 1979 till 1992 some concepts of CS have been included in the primary school and low secondary school courses – flow charts, coding, true-false, programming in Logo etc. [11, 12]. As a core subject CS concepts were introduced into high school curricula in 1986. Over the last thirty years, the school curricula have undergone significant changes. The subject of Computer Science has been moved around within the school curricula. In 2016 a new core subject "Computer Modelling" for students in third and fourth grade (9–10-year-old students) was included in the primary schools' syllabi. Teaching of the subject started in 2018/2019 school year. As of 2020 topics about computer programming are included in the new core subject "Computer Modelling and Information Technology" for the students in fifth – seventh grade. The extended timeline of CS education is presented in Table 1.

Nowadays the CS education in Bulgaria is conducted as core, elective and extracurricular courses at all educational levels, including special vocational education for professions related to information and communication technologies (ICT). Moreover, some innovative schools offer courses related to Artificial Intelligence, Robotics, Internet of things etc. A lot of private educational or IT companies offer different courses for students from 1st till 12th grades.

Table 1. Timeline of computer science education in Bulgarian schools

Period	Educational level	Description/Topics covered
End of the 1960s – till now	Math high schools	Traditionally: Algorithms, Programming. Nowadays: set of specialized courses in Computer Science
1979–1992	Experimental Primary and low secondary schools, 30 schools were involved	Basic concepts in Computer Science (primary schools) and Introduction to programming with Logo (low secondary schools) [9, 10]
1981–1986	High schools (Experimental education)	Programming with Logo or Basic
Since 1986/1987	High school	Core courses Programming with Logo or Basic in 10th and 11th grades.
1991–1994	High school	Removal of CS subject in vocational schools
1994/1995	High school	Six curricula for CS subject, depending on hardware and software equipment of the schools

(*continued*)

Table 1. (*continued*)

Period	Educational level	Description/Topics covered
2000/2001	High school	Two core subjects: Informatics in ninth grade and Information Technology – in ninth and tenth grade.
2003	Primary school	Elective course for primary schools – "Work with Computers and Information Technology". Content and software could be chosen by the teachers.
2006	Primary, low and upper secondary level	Core courses - Information Technology fifth - tenth grade, Informatics in ninth and/or tenth grade
2016	All school levels	New core subject – "Computer Modelling" in third and fourth grades (started in 2018/2019). Changes in syllabi for low and upper secondary school levels. New curricula for subjects Information technology and Informatics at high schools
2020/2021	Low secondary level	New Subject – "Computer Modelling and IT" in fifth - seventh grades, block-based and script-based programming – Python or JavaScript

3 Ecosystem in Computer Science Education in Primary School

3.1 Ecosystems in Education

The metaphor for educational ecosystem comes from the structure and organization of biological ecosystem. According to [13] "An ecosystem can be described as a community network of interactions between organisms and their environment." Transferring this definition to education, we could summarize that educational ecosystem describes the functionalities, activities, and interactions of all stakeholders in educational process with established educational environment. In [14] e-learning ecosystem is considered with three main components – human resources, technological infrastructure, and interactions between human resources and infrastructure aimed to achievement of learning outcomes. A lot of studies discuss the origin of the ecosystems in different areas. Hannele Niemi in [15] discusses relation among biological, human, business, health, educational ecosystems. The author pointed out that educational ecosystem "consists of a large number of interconnected parts, both horizontally and vertically" [15] and argues that educational ecosystem is not stable and "needs human actors, and it is dependent upon conscious human behavior" [15].

3.2 Main Components of the Ecosystem in CS Education in Primary School Level

The ecosystem in CS education in primary school level could be outlined with five components (Fig. 1):

- **Main actors** in the educational process.
- **State policy**, including national regulation, curriculum, and national educational programs.
- **Providers** of teaching and learning activities. The provider could be public or private schools, IT companies, non-government organizations (NGO), private training companies (non-school).
- **Teachers training**, including institutions approved to provide in-service or preservice teachers training.
- **Support** of students and teachers with appropriate educational content and hardware equipment.

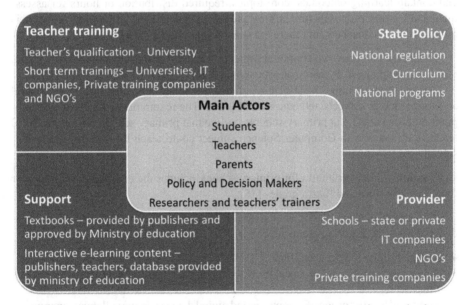

Fig. 1. Components of ecosystem in computer science education in primary schools

3.3 Main Actors

This group includes students, teachers, parents, policy and decision makers, researchers, and teachers' trainers. The main actors interact at different levels. In the center are students and teachers. Students in primary school have specific psychological and pedagogical characteristics and level of knowledge in mathematics and other school subjects. The abstract thinking for first - fourth grade students is still at a low level and that requires to use appropriate pedagogical techniques and methods. The teachers need special competencies in Computer Science and primary school education. In addition, the parents' support is very important too, considering some law requirements for using web-based learning environment, safety use of computer and internet etc. Policy and decision makers should provide adequate state educational policy. The researchers and teacher trainers give the teachers educational methods and skills needed to teach Computer Science topics in primary school.

3.4 State Policy

National Regulation. Regulations of the educational process are based on the state standards, syllabi for every grade, schedule of topics. The state standards outline competence and learning outcomes for every school level. The learning outcomes are decomposed in the syllabus for every core subject and every grade. The syllabi follow unified structure and contain learning outcomes, core topics, required distribution of hours for assessment and lessons, proposals for learning and teaching activities. The topics' schedule is developed by the teachers, but there are some requirements for its form.

In the case of elective and optional subjects, teachers must develop their own syllabi, that must be approved by regional educational authorities.

The government issues a national regulation about teachers' qualification in general and for particular subjects and educational levels. The requirements for teaching Computer Science subjects in primary schools outline that primary school educational level teachers or teachers in Computer Science subject could teach this subject in primary school.

Curriculum. The curriculum for primary school includes the core subject "Computer modeling" for third and fourth grades [16].

The accent of the syllabus of the subject "Computer Modeling" in third grade is directed towards acquiring competence for:

• Usage of digital devices and files;
• Developing animations in visual block programming environment using algorithms with loops;
• Safety and healthy usage of computers and digital devices. In the syllabus is mentioned that the creation of accounts in online environments must be under control of teacher and/or parent.

The content is outlined in four general domains: "Digital Devices", "Digital Identity", "Information", and "Algorithms". For the domain "Digital Devices" learning outcomes outline that student should "Turns OFF and ON stationary or mobile digital devices; Knows basic components of digital devices; Knows health requirements for safety work with digital devices; Gives the right and precise commands to digital devices to conduct different tasks" [16]. The learning outcomes for the domain "Digital Identity" outline that a student should "create own avatar in learning content management system; make difference between digital and physical identification; know that he/she should not provide personal data during the communication and work in digital environment; know the main threats in a digital environment and applies rules to respond to them." [16]. About domains "Information" and "Algorithms", a student should "know that data in digital devices are stored in files and folders; know the working space and the visual environment; order blocks in linear sequence in visual environment; create storytelling according to given plot using blocks in visual environment; implement loop algorithm; create animated gift card; share projects in Internet." [16]. The main topics in the syllabus are "Digital Devices", "Digital Identity", "Constructing Sequential Actions", "Constructing Repetitive Actions (Loops)", "Visual Programming Environment", "Text and Sound in Visual Environment", and "Animations".

In fourth grade the accent is on acquiring competence for:

- Usage of digital devices and information;
- File management;
- Creating interactive projects (educational computer games) in visual block programming environment using branching algorithms and synchronizing activities of the characters;
- Safety and healthy usage of computers and digital devices.

The general domains are the same as in the third grade. The learning outcomes for the domain "Digital Devices" outline that students should "know functionalities of buttons of particular device; know basic components of digital devices and how to connect end-user devices, such as robots, to them; know ethical norms for working in digital environment; know of advantages and disadvantages of digital devices for the environment" [17]. For the domain "Digital Identity" a student "makes difference between digital and physical identification and does not provide personal data in digital environment; knows the main threats in a digital environment and knows how to obtain help if it is necessary" [17]. In the domain "Information" is outlined that the student "knows the ways of receiving information and forms of presenting; knows how to save information on a digital device; knows how to present information –in form of text, numbers, audio, graphics; compares units for information measurement; knows how information is processed in digital devices; understands that digital resources could not be free of charge for using, copying and distributing" [17]. The domain "Algorithms" outlines that a student "knows the particular visual environment and creates digital content in it; implements linear algorithms in visual environment and manages characters; experiments with characters in visual environment and sets basic properties, chooses the characters and their properties according to the particular plot; develops code using blocks for character management in game; Implements looping and branching algorithms; creates project with animations of more objects, sound and text; presents the project in real and virtual environment" [17].

The main topics in the syllabus are: "Information", "Digital Identity", "Branching Algorithms", "Working in Visual Programming Environment", "Programmable devices", and "Development of Educational Games".

National Programs. Every year, Bulgarian Ministry of Education provides several national programs related to the IT in education, including subjects in Computer Science. The schools develop project proposals and apply for funding. Some of these programs are:

- "ICT in Education". This program provides software and hardware equipment, internet access for the schools, e-learning environments etc.
- "Education for Tomorrow Day". The program supports extracurricular clubs in Computer Science; teacher training in ICT implementation in education or Computer Science subjects teaching; development of interactive educational content.
- "Innovative Schools". In this program schools can apply innovative teaching and learning approaches and increase the number of classes in different subjects.
- "Digital Backpack" (https://edu.mon.bg/). This new program provides digital learning content and other e-learning services for all school subjects at all educational levels. Teachers can create and share their own digital educational resources.

3.5 Providers of the Teaching and Learning Activities

The schools – state, municipality or private apply state syllabi in mandatory courses. In addition, they can include more hours per week for computer modelling or other CS topics in the school curricula. The schools have a possibility to include extracurricular courses in the frames of National programs – robotics, computer language or device programming etc. Also, schools could extend curricula with courses for preparing students for national contests in the Computer Science area. The syllabi for the additional courses are developed by the teachers and are approved by the regional or local educational authorities.

The private non-school organizations could use their own syllabi, and in general offer courses in block programming and robotics. Usually, parents must pay for the training. Some of these educational organizations also prepare students for national contests in the computer science area.

3.6 Support

Students and teachers in primary and lower secondary schools (first till seventh grade) are supported by free textbooks in printed and electronic format, approved by Bulgarian Ministry of Education. Currently six textbooks for third and six textbooks for fourth grade in Computer Modelling are approved and used in primary schools. These textbooks are supplemented by online content, disks with resources and working books.

Additionally, an interactive electronic content is provided by publishers of the approved textbooks – every publisher provides free and/or paid e-content, teachers can develop e-content and publish it in National e-library, supported by Ministry of Education.

Teachers and students could also use well-known online environments like https://code.org/, https://scratch.mit.edu/, https://bg.khanacademy.org/.

In addition, the publishers support teachers with teacher's books with methodological learning sheets for lessons. Also, the teachers established communities in social networks. Currently the Facebook group of Bulgarian teachers in Computer Modelling has more than 6300 members and the group of teachers in Computer Science - more than 10000 members.

In general, the hardware equipment in the schools passes the requirements for teaching the computer modeling topics, but may vary widely and teachers have to take into account the current state. In fact, some schools exceed the basic requirements and have modern computers, programmable devices, 3D tools for modelling etc., but at the same time some schools have computers that only pass the equipment requirements.

3.7 Teacher Training

Pre-service Teacher Training. Teacher training is provided by universities with accredited majors by the National Agency for Accreditation and Evaluation. Universities provide bachelor and master programs for majors "Teacher in mathematics and CS", "Teacher in CS", "ICT in Primary school", Primary school education (without focus on the ICT).

It is possible to obtain qualification to teach computer science subjects in one-year post diploma qualification for people who have graduated in teachers' majors in science school subjects or in the areas of engineering, economics, physics, chemistry.

Also graduates in primary school education bachelor's or master's degree programs could teach Computer Modelling in primary school.

In-Service Teacher Training. For the career development teachers must complete training courses with assigned credits (1 credit = 16 h training). These courses could be offered by universities with accredited majors related to the school subject, IT companies, publishers, private training companies, NGOs with programs for teacher's qualification approved by Bulgarian Ministry of Education. Also, the schools can organize internal trainings.

4 Challenges in Computer Science Education in Bulgarian Primary Schools

4.1 Lack of Well-Prepared Teachers

The involvement of the new core subject "Computer Modelling" in primary school raises a lot of challenges and problems. The first challenge was related to the teachers as a main drive of the ecosystem in computer modelling education.

The teachers in the primary school subject "Computer Modelling" must be qualified in the subject content and in wide spectrum of digital competencies. They need competencies about the psychological characteristics of the students in primary school and knowledge about primary school curricula, working with parents, lifelong learning skills, diversity of pedagogical approaches suitable for primary school level.

At the beginning (2018/2019) "Computer Modelling" subject had to be taught only by primary school teachers with or without qualification in ICT. In fact, most of the teachers didn't have the necessary knowledge and skills in algorithms and programming and were unsure how to conduct their lessons. To change this, a short-term special courses for the content of the new subject were organized. Unfortunately, it became clear that the courses were not enough to provide adequate knowledge and skills for primary school teachers to teach programming concepts.

To solve the problem, in 2020 the Bulgarian Ministry of Education allowed the teachers in Computer Science area in fifth to 12th grades to teach Computer Modelling in primary school.

The universities started master's degree programs for primary school teachers in the area of IT in primary school. Courses in programming in block-based environment were included in the bachelor's degree programs. Also, a lot of short-term in-service courses were provided both for primary school teachers and for CS teachers.

In addition, the publishers of the textbooks provide teachers' guides for implementation of the content with precise lesson plans.

4.2 Abstract Concepts and Terms that Require Mathematical Knowledge from Low Secondary Level

The syllabi include a set of basic abstract concepts, used in programming as information, data, algorithm, loops, branching algorithms, variable, broadcast, logical operators, and random number. In addition, some information society concepts as digital identity, copyrights, fake news etc. are included. The concepts should be introduced in an understandable manner for the students and at the same time precise descriptions of the concepts should be provided.

The syllabi set relations to the mathematical concepts studied in the next grades such as negative numbers, coordinates, angels' metrics, random numbers. Instead of the mathematical terms, the words and examples known to the primary school students should be used.

These challenges can be solved through the application of appropriate teaching methods and techniques [18] such as:

- Focus on the properties of the concepts, not only on definitions.
- Explaining concepts by examples.
- Usage of tales and everyday life examples and analogies.
- Usage of gamified and fun elements like puzzles, challenges, anecdotes, riddles etc.
- Usage of educational computer games, simulations, or video clips.
- Usage of electronic textbooks with interactive exercises.
- Usage of appropriate unplugged activities.
- Experimenting with ready (so called "baked") code and completing of "half baked" code.
- Problem solving.

5 Conclusion

To support the proper functioning of the ecosystem in computer science education in primary schools, a lot of efforts are made by all stakeholders. Schools are provided with hardware and software equipment which is sufficient to meet the minimal requirements. The teaching process is supported through syllabuses, methodological instructions and teaching materials. Students are provided with free textbooks and interactive learning resources.

As long-time lecturers in Computer Science teacher training courses and authors of school textbooks from third till tenth grade we identified many challenges in the ecosystem of computer science education in the school. Our observations show that the crucial component in the successful implementation of the subject "Computer Modeling" in the primary school level is the qualification of the teachers in the area of Computer Science, their competencies and teaching experience. Therefore, all stakeholders in this area must focus their efforts towards:

- Improvement of pre-service and in-service teacher trainings in two main streams. The primary school teachers must obtain competencies in Computer Science at least to be able to teach "Computer Modeling" subject. The Computer Science teachers must obtain competencies how to teach in primary school level.
- Providing appropriate methodological, teaching and learning resources for teachers and students.

References

1. Kalas, I., Blaho, A., Moravcik, M.: Exploring control in early computing education. In: Pozdniakov, S.N., Dagienė, V. (eds.) ISSEP 2018. LNCS, vol. 11169, pp. 3–16. Springer, Cham (2018). https://doi.org/10.1007/978-3-030-02750-6_1
2. Falkner, K., et al.: An international comparison of K-12 computer science education intended and enacted curricula intended and enacted curricula, In: Proceedings of the Koli Calling 2019, pp. 1–10, Koli, Finland (2019)
3. Bocconi, S., et al.: Reviewing computational thinking in compulsory education. In: Inamorato Dos Santos, A., Cachia, R., Giannoutsou, N., Punie, Y. (eds.) Publications Office of the European Union, Luxembourg (2022). https://doi.org/10.2760/126955.ISBN 978–92–76–47208–7
4. European Commission, European Education and Culture Executive Agency, Informatics education at school in Europe, Publications Office of the European Union (2022). https://data.europa.eu/doi/10.2797/268406. Accessed 20 June 2023
5. K-12 Computer Science Standards (2017). https://www.doe.k12.de.us/cms/lib/DE01922744/Centricity/Domain/176/CSTA%20Computer%20Science%20Standards%20Revised%202017.pdf. Accessed 11 May 2023
6. International CS education Standards, Google for Education. https://docs.google.com/spreadsheets/d/1SE7hGK5CkOlAf6oEnqk0DPr8OOSdyGZmRnROhr0XHys/edit#gid=218360034. Accessed 11 May 2023
7. Balanskat, A., Engelhardt, K.: Computing our future computer programming and coding - priorities, school curricula and initiatives across Europe. European Schoolnet (2015). http://www.eun.org/resources/detail?publicationID=661. Accessed 20 June 2023

8. Brinda, T., et al.: Grundsätze und Standards für die Informatik in der Schule - Bildungs-standards Informatik für die Sekundarstufe I. In: Puhlmann, H. (Hrsg.), Bonn: Gesellschaft für Informatik e.V. (2008). https://dl.gi.de/items/8be548f4-643c-4893-bf5f-ea130b607322. Accessed 20 June 2023

9. European Commission, "Education in Bulgaria". https://webgate.ec.europa.eu/fpfis/mwikis/eurydice/index.php/Bulgaria:Overview. Accessed 20 June 2023

10. Garov, K.: Studying informatics and information technologies in the secondary school – state and perspectives, jubilee scientific session 2000, Paisii Hilendarski University of Plovdiv (2000). https://fmi-plovdiv.org/GetResource?id=585. Accessed 12 June 2023

11. Sendov, B.: Textbook for 4th grade. Problem Group in Education at Bulgarian Academy of Science, Sofia (1986)

12. Nikolov, R., Sendov, B.: Textbook Logo. Ministry of Education, Sofia (1983)

13. Flores-Vivar, J.M.: Evolution and trends in teaching and learning of Cyberjournalism. In: Organizational Transformation and Managing Innovation in the Fourth Industrial Revolution, IGI Global (2019)

14. Tuparov, G.: E-learning. Development and sustainability of open source learning manage-ments systems, Obrazovanie i Poznanie, Sofia, Bulgaria (2021)

15. Niemi, H.: Building partnerships in an educational ecosystem. CEPS J. 6(3), 5–15 (2016)

16. Bulgarian Ministry of Education. Syllabus in Computer Modeling - 3rd grade (2017). https://mon.bg/upload/12205/UP_KM_3kl.pdf. Accessed 12 Sept 2022

17. Bulgarian Ministry of Education. Syllabus in Computer modeling for 4th grade (2017). https://mon.bg/upload/13767/UP9_KM_ZP_4kl.pdf. Accessed 20 Sept 2022

18. Tuparova, D.: Teaching of computer programming in Bulgarian primary school - chal-lenges and solutions, in 42nd International Convention on Information and Communication Technology, Electronics and Microelectronics, MIPRO 2019, pp. 836–840, Opatija (2019)

Using Extract, Transform, and Load Framework and Data Visualization Tools to Enhance Career Services for Analytics Master's Program Student

Putranegara Riauwindu[(✉)] [iD] and Vladimir Zlatev

Boston University, Boston, MA 02215, USA
{putrangr,abamet}@bu.edu

Abstract. Tailored industry and occupation information for analytics graduates is vital to make a well-informed career decision, especially for Boston University Metropolitan College (BU MET) Applied Business Analytics students and graduates. This paper proposes an Extract Transform and Load (ETL) framework and Data Visualization method to provide students with easy-to-use and intuitive occupation information.

Multiple analytics-related industry and occupation data were extracted and aggregated from third-party sources, primarily from Lightcast and US Government Official Data. The resulting data underwent manipulation using Microsoft Power Query and Microsoft Excel and were stored in Microsoft SharePoint, with structured data in a flat table and unstructured data in a standalone file with a URL generated for linking the data. A relational database schema was then created to connect the ETL data output for visualization and analysis.

Interactive and user-friendly visualizations were created in Microsoft Power BI, resulting in two dashboards providing students with current information on the job market landscape: (i) Analytics Career Prospect, which offers data on top occupations, salary and wage information, job posting trends, required skills information, hiring industries and companies' information, education information, and job location; and (ii) Job Market Consultation, which provides a more in-depth analysis of required skills, industry performance and description, and specific job information reports such as Industry Insight, Industry Snapshot, Industry Supply Chain, Industry staffing pattern, and job posting analytics.

The resulting two dashboards provide "one-stop" search places for career research and shorten the cycle time of tedious searches.

Keywords: ETL · Microsoft Power BI · Relational Database · Structured & Unstructured Data · Data Manipulation · Career Development · Job Posting Analytics · Industry Insights

© ICST Institute for Computer Sciences, Social Informatics and Telecommunications Engineering 2023
Published by Springer Nature Switzerland AG 2023. All Rights Reserved
T. Zlateva and G. Tuparov (Eds.): CSECS 2023, LNICST 514, pp. 347–359, 2023.
https://doi.org/10.1007/978-3-031-44668-9_27

1   Introduction

1.1   Analytics: A Trending Career Prospects in a Data-Driven World

The analytics field is becoming increasingly important in our data-driven world, making it a trending career prospect for individuals seeking to impact their chosen industry significantly. With the rise of big data, according to Davenport and Patil (2012), companies are looking for experts in analytics to help them understand and make sense of the vast amounts of information they are collecting [1]. As a result, careers in analytics are in high demand, with a wide range of job opportunities available in various industries. From finance and healthcare to marketing and sports, the applications of analytics are virtually limitless.

According to a study by McKinsey Global Institute (Manyika et al., 2011), by 2025, the demand for professionals with analytics skills could exceed the supply by as much as 50 to 60 percent [2]. This trend emphasizes the need for individuals to pursue a career in analytics to meet the growing demand for this skill set. By doing so, they can take advantage of the numerous job opportunities available in this field.

1.2   Research Scope and Objectives

Given the narration above, conducting a job search in analytics can be difficult and complex. While there is a growing demand for analytics professionals, job postings in the field are also increasing rapidly. However, the job postings from one employer to another can differ significantly, making it challenging for analytics graduates to conduct initial research on where to apply, what kind of skills are required for various jobs, what possible occupations are available, which companies and industries are hiring, and where the employment locations. Hudson (2021) suggests that this complexity can make it challenging for graduates to navigate the job market and find the right fit for their skills and career goals [3].

This paper aims to propose a framework to help analytics students and graduates, especially in Boston University Metropolitan College Applied Business Analytics Master Program (BU MET ABA), in navigating the complex job market by providing provide easy to use and intuitive occupation and job reviews. The graduates can use the information to make a well-informed career decision after graduation, specifically to meet the following objectives:

1. The information must provide students with a list of potential occupations for ABA graduates in various locations in the US industry landscape.
2. The information must provide information about job trends for ABA graduates in different US industries.
3. The information must provide statistics on the potential occupations for ABA graduates within the US industry landscape in various locations, including but not limited to salary, wage, education, and experience.

The selected research framework is demonstrated with data for analytics-related industries and occupations in the United States (US) as dictated by the North America Industry Classification Standard (NAICS) and presented for the Finance, Insurance, and Pharmaceutical industries.

2 Literature Review

2.1 Career Analytics

Providing analytics graduates with insights and information about the job market and available occupations to provide them a competitive advantage in the rapidly evolving field is not a novel effort in an academic setting. This effort reflects the growing demand for analytics professionals and the complexity of navigating the job market, as employers' requirements and job postings can vary significantly.

For example, a study conducted by Wilbur and Angela Stanton (2020) suggests that the authors have performed "Career Analytics" by analyzing the skills required for an entry-level analytics position, focusing on data science, data analytics, and business analytics. The authors also identify the most in-demand job titles and functions and compare the required hard skills, soft skills, software skills, and credentials for each area. The authors wrap up the research by providing educators with recommendations on preparing students for careers in analytics [4].

Wilkins (2021) also researched the data analytics job market [5]. The author identified the most in-demand skill sets in analytics, providing insights for students, organizations, and universities. The authors argued that the findings would guide students in mastering the most relevant skills for the job market. At the same time, for the company, the information will aid them in understanding the most sought-after skills and competing for hiring. Lastly, the authors also suggested that for universities offering data analyst-related courses, the output could align their curriculum to meet the job market's needs.

The similarity between the two examples is that they both discuss the industry requirements for analytics graduates so that the students can prepare for the knowledge/skills "gap" and acquire a competitive advantage. Still, both types of research only capture the information on a specific period, resulting in a static research report. This paper will provide students with interactive and up-to-date information about the analytics industry landscape.

2.2 Extract, Transform, and Load Framework

Voluminous analytics-related industry and occupation data residing in multiple sources, a standardized framework to aggregate and collect all different data from different sources would need to be adopted to ensure scalability. The Extract, Transform, and Load (ETL) framework would suit this purpose well.

According to P. Vassiliadis' conceptual model for ETL, ETL tools are specialized tools designed to address data warehouse homogeneity, cleaning, and loading issues (Kimball & Caserta, 2004) [6]. Multiple commercial tools provide ETL functionality as a one-stop solution for all the ETL framework processes [7]. One example of a commercial ETL tool is Informatica, which offers holistic functionality to automate the data pipeline from multiple sources to the data warehouse or data lakes [8]. While most of the commercial ETL tools provide a broad range of advanced ETL functionality and cover the operations from upstream to downstream, Vassiliadis (2009) argues that ETL processes involve several key steps, including the extraction of relevant data from sources, the transportation of this data to a specific area of the data warehouse, and the transformation of the data to comply with the structure of the target relation. ETL processes also entail the isolation and cleansing of problematic tuples to ensure adherence to business rules and database constraints, and ultimately, the loading of the cleansed, transformed data to the proper relationship in the warehouse, along with the refreshing of any indexes and materialized views [9].

This paper aims to provide a solution by leveraging the existing BU MET infrastructure while minimizing the use of external commercial ETL tools and maximizing the ETL process framework discussed by Vassiliadis (2009), which will be discussed further in the Methodology section.

2.3 Database Schema and Design

As previously highlighted in Sect. 2.2, the diverse nature of data types and sources necessitates a database schema and design to connect and comprehend the extracted and transformed data effectively.

Data can be either structured or unstructured and may come from various sources. Structured data is well-organized and can be stored in a traditional relational database management system (RDBMS) for easy querying using SQL. On the other hand, unstructured data has no pre-defined format and cannot be easily stored in relational tables. Unstructured data is the fastest-growing type of data and includes data from various sources such as images, sensor data, web chats, social media messages, videos, documents, log files, and email data [10].

A collection of structured or unstructured data, organized with a central focus, is known as a database. When dealing with computer databases, the tool used to input and modify data is referred to as either a database program or a database management system (DBMS), as opposed to a manual paper-based system [11]. In comparison, a schema is a structure that connects different information within a database to create a logical connection between the data.

The proposed in this paper framework uses both structured and unstructured data with the unstructured data projected into a meta-structured table containing the unstructured data and its associated link to the hosting place.

2.4 United States Labor Landscape

Let's introduce several essential characteristics of the labor landscape in the US:

Industry Classification. Various industries in the United States are classified into several categories based on their characteristics and nature, and the classification for these industries adheres to the North American Industry Classification System. The North American Industry Classification System (NAICS) is a standardized system used by Federal statistical agencies in the US to classify business establishments, gather statistical data, and analyze the US business economy. NAICS divides the economy into 20 sectors. Industries within these sectors are grouped according to the production criterion [12].

Occupation Classification. The Standard Occupational Classification (or SOC) system is a federal statistical standard employed by federal agencies for classifying workers into occupational categories, aiming to collect, compute, or publish data. Workers are assigned to one of 867 distinct occupations based on their description. Detailed occupations are combined to create 459 broad occupations, 98 minor groups, and 23 major groups, making classification more efficient. Occupations with similar job responsibilities, and sometimes comparable skills, education, and/or training, are grouped in the SOC [13].

Registered Business. According to the latest data from the US Census Bureau, there were 6.1 million employer firms in the United States in 2019. Of those businesses, 99.7% had fewer than 500 employees, 98.1% had fewer than 100 employees, 89.0% had fewer than 20 employees, and 78.5% had fewer than ten employees. When nonemployer businesses are included, the share of firms with fewer than 20 workers increases to 98.0%, and those with fewer than ten employees represent 96.0%. Out of approximately 32.6 million businesses in the US, only 20,868 had 500 or more employees, indicating that America's economy is primarily comprised of small companies [14].

Skills Classification. There are no official skill classifications from the US government but Lightcast, one of the leading labor market aggregators and analytics, has suggested skill classification and definition. The Open Skills Library by Lightcast defines skills as abilities related to particular tasks or knowledge of specific subjects and tools obtained through education or experience. The library categorizes each skill as specialized, common, or certifications [15].

Specialized Skills, also known as technical skills or hard skills, are competencies that are mostly necessary within a specific occupation or enable an individual to carry out a particular task. Examples of specialized skills include "NumPy" or "Hotel Management."

Common Skills refer to the skills widely used across various occupations and industries, encompassing both learned skills and personal attributes. These skills may include "Communication" or "Microsoft Excel" and are also known as competencies, soft skills, or human skills.

Certifications refer to qualifications that are recognized by industry or educational bodies, such as a "Cosmetology License" or a "Certified Cytotechnologist" designation. These certifications indicate that the individual has achieved specific knowledge or expertise in a particular field or skill.

3   Methodology and Process

The proposed methodology and framework to achieve the research objective involves combining a simple Extract, Transform, and Load (ETL) framework and data visualization. This approach is distinctive because it is expected to generate dynamic output that evolves by adding new information. The resulting interactive output is designed to enable end-users to access relevant information directly instead of static, report-style output that remains unchanged as new data points emerge.

This paper's proposed methodology and framework could be summarized as Extracting and Collecting Data, Transforming Data, Loading Data to Cloud Storage, Connecting the Loaded Data, and Presenting the Data. The whole framework is illustrated and summarized in Fig. 1 below.

Fig. 1. Summary of Proposed Framework and Methodology to Enhance Career Services for Analytics Master's Program Student

3.1 Database Schema and Cloud Storage Creation

Before executing the ETL framework, a layout or Database Schema plan must be developed to meet the stated objectives first. The corresponding specific folders in the Cloud storage to host the data that went through the ETL framework must also be created first.

The database schema was created by connecting five main entities identified based on the business objective (Industry, Company, Skills, Occupations, and Location) to each other using a Relational Database model. Each entity had child entities, and the schema was made by grouping entities based on their relationships. The groups, or clusters, were then connected internally and externally, with different levels of connection (cardinality and optionality). A "bridge" entity was created to avoid complex relationships between groups. It connects two or more groups with many-to-many relationships in either one-to-many or many-to-one relationships.

The entities in the database schema were divided into two categories: "fact entities" and "dimension entities." Fact entities store transaction data from sources like Lightcast.io and the Bureau of Labor and Statistics, such as posted salary and job count within a specific industry. Dimension entities help gather information about the measures being taken, such as the industry and company. Fact entities are labeled with an "f" and dimension entities with a "d". The database schema that was developed according to the above explanation is available at the Appendix 1 Database Schema Career Services for Analytics Master's Program Student.

3.2 Collecting and Extracting Data

After the database schema was created, the first step of the ETL framework involved collecting and extracting data from various sources, primarily from Lightcast, the Bureau of Labor Statistics, the United States Census Bureau, EBSCO Information Services, and other internet sources. Data were acquired by querying third-party sources'

RDBMS, connecting to Application Programming Interfaces (API), and directly down-loading in various formats, including Extensible Markup Language (XML), JavaScript Object Notation (JSON), Comma-Separated Values (CSV), Excel File (XLSX), Portable Document Format (PDF), and Power Point File (PPTX).

The data extracted and collected including but not limited to number of posted occu-pations, salary and wages, skills requirement, company and industry posting, education requirements, job locations, company information, industry performance, occupations hiring rate, Industry Insight, Industry Snapshot, Industry Supply Chain, Industry staffing pattern, and job posting analytics., and other information.

After extraction, the data were temporarily stored in a staging area. Files that were "ready-to-use" (such as PDF, PPTX, and some XLSX files) were directly transferred to their respective folders in the Cloud Storage. Files that needed further processing (such as XML, JSON, CSV, and some XLSX files) were kept in the staging area for the next step.

For the result demonstration in this paper, the time-period of data collection is from November 2022 – March 2023.

3.3 Transforming Data

The data that needs further processing then undergoes a data transformation process. The data transformation includes but is not limited to:

1. The removal of unnecessary variables/columns in the data.
2. Variable type conversion from a certain type to another type.
3. The removal of unnecessary strings or characters within specific variables.

All data manipulation and transformation were done in Microsoft Power Query.

3.4 Loading Data to Cloud Storage

The cleaned/transformed data is then loaded into Microsoft Excel flat table entity and stored in the cloud storage in their dedicated folder based on the previously developed database schema. The cloud storage for storing the data uses Microsoft SharePoint.

Each flat table is protected so that only person who has the authority to modify the flat table to populate the flat table with new or updated information could modify the flat table.

3.5 Connecting the Loaded Data

In order to connect both the structured (Excel flat table) and unstructured data (ppt, pdf, etc.), first, the link that redirects to the unstructured data was generated. These links were then compiled into separate Excel flat tables containing detailed information regarding the unstructured data (metadata) associated with the previously developed database schema.

Each flat table, for both structured data and unstructured metadata, was then con-nected to the Microsoft Power BI. The connection and relationship between the entity/flat tables were then created based on the database schema previously developed.

3.6 Presenting the Data

The connected entity/flat table were then visualized in the Microsoft Power BI environment. Several pages of the dashboard with different visualizations were created to provide specific information to the students, such as Top Occupation, Top Skills, Top Company Hiring, Skill Deep Dive, Industry Overview, Industry, and Occupations Report. Some examples of the visualizations used were bar charts, line plots, scatter plots, tables, maps, tree maps, and other visualizations.

4 Results and Discussion

The resulting interactive and user-friendly visualizations, created in Microsoft Power BI, were two dashboards providing students with current information on the job market landscape: Analytics Career Prospect Overview and Analytics Job Market Consultation dashboard, which will be discussed further below.

4.1 Dashboard 1: Analytics Career Prospect Overview

The first dashboard created was named Analytics Career Prospect Overview. The Analytics Career Prospect dashboard offers data on top occupations, salary and wage information, job posting trends, required skills information, hiring industries and companies' information, education information, and job location.

Students can browse topics of interest at their whim. For example, what are the top occupations for analytics graduates? What are the top skills required by employers? Which companies are actively hiring and posting the most job openings? Which industry hosts the most job openings? What is the job posting trends? What are the mean and median salaries? Where are the job locations?

By using this dashboard, students can jumpstart their initial career research by finding opportunities as analytics graduates, understanding salary expectations, identifying gaps in their skillset compared to industry requirements, determining the best time to apply for jobs, exploring job openings in their preferred cities, and identifying certifications that will set them apart from others in the field. An example of a page in the dashboard is available in Appendix 2, Sample Page from the Dashboard 1 Analytics Career Prospect Overview.

Some interesting takeaways from the first dashboard were:

1. Data Scientists tops the posted occupations for analytics graduates, followed by Management Analysts and Market Research Analyst.
2. The most frequently reported range of posted analytics graduate salaries was around $67,000–$75,999.
3. The job posting for analytics graduates increased over the last three years, with most jobs posted in Q1-Q2 each year.
4. The most sought-after technical skills for an analytics graduate were Structured Query Language (SQL), Python, Microsoft Excel, Tableau, and R.

4.2   Dashboard 2: Analytics Job Market Consultation

The second dashboard created was named Analytics Job Market Consultation. This dashboard provides a more in-depth analysis of required skills, industry performance and description, and specific job information reports such as Industry Insight, Industry Snapshot, Industry Supply Chain, Industry staffing pattern, and job posting analytics.

After students perform overview research about their career aspirations in the first dashboard, they can then use this dashboard to conduct in-depth research on critical items they found in the first dashboard. For example, if students want to work in the finance industry, they can see how well it performs by looking at the Industry Performance page in the second dashboard. If students know specific skill gaps, they can visit the Skills page to find detailed explanations about those skills and where to start improving them. Suppose students want to delve deeper into each career prospect within a specific industry. In that case, they can go to the Documents page and download the in-depth reports provided by Lightcast to prepare accordingly (Fig. 2).

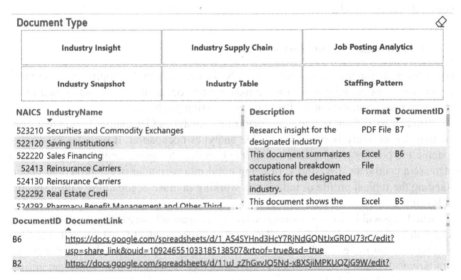

Fig. 2. Sample Page from Dashboard 2 Analytics Job Market Consultation

Some interesting takeaways from the second dashboard were:

1. There is one hire for every three unique job postings for Data Scientists, two for every individual job posting for Management Analyst, and three for every particular job posting for Market Research Analyst. Hence, the job demand for a Market Research Analyst/Marketing Specialist was relatively high in the United States.
2. Every US industry (20 NAICS categories) has had overall positive gross-output growth trends for the last 20 years. Manufacturing generally outperforms every other industry's gross output by roughly ten times.

5 Summary and Recommendations

5.1 Summary: Interactive Job Information Dashboard to Navigate the Complex Job Search Process

The dashboards, as the output from the research, are now available for students and graduates to access on the BU MET ABA Career Service Website. The dashboards were designed to simplify job research for ABA students and graduates by providing them with relevant and up-to-date information. Through the dashboards, users can easily search and navigate the job market landscape based on various parameters such as location, job title, and employer.

The dashboards provide users with critical job market insights, including industry trends, job market statistics, and salary data. The dashboards help users make informed decisions about their job search strategies by presenting this information in a clear and concise format. Overall, the dashboards are an indispensable tool for ABA students and graduates, assisting them in achieving their career goals and staying informed about the latest job market trends.

5.2 Recommendation for Next Work

Given the wide range of industries in the US, the next step in developing the dashboard is to continue populating it with more industry and occupation information and make comprehensive comparison for the built and existing products.

Another possible next step is to perform an Analytics Occupation Deep Dive, conducting deeper analysis on each possible analytics occupation. It includes examining specific job posting trends, determining the best time to apply, identifying factors that increase a candidate's likelihood of being hired in a particular occupation, and understanding the typical profile of individuals working in those occupations within specific industries.

Another possibility is to conduct Analytics Occupation Data Mining Analysis, specifically clustering and classification. This analysis aims to identify which industries and occupations are more "analytics-graduate" friendly based on their characteristics and similarities. It could give students and graduates more information on which enterprises to focus on.

Appendix

1. Database Schema Career Services for Analytics Master's Program Student

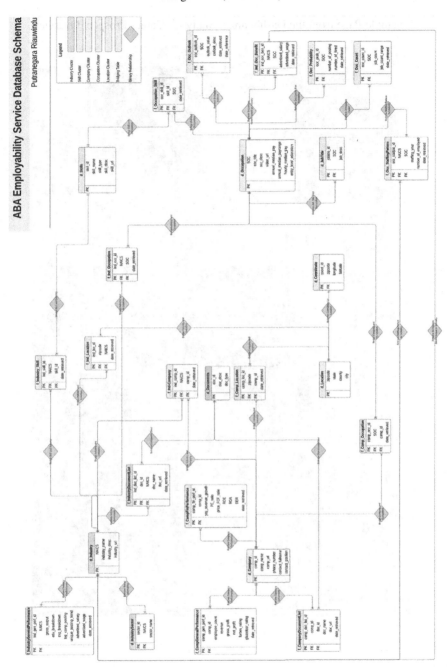

2. Sample Page from the Dashboard 1 Analytics Career Prospect Overview

References

1. Davenport, T.H., Patil, D.J.: Data scientist: the sexiest job of the 21st century. Harv. Bus. Rev. **90**(10), 70–76 (2012)
2. Manyika, J., et al.: Big data: the next frontier for innovation, competition, and productivity. McKinsey Global Inst. (2011). https://doi.org/10.1007/978-1-4614-4134-9_1
3. Hudson, D.: Tips for navigating the academic job market. Health Promot. Pract. **22**(1), 21–23 (2021). https://doi.org/10.1177/1524839920938802
4. Stanton, W.W., Stanton, A.D.: Helping business students acquire the skills needed for a career in analytics: a comprehensive industry assessment of entry-level requirements. Decis. Sci. J. Innov. Educ. **18**(1), 138–165 (2020). https://doi-org.ezproxy.bu.edu/10.1111/dsji.12199
5. Wilkins, D.: An in-depth analysis of the data analytics job market. Master's thesis. University of New Hampshire, Peter T. Paul College of Business & Economics (2021)
6. Kimball, R., Caserta, J.: The Data Warehouse ETL Toolkit: Practical Techniques for Extracting, Cleaning, Conforming, and Delivering Data. Wiley, Hoboken (2004)
7. Edjlali, R., Beyer, M.A.: Magic quadrant for data warehouse and data management solutions for analytics, Gartner (2016)
8. Mukherjee, R., Kar, P.: A comparative review of data warehousing ETL tools with new trends and industry insight. In 2017 IEEE 7th International Advance Computing Conference (IACC), pp. 371–375. IEEE (2017)
9. Vassiliadis, P.: A survey of extract-transform-load technology. Int. J. Data Warehouse. Min. **5**, 1–27 (2009)
10. Mishra, S., Misra, A.: Structured and unstructured big data analytics. In: 2017 International Conference on Current Trends in Computer, Electrical, Electronics and Communication (CTCEEC), Mysore, India, pp. 740–746 (2017). https://doi.org/10.1109/CTCEEC.2017.845 4999
11. Derclaye, E.: What is a database? J. World Intellect. Property. **5**, 981–1011 (2005). https://doi.org/10.1111/j.1747-1796.2002.tb00189.x
12. Executive Office of the President, Office of Management and Budget. North American Industry Classification System. United States (2022)
13. Executive Office of the President, Office of Management and Budget. Standard occupational classification manual. United States (2018)
14. US Census Bureau. Statistics of US Businesses (SUSB) (2019). https://www.census.gov/data/tables/2019/econ/susb/2019-susb-annual.html. Accessed 12 May 12 2023
15. Lightcast. (n.d.). Open Skills Library - Frequently Asked Questions. https://lightcast.io/open-skills/faqs. Accessed 12 May 2023

A School to Remember: Analyzing School Best Practices in the Perspective of Digital Transformation of Schools

Elissaveta Gourova[1]([✉]) [iD] and Albena Antonova[2] [iD]

[1] Faculty of Mathematics and Informatics, Sofia University, 125 Tsarigradsko Shosse Blvd, Sofia 1113, Bulgaria
elis@fmi.uni-sofia.bg
[2] Faculty of Mathematics and Informatics, Sofia University, 6 James Baucher Blvd, Sofia 1164, Bulgaria
a_antonova@fmi.uni-sofia.bg

Abstract. The digital transformation of schools aims to ensure a systematic process for adapting primary and secondary education to the level of technology innovations, preparing the next generation for new opportunities and demands. At the same time, digital transformation has to ensure complex organizational alignments beyond simple equipment implementation. School education is a conservative and slow-moving system, so a more in-depth analysis of the existing best practices can provide smooth digital transformation paths.

The present research aims to explore and analyze best practices from the perspective of digital transformation in schools. Using a bottom-up approach, in total 436 best practices are collected from 120 students enrolled in Computer Science programs at Sofia University. These students surmounted one of the most competitive university entrance exams in the country, ensuring the validity and relevance of their best practices. The study covers experiences from 85 primary and secondary schools in 42 locations in Bulgaria. The structuring of the paper is as follows. It starts with a literature overview of school digital transformation and presents the DigiLEAD project approach. Then, the methodology of the study is discussed and best practices are classified by origin (teacher, school or policy-level practices) and by impact (five-level model of quality education). The discussion part proposes different models for adopting digital technologies in schools, taking in consideration that almost 60% of the best practices come from individual teachers, teaching approaches and personal commitment. In the conclusions are summarized the key lessons learned and the limitations of the study.

Keywords: Digital Transformation · School Education · Best Practices

1 Introduction

The digital transformation is becoming an omnipresent trend, often connected to technology innovations and expected tremendous changes in the society and economy. School leaders have to consider how disruptive technologies such as Artificial Intelligence,

© ICST Institute for Computer Sciences, Social Informatics and Telecommunications Engineering 2023
Published by Springer Nature Switzerland AG 2023. All Rights Reserved
T. Zlateva and G. Tuparov (Eds.): CSECS 2023, LNICST 514, pp. 360–371, 2023.
https://doi.org/10.1007/978-3-031-44668-9_28

autonomous and collaborative robots, the Internet of things, cloud computing, additive manufacturing, augmented and virtual reality, big data analytics and others can successfully add value to their programs [1]. The digital transformation in education is often discussed from the perspective of higher education and new strategies of teaching and learning [2, 3]. However, in secondary and primary education, digital transformation has to play an even more important role in preparing society and the new generations of pupils for the new skills and competencies, needed for the future of work. It should provide systematic change management programs and instruments, aligning new technology innovations to the school organizations, teacher professional development and value-adding processes of high-quality teaching and learning. In this perspective, the ERASMUS+ DigiLEAD project engaged to develop tools for school leaders, allowing them to prepare to stay at the forefront of new digital changes, conforming to the expectations of students, teachers and society.

The present research steps on the bottom-up approach and based on best practices from school education aims to analyze the digital transformation paths. Focusing on the analysis of meaningful and efficient teaching and schooling approaches, this study aims to propose more teacher and student-focused perspective for aligning digital technologies in schools.

The paper is structured as follows. First, it outlines some challenges of the digital transformation in schools and presents the main approach of the DigiLEAD project. Next, it presents the methodology of the study, analyzing the most common approaches and practices for sourcing best practices in schools. The main criteria for content analysis, evaluation and structuring of the best practices are discussed and the results are presented. The discussion part proposes a more in-depth analysis of how the outcomes of the best practices' analysis provide models for successful digital transformation paths. At the end are identified study limitations and future directions.

2 Theoretical Background

2.1 Digital Transformation in Schools

Presently, organizations are faced with a need to adapt to the changes in the networked economy, market volatility and the fast speed of adoption of digital technologies by people and organizations worldwide. The wide use of information and communication technologies (ICT) in the economy and society has resulted in new business models, management and working processes, and new users experience – described as a digital transformation [4]. Digital transformation is understood as a change of the entire operating model of the organization – requiring reengineering of internal business processes, and the way of interaction not only among employees but also with external stakeholders – partners, suppliers, distributors, clients, etc. [3].

As outlined in [3], it is essential to develop a vision and strategy for digital transformation, and to ensure leadership capabilities to communicate it, commit employees, and guide and support its implementation and the changes in organizational processes – ways of operation and control. Subsequently, critical for the success are the readiness of the staff and its skills and knowledge. Further issues are related to the availability of appropriate tools and infrastructure.

While specific efforts were taken for the digital transformation of the economy, the educational institutions were lagging behind, and during the COVID pandemic they faced the need to rapidly change their operational procedures in order to continue smooth teaching and learning processes. Teachers had to gain new competences and adapt to digital ways of teaching and communicating with students so as to maintain the educational process [5]. Similarly, school leaders were not prepared and had to find their own ways to "upholding a sense of normalcy and care for children and families" [6]. While several actions were taken by educational authorities to facilitate online teaching, e.g. providing computers and other devices, educational platforms and software tools, as well as training teachers, the digital transformation of schools is still a challenge in many countries. Subsequently, in Europe was approved a Digital Education Action plan as a comprehensive initiative for "policies and actions on several fronts, including infrastructure, strategy and leadership, teacher skills, learner skills, content, curricula, assessment and national legal frameworks" [7].

The digital transformation of educational institutions should comprise the following processes: administration, communication, teaching and preparing lessons, students learning, reviews and examination [3]. Regarding digital learning in schools, in [8] are discussed several dimensions: technical facilities and availability of ICTs in schools; students learning activities involving ICTs, and digital educational resources; abilities of teachers to fully exploit ICT opportunities, and the use of new teaching methods and learning approaches. The availability of sufficient digital technologies is not related to their frequent use in classrooms. More important are teachers and their equipment with basic digital skills for general technology usage, research, communication, collaboration, production of content and learning via technology. Technology-related teaching skills are essential to provide students with a large variety of learning activities and facilitate their problem-solving skills. Such skills are based on knowledge of technologies and specific technological pedagogical competencies which are used for creating educational resources (pedagogical content), planning, implementing and evaluating technology use in class, and sharing experiences of technology use. Subsequently, in the education of future teachers should be placed more emphasis on the usage of technologies to enable student learning activities [8].

Most educational systems in Europe lack a strategic planning [9]. This is due to a certain extent to their centralized structure which limits the autonomy and flexibility of schools, and the role of school leaders, mainly focused on the administrative management of day-to-day activities and decision making. Moreover, school leaders lack a digital transformation mind-set and proactivity, and often are not able to understand that the primary place and purpose of technology in schools is that it can be used to transform how people think, work and communicate [10, 11].

Many studies reveal also the interactions of teachers and students during online education after the COVID pandemic. For example, [14] summarized the factors influencing the establishment of a teaching presence – related to teachers' pedagogical approach, the learning design and the facilitation. Putting the learner in the center, and teachers taking the role of facilitators helps students to engage and commit. Besides, the personalized, flexible, contextualized learning design and the use of appropriate technologies and tools help effective online learning. Digital pedagogical innovation and the changing role of teachers and students in the future are considered in [15]. The study suggests that distance learning brings greater student autonomy and higher responsibility for learning. However, digital inclusion and students wellbeing should be also taken into account by digital learning.

2.2 The DigiLEAD Approach

Partners from 5 EU member states within the DigiLEAD project considered how to support school leaders to design and implement a digital transformation strategy and Action Plans. A Strategy Toolkit on Digital transformation for School leaders was recently developed by the consortium [9] following desk research by all partners and involving focus groups with national stakeholders (researchers, teachers, school leaders, and educational authorities). The Toolkit considers specific processes in schools, and the need to support them when designing a Digital Transformation strategy:

- Creating a school vision and setting strategic objectives are of great importance in creating a successful digital transformation strategy.
- Conducting a SWOT analysis for the school is needed for analysis of the internal and external environment of schools.
- Curriculum alignment is an important section in the final school strategy as it ensures that the learning content, learning objectives, study programs, attainment targets, assessment guidelines or syllabi are aligned with the possibilities of digital education.
- Assessment plays a crucial role in how students learn, their level of motivation, and how teachers teach.
- Innovative teaching and learning strategies are essential in the overall transformation of education towards more efficient, personalized and student-oriented teaching and learning by using digital technologies.
- Infrastructure needs and adaptations focus on developing adequate and reliable infrastructure and up-to-date equipment as a prerequisite for the digital transformation in education.
- Timelines, scheduling, and ongoing monitoring are at the center of the planning and implementation of the digital transformation strategy.
- Continuous evaluation and support help to understand whether the plan is progressing within the foreseen timeframe and according to the predefined objectives, ensuring that the actions are being implemented as planned.
- Support for teachers is vital for a successful and qualitative digitalization of education, as teachers act as architects of the teaching-learning processes.
- Support for students and parents focuses on the involvement of students and parents in the digital transformation of a school.
- Privacy, health and well-being for teachers and students are pillars of digital transformation as they ensure the actors' capacity to realize their full potential.

In addition, the project team prepared a digital transformation checklist, adapted from the SELFIE tool that was produced by the European Commission [12] and the TET-SAT tool prepared within the Erasmus+project MENTEP [13]. This checklist will help school leaders with the collection of quantitative data and will enable them to first identify gaps, reflect on the current digital readiness of their school, and then evaluate the progress in the process of digital transformation.

3 Methodology Overview and Best Practices

3.1 Study Methodology

The best practices in school education are mainly presented and discussed from the top-down perspective. During the last few years, a short overview of the numerous resources of school best practices in the Bulgarian internet environment shows the common practice of teachers to present their pedagogical work at conferences and forums, conference proceedings and publications. Many collections of good practices are available through public websites (often hosted by NGOs) or as part of initiatives in specific fields (f. ex. Collection of best practices on project-based learning, best practices for integrating children from minorities and others). Furthermore, there miss a more critical analysis or academic studies of best practices, collected or sourced by bottom-up approach. This hinder the possibility to identify and further popularize the most effective and efficient good teaching and learning methods in school education.

From the perspective of new trends for digital transformation in schools, the following methodology is applied. The best practices in school education are collected from university students at the Faculty of Mathematics and Informatics (FMI) at Sofia University, Bulgaria. It should be noticed that the entrance exams on Mathematics at the FMI are among the most difficult and competitive in the country. Therefore, students revealing the best practices have a strong academic background and represent some of the best schools and teachers in Bulgaria. But more importantly, in the scope of their course work on the elective course "Knowledge Management", students are asked to carefully reflect and share personal and memorable school experiences and to analyze them from the perspective of "the school of the future".

After collecting the best practices, a content analysis is performed and the best practices are classified into three main areas (teacher initiative, school practice or policy-level initiative). Then, best practices are clustered, conforming to the five categories of quality education, as identified in [16]. More specifically, this model addresses the five key groups of criteria for quality primary and secondary education, as emerging from theoretical research [16]: (1) learning environment (psychosocial elements, physical elements, respect for diversity, collaboration, sharing and team spirit), (2) learning content (student-centered pedagogy, well-structured knowledge base, continuous curriculum improvement, interest in all students, and life skills), (3) processes (teaching, learning, assessment, support, and supervision), (4) students (involvement/participation, feedback, challenging learning activities, and improved learning outcomes), (5) teachers (knowledge of educational context, content, curriculum, and pedagogy, pedagogical skills, emotional/management/reflection skills, and teacher professional development).

3.2 Overview of the Best Practices

In total 120 BSc students in their third and fourth year took part in the best practices sourcing. All of the students were enrolled in the elective course on "Knowledge Management" and at the end of the semester, they prepared and presented a course work about the future of schools, covering both individual best practices from their own school experience and ideas about the future. The descriptive analysis shows that about 436 best practices are identified from 85 secondary and primary schools from 42 locations in Bulgaria. Responding to their study profile, most of the schools are professional or specialized mathematical high schools: in total 30 mathematical and STEM-oriented high schools, 11 Foreign language gymnasiums and 8 professional high schools, specialized in the fields of mathematics or informatics. All of the schools are public.

The good practices are not evenly distributed as some of the schools are better represented among students. As students had the freedom to emphasize and share specific experiences, all their best practices are counted separately. For example, the Pleven Mathematical High School has 52 best practices from 13 students, the National Mathematical High School has 22 best practices from 5 students, and the Sofia Mathematical High School has 13 best practices from 5 students. A significant part of the good practices covers specific school subjects and school disciplines (198 or 45%), and another (144 or 33%) of them are linked to school activities and initiatives outside the school curriculum.

3.3 Analysis of the Results

Teacher Level Best Practices
Most of the best practices can be directly linked to individual teachers' initiatives and teaching approaches. In total 264 of the best practices or about 61% of them are related to teachers' personal involvement, innovative teaching activities, personal attitude, support and mentoring to the students' success. Table 1 presents the 5 main groups of best practices on teaching level, summarized by dominating concepts.

Table 1. Individual teachers' best practices topics.

Level	Description	Number/share of best practices (n = 264)
1	Personal attitude, discipline and personalized teaching approach	38 (14%)
2	Active teaching methods	32 (12%)
3	Public discussions and debates	26 (10%)
4	Using ICT in class	24 (9%)
5	Using games and gamification techniques	21 (8%)
6	Evaluation and feedback	21 (8%)

Personal attitude and discipline – almost 38 best practices are related to the personality of the teacher, his or her personal involvement in the subject and in the role, personal examples, high requirements, strong discipline and high expectations from the students. In this group can be reported as well personalized approaches for different students (5), covering practices such as defining personalized goals, using differentiation techniques in class and organizing additional activities.

Active learning and teaching methods were discussed in 32 practices, focusing on the role of project-based learning (14), the use of active learning methods such as mind-maps and brainstorming (8), teamwork (5), a shift of the roles (student teachers) (5) and others.

Public discussions and debates are highlighted in 26 best practices, reporting different situations and forms of discussions or public debates. Students recognize that these activities challenged them to think critically, to argue better their positions, to better prepare and learn additional facts, as well as to consider the arguments of both sides and to make their own judgements. Some teachers organized public debates and discussions after showing a movie or video, for completing the literature analysis and others. These techniques are commonly linked to humanities subjects such as history (9), Bulgarian language and literature (7), foreign languages (4), philosophical studies (2) and others.

The use of **ICT in class** is reflected on several levels. About 24 practices are reported, covering the use of technologies to facilitate knowledge sharing - teachers using online platforms and repositories (7); interactive whiteboards (6) used for presenting and visualizing complex chemistry or geometry relationships. Considering specific software programs, students reported MS PowerPoint for individual and group projects, allowing them to present and raise public speaking skills (4). Specific software examples include Google Maps in Geography classes, Biology software solution Zygote Body, Khan Academy for self-learning, Duolingo in foreign language classes, Quizlet and Kahoot, along with specific tools for automatic testing of ICT tasks.

The games and gamification techniques are recognized as a substantial part of the best practices (21) covering both traditional and online games in class. Quizzes and online games (such as Kahoot!) are used by language teachers (9), as well in history, biology, mathematics and others, often for short tests and revisions before or after the class. The organized in-class competitions (10), feedback and evaluation techniques (21), allowed students to learn revisions, increased interest in the new topics or created a more relaxed atmosphere, provoking students with funny questions and humor (5).

Among the other best practices, used by the teachers to make their classes more engaging and efficient for the students are: practical experiments in class (17): STEM sciences, writing scientific protocols, work on real-life cases and experiments. Some teachers used to organize outdoor activities (14) such as visits to museums and galleries, short class excursions and trips, but in general, these practices are organized on the school level, requiring more efforts by the school administration.

School Level Best Practices
At the school level are identified about 152 best practices (35%). Conforming to the students' view, schools have to ensure additional opportunities to raise their academic skills and talents. About 35 of the best practices on the school level cover some forms

of clubs, complementary classes for talented students (such as training and preparation for national competitions), or specific extra-curriculum activities such as theatre, art and debates. Other substantial groups of school initiatives cover different types of travelling (28), international excursions, student exchange, short-term student trips, school visits to the theatre and performances, other outdoor activities. Attracting interesting experts, guest lecturers and especially foreign teachers for practicing different languages in class are mentioned in 26 practices. The school infrastructure or access to learning environments and specific digital equipment and technologies are identified in 18 practices. Festivals and school-level celebrations, school-level competitions, and sports events are also part of the good practices, creating lasting memories.

On Table 2 are displayed the clusters of best practices on school level.

Table 2. School level best practices.

Level	Description	Number/ share of best practices (n = 152)
1	School-level clubs, additional classes, trainings	35 (23%)
2	Excursions, outdoor activities, trips, visits	28 (18%)
3	Guest lecturers – alumni, foreign teachers	26 (17%)
4	Infrastructure (ICT, cabinets, classes)	18 (12%)
5	Sports activities	15 (9%)
6	Festivals and school celebrations	12 (8%)

It is worth noticing that the school learning environment and access to class infrastructure mostly include ICT infrastructure (individual PC, tablets, or access to specific equipment such as the robotics lab). Some students remember good practices such as access to classrooms and school learning environments for organizing teamwork, innovative classroom arrangements and decorations such as stickers on the walls (with appropriate formulas), students' choice decoration of the corridors, and appropriate environment for individual work.

Policy Level Best Practices
Many best practices cover general educational practices, adopted on a national level. In many cases, students cannot refer if one practice is organized by the school or by the national-level administration and policy recommendations. However, in this analysis, only 20 best practices can refer to the policy level. These cover mostly practices, related to national competitions and hackathons on different school subjects (Olympiads), compulsory internships in companies, study programs, allowing additional classes and extra curriculum activities, policies for encouraging the best students with national scholarships for academic achievements and others.

4 Discussion

4.1 The Five-Level Model

Considering the five-level model of [16], the best practices are analyzed and distributed according to one or more of the following key groups of criteria: (1) learning environment, (2) learning content, (3) learning processes, (4) focus on students, (5) focus on teachers. First, every practice is assessed following the five categories, considering how students reflect and describe their impact and their influence on the overall learning process. For example, a good practice for learning methods of a specific teacher can cover all of the five criteria: teacher used interactive screens (environment), to make presentations, videos or games (content), organizing discussions and debates (processes), focusing on students' achievement (students) and adapting and personalizing his or her teaching methods upon the results (teacher). Therefore, the presented summary of the five-level model can be reflected as a general overview of best practices' impact. As presented in Table 3, most of the best practices are reflected on the student level (355), where teachers play the dominant role. The learning environment is mainly the responsibility of the schools, along with students' activities concerning additional learning activities, excursions and competitions. On the policy level, best practices are focused on National level competitions and practice-oriented internships, examinations and curricula.

Table 3. Best practices distribution among key categories as of [16].

	Description	Overall n = 436	Teacher n = 264	School n = 152	Policy n = 20
1	Learning environment	74	28	46	0
2	Learning content	330	250	65	15
3	Learning processes	292	212	77	3
4	Focus on students	355	223	114	18
5	Focus on teachers	235	209	22	4

The visualization in Fig. 1 clearly illustrates that teacher-level best practices cover learning content, student-centered activities, learning processes and teaching improvement. At the same time, school-level activities are student-oriented, covering the learning environment and learning processes. The policy-level activities are oriented to students and learning content.

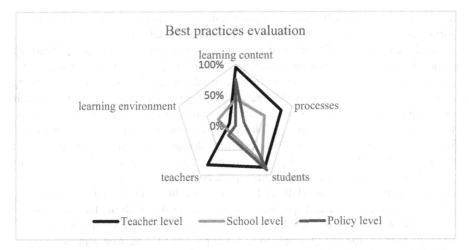

Fig. 1. Best practices evaluation and assessment by categories, following the model of [16].

4.2 Digital Transformation of Schools and Best Practices

The analysis of the best practices clearly demonstrates that students appreciate the best practices on the individual teacher level. Many students directly mention their beloved teachers' names, often speaking with respect and gratitude for people who personally motivated them and worked additionally to support their students' extra-curriculum assignments and academic interests. Students often recognize that their favorite teachers used traditional methods of teaching, making regular tests, imposing strict discipline and presenting always well prepared in class. The best teachers are proud in their profession and make a difference through demonstrating personal commitment, manifesting respect, responsibility and strong discipline in their work. At the same time, the best teachers are encouraging, open to questions and accessible, providing a personalized approach to explain, visualize and present interestingly the learning material. They are used to challenge their students, engage them in numerous activities, put high expectations and raise their confidence and resilience, motivation for self-learning and development.

In this perspective, in the first place, digital transformation in schools should support teachers to operate with more engaging tools and techniques for designing more complex learning experiences. Interactive tools can enable teachers to improve, on the one side, learning content visualization and explanation, and on the another side, to combine the online content with engaging class debates and discussions, personalizing teaching practices to students' level and applying tools for immediate feedback of the student's progress. In the DigiLEAD guidelines materials are specifically described good practices of using innovative teaching and learning methods, emphasizing on the role of both digital and in-presence activities [9]. This way, teachers should focus to design learning experiences through a complex sequence of "phygital" activities, adapting learning content and learning processes in a personalized manner [17].

More specifically, the DigiLEAD guidelines provide practical steps and action plan how school leaders and teachers can promote the use of innovative pedagogies (flipped classroom, IBL, game-based learning), techniques for learning experience design (learning personalization), competence-based learning, and design of inclusive learning activities, learning materials and assessment models [9].

At the school level, digital transformation concerns school infrastructure, learning and teaching processes, directed to students' personal and academic development. Students mention in many cases the importance of additional classes, clubs and learning competitions, raising their motivation and challenging them to learn more, applying their knowledge in practice, to network and develop soft skills, which are hardly addressed in the school curriculum. Young people clearly evaluate their limits to prepare alone for the new coming challenges. Therefore, they demand better support at the teacher and at school level – additional practice works, robotics clubs and ICT hackathons, guest-lecturers from industry and internships in companies, career counselling services and opportunities for raising skills and competences. In the DigiLEAD guidelines are addressed good practices and specific strategies for dealing with digital infrastructure needs. More resources and focus should be put on building strong communities and managing the needs of the young people to be better prepared for the new coming economy and society [9].

On the policy level, data reveal that digital transformation processes should encourage more initiatives to support new generation of students and young people in schools. It is important to highlight that students are not aware of the efforts and strategies on policy level and how they transform into school-level practices. Learning and training in the digital world require increasing personal involvement, long-term commitment and persistence from teachers and schools. Thus, policy initiatives should reflect strategies and combine different approaches for ensure successful digital transformation in secondary education.

5 Conclusion

The present study discusses good practices identified in primary and secondary education and reflects on the value-creation processes for the learners in schools. The analysis of the best practices proves that a school's digital transformation should mainly focus on students' potential to form skills and competencies in the digital world, building self-confidence and resilience.

The DigiLEAD approach for the digital transformation of schools is aligned with the main findings of the present research and proposes practical guidelines for school leaders and teachers. More importantly, the research outlines that in many cases the policy efforts remain invisible to students, but it should provide the general strategy, plan the directions and digital transformation paths, ensuring the right culture and teacher' engagement for a high-quality future education.

Acknowledgement. The authors gratefully acknowledge the support provided by the project UNITe - BG05M2OP001–1.001–0004 funded by the OP SESG and co-funded by the EU Structural and Investment Funds, and the project DigiLEAD project - 2021–1-BG01-4KA220-SCH-000032711 funded by ERASMUS+ programme.

References

1. Ebner, M., et al.: Digital transformation of teaching and perception at TU Graz from the students' perspective: developments from the last 17 years. In: Auer, M.E., Pachatz, W., Rüütmann, T. (eds.) Learning in the Age of Digital and Green Transition. ICL 2022. Lecture Notes in Networks and Systems, vol. 633, pp. 366–377. Springer, Cham (2023). https://doi.org/10.1007/978-3-031-26876-2_34
2. Oke, A., Fernandes, F.A.P.: Innovations in teaching and learning: exploring the perceptions of the education sector on the 4th industrial revolution (4IR). J. Open Innov. Technol. Mark. Complex. 6(2), 31 (2020)
3. Maytha AL-Ali, M., Marks, A.: A digital maturity model for the education enterprise. Perspect. Policy Pract. High. Educ. 26(2), 47–58 (2022)
4. Heavin, C., Power, D.J.: Challenges for digital transformation – towards a conceptual decision support guide for managers. J. Decis. Syst. 27(1), 38–45 (2018)
5. König, J., Jäger-Biela, D.J., Glutsch, N.: Adapting to online teaching during COVID-19 school closure: teacher education and teacher competence effects among early career teachers in Germany. Eur. J. Teach. Educ. 43(4), 608–622 (2020)
6. Lien, C.M., Khan, S., Eid, J.: School principals' experiences and learning from the COVID-19 pandemic in Norway. Scand. J. Educ. Res. 67, 775–790 (2022). https://doi.org/10.1080/00313831.2022.2043430
7. European Commission: Digital Education Action Plan 2021–2027. Resetting education and training for the digital age, COM/2020/624 final
8. Sailer, M., Murbock, J., Fischer, F.: Digital learning in schools: what does it take beyond digital technology? Teach. Teach. Educ. 103, 1–13 (2021)
9. Strategy Toolkit on digital transformation for school leaders. https://digilead-project.eu/toolkit/. Accessed 14 May 2023
10. Hai, T.N., Van, Q.N., Thi Tuyet, M.N.: Digital transformation: opportunities and challenges for leaders in the emerging countries in response to covid-19 pandemic. Emerg. Sci. J. 5, 21–36 (2021)
11. Gura, M.: The Edtech Advocate's Guide to Leading Change in Schools. International Society for Technology in Education (2018)
12. European Commission: European Education Area- Quality education and training for all. SELFIE (2019). https://education.ec.europa.eu/selfie. Accessed 14 May 2023
13. MENTEP project. TET - SAT. Technology-Enhanced Teaching - Self Assessment Tool. http://mentep.cti.gr/tet-sat. Accessed 14 May 2023
14. Carrillo, C., Flores, M.A.: COVID-19 and teacher education: a literature review of online teaching and learning practices. Eur. J. Teach. Educ. 43(4), 466–487 (2020)
15. Kearney, M., Schuck, S., Burden, K.: Digital pedagogies for future school education: promoting inclusion. Irish Educ. Stud. 41(1), 117–133 (2022)
16. Papanthymou, A., Darra, M.: Defining quality in primary and secondary education. Int. Educ. Stud. 16(2), 128–149 (2023). https://doi.org/10.5539/ies.v16n2p128
17. Antonova, A., Dankov, Y.: Smart services in education: facilitating teachers to deliver personalized learning experiences. In: Silhavy, R., Silhavy, P., Prokopova, Z. (eds.) Data Science and Algorithms in Systems. CoMeSySo 2022. Lecture Notes in Networks and Systems, vol. 597, pp. 108–117. Springer, Cham (2023).https://doi.org/10.1007/978-3-031-21438-7_9

TeamUp: Form Best Project Teams

Dawei Yin, Sha Hu, and Yuting Zhang[✉]

Boston University, Boston, MA 02215, USA
{davidyin,baymax,danazh}@bu.edu

Abstract. Team formation is a critical task in many contexts such as business, sports, healthcare, research, education, and more. In the academic settings, students working in teams on group projects is proven to be a very effective learning methodology. Our software engineering course features a semester-long team project as the key component of this course. However, team assignments are complex and nontrivial tasks, necessitating a careful assessment of many different factors to ensure optimal performance of the team as well as individual participants' satisfaction. Usually a predefined set of questions are used to understand participant's capabilities and preferences, and teams are formed either manually or automatically based on the results of those questions. In this paper, we propose a generalized question definition by associating each question with three factors: multiple choice/multiple answer, similarity or diversity, and option valuation, in order to consider various types of factors, provide flexibility and capture each individual's characteristics. We then propose two team performance score functions that differentiate similarity questions from diversity questions and capture each of their team formation objectives. A heuristic team formation algorithm, TeamUp, is proposed, attempting to maximize the team performance as well as participants' preferences. Through the initial evaluation we show our proposed algorithm can perform well for different team size and type of questions.

Keywords: team formation · team project · project-based learning

1 Introduction

Team formation is a critical task in many contexts such as business, sports, healthcare, research, education, and more. Whether in academic settings or professional environments, the effective team composition can significantly enhance the success and outcomes of the tasks at hand. However, team assignments can be complex and nontrivial tasks, necessitating a careful assessment of many different factors to ensure optimal performance of the team as well as individual participants' satisfaction. Usually a predefined set of questions are used

© ICST Institute for Computer Sciences, Social Informatics and Telecommunications Engineering 2023
Published by Springer Nature Switzerland AG 2023. All Rights Reserved
T. Zlateva and G. Tuparov (Eds.): CSECS 2023, LNICST 514, pp. 372–384, 2023.
https://doi.org/10.1007/978-3-031-44668-9_29

to understand participant's capabilities and preferences, and teams are formed either manually or automatically based on the results of those questions. While the question content is context dependent, we can categorize possible question types to capture different situations. In this paper, we propose the consideration of three factors and define 6 different questions types. We also propose a team formation algorithm that can take into consideration all those factors and this diverse set of question types.

Students working in teams on group projects is proven to be a very effective learning methodology in the academic setting. Particularly, in the software engineering field, almost all software is developed by teams of developers collaboratively. In order to help students experience this collaboration in real world settings, our software engineering course features a semester-long group project as the key component of this course. As our students are a mix of full-time and part-time graduate students with very diverse backgrounds, schedules, and even time zones (for the online course), and most students don't know each other before taking the class, team assignments are very challenging for the instructors. Usually the instructor and the TAs need to spend quite an amount of time on this task and there is no guarantee that the teams are formed well. The proposed algorithm can help automate this complex process and enhance possible team performance in this course and many other courses that have similar team project components.

In order to facilitate the creation of well-balanced and high-performing project teams, we need to first have a thorough understanding of the diverse preferences, skills, and characteristics of each participant. The data is usually collected through a set of predefined survey questions that participants need to fill out. Multi-choice questions are commonly used and the team formation criteria are usually to try to group individuals with the same choice for those questions. For example, the question "What technology stack do you want to use in your project?" can be used in the Software Engineering course, however, it doesn't provide flexibility for students who can use multiple technology stacks and it also doesn't capture the individual skills and capability of students in that technology stack. Multi-answer questions may be used here to allow students to choose multiple technology stacks, however, it still doesn't reflect students' preferences and capability in each of the technology stacks they choose. Furthermore, while we want to team up students that want to use the same technology stack to improve the team performance, we also want to diversify other factors in a team such as gender and work roles preferences. In our Software Engineering course, each team has different roles such as team leader, requirement leader, design and implementation leader, QA leader, and etc. We would better team up students with preferences and suitability in different roles rather than the same roles. To consider all the above issues, we associate each question with three factors: the number of choices each participant can choose, the similarity or diversity of participants' choices that should be in a team, as well as the capability or preferences value of each choice. Through these three factors we can represent a wide range of questions with a uniform definition of question, and our algorithms aim to enhance both individual preferences and team performance by considering all those three factors, in order to generate optimized team formation to promote collaboration, complimentary, and ultimately, successful project outcomes. **The contributions of this paper** is summarized as follows:

1. Propose a generalized question definition by associating each question with three factors: multiple choice/multiple answer, similarity or diversity, and option valuation. In particular, by allowing participants to assign values to options, it can capture the relative preferences or expertise of participants associated with each option. This enables more precise and tailored team compositions, allowing that participants with specific skills or preferences are appropriately assigned to project groups.
2. Propose two team performance score functions that differentiate similarity questions from diversity questions and capture each of their team formation objectives.
3. Propose a heuristic team formation algorithm, TeamUp, that attempts to maximize the team performance as well as participants' preferences. The initial evaluation shows its efficiency and effectiveness.

The remaining sections are organized as follows. Section 2 details how our research relates and differs from some other related work. Section 3 provides a detailed description of the problem, in particular defines the supported questions that consider three refactors mentioned above, and the algorithm TeamUp is described in Sect. 4. Then we used a generated synthetic data to evaluate the algorithms and show its efficiency and effectiveness in Sect. 5. Finally we conclude our paper and list some future work in Sect. 6.

2   Related Work

The TeamMaker system, developed by Layton, et al. [1] is the most similar work to ours. It forms teams based on instructor-defined criteria using a max-min heuristic. TeamMaker supports various types of questions, including multiple-choice and multiple-answer questions. While they have defined different score functions for multiple-choice and multiple-answer questions, both functions primarily rely on the number of options chosen by team members. A higher value indicates greater diversity. They differentiate similarity and diversity by assigning negative weights to similarity questions and positive weights to diversity questions. However, we argue that this score definition fails to capture the importance of measuring the degree of similarity based on the number of team members choosing the same option. For instance, in a team of 10 members, if 9 students choose one option and 1 student chooses another option, the score would be the same as a scenario where 5 students choose one option and 5 students choose another option, since both cases have two options chosen. In contrast, our algorithm defines distinct score functions for similarity and diversity questions, effectively capturing the dynamics of each question type. Additionally, we empower participants to assign values to options, allowing us to incorporate their capabilities and preferences in team formation, thereby enhancing team performance and meeting the participants' preferences.

Meulbroek, Ferguson, Ohland, and Berry [2] proposed an extension to'TeamMaker" by using the Gale-Shapley algorithm to form initial teams. However, their approach requires preference list from both students and instructors, which does not align with the general case defined in our algorithm. Thus, for team initialization, we opted simple random assignment for initial team formation, similar to the example in [9]. This choice was made to diminish the complexity of the subsequent team member swaps.

Several work only underscored the importance of heterogeneity in group dynamics and leveraged genetic algorithms to optimize team heterogeneity [3,6], [7,8]. Additionally, [4] focuses on role assignment within the group, and [5] studies optimization of team assignments in emergency departments. Our goal, instead, is to form the groups based on various factors , while taking consideration of role assignments through diversity questions.

3   Problem Definition

Suppose we have the participant set as $P = \{p_i | i = 0, ..., N\}$, and we need to form M teams $T = \{T_i | i = 1, ..., M\}$. We represent the participant p_i assigned to the team t_j as $team(p_i) = T_j$. The size of the team T_j is $|T_j|$, which is the number of participants in that team.

The team formation criteria is defined through a set of K survey questions $Q = \{q_i | i = 1, ..., K\}$, with each question q_i associated with a weight w_i. The default value of w_i is 1. We differentiate two types of questions in the formation criteria, namely similarity questions and diversity questions. Similarity questions aim to identify commonalities or preferences for the same or similar options among team members, while diversity questions focus on differences or preferences for diverse perspectives within each group. Therefore, it is intended to group participants with same/similar responses to the similarity questions and group participants with different responses to the diversity questions.

For each question q_j, we define given options as a set of options $O^j = \{o_i^j | i = 1, ... | O^j |\}$, where $|O^j|$ is the total number of given options for question q_j. In order to provide participants more flexibility and capture participants' preferences or capabilities on the given options, we define the response of each participant p_i to Question q_j as

$$R_j^i = (index(o_m^j), value(o_m^j)) | m = 1...maxO^j \tag{1}$$

where $index(o_m^j)$ is the index of the chosen option and $value(o_m^j)$ is the value associated with that option. By default, the value is between 1 to 5, with 5 representing the highest capability or preferences of the participant to that option. If the participant doesn't specify the value, a default value of 5 will be used.

$maxO^j$ is the maximum number of options that a participant can choose for question q_j. It can also be customized. A multiple choice question restricts that number to be 1 as each participant can only choose one option, while a multi-answer question enables the participants to choose more than 1 option, possibly all options.

In summary, our problem definition consider the following factors that can capture the intricacies of team dynamics and affect the team formation:

1. A weight for each question to specify the importance of the question in the team formation
2. A type (S or D) for each question to differentiate the team formation criteria in similarity questions from diversity questions
3. The maximum number of options a participant can choose to provide participants more flexibility in their response
4. The capability or preference value of the chosen option in participant's response to reflect each individual characteristic.

The goal is to form teams that can maximize the team performance as well as individual preferences.

4   Algorithm

4.1   Objective Function

In order to maximize the team performance and participants' preferences, we define the team performance score for each team T_z as the weighted summation of the team score in each question.

$$Score(T_z) = \sum_{i=0}^{K} Score_i^z * w_i \tag{2}$$

where $score_i^z$ is the score of team T_z for question q_i, and w_i is the weight for question q_i and K is the total number of questions.

As the team criteria is different in similarity and diversity questions, we define two different score functions for them:

Similarity Question: The performance score of a team T_z for a similarity question q_m is defined as

$$Score\_similar_z^m = \frac{1}{|T_z|} \max_{i=1}^{|O_m|} (\sum_{j=0}^{|T_z|} val_j^{i,m}) \tag{3}$$

where $|T_z|$ is the size of the team T_z, that is the number of participants in the team. $|O_m|$ is the number of given options in question q_m. $val_j^{i,m}$ is the jth participant's specified value for question q_m's the ith option o_i^m. If a participant doesn't choose that option, that value is 0. If the question doesn't need the participant to specify the value, a default value of 5 will be used instead.

For similarity questions, we would like to team up participants who choose the same options and maximize that similarity. In addition, we consider each individual participant's capability or preference value and attempt to maximize that value for each option as well. Therefore, we define each option's similarity performance score as the summation of each participant's value for that option. This value increases if more participants choose this option, or participants set higher option value to this option, indicating higher capability or preferences for this option. To maximize that similarity, we choose the highest option score as the question score, as the option with the highest score will be mostly the favored option for the team. If all team members choose the same option and set the option value as 5, then the team score for the question will be the highest value 5.

This can be better understood with the following example. Suppose in the Software Engineering course survey, we have the following similarity question: "Which programming languages would you like to use in your project and rate your proficiency in each programming language that you choose, with 5 being the highest proficiency." Assume that we have the response of each team member in Table 1:

Table 1. Similarity Question Example

Team Member	Java	Python	C++	R
Participant 1	5			
Participant 2		4		
Participant 3	3			
Participant 4			3	
Participant 5		3		
Summarize option value	8	7	3	0

After we summarize all participant's option value for each option, we could find the highest sum is for option "Java", which may be the favorite programming language to be used by the team. The team performance score is therefore set as

$$S = \frac{1}{5} * val_{Java} = \frac{1}{5} * 8 = 1.6 \tag{4}$$

Diversity Question: On the contrary, the performance score of a team T_z for a diversity question q_m is defined as

$$S\_diversity_z^m = \frac{1}{|O_m|}\left(\sum_{i=1}^{|O_m|} \max_{j=1}^{|T_z|}(val_j^{i,m})\right) \tag{5}$$

All annotations are the same as in the previous similarity case, where $|T_z|$ is the size of the team T_z, that is the number of participants in the team. $|O_m|$ is the number of given options in question q_m. $val_j^{i,m}$ is the jth participant's specified value for question q_m's the ith option o_i^m. If a participant doesn't choose that option, that value is 0. If the question doesn't need the participant to specify the value, a default value of 5 will be used instead.

For diversity questions, we would like to team up participants who choose different options and maximize that diversity. In addition, we consider each individual participant's capability or preference value and attempt to maximize the overall value of different options. Therefore, the team members who choose the same options do not add the additional value to diversity. Each option's value is only determined by the highest option value of all team members who choose that option. To maximize the diversity, we define the performance score as the summation of all option's value. This score increases if more participants choose different options or various participants set higher value for different options. In the most diverse case, where all options are chosen by the team with highest value assigned to each option, the value will also be 5, the highest possible value.

This can be better understood with the following example. Suppose in the Software Engineering course survey, we have the following diversity question: "Which leader role would you like to take in your project and rate your preferences in each role that you choose, with 5 being the highest preference." Assume that we have the response of each team member in Table 2:

Table 2. Diversity Question Example

Team member	Team leader	Design leader	Security leader	Testing leader
Participant 1	4			
Participant 2		5		
Participant 3	3			
Participant 4			3	
Participant 5		3		
highest option value	4	5	3	0

After we get the highest score of all participants' value for each option, we could calculate the performance score for the question as the average score of all option values

$$S = \frac{1}{4} * sum(val) = \frac{1}{4} * (4 + 5 + 3) = \frac{1}{4} * 12 = 3 \qquad (6)$$

4.2 Find Best Team Formation

In order to maximize overall team performance score and minimize the worst performance team defined above, we adopt a heuristic swapping algorithm similar to the one defined in [1] by swapping team members from two different teams if this swap can improve the performance.

First, we perform an initial random team assignments. Then we initiate an iterative process encompassing pairs of two teams to perform the swap. The swap algorithm in [1] consider all possible pairs of team, which has a n^2 complexity, where n is the total number of participants. This cause the algorithm extremely slow. To reduce the complexity and enhance the efficiency, we will consider the swap of only adjacent pairs of teams. Starting with the first adjacent pair, we probe potential member exchanges between the two teams under consideration. Upon identifying an exchange that can result in the enhancement of the minimum team score within that adjacent pair, we implement this exchange. Consequently, we then shift our focus to the subsequent pair of adjacent teams. This systematic approach of exploring and actualizing advantageous member exchanges perpetuates sequentially through all pairs of adjacent teams as described in the Algorithm 1.

In every "Pass", an iterative process takes place which can include a number of iterations until a round is completed without any team member swaps. Each Pass essentially constitutes a thorough traversal of the initial team, with the aim of achieving an optimal arrangement of team members. Given that the initial team assignments are random, we can enhance the significance of our results by setting up additional initial teams. This gives us multiple possible Pass results, and we select the pass that gives the highest minimum team score to be our final team assignment outcome.

Algorithm 1. One-time Iteration Algorithm

Input: Initial Team assignments and corresponding team scores
Output: New team assignments and team scores after swapping

1: Initialize pointer $p \leftarrow 0$
2: **while** p is not at the last team index **do**
3:     $swap\_status \leftarrow$ False
4:     **for** each member i in $team[p]$ **do**
5:         **for** each member j in $team[p+1]$ **do**
6:             **if** $swap(i,j)$ leads to improvement in the minimum team score **then**
7:                 Perform $swap(i,j)$
8:                 $swap\_status \leftarrow$ True
9:                 **break**
10:             **end if**
11:         **end for**
12:         **if** $swap\_status$ **then**
13:             **break**
14:         **end if**
15:     **end for**
16:     $p \leftarrow p+1$
17: **end while**
18: **return** TeamScores

Table 3. Results Of the Four Passes

Pass Min. Score	Team Scores						
	Te. 1	Te. 2	Te. 3	Te. 4	Te. 5	Te. 6	Te. 7
Pass 1 1.2	3.9	7.6	1.2	6.5	8.3	5.7	9.1
Pass 2 1.5	4.6	8.5	2.3	3.8	7.9	9.2	1.5
Pass 3 3.7	9.2	6.3	3.7	7.1	5.9	8.4	4.8
Pass 4 2.9	5.1	9.8	2.9	4.2	6.7	8.1	3.6

For example, divide the class into 7 teams and complete 4 rounds. Suppose the score in each pass is shown in Table 3. According to results of the four passes, the maximum minimum score achieved is 3.7. Therefore, based on the grouping result, pass 3 is our final grouping decision. This can be seen more clearly in Table 3.

5 Evaluation

This section aims to evaluate the performance of our heuristic team formation algorithm. As our algorithm differentiates similarity from diversity questions, where the goal is to group participants with the same responses for similarity questions, and group participants with different responses for diversity questions, we define the following performance metrics for each case to evaluate the performance:

For similarity questions, we assume that the option that receives the highest value from all team members will be the favorite option for the team. More members choose that option, higher the similarity. On the other hand, more options are chosen by the team members, higher the diversity. Therefore, we considered the following **performance metrics**:

1. performance score: this is calculated based on the score function defined in the previous section.
2. similarity degree: average percentage of members choosing the favored option in a team.
3. diversity degree: average percentage of choices chosen by members.

Experiment Setup: The simulation data we generate for this study serves to recreate a situation where we have 200 individuals responding to a series of questions. These responses are then utilized to assemble groups of varying sizes. The group sizes considered in our study include groups of 2, 5, and 10 participants, representing small, medium, and large groups, respectively. This experiment is repeated 10 times to increase the robustness of our findings. Each participant is tasked with responding to a total of 8 questions, each question with 5 given options. To be applicable to a broad range of real-world scenarios, we consider 4 types of questions, with 2 questions in each category. They are similarity questions with variable option value (SimVal), similarity questions without option value (SimNoVal), diversity questions with variable option value (DivVal) and diversity questions without option value (DivNoVal).

Statistical Test: We compared our TeamUp algorithm with a basic random assignment algorithm and the team-maker algorithm respectively across different team sizes. In our analysis, we employ the t-test as our primary statistical test. The t-test is a popular statistical test that is used to determine if there is a significant difference between the means of two groups. In the context of our evaluation, the t-test is used to assess whether the performance metrics of our algorithm significantly differ from the other two approaches.

Performance Score. The team performance score are shown in Fig. 1a and 1b. It shows that TeamUp consistently outperforms the random assignments and Team-Maker no matter what the team size is. The difference in mean performance scores was statistically significant, as established by a paired t-test (t(df) = value, $p < .05$), underscoring the superior effectiveness of TeamUp in fostering high-performing teams.

Interestingly, the performance scores yielded by the Team-Maker system were not only lower than those of TeamUp but also underperformed relative to random group assignments. This finding suggests possible limitations in the Team-Maker, particularly in its ability to effectively incorporate participant response option values as grouping criteria. Such an inability may potentially impede its capacity to form optimal groupings that maximize performance scores.

Similarity Degree. When evaluating the average percentage of team members selecting their preferred option, TeamUp consistently demonstrates superior performance compared to other methods. This superior performance is maintained across a variety of team sizes and for both fixed and variable option value questions. This suggests that TeamUp more effectively aligns teams according to individual participant preferences, which could facilitate improved team harmony and effectiveness.

Interestingly, as team size increases, there is a general trend across all methods indicating a decrease in the likelihood of individual team members selecting their preferred options. This is likely due to the natural dilution effect of larger teams, where individual preferences have less influence. However, despite this trend, TeamUp continues to outperform other methods, further underscoring its utility in team formation, even as team size scales up (Fig. 2).

Diversity Degree. In addition, TeamUp significantly outperforms both the random allocation method and the team maker tool when considering the average percentage of distinct options chosen by team members. This suggests that, on average, TeamUp is more effective at assembling teams wherein members favor a variety of options, in both fixed and variable choice value situations.

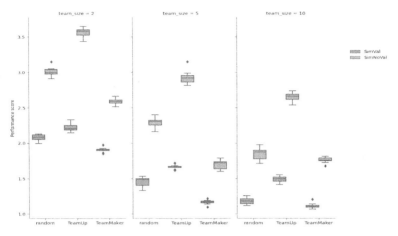

(a) Similarity question performance score comparison

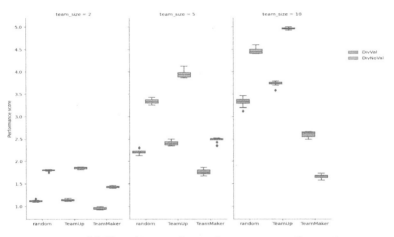

(b) Diversity question performance score Comparison

Fig. 1. Comparison of performance scores

Notably, as the team size increases under fixed option conditions, all grouping methods tend to facilitate a higher degree of diversity. This could be attributed to the increased possibility of each option being chosen as team size grows, thus maximizing the representation of different preferences within a team. This diversity is a potential asset, promoting a broader range of perspectives and skills within each team (Fig. 3).

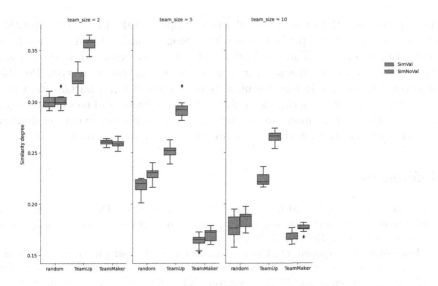

Fig. 2. Similarity Degree Comparison

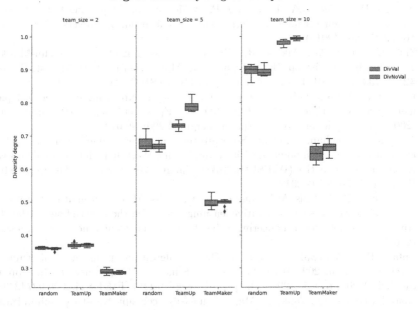

Fig. 3. Diversity Degree Comparison

6   Conclusion and Future Work

In this paper, we present TeamUp, a heuristic team formation algorithm based on survey results related to various types of questions. These questions encompass factors such as multiple-choice or multiple-answer options, similarity or diversity aspects, and the presence or absence of option valuation. Our algorithm aims to maximize team performance while accommodating the individual preferences of participants. Through initial evaluations, we demonstrate the efficacy of our proposed algorithm across different team sizes and question types. Possible improvements include implementing a more intelligent team initialization process, refining the swap method for enhanced effectiveness, and considering team size variations. Furthermore, we intend to conduct a comprehensive evaluation to further explore the algorithm's enhancements and applicability.

References

1. Layton, R.A., Loughry, M.L., Ohland, M.W., Ricco, G.D.: Design and validation of a web-based system for assigning members to teams using instructor-specified criteria. Adv. Eng. Educ. **2**, 1–28 (2010)
2. Meulbroek, D., Ferguson, D., Ohland, M., Berry, F.: Forming more effective teams using CATME teammaker and the gale-shapley algorithm. In: 2019 IEEE Frontiers in Education Conference (FIE), Covington, KY, USA, pp. 1–5, (2019). https://doi.org/10.1109/FIE43999.2019.9028552
3. Paredes, P., Ortigosa, A., Rodriguez, P.: A Method for Supporting Heterogeneous-Group Formation through Heuristics and Visualization. J. Univers. Comput. Sci. **16**, 2882–2901 (2010)
4. Zhu, H., Zhou, M., Alkins, R.: Group role assignment via a Kuhn-Munkres algorithm-based solution. IEEE Trans. Syst. Man Cybern. - Part A: Syst. Humans **42**(3), 739–750 (2012). https://doi.org/10.1109/TSMCA.2011.2170414
5. Patel, P.B., Vinson, D.R.: Team assignment system: expediting emergency department care. Ann. Emerg. Med. 46(6):499–506. Epub 2005 Sep 1. PMID: 16308063 (2005). https://doi.org/10.1016/j.annemergmed.2005.06.012
6. Assavakamhaenghan, N., et al.: Software team member configurations: a study of team effectiveness in moodle. In: 10th International Workshop on Empirical Software Engineering in Practice (IWESEP), Tokyo, Japan, (2019). https://doi.org/10.1109/IWESEP49350.2019.00012
7. Cavanaugh, R.M., Ellis, M.L., Layton, R.A., Ardis, M.A.: Automating the process of assigning students to cooperative learning teams. In: the Proceedings of the 2004 American Society for Engineering Education Annual Conference and Exposition (2004)
8. Imbrie, P.K., Agarwal, J., Raju, G.: Genetic algorithm optimization of teams for heterogeneity. In: 2020 IEEE Frontiers in Education Conference (FIE), Uppsala, Sweden, 2020, pp. 1–5, (2020). https://doi.org/10.1109/FIE44824.2020.9274243
9. Xiao, L., Huang, Q., Yank, V., Ma, J.: An easily accessible web-based minimization random allocation system for clinical trials. J. Med. Internet Res. **15**(7), e139 (2013). https://doi.org/10.2196/jmir.2392

An Empirical Study of Student Perceptions When Using ChatGPT in Academic Assignments

Vijay Kanabar[(✉)]

Boston University, Metropolitan College, Boston, MA 02215, USA
kanabar@bu.edu

Abstract. This research paper investigates students' perceptions of using Chat-GPT, an AI-based language model, in academic assignments in a project management course. The study analyzes responses to an anonymous survey that explores the value, ease of use, extent of usage, and ethical considerations of using ChatGPT in homework. The results suggest that while most students find the tool helpful, they prefer to use it only as a supplementary resource. Students are concerned about actual learning and whether critical thinking skills can be successfully acquired when AI-based tools are used to generate essays. The survey reveals that student reaction teethers between acceptance and rejection. The paper concludes by assessing the deliverables from students and guides the informed use of tools such as ChatGPT in traditional college courses.

Keywords: AI Tools · ChatGPT · Teaching and Learning

1 Introduction

In the aftermath of ChatGPT's introduction in November 2022, every instructor and professor, regardless of their primary discipline, is suddenly facing a new reality—do we embrace generative AI Tools in our courses or ban them outright? Plagiarism was evidently a big risk and was being raised all around in academia. Even though many promising tools to detect the use of tools like ChatGPT emerged on the horizon, none of them provided the ironclad guarantee that educators need when assessing student deliverables. It was clear by early 2023 that banning such tools would not be a workable strategy. Faced with this new reality, faculty in individual departments and programs were left to use their best judgment to address such tools within the context of their coursework.

In this paper, we provide details of how ChatGPT was used in an assignment. We follow it up by testing two hypotheses – a) an assessment of student perception of its use in academic coursework and b) the ethical use of ChatGPT for learning. The paper will contribute to the emerging knowledge on using AI Tools in academic work.

© ICST Institute for Computer Sciences, Social Informatics and Telecommunications Engineering 2023
Published by Springer Nature Switzerland AG 2023. All Rights Reserved
T. Zlateva and G. Tuparov (Eds.): CSECS 2023, LNICST 514, pp. 385–398, 2023.
https://doi.org/10.1007/978-3-031-44668-9_30

1.1   AI and ChatGPT

Before addressing how to adapt and work with the new reality, let us introduce AI and describe how ChatGPT works. AI stands for artificial intelligence; from our context, it is intelligence captured in software and exhibited by it. The Oxford Dictionary defines intelligence as "the ability to acquire and apply knowledge and skills." With human beings, this process begins very early on. Babies recognize objects and learn to communicate and manage them early in life. They begin building a vocabulary database to obtain what they seek early on. It is inevitable that as they become adults, their vocabulary and natural intelligence will be impressive. Since the earliest AI systems were designed, our goal has been to mimic human beings' generative and conversational intelligence. IBM's Watson, one of the earliest successful AI systems, claims it is one of the first AI chatbots—that it is easy to use and that Watson understands natural language and human conversation very well [1].

This is an excellent segue to introducing ChatGPT. According to Open AI the vendor for this product, this AI tool should be known as "Chat with GPT". Its strength is its competency as an interactive chatbot that uses artificial intelligence to generate human-like responses to user input.

GPT stands for Generative Pre-trained Transformer. The term Generative implies that words are generated, Pre-trained because the AI system needs to digest tons of data and information from provided databases. Transformers provide impressive text generation to image creation abilities. Transformers improved upon the previous generation of neural networks—known as recurrent neural networks—by including steps that process the words of a sentence in parallel rather than one at a time, making them faster [2]. In other words, the ChatGPT transformer does not process words sequentially, one at a time, but instead processes the entire input simultaneously. Due to this and the thousands of hours engineers invested in fine-tuning and training the GPT models, ChatGPT can answer any query you ask fluently. This is the perfect time to state that not all its responses are accurate or truthful. The term hallucination describes the state in which a GPT gives completely incorrect responses.

1.2   Understanding GPTs

GPT uses machine learning techniques to analyze sizeable human language datasets and generate contextually appropriate and linguistically sophisticated responses. The core of an A.I. program like ChatGPT is a significant language model: an algorithm that mimics the form of written language. Let us trace ChatGPT to a case study vividly described as Baby GPT by Bhatia see [2]. In this article, a BabyGPT—which has no data at all, to begin with, is pre-trained by reading the complete works of Jane Austen. It trains, encodes, or learns just the 800 thousand words in the provided text—and nothing else. After the first iteration of training, Baby GPT produces total gibberish when asked to answer or auto-complete the prompt: "You must decide for yourself," said Elizabeth.

Before training: Gibberish. But after 500 rounds—or about a minute on a laptop—it can spell a few small words such as the following the sample text:

"You must decide for yourself, said Elizabeth, ra but riteand the uth this hat say not shnd she for the seer refer of in he he was atte.." [2].

After 30,000 rounds, an hour into its training, BabyGPT is learning to speak in full sentences even though some of the generated sentences do not make sense:

"You must decide for yourself," said Elizabeth, rather repeatedly; "that is very agreeable displeasure, they will ever be a lively young woman as it will be more disagreeable." [2].

In just an hour of training on a laptop using *nanoGPT*, the language model created by Andrej Karpathy, went from generating random characters to a very crude approximation of language.

Other tools like Google's Bard and ChatGPT 4 are currently available. However, our paper focuses on ChatGPT 3 as it is freely available, and students have ready access to it. GPT-3 is very powerful–it has 175 billion parameters, making it a potent language model. This model demonstrated impressive performance on various natural language processing tasks and has been used in various applications, including chatbots, language learning tools, and content creation platforms.

1.3 ChatGPT in Education

Academics and practitioners have started exploring the use of ChatGPT for research and real-world applications [3–9]. When we started researching this topic, only a few papers were available. Newspapers and Media headlines were the sources to go to for an understanding of the role of ChatGPT and education. Since then, a search of Google Scholar reveals an explosion of work done with ChatGPT. The papers reflect a rich variety as well, such as: "Education in the era of generative artificial intelligence (AI): Understanding the potential benefits of ChatGPT in promoting teaching and learning",

"ChatGPT for education and research: A review of benefits and risks.", "Role of ChatGPT in education." or "What is the impact of ChatGPT on education? A rapid review of the literature" [17–20].

Beth McMurtrie, in her blog in the Chronicle of Higher Education [21] describes how academia reacted to a semester of dealing with generative AI, "Some faculty members enthusiastically embrace a future in which these programs become part of everyday life, because they can help reduce time on routine tasks, function as a personal tutor, or kick start ideas for essays and research papers. Many—including some of these AI enthusiasts—are deeply worried that students have been handed a powerful tool that comes without a training manual, so there's no way to tell whether it's producing insights or inaccuracies. They also fear that students may become willing to cede the difficult work of critical thinking and analysis in favor of a time-saving device that can churn out a quick discussion post or essay." In this paper, we refrain from further expanding on the significance of generative AI in education as it is out of scope. However, the above makes it evident that ChatGPT will be a critical tool to explore in academia.

2 Using ChatGPT for Research and Assignments

In this section, we describe how and why ChatGPT was introduced to students to assist them with their assignments. The earliest media stories fascinatingly described the potential and ability of ChatGPT to pass exams. Evaluating ChatGPT's ability to solve higher-order questions on the competency-based medical education curriculum in medical biochemistry, Ghosh & Bir demonstrated research results indicating that ChatGPT has the potential to be a successful tool for answering questions requiring higher-order thinking in medical biochemistry [5]. ChatGPT has passed several exams in different fields, including law, business, and medicine. For instance 2023, ChatGPT passed a law exam at the University of Minnesota Law School, a business exam at the Wharton School of Business, and a clinical reasoning exam at Stanford Medical School [10].

Our own research providing ChatGPT tests and assignments from previous semesters yielded remarkable results. In each case, ChatGPT scored very good to excellent grades. With such promising results, we decided to unbridle the use of ChatGPT for student use in assignments.

A range of emotions swelled in academia early in our semester, ranging from "ban the use of AI" to "embrace it." There were good points made for each sentiment. But advances in the field were moving at breathtaking speed. After substantial research and brainstorming with colleagues, it was evident that the use of ChatGPT in courses I coordinated needed to be addressed.

With headlines such as *ChatGPT is about to revolutionize the economy. We need to decide what that looks like* (MIT Technology Review) [11]; we indeed decided to move forward to encourage students to leverage the use of ChatGPT in their assignments.

The following two points prevailed in motivating our approach to allow the use of ChatGPT by students in their classwork.

- As documented earlier, GPT was undoubtedly intelligent– passing exams across disciplines with flying colors. So, why not allow students to tap into GPT as a research tool? Instead of doing a Google search and synthesizing the links, students can now obtain a preliminary overview of the research topic associated with the assignment. ChatGPT is highly versatile at brainstorming, which is not possible with results from search engines.
- A second consideration is the reality of student life. Widely known as *student syndrome*, it refers to planned procrastination, when, for example, a student will only start to apply themselves to an assignment at the last possible moment before its deadline [12]. GPT can amplify abilities and productivity equally for beginners, experts, and everyone in between--given a request for any information that you might ask a human assistant, GPT comes back instantly with an answer that is likely between good and excellent, enhancing productivity [13] if students are prone to last-minute research and might do a sloppy job, why not provide them access to an AI researcher – ChatGPT, in this case, to function as their research partner. Group projects have strengths, but many assignments must be completed individually. So ChatGPT can be that silent "artificial" coach, mentor, or team member.

2.1 Introducing ChatGPT

A private remark by a student concerning ChatGPT, which was alarming, moved me:

> "Professor, my friend got 10/10 on an assignment, while I got 8/10. He used ChatGPT, and I did not."

It was implied that this student got a better grade due to the use of AI and this was unfair.

To provide a level playing field, I identified a business analysis assignment in my project management course that could leverage the use of ChatGPT. Details of the course are provided below:

University: Boston University
Course: AD 642 Project Management
Discipline: Administrative Sciences (Business/Management)
Nature of Assignment: Complete a Business Case – especially a financial case for investing in a project. ROI and NPV calculations were done. Budget calculations were derived from MS Project estimates of work packages.

With an assignment identified, the first inquiry on this topic was to determine what percentage of the students are familiar with ChatGPT. A show of hands in the classroom in mid-February 2023 revealed that less than 50% of the students were familiar with or were actively using ChatGPT. Therefore, the next step was to tutor students to create accounts and demonstrate the use of the tool. This was a straightforward process. Students quickly created accounts via the URL https://chat.openai.com and typed in sample queries.

The next task was to describe how to cite the work. This proved to be a challenge for us. We use the APA style for citation, and as of mid-February 2023, there was no homogenous recommendation for APA citation. But, after some research, example styles were given to students to use in their assignments.

2.2 Prompt Tutorial

Since many students were new to AI tools, an introductory tutorial to prompt ChatGPT was provided. The prompts pertain to a business case analysis for a scenario that all students are familiar with – investing in higher education. Students were asked to reflect on their education and provide a financial analysis from a pre-mortem perspective. The final deliverable was a business case. Students were asked to personalize to the real-life scenario as much as possible to prevent the risk of a generic submission from ChatGPT. They were asked to conduct research about the job market in the country they came from and most likely returning to for employment.

The Table below describes a few sample prompts explored in class (Table 1).

Table 1. Key Domain Tasks Addressed in Revised Project

Introduction	Prompt: "Research the background, purpose, and overall context of pursuing a master's degree in the USA and summarize your findings to set the stage for the business case."
Market Overview	Prompt: "Analyze the demand for master's degree holders in the USA job market, focusing on specific industries and sectors Include trends and statistics that support your analysis using a tabular format."
Cost Analysis	Prompt: "Identify the costs associated with obtaining a master's degree in the USA, including tuition fees, books, and health insurance."
Financial Benefits	Prompt: "Determine the financial benefits of obtaining a master's degree in the USA, such as salary increases, job opportunities, and promotion potential. Provide data that demonstrate these benefits and compare them to those who do not hold a master's degree."

2.3 Research Hypothesis

A research hypothesis was identified to test if the goal of introducing ChatGPT in the assignment was successful and to answer other questions pertaining to ethical use of ChatGPT in education.

Hypothesis: Using ChatGPT in academic assignments positively influences student learning outcomes in the classroom.

The simple hypothesis can be tested through a survey and analysis of the data from the responses. Grades and other qualitative student feedback would also be examined to validate that the learning outcomes were achieved.

A more intriguing hypothesis we need to address is whether using ChatGPT as a tool is ethical. The traditional learning acquisition processes, that is, "the human ability to think, to reason, to plan, to perceive, to adapt, and to perform induction, deduction, logic as well as to communicate, all ordinary abilities of human intelligence might not possibly be employed" when we use ChatGPT [14]. What is students' reaction to learning and doing academic work using AI? It is surely a paradigm shift from the traditional way of conducting research. We need to research if students have varying reactions to the use of ChatGPT in academic work and how they perceive its use as a research tool.

Hypothesis: Students' perceptions of using ChatGPT as an academic tool are affected by ethical concerns as this learning mode is a departure and a paradigm shift from the traditional research methods.

This hypothesis can be tested through a simple survey asking students to what extent they consider ChatGPT ethical (from a learning perspective).

3 Survey

A simple survey was designed to test the hypothesis. See Appendix A for details. A key point to note is that the survey was made anonymous. The anonymity of the survey was meant to encourage honest responses from students. The survey asks students what percentage of their assignment effort came from ChatGPT – this is a reasonable question to gauge the level of contribution from ChatGPT. This information can help provide insight into how heavily students rely on ChatGPT to complete their assignments.

Essentially, the survey instrument aims to test the hypothesis that AI tools such as Chat GPT are helpful for academic research and assignment work. Within this context, we were curious to find out if students were using output from the GPT as is or modifying it. If it is providing accurate responses, much re-prompting might not be necessary. Our goal was to collect information on that as well. Did they prompt more than once? Twice? More than Three times.

A second hypothesis that we tested was the ethical aspect of using ChatGPT.

The final question is open-ended and seeks their frank input. Students are more likely to share their true thoughts and experiences without fear of retribution or judgment if the survey is anonymous.

4 Survey Results and Findings

The study's results are shown below. The comprehensive feedback from our survey respondents provided invaluable insights into using ChatGPT for homework assignments. The data sheds light on the perceived value of ChatGPT as a study tool, the ease or difficulty of eliciting helpful content when using ChatGPT, the extent to which ChatGPT-generated text was incorporated into final papers, and the ethical considerations surrounding its use. What is insightful is the students' additional comments –they offer a rich understanding of their experiences and attitudes toward ChatGPT, both positive and negative.

In the following paragraphs, we will delve into the specifics of these responses, discussing our observations and interpreting the implications of these findings. We have left the pie charts from Google Forms results as-is for convenience. The Bar charts could have illustrated the same more intuitively. The survey was anonymous, and students answered selectively.

For the first question, *"How would you rate the overall value of using ChatGPT in your* homework assignments?".

- Extremely valuable: 4 respondents
- Very valuable: 14 respondents
- Moderately valuable: 11 respondents
- Slightly valuable: 6 respondents (Fig. 1)

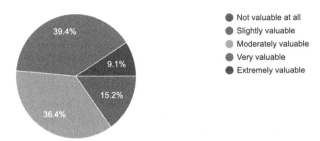

Fig. 1. Overall Value of ChatGPT

Comments: Most respondents found ChatGPT valuable for their homework assignments, with most rating it as either "very valuable" or "moderately valuable."

Was it easy to prompt ChatGPT to generate helpful content for your assignments? Or did you try several times before you got the correct output?".

- Prompted once: 6 respondents
- Tried variations (two times): 16 respondents
- Tried three times or more: 9 respondents (Fig. 2)

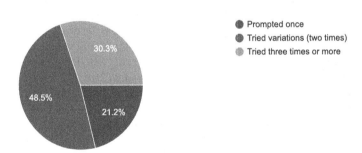

Fig. 2. Prompt Attempts to Obtain Desired Output

Comments: Many users needed to try at least a couple of times to get the desired output from ChatGPT for their assignments. Most respondents tried variations of prompts twice, while many had to try three or more times. ChatGPT gives impressive results on the first attempt in most cases. But it is possible that students tried a variation of the professor's suggested prompts.

Approximately what percentage of the content in your final paper includes direct quotes or paraphrases from ChatGPT-generated text?".

- 0%: 3 respondents
- 1–20%: 17 respondents
- 21–40%: 6 respondents
- 41–60%: 6 respondents (Fig. 3)

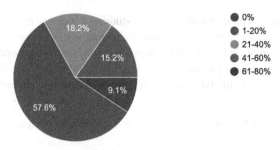

Fig. 3. Percentage Use of ChatGPT in Assignment

Comments: From these results, most respondents used a smaller portion of ChatGPT-generated text in their final papers, with most reporting 1–20% of the content as direct quotes or paraphrases. A smaller number of users relied more heavily on ChatGPT-generated content, with 21–40% and 41–60% usage reported by a few respondents. No respondents reported not using ChatGPT-generated content (0%) in their final papers. This suggests that while ChatGPT is a helpful tool for students, most users prefer it as a supplementary resource rather than a primary content source for their assignments.

To what extent do you consider using ChatGPT in your homework assignments ethical? (Focus is on learning perspective).

- Completely ethical: 5 respondents
- Somewhat ethical: 8 respondents
- Neutral: 15 respondents
- Somewhat unethical: 4 respondents
- Completely unethical: 2 respondents (Fig. 4)

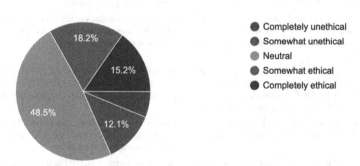

Fig. 4. Concerns About Using AI to Do Scholarly Work

Comments:
Almost a quarter of the students perceived the use of ChatGPT as unethical. With some strongly objecting to the use of ChatGPT. Note: This conversation occurred spontaneously in class when ChatGPT was introduced as a recommended tool.
Any comments on the use of ChatGPT in assignments?

While the previous questions did not allow students to provide feedback, this question succeeded in obtaining insight that revealed interesting student observations. We list the actual responses below, and for ease of comprehension, we have grouped them into two columns, as positive leaning or guarded comments in Table 2. Note: The comments in the two columns listed in the table are comments from different students.

Table 2. Comments From Students Grouped by Categories

Positive Leaning Comments	Guarded Comments
I think this assignment is useful to practice our prompt questioning and structuring for future ChatGPT use in courses	ChatGPT is not so helpful for me right now, compared to using Google search or Wikipedia
If one uses it to enhance their own work, it should be considered it's fine to use ChatGPT (for the future as well)	I worked more with Bard found it more intuitive. It can be implemented for easier navigation on research paper and sources
The use of ChatGPT can provide a higher value to the students, but only if the student already has some knowledge about the topic	AI can bring you some wrong information. The student must be able to determine if this information is right or wrong
I think ChatGPT is very useful. However, I believe that students cannot use it to write the entire paper. Honestly, I didn't fully use ChatGPT for the assignment	ChatGPT is a dangerous tool. It doesn't reflect the knowledge of the student. (i.e., it misrepresents how academically strong the student is. The assignment results seem to show that a student has strong skills when ChatGPT is used. Academically, this is unfair; it doesn't represent or show the person's critical mindset
It was helpful to come up with ideas Not a good response was obtained always, but somehow helpful	It was weird for us to have the "premade" prompts, as it takes away the critical thinking of the research. I think we should decide, our own prompts
Personally, I think chat GPT is helpful, providing ideas you never thought of before. Let students decide if not to use ChatGPT and when to use it	It has helped me a lot in my Business Analytics foundations course because I had no background knowledge in programming
It works great as a personal tutor. It is completely ethical and will be the new trend of academic learning. Soon, it will be as normal as people using Google today	For all student users, my advice is, just don't let ChatGPT dominate your ideas, and always keep your own thoughts
Every tool once launched in the world had questions of usage initially, whether it was Word, PowerPoint or Excel. Now, Chat GPT is a good tool for everyone as it makes searching simplified and easy	It should be used to understand and refer to but not rely on it fully. I think using ChatGPT is a big progress. It's not cheating, it's just a new tool
You need to learn how to train AI to get the answer you want. The education system needs to adapt ChatGPT	ChatGPT can provide a clear outline. Very helpful for getting actual facts and we don't have to waste time searching for information
Technology and Innovation cannot be disregarded, proper use of such things is necessary	In an assignment, ChatGPT can only be useful to some degree. It won't generally provide accurate or precise information that we can use in a paper. For my assignment it didn't generate precise info on foreign countries for example

(continued)

Table 2. (*continued*)

Positive Leaning Comments	Guarded Comments
Using ChatGPT can help to complete the assignments to a certain extent and improve efficiency. However, it's also important that students are using ChatGPT in the right way	Although it was highly beneficial, preserving (developing) our critical thinking skills is equally important. Though using ChatGPT is kind of convenient and quick for generating content, it is still important to read some authentic articles about the information you need for the essay
ChatGPT is a very helpful tool and can help you with research your topic in-depth and can save time when compared to finding different sources individually. However, later you must read and verify the content provided and not simply just copy and paste	We must leverage the tool, but we should learn the material as well
It is a very helpful tool not only in doing homework but with professional projects too. And it will make research easier	
I used it for the brainstorming stage only	

5   Hypothesis Analysis

Hypothesis 1 was inferred from several questions and other informal comments from students. We can determine with a certain degree of confidence that using ChatGPT in academic assignments positively influences student learning outcomes in the classroom. The average class grade for this assignment compared to the previous year was 12% better. The reasons possibly included the following:

a) Increased access to information about the subject matter: ChatGPT can quickly provide students with information on a particular topic (business case analysis involving financial analysis in our assignment), allowing them to learn more efficiently and effectively.
b) Enhanced critical thinking skills: As students use ChatGPT to research and generate content, they might have evaluated other dimensions they did not think of—for example, the longer-term value of investing in education.
c) Improved writing skills: Using ChatGPT to generate content, students were exposed to new vocabulary and writing styles, which helped help them improve their writing skills and resulted in a better paper.
d) Engagement with virtual research: Using ChatGPT to generate content can make the research process more engaging and interactive for students, potentially leading to increased motivation and participation. Students were motivated to finish the assignment as they could visualize the final product.

As noted in student comments, a lot of work and preparation must occur before ChatGPT will be a helpful tool.

Hypothesis 2, we cannot conclusively determine from one single question in the survey. The survey indicates the respondents' general attitudes toward using ChatGPT in academic work. Note that there is a split in attitude, with approximately 25% in favor and 25% opposed with 50% neutral. A more comprehensive study design would be required to test the hypothesis properly. This would involve a larger sample size, a broader range of questions, and more objective measures of academic performance.

Please note that while a larger sample size would have been preferable, the limited class size was a constraint in this case. However, we made efforts to ensure the reliability of the results by encouraging all students in attendance to complete the survey to form reliable research conclusions about the population.

6   Conclusion

The survey and informal conversation with students reveal that the students are quite impressed with the ability of ChatGPT to act as a research partner and help them in many ways. While we did not survey the role of ChatGPT as a tutor, this is a key aspect that needs to be explored further when we redesign the curriculum. For instance, the instructor is freed up from the responsibilities of explaining mundane terms but yet critical concepts, such as NPV or Discounted rate, to students. Ascione reports, "Tutoring has long been a dream of people in tech. This is something we're already starting to see unfold [15]".

An interesting observation that needs to be explored further is productivity or simply motivation provided by use of ChatGPT in the course. Unlike the previous semesters, we had students complete the homework on time and schedule. A skeletal output was generated from the prompts provided by the instructor to consider. So students had a head-start. Excuses such as "I have Covid, please give me another week" did not appear in our inbox this time. Therefore, an unexpected benefit of using AI tools is that it appears to help students overcome the *Student Syndrome*. As vividly stated by Hoffman [13], student syndrome is that students start work only when the deadline is approaching. ChatGPT helps the student successfully start and deliver much closer to the finish line than if they did not use generative AI tools.

We pride ourselves on introducing students to the latest academic tools and techniques. Generative AI represents yet another computational invention that can elevate a student's distinctive capability in education. Therefore, introducing and demonstrating tools such as ChatGPT to students behooves us. Unfortunately, we open the floodgates in doing so, and there is no going back. It is not conceivable that students will see a working demonstration of ChatGPT and then not leverage it further for their research work to complete assignments. Therefore, an AI Policy must be documented in our courses to provide a level playing field.

Eventually, students will get good at using tools such as ChatGPT. The challenge for educators will then go beyond simply mentioning Chat GPT or Google's Bard as a tool that can be used in the course. It means that from a pedagogical perspective, instructors must integrate AI into their curriculum. They can emphasize active and experiential learning and show students how to use AI tools and technology.

As anticipated, the research validates the debate about the "ethical use" of ChatGPT in education. Using GPT to do research and ethics. GPTs have limitations. They don't learn facts or principles that let them use commonsense reasoning or make new inferences about how the world works. When you ask a question, it has no awareness or insights into your intent -- it's not making factual assessments or ethical distinctions about the text it is producing: it's simply making algorithmic guesses and more to compose in response to the sequence of words in your prompt [13].

Students consider using ChatGPT unethical to use. This aspect needs to be explored in considerable detail in future research. Not exercising the traditional approach to conducting research or homework was troubling to many students. It goes against students' and researchers' ability to learn and innovate. While they appreciate Generative AI they seem to have misgivings. There is also a concern about bias and misinformation. Consider the statement from Leandro Maciel [14] "In addition to this philosophical issue (about consuming output from AI), there are also unwanted effects such as the generation of misinformation, the dissemination of fake news, and even the promotion of plagiarism. ChatGPT consists of an associative system whose content is not generated by real knowledge. ChatGPT does not provide information checking (uneven factual accuracy) as well. The technology may generate incorrect information and may produce harmful instructions or biased content, as pointed out by the ChatGPT platform itself (Source: https://openai.com/blog/chatgpt/. Access on Feb. 14th, 2023.)

We conclude by giving ChatGPT the final word on the ethical use of ChatGPT for student assignments and what I must do next as instructor. I chose to prompt ChatGPT for a response to my question: *How do I react to the concern from a small segment that students should not be using ChatGPT to do assignments?* ChatGPT replies [16]. When addressing concerns from a segment of students who believe that using AI for the assignment is not appropriate, consider the following steps:

1. Acknowledge their concerns: Recognize the concerns raised by these students and emphasize that you appreciate their engagement and feedback.
2. Clarify the purpose of using ChatGPT: Explain the educational objectives behind incorporating ChatGPT into the assignment. The goal is to enhance the learning experience, improve research efficiency, and provide new perspectives rather than replace independent thinking or traditional research methods.
3. Highlight the benefits: Discuss the potential benefits of using AI-based tools like ChatGPT, such as saving time, generating new ideas, or providing a different perspective.
4. Set clear guidelines: Establish clear guidelines for using ChatGPT, including how to cite and credit any information obtained from the tool properly and verify the generated content's accuracy and reliability.
5. Encourage critical thinking: Emphasize the importance of developing critical thinking and problem-solving skills, and remind students that ChatGPT should be used as a supplementary tool rather than a substitute for their own thinking and analysis.
6. Provide alternatives: For students who remain uncomfortable with using ChatGPT, offer alternative research methods or resources they can use for their assignment.
7. Monitor and evaluate: Continuously monitor the use of ChatGPT in assignments, evaluate its effectiveness and impact on students' learning, and make adjustments as needed.

References

1. IBM, Watson Assistant: Build better virtual agents, powered by AI. https://www.ibm.com/products/watson-assistant. Accessed 10 Feb 2023
2. Bhatia, A.: Let us show you how GPT works—using Jane Austen. N.Y. Times (2023)
3. Branum, C., Schiavenato, M.: Can ChatGPT accurately answer a PICOT question? Assessing AI response to a clinical question. Nurse Educ. **48**(5), 231–233 (2023)
4. Fishman, E.K., Weeks, W.B., Lavista Ferres, J.M., Chu, L.C.: Watching innovation in real time: the story of ChatGPT and radiology. Can. Assoc. Radiol. J. (2023). https://doi.org/10.1177/08465371231174817
5. Ghosh, A., Bir, A.: Evaluating ChatGPT's ability to solve higher-order questions on the competency-based medical education curriculum in medical biochemistry. Cureus **15**, e37023 (2023)
6. Graber-Stiehl, I.: Is the world ready for ChatGPT therapists? Nature **617**, 22–24 (2023)
7. Gupta, R., et al.: Performance of ChatGPT on the plastic surgery inservice training examination. Aesthet. Surg. J. (2023)
8. Hasnain, M.: ChatGPT applications and challenges in controlling monkey pox in Pakistan. Ann. Biomed. Eng. **51**(9), 1889–1891 (2023). https://doi.org/10.1007/s10439-023-03231-z
9. Singh, S., Djalilian, A., Ali, M.J.: ChatGPT and ophthalmology: exploring its potential with discharge summaries and operative notes. Semin. Ophthalmol. **38**(5), 503–507 (2023)
10. Kelly, S.M.: ChatGPT passes exams from law and business schools: CNN business. CNN (2023)
11. David, R.: ChatGPT is about to revolutionize the economy. We need to decide what that looks like. MIT Technology Review. MIT Press, Boston (2023)
12. Wikipedia Projects, Student syndrome - Wikipedia (2022)
13. Hoffman, R.: Impromptu. Dallepedia LLC, North Haven (2023)
14. Maciel, L.: Editorial: ChatGPT and the ethical aspects of artificial intelligence. Revista de Gestão **30**, 110–112 (2023)
15. Ascione, L.: 3 academic leaders weigh in on ChatGPT's place in higher ed - eCampus News. eCampus News (2023)
16. OpenAI. [ChatGPT's response to the question: "How do I react to the concern from a small segment that students should not be using ChatGPT to do this assignment?"]. https://chat.openai.com. Accessed 5 May 2023
17. Baidoo-Anu, D., Owusu Ansah, L: Education in the era of generative artificial intelligence (AI): understanding the potential benefits of ChatGPT in promoting teaching and learning. Available at SSRN 4337484 (2023)
18. Sok, S., Heng, K.: ChatGPT for education and research: a review of benefits and risks. Available at SSRN 4378735 (2023)
19. Biswas, S.: Role of ChatGPT in education. Ann. Biomed. Eng. 1–2 (2023)
20. Lo, C.K.: What is the impact of ChatGPT on education? A rapid review of the literature. Educ. Sci. **13**(4), 410 (2023)
21. McMurtrie, B.: Teaching: Reckoning with ChatGPT. Chronicle of Higher Education. https://www.chronicle.com/newsletter/teaching/2023-06-22. Accessed 22 June 2023

Value-Added Grading of AI-Assisted Papers

Eric Braude$^{(\boxtimes)}$ (iD)

Boston University, Boston, MA 02215, USA
ebraude@bu.edu

Abstract. The advent of AI generators such as chatGPT is significantly affecting the workplace as well as teaching and learning in higher education. This includes education in systems analysis, design, and programming. Working IT professionals will routinely rely on AI generation, we believe. Consequently, students should learn to leverage AI tools. We describe a way to prepare systems analysts and developers for a professional environment in which AI generation is ubiquitous and we explain an approach to evaluating graduate work prepared with the aid of AI generation. It is based on the *value added* in students' work: their chosen prompt sequences and their edits, deletions, and additions to AI-generated material. Although professionals are judged by their products, we believe that value-added will be a key professional goal in the AI-rich environments of the future because it distinguishes the end-products of professionals who better leverage AI.

Keywords: Assessment · IT education · Grading · Prompt engineering · Systems analysis and design · AI generation · Software development

1 Introduction

After much anticipation and discussion (e.g., Floridi and Chiriatti [2]), chatGPT was released in November 2022 and is affecting the workplace, as well as teaching and learning in higher education. This includes education in systems analysis, design, and development. Professionals are judged by their products, but we believe that value-added will be a key professional goal in the AI-rich environments of the future because it distinguishes the quality of the end-products of those who better leverage AI. Software systems professionals will routinely rely on AI generators, and students should learn to fully utilize these tools.

The use of tools in higher education is frequently encouraged, and we typically assess student work by inspecting the end-product. AI generation, however, is powerful enough to do at least some of the significant work we traditionally expect from students. For example, even the following prompt to chatCPT generates a complete, albeit simple, game that "will help you grasp the concept" of a full game: *Give the Python code for a console-based videogame to save the Earth from environmental collapse*. Additional prompts can make the game increasingly challenging.

Although some instructors claim to easily detect AI-generated material, and although tools exist that claim to detect it, such tools are not sufficiently reliable (Sadasivan

© ICST Institute for Computer Sciences, Social Informatics and Telecommunications Engineering 2023
Published by Springer Nature Switzerland AG 2023. All Rights Reserved
T. Zlateva and G. Tuparov (Eds.): CSECS 2023, LNICST 514, pp. 399–406, 2023.
https://doi.org/10.1007/978-3-031-44668-9_31

et al. [8]) and we can't fairly convict students of plagiarism without proof. Neither suspicion nor tools supply such proof. In any case, we believe that the use of AI should be encouraged and rewarded, not punished. Approaches to assignments and evaluation must adapt.

The unprecedented[1] nature and dynamic of AI generation is such that very early study of its effects on education, and corresponding practical adjustments, despite being necessarily incomplete, are called for without delay: hence this report and work-in-progress.

We began this work with a course, "Systems Analysis and Design," which started in the second week of March 2023, four months after the introduction of chatGPT. We continued it in a course on Advanced Java Programming, beginning in May.

We identified the following research questions.

1. How do we educate software systems professionals for an environment in which AI generation is ubiquitous?
2. How can we avoid passive, over-reliance on AI generation, where students do not sufficiently absorb the required concepts?
3. Is there a way to effectively evaluate the systems analysis or programming knowledge of graduate students when they use AI?

Our response to the first question was to incentivize students to leverage AI generation to the full throughout the course and to provide guidance on prompts, as exemplified in Sect. 1.1 below. Our response to the second and third research questions was to evaluate student work based on their *value added*—their own prompt sequences and their improvements to the resulting chatGPT end-products.

Students were permitted to opt out of using AI generation upon request, but they were required to justify this.

1.1 Prompt Guidance

Prompt advice—now ubiquitous on the Web—was shared throughout the term, specialized to systems analysis and programming. The following were typical.

GENERIC PROMPT ADVICE[2]:
Be specific about word count and make it higher than you will eventually need. Understand the chatbot's limitations. Use clear and concise prompts. Ask the AI to add more when you need more. Ask the AI to reformulate its response if you need it. Use key words. Keep it simple. Review AI output for accuracy. For code generation, request pre- and postconditions; request tests.

METAPROMPT EXAMPLES

- *I want to create a role-playing video game and I need its overall states and transitions. Give me some chatGPT prompts to get the best results.*

---

[1] Hundreds of the world's most prominent AI scientists signed a statement in May 2023 that "Mitigating the risk of extinction from AI should be a global priority alongside other societal-scale risks such as pandemics and nuclear war." (https://www.safe.ai/statement-on-ai-risk).

[2] Edited from https://www.elevatodigital.com/10-tips-and-tricks-for-using-chatgpt/.

- *What are some helpful prompts that I might ask you (chat GPT) about project risks?*

PROJECT IDEA EXAMPLE
Give a numbered list of 8 to10 requirements for a role-playing video game about conservation, resident on a PC. Use "shall." Be precise.

CODE IMPROVEMENT EXAMPLE
Reorganize the following code to make it more modular, more readable, and with less nesting. Leave the comments intact.

CODE GENERATION TEMPLATE EXAMPLE[3]
I want you to act as a grandmaster Java software developer who has extensive experience writing Java code for mission-critical Java applications and is capable of teaching Java to other advanced Java users. I will give you a specification of different aspects of a Java application, and I want you to reply with Java code using one code block per Java class. I want you to reply only with the Java code and nothing else. Do not write explanations. I want you to provide an "Intent" comment just above each Java class that explains the intent of each class. Use no more than two sentences for each of these comments. This comment must not include any implementation details and must not mention the name of any Java classes. The following is a bad example which includes the name of a class: "The intent of this class is to average ten numbers using the NumbersList Class". Do not follow that example. Instead, say: "The intent of this class is to average numbers". Exclude implementation details, do not mention what classes the implementation will use, and include only the intent of the class. For each method that is not a getter or setter, I want you to provide preconditions and postconditions. A precondition is something that must be true before the method executes. A postcondition is something that must be true after the method has been completed.

We continue to work on testing and improving our advice (e.g., is anything lost by prompting "Provide ..." instead of "I want you to provide ..."?).

2 Related Work

Finnie-Ansley et al. [1] compare AI-generated code with that produced, unaided, by students, as well as the effect of prompt variations on the code output—related topics but not our goal here. They note that "we cannot put the genie back in the bottle. The question arising for the computing educating community ... is how we engage with the challenges and opportunities presented by the by the increasing effectiveness of machine learning tools ..." Finnie-Ansley et al, along with many researchers, suggest having students critique the output of AI generators. AI generation critique is somewhat incorporated in our approach in that students must inspect AI-generated material before they can add value to it.

Using chatGPT to *create* assignments has been discussed by several researchers (a recent example is Zhai [6]), but, while related, this was not our goal. An early use of AI in education has been to grade, or assist in grading, papers (e.g., Stanyon et al [3],

---

[3] We are indebted to Warren Mansur for this prompt example, slightly edited.

Restrepo-Calle et al [4], and Zhai [6]). Many researchers have investigated the *detection* of cheating via AI generation. So far, this has had mixed results (e.g., Khalil and Er [5]). Plagiarism detection is not our approach, however.

Finnie-Ansley et al suggest placing "more emphasis on code review, or evaluating code." This is consistent with our view and approach. They ask the question "How can an educator differentiate between a student who tried, but ultimately failed to get the correct answer and a student who simply generated code using (an AI)?" Our work deals with this question.

3 Approach

Students in the spring 2023 Systems Analysis and Design and Advanced Programming courses were required to leverage AI generation as much as they could—to "push" it. They could request to opt out with justification, however, which we told them was likely to be approved. Prompt engineering examples were provided as in Sect. 1.1. We emphasized specificity, focus, and hyper-prompting. *Specificity* includes being explicit about the word counts and literacy level of outputs, requesting a format such as numbering, and using template-like underscores in prompts. *Focus* concerns applying one aspect at a time, although this is not always desirable. *Hyper-prompting* includes asking chatGPT for effective prompt suggestions.

Assignments were in essay or project form (in particular, not multiple choice). The assignment grading criteria were based on students' value-added, as follows for the systems analysis class:

1. *Your contributions to clarity*
2. *Your contributions to technical soundness*
3. *Your contributions to thoroughness & coverage and*
4. *Your contributions to relevance*

For the advanced programming class, the criteria consisted of contributions to clarity, implementing requirements, and technical correctness.

Student work was evaluated via their prompt sequences, together with their edits—including additions—to chatGPT's output produced by their prompts. Because this material can be voluminous, the student's summary of their value added was required to be listed first, the remainder acting as documentation of the claims made.

Students were provided with an MS Word template for their assignments that included sections for their responses to specific topics. We tried two formats for this, mindful of the large resulting quantity of text. The first template format, shown in italics next, supplemented the template with an MS Word 'note' of variable length, where students were requested to provide their prompt sequence and the text resulting from it.

Class Model
Provide a class model for the system, maintaining the system scope you determined. Your solution should have roughly 12 classes. (When complete, a real design typically may contain hundreds of classes, but your submission must focus on the scope you have chosen.) Your class model should show classes and their relationships. To add clarity to

your diagram, provide key attributes and methods. (You do not have to list every attribute and method, just the most important ones.) Label clearly.

Your class model and notes replace this.

Replace this with the chatbot text from which you edited your response or with "no AI used for this part."
MY SEQUENCE OF PROMPTS:
(Expand this text box downward to work on, but please restore it to just the first line when done.)
1.

An improved format provided an ordinary MS Word headings for this purpose because these are collapsible, and this solves the volume problem. The usual plagiarism rules apply to prompts: copied ones had to be acknowledged.

4 Results

Besides describing methods used to deal with AI generation, this study includes three small surveys in the Spring 2023 Systems Analysis class. The purpose of the latter was to frame hypotheses, to suggest measurements in future studies, and to learn what questions to ask in a large-scale investigation.

Every student in the Systems Analysis class and, at the time of writing this, the Advanced Programming class, opted to use AI generation on every assignment, despite having the option to avoid it. About four of the sixteen students in the former class had not tried chatGPT when the class began. Initially, only a small minority in that class felt comfortable leveraging AI generation to the maximum extent.

Identifying survey question phraseology in the AI-assisted environment was one purpose of our study. Students were surveyed three times in the Systems Analysis class, using similar questions. The first survey was conducted two weeks after the seven-week course began; the question was "How effective is the integration of chatbots into the assignments?" The results are shown in Fig. 1. The second survey was conducted four weeks after the course began. The question was "How helpful or unhelpful for your learning is the option to use a chatbot for assignments (compared with having it prohibited)?" The results are shown in Fig. 2 The third survey was conducted six weeks after the course began, the question being "How helpful or unhelpful for your learning is the option to use a chatbot for assignments (compared with having it prohibited)?" The results are shown in Fig. 3.

The final exam in the systems analysis course was proctored, and AI generation was prohibited. There were no significant difference in grades when comparing the finals with the assignments.

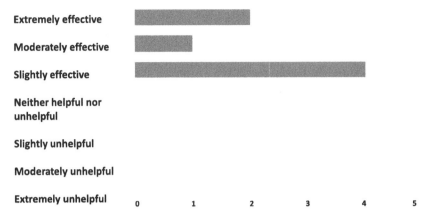

Fig. 1. Results for "How effective is the integration of chatbots into the assignments?" (week 2)

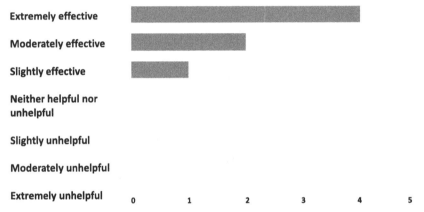

Fig. 2. Responses to "How helpful or unhelpful for your learning is the option to use a chatbot for assignments (compared with having it prohibited)?" (survey 2, week 4)

5   Analysis

This study concerns the learning that students experience in the AI-generation era and the design of assignments to promote such learning. Our approach, *value-added*, and students' reaction to it—and to using AI generation—was the specific subject.

Students showed an interest in using chatGPT throughout both courses. In the beginning, several students submitted work with only minor edits to AI-generated output, but this changed as we emphasized that credit would be given only for their value added and as they became accustomed to appropriately leveraging chatGPT. We don't want a student to edit just for the sake of editing, however: either the grader can show that added value is possible—otherwise the student's response contributes neither way except insofar as the prompt is added value.

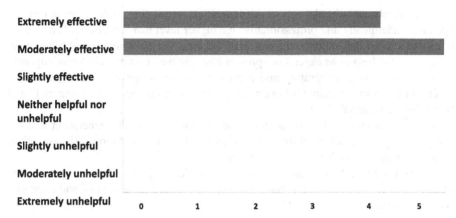

Fig. 3. Responses to "How helpful or unhelpful for your learning is the option to use a chatbot for assignments (compared with having it prohibited)?" (survey 3, week 7)

As Figs. 1, 2, and 3 show, there was evidence of a growing appreciation among students for the value of AI generation in the systems analysis class.

Although a formal comparison is yet to be performed, we were encouraged by the apparent consistency of grades when compared with the proctored, non-AI-assisted final exam in the systems analysis class. This suggests that over-reliance on AI generation may have been mitigated.

6 Conclusion and Future Work

The experiment suggests that students may welcome AI generation as a permanent part of their education and professional practice. The results encourage the hypothesis that the careful adding of value to AI-generated material promotes learning. The small sample size and experiment informality, however, do not *prove* these conclusions, and a side-by-side evaluation comparing our approach with a credible alternative and significant number of students remains to be performed.

When introducing chatGPT-assisted work in the cited courses, we avoided discussing prompting itself (prompt engineering) in a dedicated module, fearing that this would detract too much from the course subject matter. Instead, we disseminated information such as that in Sect. 1.1 throughout the course. This is not unreasonable, but a tutorial on the use of chatGPT might have saved time discussing the tool.

Compared with evaluating students' products alone, inspecting their prompts and edits increases grading time. Primarily reviewing students' own accounts of their value added mitigates this time problem. But the past may be irretrievable in any case: AI generation makes it possible to generate much greater volume, which will take more time to evaluate in any case.

As prompting becomes increasingly important, the clear use of (natural) language increases in importance for students in technical fields like systems analysis and software development.

More fundamentally, the use of AI generation means that students must learn to operate, academically and professionally, at a higher level than heretofore. Rather than think like a "classical" individual contributor, students and practitioners will function, in effect, with the help of an eager, ever-present assistant who is extremely knowledgeable in, and very good at integrating and expressing specifics that have been created by others. In other words, they will operate at a "contributing technical managerial" and "contributing editorial" level.

Critical thinking is key to dealing with chatbot output: AI generation encourages teaching and learning at the *evaluate* end of Bloom's taxonomy [7]: *remember, understand, apply, analyze, evaluate*, and *create*.

We propose that the approach to incorporating AI generation in learning described in this paper forms a reasonable basis for moving forward in various IT and computer science courses.

Acknowledgement. The author is indebted to the facilitators in the two classes mentioned who evaluated, or are evaluating, student assignments with the approach described here: Pamela Farr, Kuang-Jung Huang, Tony Lucarelli, and Warren Mansur.

References

1. Finnie-Ansley, J., Denny, P., Becker, B., Luxton-Reilly, A., Prather, J.: The robots are coming: exploring the implications of OpenAI codex on introductory programming. In ACE 2022: Proceedings of the 24th Australasian Computing Education Conference, pp. 10–19 (2022). https://doi.org/10.1145/3511861.3511863
2. Floridi, L., Chiriatti, M.: GPT-3: its nature, scope, limits, and consequences. Mind. Mach. **30**(4), 681–694 (2020). https://doi.org/10.1007/s11023-020-09548-1
3. Stanyon, R., Martello, E., Kainth, M., Wilkin, N.K: Demo of Graide: AI powered assistive grading engine. In: L@S 2022: Proceedings of the Ninth ACM Conference on Learning @ Scale, pp. 466–468 (2022). https://doi.org/10.1145/3491140.3528263
4. Restrepo-Calle, F., Ramírez-Echeverry, J., Gonzalez, F.: Uncode: interactive system for learning and automatic evaluation of computer programming skills. In: EDULEARN18 Proceedings, pp. 6888-6898 (2018). https://doi.org/10.21125/edulearn.2018.1632
5. Khalil, M., Er, E.: Will ChatGPT get you caught? Rethinking of plagiarism detection. arXiv: 2302.04335 (2023)
6. Zhai, X.: ChatGPT for next generation science learning. crossroads. ACM Mag. Stud. (XRDS) **29**(3), 42–46 (2023). https://doi.org/10.1145/3589649
7. Bloom, B.S., Engelhart, M.D., Furst, E.J., Hill, W.H., Krathwohl, D.R.: Taxonomy of Educational Objectives: The Classification of Educational Goals. V. Handbook I: Cognitive domain. David McKay Co., New York (1956)
8. Sadasivan, V., Kumar, A., Balasubramanian, S., Wang, W., Soheil Feizi, S.: Can AI-generated text be reliably detected? arXiv:2303.11156v1 (2023) https://doi.org/10.48550/arXiv.2303.11156

BU MET ABA Program to Quantitative Trading in Energy Market

Hanbo Yu[✉]

Department of Administrative Sciences, Boston University, Metropolitan College, Boston, MA 02215, USA

yuhanbo@bu.edu

Abstract. This paper presents a study conducted by the author during his enrollment in the Applied Business Analytics program at BU Metropolitan College from September 2019 to January 2021. Equipped with the acquired techniques and skills, the author subsequently joined a high-tech energy company and engaged in quantitative trading to capitalize on the financial opportunities presented by the DART spread. The paper provides an overview of the New England wholesale energy market, including an explanation of how the DALMP and RTLMP are settled, highlights extreme market events, and discusses the market's chaotic nature. The author further describes the qualitative and quantitative approaches employed, such as machine learning, statistical analysis, and data mining, which enabled him to achieve an impressive annual rate of return of 25.52% and a peak daily rate of return of 334.87% (translating to net earnings of $100,462.36 within a single day) through quant trading.

Keywords: Quantitative Trading · Wholesale Energy Market · DALMP · RTLMP · DART spread · volatility · rate of return

1 Bridging the Gap: The Intersection of BU's MET Applied Behavior Analysis Program and Quantitative Trading

The author was admitted to Metropolitan College's Applied Business Analytics program at Boston University (hereinafter referred to as BU MET ABA Program) in September 2019. After one year and a half's study, the author graduated in January 2021, subsequently joined a high-tech renewable energy company, and started to work as an energy market analyst and quantitative trader. The author mainly focused on the wholesale energy market in New England, studied the market rules, conducted extensive data analytics using the techniques and skills he obtained from the BU MET ABA program, and exceeded his annual revenue goal of 3.39 million by 34.31%. This paper mainly introduces how the wholesale energy market in New England works, DALMP and RTLMP, and how the author conducted quantitative trading to obtain financial benefits from DART spread.

© ICST Institute for Computer Sciences, Social Informatics and Telecommunications Engineering 2023
Published by Springer Nature Switzerland AG 2023. All Rights Reserved
T. Zlateva and G. Tuparov (Eds.): CSECS 2023, LNICST 514, pp. 407–416, 2023.
https://doi.org/10.1007/978-3-031-44668-9_32

2 New England Wholesale Energy Market Overview

2.1 Introduction to the Wholesale Energy Market, DALMP, and RTLMP

The energy market in New England (Massachusetts, Connecticut, Rhode Island, New Hampshire, Maine, and Vermont, six states in total) area is operated and monitored by the Independent System Operator New England (hereinafter referred to as ISO-NE).

In the ISO-NE wholesale energy market, electricity is bought and sold in two different markets: the day-ahead market and the real-time market. The day-ahead market is used to plan and schedule electricity generation and consumption for the next day, while the real-time market is used to balance supply and demand in real time based on actual consumption.

The energy market in New England is a clearing energy market, and ISO-NE uses economic dispatch to balance demand and supply[1]. ISO-NE dispatches all generation resources in an economic merit order, i.e., resources that submit the lowest price will be dispatched first, and when demand (load) increases, higher-priced supplies (generators) will be dispatched next, and highest-priced supplies (peak facilities) will be dispatched last.

Under this mechanism, supplies are stacked up incrementally from the lowest price to the highest price with different supply quantities. When the demand meets the supply, the market will clear, some supplies with low prices will clear the market, some supplies with high prices will not clear the market, and some supplies with certain prices will partially clear the market, as shown in Fig. 1.

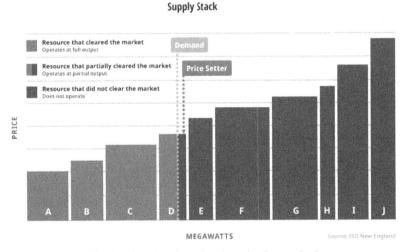

Fig. 1. How do prices clear in a clearing market?

Since there will be a supply stack that is "on the margin", the energy clearing price in New England is called Locational Marginal Price. This clearing mechanism is the same across the day-ahead market and real-time market, therefore, there are two prices in the wholesale energy market, one is Day-Ahead Locational Marginal Price (hereinafter referred to as DALMP), and the other is Real-Time Locational Marginal Price (hereinafter referred to as RTLMP).

The DALMP will be a fixed price for the specific hour, for example, between 1 pm and 2 pm on a certain day (hour ending 14), DALMP is $17.26/MWh. The RTLMP may change every 5 min based on real-time supply and demand, and after each hour, an hourly-average RTLMP will be calculated for settlement purposes. This hourly-average RTLMP may be higher or lower than the hourly DALMP, and for over 99.9961% of the time (there is only 1 h in recent 3 years that the DALMP and RTLMP are the same for the same hour), RTLMP and DALMP will be different for the same hour.

The difference between the DALMP and RTLMP is called the Day-Ahead-Real-Time spread (hereinafter referred to as the DART spread). Since most times the DART spread is not 0, it is possible to financially gain the benefit from the DART spread.

2.2 Attributes of DALMP and RTLMP

The wholesale energy market in New England is free, however, ISO-NE has its own market rules. Some may think that generators can bid whatever price they want, on the contrary, they cannot simply do that. All generation resources must bid with their variable costs[2]. Generators that use different fuels will have different variable costs, for example, for some renewable fuel generators, their variable costs can be low or even zero (PV, hydro, and wind); nuclear units usually have relatively low variable costs as well; natural gas units have higher variables costs, and coal and oil units can have even higher variable costs.

For most times, the marginal supply stack is the natural gas units, which settles the DALMP. Different units have different heat rates, and the variable costs of natural gas units will be:

*Bidding Price = Gas price*heat rate + some fixed costs*

Therefore, the DALMP is mainly driven by natural gas price and demand level and will not be negative in most regions/areas/interconnection nodes, unless in some certain areas/interconnection nodes, renewable resources are the marginal supply stack.

On the other hand, RTLMP is balancing the demand and supply in real-time, and when real-time demand is lower than day-ahead demand and real-time supply is higher than day-ahead supply, RTLMP will be lower than DALMP.

On the other hand, if real-time demand is above day-ahead demand and real-time supply is below day-ahead supply, RTLMP will be higher than DALMP. This may last very shortly, as ISO-NE will try to dispatch available resources to offset this supply shortage and keep the whole power grid system stable, however, this may last long enough if the supply is not offset, even to 48 h.

Sometimes, RTLMP can be as low as $0/MWh, or even negative. This usually happens in the spring and fall months, such as late April, early May, late September, and early October, when solar irradiation is strong and PV output significantly reduces the system demand.

RTLMP can also be as high as $900/MWh. Historically the highest RTLMP record within the last 5 years was $2632/MWh, which occurred on December 24th, 2022, between 6 and 7 pm. The negative RTLMP and extremely high RTLMP are usually relevant to extreme events of the system, known as Minimum Generation situation, and Capacity Scarcity condition.

2.3 Extreme Events: Min Gen and OP-4 Event

The wholesale energy market in New England can be volatile, and ISO-NE's top priority is to balance the electricity supply (generation) and demand (load). The Day-Ahead market is relatively more stable than the Real-Time market since things can change fast in real-time, e.g., some generators that have Day-Ahead generation obligations but did not show up due to unit trip/malfunction, some Day-Ahead demand did not show up due to unexpected sunny and warmer weather, some Real-Time demand emerged due to sudden temperature drops or raises, etc. Although ISO-NE was trying its best to maintain stability, every participant in the market, no matter supply or demand and how small they are, can be a snowflake that contributes to an avalanche.

ISO-NE has a considerable amount of capacity reserve: they usually have an approximate 28,000 MW capacity reserve2 while the annual highest demand for the last 5 years was 25,559 MW which occurred on August 29, 2018, between 4 pm and 5 pm[3]. When supply is below demand, ISO-NE will dispatch some fast-start generators to meet the demand; and when supply is above demand, ISO-NE will dispatch some generators to back down to shed some supply.

This operation strategy worked fine most times, however, there are some certain times that ISO-NE cannot shed enough supply to match the demand, then the supply will be above demand for several hours until demand increases to match the supply level. When that happens, it will trigger an extreme event named "Minimum Generation Emergency", hereinafter referred to as Min Gen, which means that the Minimum must-run Generation/Supply is significantly higher than the Demand/Load. When a Min Gen is triggered, the system-wide RTLMP will drop to 0 or negative, until demand raises, and Min Gen is canceled. The main cause of a Min Gen is usually an operation strategy named "Posturing".

When ISO-NE is foreseeing extreme weather to occur in 2 or 3 days, they will try to dispatch all generators to meet the potential demand. Since not all generators are fast-start, it will take 24 or even 48 h to get some generators to ramp up, and these generators cannot back down until the extreme weather passes. Other generators cannot back down such as Nuclear Reactors, combined with winds or hydro that have a production tax credit that makes sure the owners of the generators get paid no matter what the RTLMP is, supply will exceed demand significantly, and a Min Gen may be triggered.

Table 1 below is an example of how ISO-NE postures supply to counter extreme weather:

Assume that Day 3 ISO-NE is seeing a 20,500 MW demand/load, then ISO-NE will start dispatching all slow start generators from Day 1. As time flows, the Must Run MWs will continue increasing as these slow-start generators ramp up to their maximum capacity. By Day 3, when the extreme weather comes in, ISO-NE will have enough supply to meet the demand and keep all lights on across the New England area.

However, in the middle of Day 2, between 10 am and 4 pm, the system load can be only 10,000 MWs or even lower, when temperatures are mild, PV outputs are high,

Table 1. How ISO-NE postures supply to counter extreme weather

Date	Must Run MWs	Fast Start MWs	Total Available Supply
Day 1	8,000	8,000	16,000
Day 2	11,000	8,000	19,000
Day 3 (Extreme weather day)	13,000	8,000	21,000

and decent wind and hydro outputs. This will trigger the Min Gen situation since the Must Rum MWs are at least 1,000 MWs higher than the system demand. RTLMP will drop to 0, and even negative, while DALMP will stay positive. This will bring a great opportunity to get DART spread.

Another extreme event is the contrary of Min Gen. It is named the Capacity Scarcity Event and will happen when ISO-NE cannot provide sufficient supply to meet system demand. This is a rare event compared to Min Gen and will cause serious problems such as electricity outages in several regions, blackouts, and even casualties when combined with extreme weather.

When a capacity scarcity event occurs, ISO-NE will trigger Operation Procedure (OP)-4, which is trying its best to offset this capacity shortage, including raising the RTLMP via real-time generation auctions. RTLMP will be much higher than DALMP and can last several hours. Usually, peaking facilities (also known as peakers) which are usually natural gas units and have extremely high heat rates will be picked up, and push RTLMP to around $800/MWh, and even to over $2000/MWh.

Min Gen occurred more than OP-4 in the last 5 years. There is only one scarcity event that triggered OP-4 in the last 5 years, and it happened on December 24th, 2022. A cruel cold snap hit New England, including New York State, Quebec, and New Brunswick in Canada. A huge chunk of generation tripped offline due to extremely cold weather, and they could not come back online fast since most operation and maintenance workers were not working since it was Christmas Eve. A similar thing happened to New York State which has its independent system operator known as NYISO, and NYISO, Quebec, and New Brunswick also cut their exports to New England to reserve their energy. Suddenly, energy is short in the whole northeastern area of North America, ISO-NE could not borrow or purchase any extra energy from outside, or inside. The situation worsened during the evening peak hours, from 6 pm to 8 pm when system demand kept climbing and supply was in severe shortage. ISO-NE implemented OP-4 to raise RTLMP to encourage suppliers to offer enough generation to meet the demand, RTLMP went to $2,632/MWh and was historically highest in the last 5 years while DALMP was around $320/MWh. This situation was finally resolved the next day, and luckily, this capacity scarcity event did not cause any casualties and all lights were on during Christmas.

On the other hand, Min Gen occurred 4 times from 2023 until May[4]. Predicting these extreme events is one of the key components to obtaining the financial benefit of DART spread, and it is also very important to understand what caused these extreme events.

2.4 Financial Transactions to Get DART Spread, INC and DEC

ISO-NE provides official ways to obtain the DART spread through Financial Transactions/Trading. However, conducting the financial trading will require certain Financial Assurances since there can be potential losses and collaterals must be withheld for hedging. If the financial transactions exceed the financial assurance limit, ISO-NE will cancel all transactions.

ISO-NE provides two types of financial transactions: Incremental (hereinafter referred to as INC), and Decremental (hereinafter referred to as DEC). INC allows traders to sell energy with DALMP and buy back with RTLMP, and DEC allows traders to buy in energy with DALMP and sell with RTLMP. INC and DEC do not require physical dispatches of energy, since these transactions are selling some amount of energy during some hour and buying back the same amount of energy during the same hour, no actual generation/consumption of energy will occur. For example, there is one INC transaction for 8 MWs for Hour Ending (hereinafter referred to as HE) 8, and DALMP is $23 and RTLMP is $22, this transaction is selling/generating 8 MWh energy with $23 and buying/consuming 8 MWh energy with $22, no net generation or consumption will occur.

The equations of the financial benefit of INC and DEC are below:

For INC:

Net Earning = MWs * (DALMP-RTLMP)

For DEC:

Net Earning = MWs * (RTLMP-DALMP)

If some INC transactions are cleared and DALMP is above RTLMP for the same hour, some net earnings will be realized; however, if RTLMP is above DALMP, some losses will be realized. Similarly, if some DEC transactions are cleared and DALMP is below RTLMP for the same hour, some net earnings will be realized; however, if RTLMP is below DALMP, some losses will be realized. The losses will result in negative net earnings.

Financial transactions can be profitable, but also risky. All financial transactions must be made before 10:30 am on the prior day, i.e., if a trader is going to make some INC/DEC for Day 3, all bids/offers/transactions must be submitted before 10:30 am on Day 2, and no real-time adjustments or cancellations will be available during Day 3. Therefore, although INC/DEC does not dispatch real energy, a physical or financial hedge will be helpful.

2.5 Chaotic Nature of the Wholesale Energy Market, and Information Asymmetry

Figure 1 is a good resemblance of how the wholesale energy market works. The Day-Ahead energy market makes good plans to balance supply and demand, nonetheless, the supply and demand can change in real-time. Some supplies that have day-ahead obligations can malfunction and trip offline, some external imports can be cut off due to some system problems such as a Quebec Hydro transmission line broken or under unplanned maintenance, some nuclear plants can have some emergent technical issues, some PV panels are performing less than expected due to unexpected overcast weather, etc. Demands are similar, some extra demand can show up due to unexpected hot or cold weather, or some demand facility decides to consume a huge amount of energy when they see low RTLMP. Demand can also be severely below forecast due to a warm, windy, and sunny day, when PV outputs are strong, just like what happened on April 16th, 2023, in California, system net demand hit zero and even negative due to strong PV and wind output while forecasted system demand was around 7,000 MWs[5].

A lot of events can happen without any forebode, and this reveals the chaotic nature of the wholesale energy market. Some generation outages are planned or scheduled, and ISO-NE will release this information for transparency purposes; some outages cannot even be predicted. Every participant's bidding behavior may affect the whole energy market, for example, as small as 10 MWs extra generation may set RTLMP to $0 from $18, and 10 MWs extra demand may set RTLMP to $200 from $40.

No participant in the energy market can have all the information. Some participants/traders will have more information, and some will have less. This will cause an information asymmetry[6], and participants/traders who possess more information will be likely to make better decisions. To obtain the financial benefit of DART spread, more information will be helpful for traders to achieve their goals.

3   The Author's Approach to DART Spread Analysis

As a quantitative trader, the author utilizes different methods some of which he obtained from the BU MET ABA program and some of which he learned by himself to analyze DALMP and RTLMP. There are over 1,200 grid nodes that can settle DALMP and RTLMP in New England, most nodes will have similar DALMP and RTLMP for the same hour, while some nodes' DALMP and RTLMP will clear differently due to renewable energy impacts such as solar, wind, and hydro, or system conditions such as transmission line outage, transmission constraint, etc. The author collected DALMP and RTLMP for the last five years for the New England Hub node (near Boston), and some nodes that have higher volatility in northern Vermont and Maine. The author then conducted the statistical analysis and found that the annual average DALMP was above the annual average RTLMP for the last 5 years, except for one day that had the capacity scarcity event, December 24th of 2022. A naïve rule that just bid in INC without any other analysis will make a small amount of financial benefit each year, though taking a lot of ups and downs in the process.

However, if that day of scarcity event was counted, RTLMP will be above DALMP for the fiscal year of 2022, and that will result in severe financial loss for that year. The naïve rule is not optimal, since one scarcity event will wipe out the whole year's net earnings, and simply applying it is against scientific thinking and will not be accepted by most organizations.

Although the naïve rule does not work well, it does provide the insight that DALMP is likely to be higher than RTLMP. The author then switches to supervised machine learning to get a better forecast of DALMP and RTLMP and uses that forecast to make trading decisions.

Since the wholesale energy market is a clearing market, demand plays a crucial role in the DALMP and RTLMP. The fortunate part is that ISO-NE does provide an hourly demand forecast for the next three days, and it is the guideline of how DALMP is cleared in each node; the unfortunate part is that ISO-NE admits, its demand forecast is not accurate enough[7], and may cause volatilities in the wholesale energy market. When demand gets lower, it gets more likely that RTLMP goes negative since Min Gen may be triggered; when demand gets higher, it is more likely that RTLMP goes above DALMP, and even several times higher since an OP-4 may be triggered. The author is using ISO-NE's official real-time demand as an input for the supervised machine learning model and using ISO-NE's official demand forecast as an input for DALMP and RTLMP forecast.

Another important input variable is the Pipeline Natural Gas Price at Algonquin City Gate of Boston. Since most times Natural Gas units are marginal units, and all natural-gas units must bid with their variable costs, higher gas prices will result in higher DALMP and RTLMP, and the higher the natural gas price is, it is more likely that RTLMP is also much higher than DALMP. The author uses historical Algonquin City Gate natural gas prices as an input and uses estimations of future natural gas prices from the ICE platform for forecast purposes.

Different hours, weekdays, and wintertime shifts are also valuable input variables. For example, 8,000 MW demand for HE 18 is usually the lowest point of the year, while 8,000 MWs for HE 13 can happen 40 times across the whole year. Weekdays usually have higher demand, and weekends and holidays usually have lower demand. The wintertime shift also plays a critical role since this will shift the hour.

With all these necessary inputs, and public nodal DALMP and RTLMP gathered the author went through the process of model selection. The author tried different supervised machine learning models, such as Multiple Linear Regression, Polynomial Regression, Lasso and Ridge regression, K Nearest Neighbor regression, Random Forest, Gradient Boosting regression, Artificial Neural Network (Tensorflow), etc., and utilized cross-validation methods to minimize the loss. After hyper tuning all those parameters for those models, the author noticed that the Gradient Boosting regression model has the lowest cross-validation mean-absolute-error (hereinafter referred to as MAE) of 3.43 for DALMP and MAE of 9.36 for RTLMP. The higher MAE of RTLMP proves the chaotic nature of the energy market since RTLMP can be more volatile.

4   Quantitative Trading Performance

The author started quantitative trading to get DART spread in May 2022, after extensive analysis and market rule studies. At first, the author was acting conservatively, bidding small MWs of INC/DEC, such as 2 MWs for an hour and 4 h for a trading day. Then after some successes, the author started to increase the bidding amount, to 8 MWs for each hour, and up to 24 h maximum per day.

The rate of return is a key performance indicator of trading success. The usual calculation of the rate of return is:

ROR = (Revenue-Cost)/Cost

However, when some INC transactions were cleared and RTLMP went to 0 or negative, the cost can be 0 or negative, and ROR will be an error or negative, which does not make a good sense of how the performance was. Therefore, the author was using a different approach to calculate the rate of return.

For INC transactions, the ROR will be:

ROR = (DALMP-RTLMP)/DALMP

For DEC transactions, the ROR will be:

ROR = (RTLMP-DALMP)/DALMP

And for the year 2022, the author obtained a 25.52% rate of return for quantitative trading. This ROR is a year-flat rate, and cannot be compounded intra-year, however, for future years, this ROR can be compounding since net earnings are going into bidding costs for future transactions.

The author's highlight spot was December 24th, 2022, when the capacity scarcity event occurred. The author saw a cold snap attacking New York State, New England, Quebec, and New Brunswick and deemed that there may be a huge chunk of generation outages occurring and they could not come back online soon enough since it was Christmas. The author then submitted big amounts of DEC transactions with a $30,000 bidding cost; the market proved the author's decision correct, and even better, a capacity scarcity event occurred and RTLMP went off the charts. The author made a $100,036.24 net profit within one day, and the Rate of Return of that day was 334.87%.

5   Conclusions and Next Steps

The author was successful in quantitative trading, with a compounding annual rate of return of 25.52%. The techniques he obtained from the BU MET ABA program played a key role in his success, and it proves that the BU MET ABA program is competitive, helpful, and can create new opportunities when combined with domain knowledge in other areas.

The author is not satisfied with ISO-NE's official demand forecast since it is not accurate enough which is admitted by ISO-NE and is a crucial input for supervised machine learning models. The author is trying to build his own ISO-NE demand forecast model and aims to have better forecasts for DALMP and RTLMP. The author is also considering using techniques such as deep learning, reinforcement learning, etc. to decrease the losses of machine learning models to get better forecasts.

The author is also aiming to study the New York State energy market managed by NYISO, the California energy market managed by CAISO, and the Texas energy market managed by ERCOT. These markets have higher volatilities compared to ISO-NE yet have similar market rules, and can achieve a higher rate of return if the right decisions are made.

References

1. England, I.N.: How resources are selected and prices are set in the wholesale energy markets (n.d.). https://www.iso-ne.com/about/what-we-do/in-depth/how-resources-are-selected-and-prices-are-set
2. Real-time maps and charts. ISO New England - Real-Time Maps and Charts. (n.d.). https://www.iso-ne.com/isoexpress/web/charts
3. Energy, load, and demand reports. ISO New England - Energy, Load, and Demand Reports (n.d.). https://www.iso-ne.com/isoexpress/web/reports/load-and-demand
4. England, I.N.: Power system forecast and status (n.d.-b). https://www.iso-ne.com/markets-operations/system-forecast-status
5. Weaver, J.F.: Driven by solar, California's net demand hit zero on Sunday. pv magazine USA (2023). https://pv-magazine-usa.com/2023/04/20/driven-by-solar-californias-net-demand-hit-zero-on-sunday/
6. Akerlof, G.A.: The market for 'lemons': quality uncertainty and the market mechanism. Q. J. Econ. **84**(3), 488–500. The MIT Press (1970). https://doi.org/10.2307/1879431.JSTOR187943
7. NEPOOL participants committee report - ISO New England (n.d.). https://www.iso-ne.com/static-assets/documents/2022/07/july-2022-coo-report.pdf

Author Index

© ICST Institute for Computer Sciences, Social Informatics and Telecommunications Engineering 2023
Published by Springer Nature Switzerland AG 2023. All Rights Reserved
T. Zlateva and G. Tuparov (Eds.): CSECS 2023, LNICST 514, pp. 417–418, 2023.
https://doi.org/10.1007/978-3-031-44668-9

Printed in the United States
by Baker & Taylor Publisher Services